ON FOOT
through
AFRICA

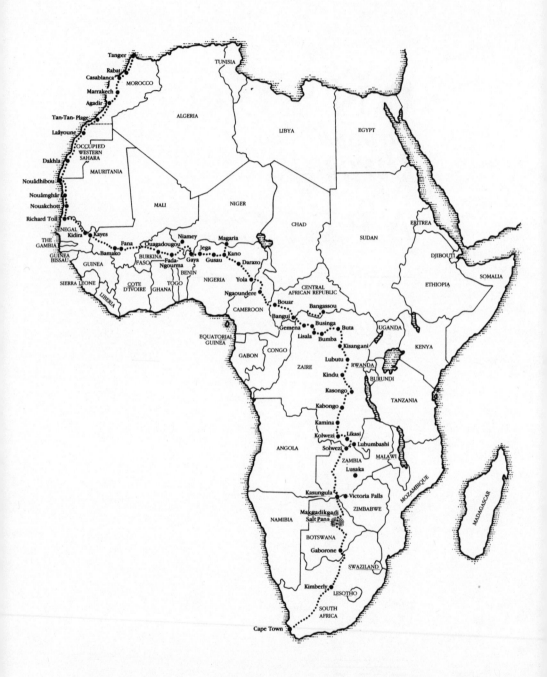

Between 2 April 1991 and 1 September 1993, Ffyona Campbell walked every step from Cape Town to Tanger, a total distance of 16,088 kilometres.

ON FOOT
through
AFRICA

Ffyona Campbell

TED SMART

Also by Ffyona Campbell

Feet Of Clay

The right of Ffyona Campbell to be identified as the author
of this work has been asserted by her in accordance with
the Copyright, Designs and Patents Act 1988.

First published in Great Britain in 1994 by
Orion
An imprint of Orion Books Ltd
Orion House, 5 Upper St Martin's Lane,
London WC2H 9EA

This edition produced for
The Book People Ltd
Guardian House, Borough Road
Godalming, Surrey GU7 2AE

A CIP catalogue record for this book is available from the
British Library

ISBN 1 85797 946 X

Filmset by Selwood Systems, Midsomer Norton

Printed in Great Britain on paper made from recycled pulp
by Butler & Tanner Ltd, Frome and London

For my father
and
for the men who were with me

'The possible is not what you can do
but what you want to do'

Ian Fleming

Driver: 'So why are you doing this, anyway?'
Walker: 'Because I said I would.'
Driver: 'Who did you say it to?'
Walker: 'Myself.'

Acknowledgements

Among the hundreds of requests I made for money, products and help over a two year period there were a small number of people who had the guts to say yes. I'd like to thank them not just for their help (which was greatly appreciated) but for their faith in me. It is thanks to them that I got to the starting block.

My financial sponsors were: Scholl, Bill Skerrett, You Magazine, Nick Gordon, Hi-Tec Sports, Niagara Therapy, Nicholas Duncan, Tony Seaney, Freddie Mitman, John Paul Mitchell Systems, Harold Leighton, Sabona of London, Detmar Hackman.

Product and services sponsors were: De Beers, Olympus Optical, Berghaus, Snowsled (Ventile), Ever Ready, Coleman, British Airways (vaccinations), Parlour Products, Safariquip, Survival Aids, Blacks of Manchester, Schwartzkopf, L'Oriel, RPM Records, Piz Buin, CCS Camera Care, Raleigh Industries (Nigeria), Graham Plain (SARBE).

Yet more people gave their time during the planning stage, for sponsorship contacts, route and logistical advice and a thousand other details without asking for anything in return. I would especially like to thank: Michael and Mariantoinetta Asher, Col. John Blashford-Snell, Warren Burton (Encounter Overland), Belinda Boyd, Lord and Lady Chelsea, Chris Cook, Jerry Callow, Lord and Lady Coleridge, Nick Cater, Simon Costain, Nicholas Duncan, Judy Drake, Capt. Robert Guy, Abel Haddon, Andrew Harwich, Jim Hargreaves, Mark Harvey, Brian Hanson, Sally Hancock, Alan Hooper, Paul Harris, Anthony Howard, Tony Jones (Encounter Overland) and Stan, Trevor Jones, Phillip Jones, Dr Ken Kingsbury, Mark Lucas, Luly Thomson, Alan Massam, Renske Mann, Iain McDonald, Andrew Muir, Jean-Pierre Peulerée, Richard Robinson, Major John Reeve, Jonathan Shalit, Alison Scott, John Stevens, Richard Snailham, Pippa Snook, Kurt Sartorious, Bertie Way, Shane Winser, Anthony Willoughby, Graham Wallace.

During the walk, I would like to thank the following people for their kindness, many of whom put themselves to considerable inconvenience to help us: Vasilios Anagnostellis, Helga Baak, Karen Baak, Harold, Karen and Cherina Blackburne, Nick Byers, Del and Jack Craig, Rene Craane, Brian Donaldson, Kevin Grotts, Chris Hill, Zaven Keorkinyan, Mr and Mrs Gordon Pirie, Sir and Lady Allan

Ramsay, Janet and Ali Reda, Jeff Roy, Johnnie Simpson, Dan and Libby Simpson, Andy Sutcliff, Stephanie Sweet, Col. Adrian Wray.

From Survival International, I would like to thank Stephen Corry, Honor Drysdale and Charlotte Sankey for their enthusiasm.

On the home front, I would like to thank my patron, Robin Hanbury-Tenison OBE for his support and Robin Allen for his silent patronage and his faith in my walk. Thanks to my father for listening and to my mother for handling the press with such humour – at last you can read about all the things I wouldn't tell you! And Max Arthur, for encouraging me when I was down and for celebrating when I wasn't. Martyn Forrester for his support. Luly Thomson for her initial enthusiasm and my sister, Shuna, for running the logistics for eight months without cracking up.

In the gestation of the book, I would like to thank the world's number one writer's hero, Mark Lucas and his better half, Lavinia Barnes; and Yvette Goulden and Nick McDowell at Orion for their enthusiasm.

But, if I hadn't had good people with me I'd be dead and eaten by now or sitting in a corner staring at a wall. Very special thanks go to those who went the extra mile: Bill Preston, Blake Rose, Raymond Mears, Tom Metcalfe and Peter Gray.

My greatest admiration is for the African people themselves, theirs is a tougher road than mine ever was – because people want to change them.

Ffyona Campbell

The *Guinness Book of Records* has a set of rules defining the walk around the world: you must begin and finish in the same place, cross four continents and cover at least 26,400 kilometres. Two men have done it, stopping as I have done and working between walks, but no women.

My Transworld Walk began at John O'Groats when I was sixteen. With my hair in dreadlocks and a hamster in my pack I walked 1,600 kilometres to Land's End in forty-nine days; an average of forty kilometres a day.

Two years later I walked across America from New York to Los Angeles. I was eighteen and it was my first experience of paranoia. At every town, it seemed, my sponsor threatened to pull out. But I did the 5,600 kilometres in 151 days; an average, again, of forty kilometres a day.

Australia was next. 5,100 kilometres from Sydney to Perth, in a planned 150 days. I spent two years getting the finance together, but on the eve of the walk my main sponsor called me up and said, 'Hello Ffyona. I've been in contact with our Australia office who are running a promotional event which clashes with yours. I'm afraid we're going to pass on this opportunity.' In short, I didn't have enough money to walk across the continent at forty kilometres a day, so I walked eighty kilometres.

The toughest part of that journey was the 1,600 kilometres across the Nullabor Plain. It was the training ground – the mental training ground – for Africa. I learned never to think of the end of the journey or even the end of the day.

My two successful predecessors had crossed Europe, Asia, Australia, and America. I decided to substitute Africa for Asia; I like to walk from one end of a continent to the other and too many parts of Asia were impassable.

My good friend Anthony Willoughby suggested I take the old

explorers' route, Cape Town to Cairo. Drawing a straight line between the two, I didn't have to be Foreign Secretary to foresee a few complications: there was a major war in Sudan for a start. But I took the view that I would just have to hang loose and be ready to sidestep the hot spots when they ignited.

After some research into water and food availability, I discovered there were several long stretches where there wasn't likely to be much of either. I would need back-up. I am not a traveller; I do not wander where the fancy takes me. My expeditions are more focused. The planned route covered 10,000 kilometres (6,300 miles), which would take me a year to walk at my usual speed. I had never been to Africa and I didn't want to recce it: if you don't know how bad it can get you always think tomorrow will be better.

I decided on a vehicle and two drivers, which I hired from One Ten Expeditions, a company specializing in expedition support. I paid for a fully equipped Land Rover, fuel, documents and drivers' flights, wages and food for a year. My office back-up came in the form of Luly Thomson, who had been Bob Geldof's right-hand man during Band Aid. She was fun to be around, and provided good, old-fashioned moral support. I hoped that she would also keep family and friends updated on my progress, and sponsors informed.

All my walks have benefited a charity because they are vehicles which can – so why not? This time I wanted a charity which benefited people in the countries on my route. There were plenty covering Kenya, Tanzania, Zimbabwe and Nigeria but little in between. Then, through my investigations, I came across Survival International, an organization which lobbies for the rights of threatened tribal peoples.

Now all I needed were the sponsors themselves, and I spent the next two years looking.

My aim was to get one major sponsor, since smaller ones often want more than their pound of flesh and rarely get satisfactory returns. I've been turned down only once for sponsorship when I've actually got in front of the decision makers, but now nobody wanted to meet me. The recession was biting hard, Saddam Hussein had invaded Kuwait, and the charred remains of a British girl, Julie Ward, had just been found in a Kenyan game park. Companies don't like sponsoring individuals at the best of times because of the high chance of failure, and no one wants their logo on a dead body.

Almost in desperation, I went to the British Footwear Fair at Olympia in August 1990, hoping to meet marketing directors. It was the wrong fair; all high heels and slingbacks. Kids' slippers with elephant motifs were about as African as it got. But Hi-Tec was there, standing out like a stubbed toe. I picked up their hiking boots and read the blurb. 'Tested on expeditions around the world,' it said.

So I asked the guy on the stand: 'Which expeditions?'

He didn't know. I told him about my walk and said that if he really wanted to test them, he should sponsor me. Luly and I were invited to make a follow-up presentation to him at his office, which we did. The meeting went well and they agreed to get back to me within a fortnight.

Three months later I got a call to say no. I heard this on a Friday night, but by Monday morning I'd got them to put in half on the basis that I would come up with the rest by the end of February. Just £25,000 to find in two months, then.

Nick Gordon, the editor of *You* magazine, went some of the way to bridging that gap over a round of carpet golf in his office. I was very glad he came straight to the point because I can't play golf and it was my throw.

I went to Sydney in early February to promote *Feet of Clay*, the book I had written about my Australian journey. I worked my way west, hoping for a miracle. A sports injury equipment salesman heard me on a radio chat show in Perth, while driving home from the office. He called me up with an offer: a free massage in my hotel room. My first reaction was to tell him where to shove his sports injury equipment, but I accepted dinner. Across a candlelit table I asked him for sponsorship and he said he'd get on to it. I said I'd heard that one before.

I was tannoyed at the airport the next morning. Nicholas Duncan had persuaded his company, Niagara Therapy, to put in 5,000 Australian dollars. With two weeks to go before I headed for Africa, I was still £12,500 short.

When I got back to One Ten Expedition's office in London there was a box of shampoo waiting for me, sent by the marketing director of John Paul Mitchell salon hair care products. 'Because I heard your voice on the radio and thought you must have beautiful hair,' said the accompanying note.

I called him up, thanked him and asked him for money. Four days later we met in Kensington and he agreed to put in £2,000 then and there and £2,000 at the end of the walk. We said goodbye and I went back to my car to find it had been broken into. I'd left my briefcase in there with my passport, credit card and keys. I cancelled

my credit card but I couldn't get out of the car park because I had
no cash. Then I remembered that my boyfriend's mother had given
me £20 for my birthday to buy a towelling dressing gown for the
trip – much more practical than a towel – and I'd stuffed the money
into the ashtray.

I was still £10,500 short on my original budget, but decided I
couldn't hang around any longer. There was nothing left in the pot
to pay Luly, but she very gallantly decided to continue working for
me and be paid later. The One Ten Land Rover was duly shipped
to Cape Town, loaded up with kit and food stores for the remoter
places, in time to start on 2 April 1991. Towards the end, the pages
in my diary looked like a wall of graffiti, until the final day, when the
scribblings were given a priority number:

1) sew badge on late jacket 2) get reshaped insoles from Simon 3)
to bank, get replacement card, cash, T/C 4) Phone Aunt Rabbit
5) sign four (six?) cheques for Nic re old parking tickets 6) Mark
re photo agreement 7) put car in bin 8) take back video 9) clean
flat of perishables 10) bone for Fraz 11) PACK! 12) record ans
machine mess – 'Hello, this is Ffyona Campbell, I've gone for a
walk ...'

I never like saying goodbye, especially to men I've fallen in love with.

Six months earlier, I'd taken a one-week course at Raymond Mears' bushcraft 'school' in Surrey. An expert outdoorsman, Raymond lectured and wrote extensively on his subject, and had set up and run the selection weekends for Operation Raleigh. He followed the philosophy of the North American Indians and had a deep affinity with their ways. It only took me a day to two to realize that I had a deep affinity with his.

The day before I was due to leave for Cape Town was also the day before Raymond started teaching another bushcraft course, so our farewells took place in Selborne. None of the students had arrived yet, and we spent the night in the woods alone. Raymond gave me the tooth of a fox we had known. He'd dug up the skeleton and had boiled it white, then threaded a piece of coarse rawhide through the top to make a necklace. It was to protect me. He'd made one for himself, too, and we put them on each other.

Raymond had also made a sheath and antler-horn handle for the carbon steel neck-knife he had specially commissioned for me from Wilkinson Sword. He had dyed the cord deep red to show that I'd earned my spurs in bush-craft skills. Finally, he gave me his moccasins. Then I prepared my medicine bundle. I felt it was important to play out these rituals; they made me feel special, like being let in on a secret.

When I drove to Heathrow the next morning I was crying. My parents had flown up from Devon to see me off, and my sister Shuna had come down from London. We women sobbed our way through the departure lounge. It was ridiculous, really, us making such a fuss. But I missed Raymond's counsel and comfort already, and I was frightened of Africa.

I flew to Cape Town with my firebow on my knee and my knife

at my right-hand side: *Draw it with honour, Fi, sheath it with courage.* My fox's tooth was around my neck. None of these totems shielded me from my first brush with African bureaucracy.

'Would you mind not stamping my passport?' I asked the immigration official, a white. 'I'm travelling up through Africa and will be refused entry into some countries if they know I've visited South Africa.'

It seemed a normal enough request, but with stamp poised he said in a brutally clipped accent, 'Well, you should have got a letter of authorization from the Embassy in London.'

'I had tea with the ambassador,' I said. 'He didn't mention this.'

For a terrible moment it looked as though the walk was over before I'd taken a single step. Then, with a highly theatrical sigh, he took the sheet of paper I had offered him and brought down the stamp.

The South African media were waiting for me outside, gathered around a banner from Hi-Tec that said: 'Just don't quit.' They wanted me to do some bimbo poses in shorts and running vest. I didn't mind the sporty image: it somehow delayed the shock of khaki and the real Africa, and I guessed it would make people I met in civilization more comfortable if they could put me in a box.

As Brad, the managing director of Hi-Tec's South Africa operation, drove me to my hotel, he dropped a bombshell: he had delayed the start of the walk by two weeks because he wanted me to do some promotional odds and ends.

'You'd have to wait anyway,' he said. 'The funds haven't come through from London.'

'Why not?'

'Because of the exchange rate rules. You wanted it in sterling.'

'Well, I can hardly walk the length of Africa with a purseful of rand, can I?' I said through gritted teeth.

That night, the moon was full and I sensed Raymond's presence strongly. We had made a pact to look at the moon to 'talk' to each other. It was a North American Indian idea. I was clinging very tightly to this sort of stuff; I knew I had built him up in my mind as someone to walk towards. I needed something very powerful to pull me onwards, especially since I no longer had the hatred for my father, which I had used to fuel my Australian walk, to fall back on. He had dealt me the worst blow possible after the end of the Australia walk by bestowing praise on me, which left me standing at the bottom of Africa without a reason to walk to the top.

3

23 March: *Under the Southern Cross again, and the distant dawning hum of insect life around the edges of the night – yet the yellow glow of the setting sun is still present in the west. Africa must be a very different kind of walk. This will be more than notching up miles; it will be a time to learn, to shape my future. The road home has never been longer nor so dear. This is my walk, my journey and my apprenticeship to life.*

Brad introduced me to Andrew Muir, who ran the Wilderness Leadership School. Its aim was to get people from different ethnic, economic and social backgrounds together in the outdoors, to show them that they could get along. In the process they were taught about the wilderness, how fragile it is and why it must be maintained.

The following day Oliver Ryder, one of the drivers, flew in from London. He wasn't due for another week, but he said he'd got bored. Just twenty-one, Oli was a gangly six feet seven. His brown hair was City interview length, and he had clear blue eyes and a deep, upper-class voice.

At 5a.m. the next day he left with me, Andrew and Andrew's girlfriend for the drive to a farm in the Karoo. Andrew wanted to meet a group of Bushmen who had been brought down from Namibia by some farmers – the Bushmen wanted to live in their traditional way, having escaped from virtual slavery at the hands of some Portuguese. Andrew also wanted to investigate why the South African farmers had given the Bushmen a home, and find out if he could train some of the men to become guides for the Wilderness Leadership School.

We spent two days there. It didn't take us long to figure out that this wasn't a mission of mercy: the farmers had built 100 holiday bungalows in the semi-desert and wanted to attract visitors. The Bushmen were the attraction, and their story had attracted the media.

The previous day they'd been taken to Cape Town for a photo shoot. Dressed in their skins, they had been paraded around. It was degrading. They had forgotten many of their skills and could not hunt. The Elder, Davit, was hitting the booze. The women, as always, were keeping things together.

The farmers had built the bungalows on a sacred site. There was a natural spring amongst the sandstone rocks, covered with Bushmen art. The farmers had laid down concrete and turned it into a swimming pool with a tiled floor and ladders.

As we were leaving I saw a spitting cobra under a rock. Shiny black and frightened, it fired its venom at the manager but he was saved by his glasses. Some local boys tried to catch it, but they were unprotected by spectacles.

'It doesn't matter,' the manager said, 'there's lot of them around.'

I didn't understand. 'Spitting cobras?' I said.

'Boys,' he laughed.

Andrew also took me to two shanty towns outside Cape Town.

Total population of Khayelitsha and Crossroads: 15,000.

Total number of toilets: 2.

Children ran in and out of the piles of burning rubbish, touching our skin, laughing and curious.

When we left the compound we saw several young boys painted in white chalk standing by the motorway. It was a part of their circumcision ceremony, Andrew explained; they must spend two weeks alone in the wilderness using all the skills they had learned to stay alive. But these boys didn't have any wilderness to go to, so they stood by the motorway.

While researching the route back in London I had been told about Pippa Snook, a water engineer who wanted to follow Livingstone's footsteps by motorbike. She lived in Devon and we had tried to meet up, but when I drove to her house in a gale, the road was blocked by a fallen tree. I now got a call from her saying she was in Durban and hitching down for the start of the walk. When she arrived, we spread out the map and she told me point blank that I couldn't walk forty kilometres a day through much of Africa. She'd been up through Zaire but the route I intended was apparently impassable for vehicles.

'We'll cross that bridge when we come to it,' I said.

'Bridge?' she said.

*

The Land Rover arrived at the port. However, the bill of lading, carnet and other bits of paperwork did not. They had been couriered from London by DHL several days before, but the local office could not trace them. I did some tracing of my own. I found they were in Johannesburg, and couldn't get to us for another three days. I was beginning to get a feel for African efficiency.

Charles Norwood, the owner of One Ten Expeditions, had omitted to tell me that Oliver would be leaving in Zaire because he had a job in the City waiting for him. Of the other driver, Gerry Moffatt, he had told me nothing except that he was Scottish and a good guy – no clues on how long he would be staying. Charles really knew how to make a girl relax.

Charles and Gerry Moffatt arrived and the four of us went out for a meal with Brad and his wife and various Hi-Tec people. The restaurant we went to was unlicensed, but the owners had come up with a novel way round the problem.

'Oh, sir,' the waiter would say at appropriate intervals, 'do you mean that bottle of dry white wine you left outside? Let me fetch it for you.'

Charlie gave me a quiet pep talk about taking every day as it came. He'd been with me during the final rewrite of *Feet of Clay* and knew how much I'd missed of Australia because the journey was so fraught with physical pain and there had been no time to look around. He told me I must have fun because the journey was so long.

I looked up the table at Gerry. Twenty-six and five feet eight, he looked strong and wiry, and his hazel eyes were highly communicative. Charlie told me that he ranked in the top five kayakers in the world, and was an expert climber and skier. He'd been a driver and white water raft guide with Encounter Overland for the last four years. He appeared very sociable, with an infectious sense of humour expressed with a high-pitched voice and strong Edinburgh accent. He drank too much, and he smoked too much. No doubt about it, he was the life and soul of the party. I knew he was just the sort of person I was looking for, but I voiced my concern to Charlie about his boredom threshold. He didn't hear me.

Sunday was spent putting the stickers on the Land Rover and sorting out the equipment. Charlie indicated that Gerry and Oli should do the sorting and packing.

'This is their job,' he said. 'They have to set up a working routine, and it will give them a go at working together before hitting the road.'

It was the first of several signals to me that I should butt out of the back-up system.

That evening we sat in a street café with a piece of paper each and delegated jobs: arranging a police escort out of Cape Town since there would be a group of race walkers with me for the first hour; working out a route through town; paying the hotel bill; getting insurance.

I went to bed early with a bottle of brandy. I called my family and Raymond and told them I loved them. Then I had a long, hot bath, got very clean, watched TV, enjoyed the privacy of being behind a locked door, and consciously savoured everything I was about to do without, like flushing the loo, lying on the bed without being bothered by mozzies, and drinking out of a glass.

I felt as if I had turned my back on a secure future with the man I loved, and a stable and easy life – everything I had walked halfway around the world to achieve. I'd never experienced so much hype around the start of a walk and felt very nervous that I couldn't pull it off. I was scared of Africa and scared of the walking – mainly because I hadn't trained in Hi-Tec shoes. It takes about 300 kilometres to decide whether a pair of shoes will work and I hadn't walked more than eight kilometres in one stretch in the last six months because I had been working so hard to get the money and organize the logistics. It takes so long to get it all together that once everything's ready I think, 'Thank God that's over: but then comes the realization that I've got to go and do the walk. And I hadn't done *any* training.

I went through a kind of mental warm-up routine that night, reminding myself to take one day at a time, never to think of the end, to remember to laugh and have fun, not to look at the ground but keep my head up and look around. I felt better when I remembered that my daily schedule was only half what I had walked in Australia; then, I'd been forced to cover such ridiculous daily distances that I had reached Perth a mental and physical wreck.

We got up early and had a final logistics meeting. We were to be at the Camps Bay Hotel, opposite the Atlantic beach, at 10 a.m. for Hi-Tec's start celebrations.

I went to a bank and stood in the queue for forty-five minutes to get money out on my credit card. Charlie organized the insurance and Gerry and Oli went shopping. While they were walking along the street Gerry bumped into a lamp-post. There was a clang as it made contact with the metal plate in his head. Not knowing what had hit him, he got up fighting.

Oli rode the bike to Camps Bay and Charlie, Gerry and I drove in the Land Rover. We spent some time on the beach, drinking champagne cocktails with the Mayor of Cape Town, the De Beers rep and various other dignitaries. Mavis Hutchinson, nicknamed 'The Galloping Granny', was there to walk the first ten kilometres with me; she'd walked across America and Britain whilst in her fifties. There was a good media turn out but there were only so many times I could run in and out of the ocean. I did one last one, just for me, saying to myself: 'The walk begins.'

Gerry was videoing it, Charlie was photographing it. I turned to the video camera and said, as I have always done before the start of a continent: 'Don't worry Fi, you're just going for a walk.' Then I half-filled a 35mm film canister with sand. I would fill the rest of it when I reached Cairo, with sand from the Mediterranean.

I walked onto the grassy bank where the Land Rover was festooned with Hi-Tec logos. We lined up for team photos and the mayor presented me with a scarf. I gave a speech, not a very good one, about the importance of sport as a way of uniting people.

Then I thanked everyone and said: 'I'm off!'

Everyone thought I was just doing dummy runs for the cameras and stayed around drinking champagne and eating canapés.

But I had started.

Ten minutes later I got a stitch. After the walking entourage had stepped into the airconditioned cars that were waiting for them, I hammered on through the centre of Cape Town, feeling hot and wobbly. Oli caught up with me on the bike. We pressed on through some rough industrial areas and then out into that awful mess that characterizes the outskirts of every town.

We stopped that evening in Goodwood, where the Holiday Inn had agreed to put us up. I'd only done twenty-seven kilometres but we'd started very late. The shoes were fine so far but a shin splint had started in my right leg. I'd suffered from them very badly during the first two weeks of the Australian journey and couldn't face going through that kind of pain again. I'd had a pair of insoles made to correct the pronation in my gait and reduce the risk of the injury recurring, but they obviously weren't working: I usually got shin splints in the hills, but here the terrain was flat. It scared the shit out of me.

We showered and Charlie and I had a chat about money. He

wanted payment for bringing down my equipment in the Land Rover, even though it hadn't cost him a penny. He said that if he hadn't done it, I'd have had to pay somebody else to do it. I said that I'd paid him £25,000 for the full hire of a Land Rover for a year, including drivers. He was over budget, he said, because the passengers he'd planned to bring to South Africa had backed out, and instead of making a profit on bringing down the Land Rover overland, he'd spent £2,000 more on shipping. He asked if I could help out by paying for the drivers' food. I finally agreed when he assured me that food in Africa was very cheap. Little did I know.

I'd decided that, as in Australia, the sections would be called 'quarters'. On the Sydney to Perth walk I had had five sections to do a day, but could never get used to calling them 'fifths'. My planned routine for the first two weeks was to walk two and a half quarters each day: sixteen kilometres to breakfast, sixteen to lunch then eight to day's end at around 2p.m.

Much to my annoyance, Charlie insisted that one of the drivers walk with me at all times – but he knew Africa, I didn't.

I walked with Gerry the second morning. Habitation petered out into fast food chains, then the dregs of old railways rusting and grass scrubby with red dust, and then white gum leaves – my old friends. I was hot, dehydrated and irritable.

Walking is uncomfortable. When you're getting shin splints, blisters, nails coming off, muscles stiffening, sunburn, diarrhoea and body sores, it's difficult in the beginning to calm yourself and not be annoyed with the drivers, even if they're not doing anything wrong. To some extent my annoyance this time round was alleviated by them each walking a quarter a day with me, but when I stood up at the end of a break to face another painful sixteen kilometres of road, knowing that all they had to do was slide behind the wheel of the Land Rover – well, it got to me. I envied them being able to drive. I envied them the enjoyment and anticipation of a new day without blisters. It's lonely out there, without anyone to share the grumbling and soften it with humour. Getting into a break and peeling off the shoes and socks alone is lonely. I'm in pain and I don't really want to do it anyway – but I am the one who makes the journey move forward, so I can't let up. I have to have a very strict routine or I wouldn't cover the distance. I'd been working for myself for two years; if I didn't want to do something, I just didn't do it. That works in the city; life generates its own momentum. But on the road, nothing takes place unless I walk to it.

I had spoken to Robert Swan, the polar walker, about back-up – he thought it was a fabulous idea to get to day's end and have the camp set up.

'Yes, that's nice,' I'd said, 'but how would you feel if you were plodding along in pain, cold and exhausted, knowing that a snow mobile was up ahead with all the other team members inside, all cosy and warm, drinking hot chocolate and enjoying a laugh?'

Ran Fiennes was running a river in the wilds of Canada while being filmed by a crew on the bank who were struggling with heavy camera equipment. The director wanted to hire pack horses for them, but to Fiennes' mind the ethics of the expedition, a river journey, excluded outside support. 'I can hardly expect my guys to stumble on with heavy backpacks when there are ponies a few yards behind us which could happily take all our gear as well as yours,' he said. He got a lot of flak about it, but I saw his point.

Charlie walked with me in the afternoon. He talked of paragliding and we watched the thermals building up behind the hazy, jagged mountains far in the distance. The road became more like the Africa I had looked forward to. There were dirt verges upon which I walked to help the shin splints ease. Trucks carried workers who stood up in the wind, waving to me. I saw women and schoolchildren, one carrying a box of newspapers on her head. She probably lived in the shanty town we had passed a little earlier. The town was full of rubbish, for they are granted no garbage collection and must burn what they can and scatter the rest. The buildings were made of corrugated iron and wood, some with a single glass pane. Small children waved and laughed at us. They were the first to wave at me since I began, and one gave the clenched fist of salute of Black Power.

Paarl loomed in the distance with its rounded hilltop rock and painted monument to the Afrikaans language.

A BBC camera crew was still hovering around. They arrived just as Charlie and I reached a junction and were debating the route. We took the road we thought was right, waiting for the Land Rover which carried the map. It was my fault – I should have taken the map with me or at least memorized the route because I couldn't rely on the Land Rover to be there at every turn just yet. The drivers hadn't worked out their timings and in a car you don't understand the importance of distance – being a couple of kilometres over doesn't worry you. Half an hour later the Land Rover caught up with us: we'd gone the wrong way. Wasted steps.

The boys had secured us a place in a camp resort for free. I marked the road at the end of the day with orange spray paint and we drove to the campsite. I am fanatical about walking every step of the way, so the road had to be marked well enough to find again in the dark the next morning. I found it easiest to walk to an object like a tree or a telegraph pole and touch it that night, then start by touching it again the next morning.

The campsite was lovely, green with lots of flowers. The evening light in South Africa is golden and lasts for at least an hour. I was very stiff that evening and Gerry massaged my legs after I'd stretched.

It was Oli's turn to cook. Instead of asking what I could do to help I just mucked in and started cutting up the cheese while he put the macaroni on the petrol stove. Charlie again took me aside and told me to leave the boys to do their thing. I felt embarrassed; it showed I didn't know the score. But on my walks I want to be involved with the camp because it makes me feel like I am part of the team, part of the process of setting up a home. I need to absorb myself mentally and physically in something other than walking. Repeating the same movements with my body for eight hours a day and then sitting down, doing nothing but writing or dressing my feet, means that I become clumsy. In Australia, there wasn't any time during the 120-hour walking week to do anything in the four-hour nights but syringe blisters, eat and sleep. It was a journey, not a way of life. But on the rest days, nothing gave me more pleasure than cleaning out the back-up van and making a place in the bush. The back-up driver, David, had certainly not objected.

As the sun set, the camera crew said their goodbyes. The frivolities were now over. I envied them their freedom to leave.

4

At 5.30a.m. I was woken up with a metal mug of tea handed into my roof tent. Hey, nice touch, guys! After a breakfast of fruit I set off half an hour later, at dawn.

It was two hours before the Land Rover passed me on its way to the first break; the boys hadn't sussed yet that it was more relaxing to pack up quickly, get ahead and have their breakfast while waiting a couple of hours for me to catch up.

I like walking very fast – eight kilometres (five miles) per hour. The exercise gives me a high and it means I get the walking over with quickly. My plan was to walk sixteen kilometres and meet them at breakfast. I'd take a break of half an hour, and set off while they packed up. While I was walking the next sixteen kilometres they'd pass me again, and meet me for a lunch of sandwiches, pasta or leftovers and tea. After an hour, I'd set off for the final quarter and meet them again for evening camp. The boys had to get into the habit of measuring distance very precisely – they pressed the mileage gauge each time they left a break, but if they had to go into town either ahead of me or back, they had to remember to compensate.

People imagine for some reason that the back-up vehicle crawled behind me every inch of the way. This is a good way of pushing both back-up and walker to the point of suicide. In fact, it was very important that it kept away from me so I couldn't hear or see it, and *ahead* of me, because if they broke down behind me I would be stranded with only what I carried – a small day pack with a plastic, one-litre water bottle, loo paper, a small plastic bottle of talc for body sores, bananas, sunglasses, zinc for my nose.

I set out for Ceres, Charlie walking with me for the morning as, side by side, we matched step and talked about his times in Africa. Nothing appeared to faze him because there was always a solution.

He was a good bush mechanic and in many ways he treated life like he did the engine of a Land Rover. Whatever the problem, it could be fixed – just give him the right spare parts, the tools and a strong right arm.

There were burnt wheat fields on both sides of the road, black and ochre palettes divided by the ribbons of steel of the railway tracks that had shadowed me for several days. A train driver waved to us, chugging his arm like a speed walker and smiling broadly. The mountains kept their distance on my right, never seeming to come any closer.

Gerry found us a good camp ground, although he had to use his considerable charm to convince them to let us stay. We had tents to pitch and the owners only accepted caravans. The air was quite cool by late afternoon and we were in a bowl between the mountains and vineyards on many of the slopes. This was one of South Africa's best known wine-growing areas and the only place where grapes were sometimes harvested at night to give them a special flavour.

This produce had to be sampled, of course. Gerry cooked a chicken casserole and afterwards, almost reverentially, Charlie opened the bottle of whisky he'd been carrying with him since he left London. It disappeared with surprising alacrity but the boys cheered up when the boss of the camp ground arrived with a bottle of brandy. This was washed down with a bottle of red wine, one of sparkling and two of grape juice.

A local Boer had arrived wearing a khaki uniform with epaulettes. Small and thin with a meanly trimmed moustache, he was a loutish, opinionated snob who became increasingly angry as the boys grew steadily pissed and kept interjecting during his monologues about white colonial rule and the savagery of the 'blecks in South Efrica'. He told us about a recent earthquake, but said it wasn't too bad – nobody died. A few blacks were killed, but nobody died.

In the throes of a severe hangover the next morning, Gerry looked ready to sell his soul to anybody who could take the pain away. To make matters worse, a howling wet wind blew from the southeast, bending sapling trunks almost sideways and threatening to carry away anything not tied down.

This was the toughest mountain section so far – the crossing of Michell's Pass, which had been built during the gold rush of the 1880s to service the ox-carts driven up to the Transvaal by men who dreamed of finding their fortune a few inches beneath the earth.

To the right of us, deep in a gorge, Gerry heard white water thundering over the rocks. He told me the story of his restructured feet. Ten years earlier, at the age of sixteen, he'd gone kayaking in Austria. He came over a rapid and plunged into a pool at the wrong angle. The kayak nose-dived into the rocks, hurling his body forwards so that his feet were forced into the narrow point. His toes were bent back over his feet. His wrist and ribs were broken and he fractured his skull. Worse was to follow.

Lying unconscious under water, still trapped in his kayak, Gerry was swept downstream for over a minute, his head being bashed against submerged rocks. Finally caught in an eddy, he was pulled to safety and given mouth-to-mouth resuscitation.

Although lucky to be alive, Gerry had no medical insurance and he knew the hospital bills would be too much for him or his parents. He told doctors that he had a flight booked to Scotland and discharged himself from hospital. Instead, a friend drove through the night for fourteen hours while he lay on the back seat in agony. Back in Britain, a metal plate was inserted in his head and his feet were rebroken and set in plaster. They were never the same again.

There was so much latent energy in the mountains rising around us; so much power in the rugged peaks that were cooled by the clouds. It reminded us both of Glen Coe in Scotland, where we each had different experiences of the cold and wet that enfolds it.

Baboons scattered into the higher ground as we passed and we picked up stones ready to defend ourselves. They don't normally attack but the fangs of a baboon can pull down an antelope and, young or old, they show little fear of humans. If food is around they'll find it, even if it means opening car doors or unfastening the ropes on a trailer tarpaulin.

A large male watched us pass, staring intently at the funny Gore-Tex'd couple, and then rolled several large stones down the cliff face to see if he could make us scurry.

Pushing up those long contours felt good and I kept up a fast pace. During those first few days I had been preoccupied with my own fitness and fears. I was working hard at training my mind not to think ahead or else I'd panic at the enormity of the distance. I would need it to keep me going steadily through the rainforest, when living conditions would get bad, stress mounted and there was no way to stop and get off. I did panic sometimes on walks and I'd have to pull in the reins and control myself. Sometimes the hardship is the easy stretch because there's something tangible to battle with, the easy stretches are not always as they seem. The mind is what gets me through – the body just follows. It helps if the body is in good condition for the task but my body was soft – I was used to eating plastic-wrapped food from the supermarket, having showers every day, not being bitten by insects or spending all day in the sun.

I didn't have time in all of this to consider how Oli, Gerry and Charlie were coping. This was all very new to them and they were learning every day. Being back-up on a walk is a vital job but the pace is slow. The adrenaline rushes that come with an adventure don't happen every day and the miles creep along rather than get eaten up. The job itself, once learned in a few days, is very boring.

Gerry, in particular, didn't seem to understand about pacing yourself and not looking ahead to months of the same – I had tried to explain this idea as a way of dealing with the pace but had been rebuked for trying to teach an overland veteran how to suck eggs. It was an odd set-up for him in other ways, too. I had spent two years planning the walk; he had just arrived. Yet I didn't know anything about Africa and he did. At the same time, because it was my walk, I was getting all the attention: he was taking the lead, yet not receiving any public or private acknowledgement from me for it.

There were rumblings of dissent within the ranks. When I told Gerry how well he'd done walking that morning this was construed as me being patronizing. And when, cold and wet, I asked Charlie and Oli for a cup of Bovril for the two of us, they had just looked at each other as if to say, 'Who does she think she is?'

Gerry tried to help. 'C'mon guys, it'd warm us up as we're quite cold.'

Finally a kettle was boiled and Charlie and Oli stood out in the rain in protest while Gerry and I sat in the Land Rover. It was totally unnecessary. In only a few minutes they could have rigged up the tarpaulin and kept out the rain.

I'd write at each break, which the boys also seemed to find irritating, especially when there were tensions. Then I'd get out my day bag and set up a small mirror and apply lashings of moisturizer, zinc on my nose and suntan cream. I got ragged mercilessly for it but my skin couldn't take ten hours of sun.

We had a long way to go and it didn't augur well that already petty jealousies and tantrums were surfacing. I was glad that Charlie would only be with us for the first two weeks. He could be moody and uncommunicative and it didn't help morale.

That night we camped under tall pines and had rice and bolognaise for supper. The evening was windy and cold. I snuggled underneath my duvet, curling into a ball as I listened to the trees groaning. Now that the veldt had arrived it felt more like Africa. It was huge and, alone in my cocoon, I felt smaller than ever.

My roof tent was made of yellow, middleweight canvas and folded in half across its width to lie flat on the roof rack. Our sleeping bags, thermorests and tent went on top and a heavy plastic, dark blue tarp fitted over all of it with a rope running through eye holes around the edge which slipped under hooks. To set it up, I'd climb on top of the spare wheel on the bonnet, grasp the side of the wooden base board and pull up and then down over my head. The board projected two feet over the bonnet, the tent folding out automatically with two U-shaped metal poles which form a fan shape.

There was a foam mattress two inches thick, covered in a dark blue cotton case. I hate sleeping bags – they're too restrictive, hot and slithery. I always take a duvet and sheets. It was the duvet I'd been given when I was six and first went to boarding school. There were two flap doors, one on each end. At the back was the row of water and diesel jerry cans and a space where I kept four dark blue nylon stuff sacks with my clothes so that I could get dressed up there. On many clear nights, I'd flip the door flap over the top, put my pillow on the stuff sacks and lie under the stars. The door and the four triangular windows had mosquito netting covers but they were so weak they split. It was not mozzie free. In the heavily infested areas I would hang a net inside from the roof struts and tuck it under the mattress. However, the joints at the side let mozzies in. It was the cheapest on the market; for a few quid more I could have had a waterproof, insect-free zone.

Along the side at the back I had a laundry stuff sack, my bow drill and my bits bag of little treasures which I never used. I put my shoes in the space between the floor board and the Land Rover's roof. I loved my tent. It was a sanctuary and lying inside with my head torch hanging from the roof strut it glowed warm yellow, my favourite colour. The only setback was going to the loo in the night, which meant climbing down.

Because Ceres is in a bowl surrounded by mountains we had to leave it via a pass, similar to the one we had entered by. It was all uphill for the first fifteen kilometres through Hottentot's Kloof, which I reached in the growing light of the morning. I walked alone this time with Charlie taking pictures from the Land Rover, using the rugged peaks as a backdrop. The morning light threw long shadows and made the mountains appear to be covered in old brown velvet against a perfect blue sky. The sun was bright as I faced it walking east.

I pounded hard up mountains steep enough to burn out the gear boxes of cars and trucks. My speed increased with an incline – nine kilometres per hour uphill in top speed. Something had to give.

A shin splint began to develop in my right leg, which was unusual because normally it was my left one that gave me problems. At the same time my energy level was low and I was pleased to see the Land Rover parked for pictures at regular intervals where I could eat fruit and recharge.

I didn't wear a watch because I'd keep looking at it and time would drag on. I'd know when a break was coming up because at around thirteen kilometres my thighs would stiffen and I'd get a bit light-headed and out of energy. I'd anticipate the Land Rover over each horizon, which got very frustrating if I'd been in daydreams and didn't know what time it was. I found that if I ate a banana just before I set off, by eight kilometres I couldn't taste it in my mouth so I knew I was half-way.

Seeing the Land Rover was always such a joy if it was a surprise – it gave me a sense of looking for treasure three times a day. It was also my way of proving I never cheated because I would get to the breaks at exactly the same time give or take ten minutes depending on heat, terrain and diarrhoea – impossible if I had cheated.

As I reached the summit and stood on a small flat plateau the mountain peaks to my left rose still higher. There was a small orchard on a burnt scrap of land and a lone apple tree grew on the verge dropping its fruit for the birds and insects.

The view was glorious and I was filled with a sense of achievement after the slog. I spied a furry animal dashing into the scrubby bush and stalked after it. It was only a pale ginger cat, half-starved and frightened even though it had refused to get off the road when the Land Rover passed. A jackal barked in the distance and I realized that my ginger tom had every reason to be scared.

The boys had cleverly parked so that the shade fell on the opposite side of the Land Rover from the road so that we could eat in privacy. They'd set up the camping table, made of white formica with a dark blue edge and two U-shaped legs which folded flush underneath. This was set up against the Land Rover for stability. We had three fold-up camping chairs, two with padded seats and back and one with thick plastic netting. The last was useless in mozzie country – they'd hovver underneath and bite ya bum.

Beside the table was the red day box which contained ceramic plates, metal mugs, cutlery, condiments, herbs, spices and jars – Marmite, marmalade, African margarine which has to be virtually boiled before it will melt, a chopping board, a bottle of potassium permanganate and one of Chloromin T. The former was for washing fruit and veg – you soak them for forty minutes in a light solution – and the latter to give the electric pump a hand in purifying water which was severely stagnant. Just the edge of a matchstick per jerry was enough. We drank a lot of tea when the water was good but I switched to coffee when the water was too saline or too dodgy and needed more chlorine.

There were three plastic washing-up type bowls in a row – one for hands and body, one for fruit and veg (potassium permanganate stains everything brown even though it is purple), and one for washing up. We rinsed things in the vegetable bowl.

Some of the kit Charles had chosen was ridiculous. The Coleman double-burner unleaded petrol stove clogged constantly because there wasn't any unleaded fuel. I didn't know why they didn't cook on wood – a campfire is much easier, more jolly, can accommodate more pots, there are no gadgets to clean afterwards, no soot, and it smells nicer. But Charlie got one thing right. The water purifier was a good bit of kit – an electric pump which ran off the Land Rover's second battery and purified the water using a charcoal filter system with an ultraviolet light to kill anything left. It had a shower head and water came out under enough pressure to produce a decent spray.

At first break Gerry massaged my right lower shin and applied a Spenco bandage. I slipped into a size 8 shoe for the right foot and began walking again. It didn't take long to feel the downward slope catching at my calves and I felt the telltale hell of a shin splint. This, I knew from experience, was not going away.

Charlie urged me to stop but I continued until I was absolutely sure and then pulled up. It was the only sensible thing to do, particularly as the trip had only just begun and there was such a long way to go. I stopped after only sixteen kilometres.

We'd been on the road for six days, and nobody took any convincing about returning to the caravan site at Tulbagh for the rest day, where we knew we could relax in a free chalet and swim in the pool. I marked the side of the road with orange paint and clambered into the Land Rover, nursing my right shin.

Gerry walked with me as we put the mountains behind us and entered the Little Karoo, the semi-desert, with its open bushland clinging to sandy soil. For the first time we carried a water bottle, toilet paper and camera in a day pack. The boys had gone off to Ceres to collect my shoes and insoles, and to telex London and wait for the reply. They were due back by midday.

My leg hurt less and less as the road flattened and became a dirt track. I liked it but there was little space for daydreams when walking in company. In the distance we could see a faded mountain range and Gerry and I bet on reaching it before nightfall. Although I preferred walking alone, Gerry made me laugh and kept my spirits high. For as much as I enjoyed my own company, he was gregarious in the extreme.

It was dusty work walking with a headwind that acted like calamine lotion and took the heat from the sun in a cloudless blue sky. We averaged seeing a car every hour. As I unhooked the water bottle again, I told Gerry how stupid it was to be walking in the semi-desert with so little water and so much faith in the timekeeping of the boys. I wondered how long we could survive if they didn't turn up at midday. There wasn't enough water to turn back.

Our saliva was already thick and the last drops of water were warming in the bottle when Pippa Snook arrived in a dilapidated Land Rover with two Israelis we'd met the day before. It was pure chance.

They also had little water. The girls had insisted the driver fill up in Ceres but they were short of time and decided to push ahead to Sutherland. We drank and filled up our bottle then set off again with Pip striding along beside us. The Israelis' Land Rover caught up with us again and sacrificed more of their limited water. Pippa was worried about us in the desert, but I reassured her that the boys would catch up with us soon. She left.

There was no shade, and it was pointless to stop until we found some. But as we paced onwards, growing more and more dehydrated and increasingly quiet, a gnawing fear began to beat time with my steps. I kept looking behind and listening for the sound of the Land Rover's engine. The lack of water and uncertainty had gone beyond a joke. If I'd been alone I would have been furious, worried and probably in tears.

Another hour went by and still there was no sign of them. Suddenly the thought of perishing in the desert loomed large. This was madness but there was nowhere to go but onwards. It had been hours since we saw the last car and the bottle was again down to its last few drops.

Gerry's head had dropped and he paced with his eyes on the toes of his restructured feet. We had no energy left to talk. This was rapidly becoming a matter of survival. I spotted a tree in the distance and we pushed forward, hoping to shelter in the limited shade until the boys arrived.

And then I heard the engine. Oli and Charlie were full of smiles. There was no telex. They'd had to fix a puncture and repair the wheel. As I swallowed a litre of water, I thought of what would have happened if Pippa's Land Rover hadn't found us. That would have been a story for the newspapers back in Britain. 'Intrepid Walkers Perish in Desert.'

We'd walked almost the entire day's schedule but it would have been a battle without winning if I didn't complete the day. Gerry was game and after several litres of water and a sarnie, we set off for another three kilometres. At day's end, Gerry and I rode on to the campsite, sitting on the spare wheel of the Land Rover and laughing like mad people.

5

C harlie was leaving.

His parting words were: 'Take good care of the boys,' and I felt guilty. They had taken such good care of my meals and my wellbeing and I could do little for them in return. Right from the beginning Charlie had insisted that somebody always accompany me each day for security, but I didn't like them walking with me. On the other hand, I didn't know Africa yet, they enjoyed the exercise, and I didn't have the heart to refuse them.

Though Gerry and Oli's lives had gone in totally different directions, their paths had crossed in Africa on my walk. I envied both of them: each had had one home and one school.

Oli had had a fabulous childhood. He loved school and university – partying on and never having to work too hard to pass. There was a job already waiting for him at Kleinworts in London, one of five he was offered. He told them to wait and disappeared to Africa. This was his big adventure before settling down.

Gerry came from an intellectual family. He went to a Catholic school and then, at sixteen, left a family of four sisters and set out into the world. His life had been one long expedition ever since.

My upbringing compared so starkly with theirs. I suppose my father took the decision to get his daughters through the system however he could, but he was so financially stretched, I guess he assumed that school would take care of us as people. Perhaps he might have been more interested in us if we had been boys. All I know is that I missed out. I grew up on the outside looking in. Sport, skiing, sailing, riding, climbing – you name it, I never had the opportunities to do it because we were always moving and my parents liked to live in remote places. So I made my own adventures, always alone because there weren't any other kids around. I cycled and walked, taking my painting things with me and poured my energy into organizing new missions. Our household was typical of the military family; we had this mentality that we were waiting for something to change it all, 'when we get to the next house ...' But I didn't want to wait for them; I was bursting with energy to explore and be challenged; I was so utterly bored. I wanted to see the world and the only way I knew how was to walk.

People often asked me about my motivation. 'Why do you want to walk around the world?' 'Why Africa?' If I was lucky they stopped short of calling me crazy. I had many different answers. Often they changed with my moods. But in truth I needed my rite of passage, I needed to make a journey which would lead me through adolescence and into adulthood, earning respect for myself along the way. Native people understood it, but the constant questioning by my own people made me confused.

The low scrub growing out of the ochre-coloured earth was like the saltbush of Central Australia, devoid of shade or respite from the sun. The horizon was a line of mountains painted in various shades of purple and rimmed with reds as the sun rose and the clouds lifted like sheets unveiling a painting.

My new insoles had raised my foot, causing the top to press painfully against the laces and begin to swell. Another shin splint beckoned. I pushed back the hot tarmac under a belching sun and dry wind as the road climbed the mountains towards Sutherland, the highest town in South Africa. By the time I reached 1,800 metres, one foot was painfully swollen and my hair was plastered flat against my scalp. There was no joy at all until I saw a road sign announcing: 'Danger ahead – rough track. Fasten seat belts and remove all dentures.'

Gerry went to get ice in the town and found none. He improvised and bought several bottles of cold beer and I put them against my elevated foot at each of the breaks. I had started at seven that morning, far too late to escape the heat, and I could feel the 'one-hour-to-go' syndrome haunting me. I hated it.

I pushed along the dirt track with the wind in my hair, the sun on my back and daydreams drifting in and out of reality. A cinema played inside my head, urging my feet to follow. This daydreaming keeps me sane. I can enjoy the cool of the dawn, and the wild beauty of this sunburnt land, but slip into in a trance during which time passes more quickly. At the beginning of a walk I give myself permission to daydream without limits, build up people and play out scenes of my future life. Anything goes as long as I get to the end.

Then I must deal with sorting out fantasy from reality.

To add to the pain, or perhaps because of it, I missed Raymond dreadfully. We'd been together six months, long enough for me to be heartbroken at leaving him, and desperate enough to want to get home. I loved Raymond's affinity with the natural world. He seemed as comfortable in the forest as a brown bear. Amid the trees, miles from the nearest town, his eyes became firm and bold. He was still there in my daydreams, drawing me on. He was a constant, like a photo carried into battle.

6

I walk six days then have a day off. I call it a rest day but it's only a rest from walking, not from the trip. We all wash our clothes, bodies, clean up the kit and scrub down and repair the Land Rover. Now that Charlie had gone, I'd cook the supper on the eve of the 'weekend' and then get up first and give the drivers tea in bed and make breakfast the next morning. In the early days my bush cooking was awful, so for the drivers it was the last hurdle of the week to endure before the rest day.

I filled in a witness book at the end of each day for *The Guinness Book of Records*. It noted my position and the day's distance and a witness's name and address if we found someone during the day. It was a great boost to me to look down the column of daily distance and see a constant line of full days. In the first two weeks I walked forty kilometres a day but we got to day's end at 2p.m. and began to get very bored. So I added another eight kilometres each day. This meant I was gaining one day ahead of schedule every five. I stored these up as a reserve for the delays in border crossings, breakdowns, or illness.

Slowly I was beginning to enjoy the freedom of wandering over dirt tracks littered with the footprints and spoor of the creatures that thrive out there – traces that were now being added to by my team.

Poor Oli had been teased mercilessly by Gerry about his constipation and I was just as prone to getting blocked up. Perhaps it was the alcohol. After supper, as we sat around the campfire, Oli would sigh and with a trowel in one hand and a roll of toilet paper in the other head off into the darkness, hoping that he would finally get a result. After much grunting and teeth grinding he returned, disappointed.

Aside from fresh fruit and vegetables we were almost entirely self-sufficient. Every bit of spare space in the Land Rover was taken with supplies, pots and pans, tents, jerry cans of water and fuel, spare parts and our personal items. Each afternoon when we made camp, Gerry would immediately begin checking the vehicle, topping up the oil and water and running a few diagnostic tests. Our brush with disaster in the Little Karoo made me concerned about the Land Rover breaking down and not being there at the breaks. Meanwhile, Oli would begin setting up the tents and they took turns cooking supper.

Gerry had years of experience turning a can of Spam and bag of rice into something edible. With a few herbs and spices he seemed to make everything taste good, including my favourite egg pasta with tomato and lashings of salad cream. Oli, however, was the sort of cook who believed the guy who invented Marmite should get a Nobel Prize.

Every evening or in the morning before we broke camp, a hole had to be dug and the rubbish buried. Gerry was a little manic about it. He told Oli to bury the pepper grinder when we ran out of peppercorns and the cheese grater when we ran out of cheese. Whatever happened, we were sure to leave no trace of our passing save for the cold ash of the campfire. Already I'd noticed how much litter lay beside the roads: cigarette packs, cans of soft drink, plastic bottles, all carelessly tossed from passing cars. If more people walked these roads, they would see how their jetsam spoils the countryside.

Some rubbish, however, was recyclable. The boys quickly discovered that the blow-up silver bags inside wine boxes made wonderful pillows. This, of course, became a good excuse to drain the contents quickly.

The 7a.m. Cape Town to Jo'burg flight passed over ten minutes later than usual. It was a small sign that we were getting somewhere, and the Karoo was being conquered.

Arcs of dust were thrown up by every approaching car and billowed like rocket tails. Even though you can see the telltale cloud from miles away across the flat plains, it would be easy for an accident to happen.

I had slept poorly, kept awake by locusts that sounded as if they were powered by lawn mower engines. Thankfully, it was a cooler morning but I still put lashings of Vaseline on my cracked lips. Dodging the dust clouds as I walked with Gerry, I daydreamed.

I barely noticed what appeared to be a piece of firewood on the road and stepped straight over it. Gerry stopped dead in his tracks.

'It's a snake,' he said, edging sideways.

I laughed. 'Don't be silly.'

'Look! Look at its tongue. There! See it?'

Sure enough I saw the telltale dart of a tongue tasting the air.

'Christ! I almost kicked it,' I whispered, jumping backwards as the brown snake shimmied slowly and disappeared into the bush.

Later we discovered that if either of us had been bitten we could have stopped breathing within the hour.

The Great Karoo made me feel far more welcome than its little brother, although the terrain was much the same – small, spartan bushes along dry riverbeds and the occasional bore pump. This is a sandy land with rugged hills showing their layers in craggy lines. Since the beginning I'd been looking for scenery that matched my idea of the real Africa. So far I had walked through places that reminded me of the Mediterranean, Australia, Scotland. Now these hard, flat mountains and desert floor looked like southern Idaho, the traditional backdrop to countless Western movies.

There are sheep farms every thirty to forty kilometres in the Karoo, or wherever there's an oasis. One farmer saw us on the track and took us to his home for a *braai* (barbecue) of herby lamb sausages, a shower and a clean bed. Then he called his friend forty kilometres up the track to go out and find us that evening. A chain of hospitality was set in motion.

The Afrikaaners drink heavily and when they're pissed they want to talk politics. They haven't met many foreigners and are eager to explain the complexities of their situation in a way that the international press seems to ignore. It was quite an eye-opener. Sometimes their hospitality was exhausting. Sometimes all we wanted to do was have a quiet bush camp under the stars. Gerry was a very sociable guy and the hospitality we received was largely due to him. But I could already tell from his constant talk of future plans that he realized he was stuck and was fighting it.

He gave up when we hit Canarvon. We drove to the town for a few beers and I was asked to report to the Municipality Building. The mayor had heard we were coming and wanted to offer us free hotel rooms. Dangerously, the bar was also complimentary and the boys needed no second invitation. After the third or fourth beer, they commandeered the pool table and organized a tournament. Unfortunately, they included a local who proved to be the district champion for the previous two years. From what they told me the next day they were alone in a bar full of men who would have been right at home in brown shirts and army boots.

The next morning, as I walked through a shanty town on the fringes of Canarvon, the stench of dead animals carried to us like a gust of wind and nearly made me gag. Little kids in scraps of clothing played in the dust, lifting their gorgeous brown eyes as I passed. They waved and laughed with so much joy it made me despise the men we'd met in the bar the previous evening.

A walk was all I could see in my life. Nothing else existed until I finished. As I listened to Oli telling me what he'd do upon his return – drink a pint of bitter, drive his father's car fast and listen to the birds in the garden – I realized what a desperate and tenuous grasp I had on them both. I wanted them to enjoy the journey and not feel caged. Yet the very nature of their job precluded this – driving for only ten minutes every three hours. They wanted me to see us as a team but we didn't share the same goal and they weren't making anywhere near the same amount of sacrifices for even their short time on the trip. The strain of the easy days through South Africa broke their morale. The more they hated it, the more I was the focus of their hatred.

That night I drank in the scent of moon flowers and geraniums and tasted prickly pear, a yellow fruit with black seeds that is farmed over large areas of the veldt. I peeled off the skin with a knife because of the prickles. It was sweet.

The man with the most water wins in the desert. Some are very rich. One farm we passed had turned the scrubby desert into a shade-drenched valley thick with palms and heavy trees with moist leaves and thick trunks. The cool whitewashed farmhouse was decorated with brilliant bougainvillea.

Oli and I peered hard through the trees to see the stone walls and little grassy paddocks dotted with plump sheep. They were proper sheep, not the scrawny, black-faced variety that flock together in the dry scrubland. Around the corner the temperature rose by another ten degrees and we were out in the desert again.

This area of the Karoo is littered with dinosaur fossils. The high flat mountains that surrounded us mark where the earth's crust once reached. I watched a lizard haring across the road and into the graveyard of his prehistoric ancestors.

We had made the decision to push on for a couple of days to get to Prieska for the rest day. This, coupled with the additional five kilometres a day, was a mark of how well the mind games were working for me. I was relaxing into the rhythm of the walk and not fighting it as the boys were.

I love the silence of the dawn with only the crunching of my feet and the hum of my anxieties. The peace was shattered when a couple of young Hottentots came racing around a corner in their horse-drawn buggie like joyriders. They came to a sheepish standstill when they saw me. Maybe they were test driving it.

By first break I realized there was a cigarette emergency. We had less than a packet between us and were ninety kilometres from anywhere. I was also beginning to hallucinate about my favourite foods. I saw a cloud shaped like a Cornish pasty and half a case of wine. Then there were two bucket-like mountains and I longed for warm pitta bread with cheese and onion.

That afternoon we went in search of a bore hole and a swim. For days they had been dotted about the landscape and it didn't occur to us that we could use the precious water to cool off and clean ourselves. Now, finally put right, we went from hole to hole, only to find them surrounded by sheep droppings and covered in a scum of dead flies and insects. Covered in sweat and dust, we had to laugh.

The boys were hung over when I woke next morning and began walking. During the night, dreadfully homesick again, I had decided to continue trying to cover forty-eight kilometres a day for as long as possible. It would knock forty days off the walk and bring me home sooner. While the land was so flat, the task seemed reasonable.

It was still dark at 6.15 but I had the glorious sunrise to enjoy. I didn't want to think about the boys sleeping off their whisky and beer as I was out walking.

By mid-morning, the flies swarmed around my face, only my sunglasses preventing them from reaching my eyes. Sometimes I saw foxes with white tips to their tails. Sometimes I smelt death nearby. Grasshoppers flew before my feet like puffs of sand kicked up on a beach.

7

After eight days of solid walking – the longest stretch so far – we arrived in Prieska. Tall pale gums lined the banks of the Orange River and, labouring beneath them, was an old man forever raking up the leaves. It was good to be near trees again.

That morning I'd seen my first weed cricket, a beetle in a morning suit piped with yellow. The locals call them tok-toks because of the sound they make, rubbing their hind legs together. The one I saw was from a swarm blown out of the bush by the high winds from the north that also brought rain. When Gerry drove ahead to buy food in Prieska he struck a swarm five kilometres wide. Soon I, too, was crunching them underfoot, listening to the awful pop and leaving a trail of yellow goo.

My sponsorship money didn't allow us the extravagance of a bed and shower very often; for those luxuries we had to rely on people's generosity and spirit of adventure. Over the next few nights we cooked dinner for the mayor and his wife in exchange for using their video machine; got pissed with scientists from a nearby ammunition-testing range; and a guy drove seventy kilometres with a case of beer just to meet us.

It continued raining throughout the rest day. I got in the cab of the Land Rover and Gerry came and sat beside me. We spoke of the tense atmosphere of the previous week. He felt I was mad at him.

'No,' I said, 'I just need space. With all the people around I haven't been able to be by myself.' The burden of discontent in the back-up was something I just couldn't be bothered with – they either listened to my advice about pace and got on with the job, or they would just have to put up with my distancing. I was going all the way.

Gerry fell silent and we listened to the rain against the metal roof and watched it splatter on the windscreen.

'I'm scared about Zambia,' he whispered. 'There's some heavy duty shit happening there and we're going to be very vulnerable. Perhaps we should recruit a military man to take us through.'

'A bodyguard?' I asked.

'Call it extra protection. Zambia is cowboy country. The true lawless wilderness. We could disappear in the bush and nobody would ever find a trace of us or the Land Rover.'

I felt strangely reassured. For all his drinking and partying, Gerry's mind was still very much on the job.

That night after supper as the rain continued to fall, we lay out and listened to the World Service news. I got tearful during the report of our sailors returning home after the Gulf and at the plight of the Shiite refugees in Iran.

I was pleased to leave Prieska's hospitable but ignorant and bigoted population behind. Our next rest day wasn't until Kimberley and I wanted to push hard until then.

It was good to be outside again, eating sandwiches in the open air and squatting in the scrub. Toilets are so restrictive. First you have to find one and they're often filthy. I was getting very good at squatting and digging a hole with my heel to stop the splashback. There's nothing worse than walking in wet shoes.

Oli announced that he was going to leave in Lusaka, just six weeks away, and not in four months' time as I had thought. Lusaka was the only place for him to fly out from or else he'd have to be driven back down through Zaire because there was no public transport. I had no idea who would replace him. Charles, when I phoned him, didn't know either. His forte was seeing an obstacle across the road and dealing with it, not planning ahead. He left it up to Luly – but it wasn't her job and she had a living to make. I felt that the walk wasn't being taken seriously, and it pissed me off.

I worried about Gerry. I had the impression that he was still having trouble accepting my overall authority, quite probably because I didn't know a thing about Africa or Land Rovers. It was a new position for him. When he worked for Encounter, he controlled the trips and was always in charge. But this was different. This was my show. Yet in all our meetings with people so far, it was Gerry who shone, as if the entire project centred on him, along with its ultimate fate.

On the other hand I didn't care what other people thought. This was my walk and its success was in my hands, or more importantly, on my feet.

*

The avocado sandwiches looked as though they had been filled with pulverized tok-toks, but I didn't care. All morning I'd dreamed of pancakes and chocolate syrup and cappuccinos with inch-thick frothy heads.

Sixteen kilometres north of Prieska, on a flat stretch of road bordered by farmland, Oli spotted a small deer trapped in a barbed-wire fence. Its head and one foot were caught on one side of the fence, making it impossible for it to escape.

Approaching quickly from the other direction were two black men. They crossed onto the verge, obviously planning to put fresh meat on the dinner table that night.

Gerry heard Oli's cry and leapt out of the Land Rover. He sprinted across the verge and threw his arms around the frightened animal's neck as the opportunist hunters prepared to stone it to death. The deer let out a pitiful yelp and squirmed in Gerry's arms as he tried to untangle the barbed wire. It had cuts over its eyes that bled like red tears.

The men shouted angrily, thinking that we were trying to steal their prey, and looked totally bemused when Gerry lifted the deer to his chest and then set it down on the far side of the fence, where it bounded to freedom.

Only afterwards did I wonder if those men were going home to hungry families with nothing to put on the table.

Two ostriches joined us for breakfast, thankfully on the other side of a fence. Tina Turner was playing on the Land Rover music box and they danced in time to her.

After lunch we crossed the Orange River, running brown because of a manmade dam that was used to irrigate nearby farms. The boys wanted to swim but decided to postpone it for an hour until I finished the last quarter. That was decent of them – it's pretty tough going to see your back-up team wet from a swim when you're wet from sweat.

That night we held a team meeting. Charlie had told me before he left to make sure that everybody had a chance to air their grievances. We talked about the standard of the meals and how much the budget was to cover. Some of the complaints were pedantic, but it was best to have them aired.

Afterwards Gerry and I sat on the bonnet of the Land Rover and talked until late. He pledged to go as far as Kisangani in Zaire, rather than leave the trip in Lusaka with Oli. Zambia and Zaire would be the real test and he wanted to make sure I was OK.

'I will be sick with you, lose weight with you and go through hell with you,' he said. 'Just remember I'll always be there.'

After all the effort of finding some kind of equilibrium in this team, it was reassuring to know it wasn't to be wasted.

8

The walk began pre-dawn when the moon was big and orange, moving in and out of the clouds. I wanted to push past the town of Douglas towards Kimberley, where a bag of mail would be waiting.

Douglas is an empty farming town surrounded by semi-desert and irrigated farms that had none of the atmosphere of privilege or gratitude that marked the farms in the Karoo. Thankfully, the great desert plateau was now behind me – the first geographical hurdle had been conquered.

This was true backwoods South Africa. The coloureds lived next to the blacks and the blacks lived next to the whites, but the chasm was as wide as the Rift Valley. When calculating the town's population of 1,500, nobody bothered counting the 5,000 blacks and 1,000 coloureds living there.

I like the bush. I don't like towns; I don't like walking on the outskirts because they're dirty. As the clouds closed overhead, I passed the cinders of the railway tracks, the telephone exchange, and the obligatory scrum of young boys playing football on a dusty strip of ground.

Crossing the Piet River I tossed in a stone and made a wish to the Road God of Thirst. All around me he was feeding the greedy soil with spinning sprinklers.

It was Sunday and there were no shops open. We had to make do with what we had left over and break into our limited stores. The atmosphere was oppressive and I found myself wishing it would rain.

Everybody was subdued during the breaks; the boys were tired and fed up. I'd begun to settle and because I had trained my mind not to think of anything further ahead than the next horizon, the boundaries of my world were very small. This is the biggest difference between me and a traveller. I don't look around, observe or think ahead in the beginning – if I did, I would be crushed by the enormity of the journey in front of me. It takes a long time to look out and it isn't measured in kilometres on a map.

I was pleased to get out on the road by myself. In blazing heat and sapping humidity I pushed between carpets of thick yellow grass the colour of my hair and listened for the hiss and rustle of industrious and invisible insects.

That night we stayed at the Orange River Resort – along with several million mosquitoes. I woke with a sore bum and a bad case of the runs. Even though I'd smothered my buttocks with talcum powder before going to bed, it made no difference. As the landscape changed, offering trees and brown long-horned cattle, I pushed on through the pain. My arse began to burn and no amount of talc was going to put out the fire. Doubts and tears of misery flowed as I felt my bowels loosen. My hands had swollen and I could hardly write my notes during the rest breaks.

The last quarter was sheer hell. There were hot coals between my buttocks. Lashings of talc and loo paper eased things slightly but it wasn't until I saw the tall towers of Kimberley in the distance, beyond two hills that shimmered in the heat haze, that my confidence rose.

Slumping down into a chair I screamed and stood bolt upright. Gerry laughed and handed me a mug of wine.

'What's the occasion?' I asked.

'Well about five clicks back you passed the thousand kilometres mark.'

'And you let me keep walking?'

'You looked like you were having so much fun.'

The first bottle was finished before the cork had a chance to dry. A second was opened and then a third. By 7 o'clock we were all smashed and I was wearing the contents of one bottle like a triumphant Grand Prix driver.

Next morning, I tenderly took the first few steps, fearing another day of pain. I wanted to run into the arms of Kimberley, where I could sleep for two days and fix my aches and rashes. The towers I'd seen yesterday looked further away, an optical illusion created by the flatness of the land.

It wasn't until midday that I finally walked through the outskirts of town, where the pavements ran up and down and turned my legs to jelly.

Kimberley had the smell of burnt sunbed skin and looked like a Western film set. I walked right through town and out again along the road to Johannesburg. No one nodded or tooted their horns. We passed the 'Big Hole', a famous landmark of South Africa's diamond mining industry. At day's end we turned back and rode the Land Rover into the town where Kevin from Hi-Tec was waiting with letters from home and the possibility of a cold power shower.

We had rooms arranged at the Kimberley Club, an old colonial building owned by De Beers. For some reason mine was awful but the boys had superb suites with showers. I was almost too tired to care; or to bath; or to lean down and pick up the schedule that had been slipped under the door.

I exploded. The public relations officer for De Beers had arranged a full two days of interviews, receptions and appointments, starting at 6.40a.m. and ending with 'an evening of leisure'. I couldn't believe it. Everybody wanted a pound of flesh and all I wanted to do was rest. Showing remarkable restraint, I thought, I explained that there were only two appointments on his list that I would like to keep. I would do the lunchtime reception and the tour of the Big Hole.

The freelance journalist from the local Kimberley newspaper didn't appreciate my stand. She was one of those pent-up, highly organized committee types who react to every problem as if it is total, unmitigated disaster. She shouted furiously down the phone at my refusal to cooperate. Gerry handed me my second beer and I giggled at her high-pitched whine. Her main irk was that she wouldn't be able to get a photograph of me for Thursday's paper unless we shot it in the morning. But there was no way I was getting done up to perform at 9.30a.m. I was already committed to a poster shoot for Hi-Tec on Friday morning at 6.30a.m., which left me only one lie-in, and I wasn't giving it up. After another two beers I began to relax and laugh, mellowing out as we listened to the frogs croaking outside in the moonlight.

We were in the bar at the Kimberley Club with all its dark wooden beams, marble floors and shiny brass carpet rods. The walls were covered with photographs of gold miners and military men – pioneers whose courage had shaped history. These same men with their starched upper lips had shunned women's company and shut out the problems of their world when they drank here.

Out on the covered balcony that stretched the length of the old brick building, there were palm trees in whitewashed earthenware pots and mahogany doors with brass handles and railway carriage curtains to block out the heat of the day.

It didn't come much better than this, I thought. And if I could have frozen that moment and carried it with me in my day pack, it would have kept me from going crazy when things got tough.

The following day, when I phoned London and spoke to Luly, she told me she had received a fax from the boys saying that morale was very low and they wanted out. Gerry had asked to leave in Lusaka because he was bored.

I was furious.

Confronting him in Oli's presence I asked him: 'Is it true?'

Gerry didn't bat an eyelid. 'Yes, if Charlie agrees. I didn't want to say anything to you because if I had to go to Kisangani I didn't want you to feel my heart wasn't in it.'

'But why?'

'I've had to do a lot of things I didn't want to do, but hey, it's a job.'

Ignoring his pleas to sit down, I left to find some space. When Gerry finally found me, I asked for the real reason.

He wanted to get back to the UK to organize the first raft trip the length of the Bramaputra river because a group of Americans were planning an assault and he didn't want to be beaten. Gerry had his own dream and could never find fervour or passion for somebody else's. I couldn't find fault with that; I couldn't do it either.

The decision about whether Gerry could leave would be made in London. It would mean Charlie putting more money into the trip, so I told Gerry that if he couldn't pay for his airfare, I'd give him the money. I wanted him off the trip, for both of us.

Gerry always talked of us as a team. I liked the idea, but it just wouldn't work. I learnt early on not to talk to the boys about what I'd experienced on the road – they didn't understand. Similarly, I couldn't relate to their anecdotes, felt removed from their experiences. If you're not doing the same jobs you must at least have the same goal. I had no option but to stick with a sometimes boring, tiresome and repetitive dream, but he could leave and plan new adventures. The cautious journey of getting to know each other was over, replaced by the knowledge that it wasn't going to work. Now the end grew closer and bigger as it approached.

I told myself I didn't care. 'I like it out here. I'm getting seven hours of exercise a day in the outdoors, I'm in the company of a couple of guys who can be fun and I know exactly where I'm going. What more could I want?'

*

For the next two days I had to play the perfect corporate billboard, plugging my sponsors, smiling for photographs and dignitaries.

Cosmopolitan magazine asked me what I would do if I woke up one morning and found out I was a man.

I said: 'I'd have a sex change.'

We had been told by De Beers that we would dine at the club with various directors and must wear jackets. It was quite a feat for the boys to bring jackets and keep them clean for this occasion. We spent several hours getting ready. The PR woman for De Beers arrived to say lunch was now just for the four of us and she was in jeans.

As we ate, I told her how fitting I thought it was for De Beers to become involved with me. Cape Town to Cairo was the traditional route for crossing Africa overland. One of the first to do so was Ewart Grogan. He wrote a book, *From the Cape to Cairo on Foot*, a title which slightly glossed over the fact that he took trains and boats wherever possible. He did it to test the feasibility of Cecil Rhodes' Cape to Cairo railway. Rhodes was the founder of De Beers – he made his money initially by importing an electric pump to Kimberley and renting it out to the diamond prospectors whose claims often filled with water. He bought out everyone and formed De Beers, which was named after the two brothers who owned the land before diamonds were discovered.

Grogan's other reason for the journey was to prove himself worthy of the woman he loved and wanted to marry. He met her while recuperating from sickness in New Zealand. He asked for her hand but he had no prospects and her father dismissed him. If he walked the length of Africa, he asked, would he be worthy of Gertrude? He reached Cairo and married her and they went to settle in Kenya as one of the founders of the British protectorate. The rumour there was that Grogan would have walked twice the distance to be rid of her.

My research into other walks through Africa brought up an Australian, Ronald Monson, who walked from Cape Town to Cairo in the 1920s – all the way, bar four days. The swamps in Sudan forced him to take a boat. Like Grogan, he hired teams of African bearers to overcome the logistical problems yet they received little, if any, recognition.

De Beers had very kindly offered to provide me with hospitality in Cape Town, Kimberley (largest diamond mine hole in the world), Gaborone (capital of Botswana and central diamond sorting centre),

Orapa (active mine), Lusaka (capital of Zambia) and Kinshasa (capital of Zaire) for my month off half-way.

That night, Gerry got word from Charlie that he could leave the trip in Lusaka. He was demob happy and gave me a hug. I was nervous about going back on the road again – so much had changed in just a few days. But we'd been in one place too long. It was time to move on.

I decided to walk the next twelve days straight, without a rest day, so that we could spend an extra day in Gaborone at the De Beers guest house for directors.

It's very important for me to have short-term destinations but not to build them up in my mind. Two weeks ahead is really the maximum. But sometimes I couldn't keep the excitement in check, especially over the possibility of a Coke. After weeks of nothing, we'd get to a small town and see the Coca Cola sign. Yeeha! But, 'No Coke, only Fanta', and warm orange is far more sickly than warm vegetable extracts. It became the saying when we were let down.

Every day was a push. I got the feeling that I was walking the 'world around' like a guy rolling a log on a river with his feet. Looking forward to something on a walk isn't like looking forward to the school holidays, which will happen no matter how little work you do; on a walk it's footsteps away, not time. I envied the boys over this. They were waiting for the holidays; I was walking the world around to get us there.

I felt like I was dragging a great weight. I noticed this most if I turned around and looked at the road behind me and walked back a few steps: it felt like running downwind instead of head on into it.

We had 800 rand to last us two weeks till we reached the border of Botswana and the town of Gaborone. I didn't want to change any more sterling. To reach Gaborone by 16 April meant walking forty-seven kilometres each day for a fortnight. No problem. We had four cases of wine donated by the South African Wine Growers Association because they heard we liked it, and it had to be drunk before crossing the border.

We'd taken two extra days off in Kimberley and miscalculated how far I'd covered in the first few weeks. Distances were now crucial. If we didn't reach Botswana before the 18th, the border would be closed for a public holiday weekend.

It was good to be back on the road, although I had stomach cramps and my blood sugar level felt low. Kilometre markers on the train track which ran parallel to the road gave me some sense of distance, but they made the walk seem slower. I ignored the signs, concentrating instead on the subtle changes in scenery – the chestnut cows with white faces sticking up from the yellow grass, the medieval-looking beetles scurrying through patches of low scrub, and hanging bird's nests that looked like Christmas decorations in the trees.

I received our first donation – five rand from a lone driver who had heard about my walk from a newspaper in Kimberley. Close behind, a car load of wrinklies clapped as they drove past.

Gerry had hit the nail on the head when he described boredom as the killer: 'Hey, the greatest decision I have to make each day is whether or not to curry the vegetables.'

That is the greatest challenge of a walk, not the physical side. Unless Gerry could greet the Road God of Distance with humility, respect and submission, his battle against boredom would rage hard and eat him up over the next eight weeks to Lusaka. He would miss the joy of travelling so slowly across a continent. Already, his eyes were shut.

The dawn was pink with dust and clouds threw shadows across the few maize fields. Corn was ripening in the fields and in places I could see sunflowers, past their prime. Cyclists often passed, brown riders in faded wind-puffed western clothes riding heavy steel bikes. We finally left Cape Province and I walked into the Transvaal. The change was announced by a very modest sign.

All morning I'd daydreamed about renting a cottage on Dartmoor where my writing room had whitewashed stone walls, flagstone floor and a white desk in the centre with a fax, photocopier, coffee percolator and white Apple computer. There was a daily sweeping downstairs and a Mercedes in the driveway. I'd had this dream in Australia, but it was losing its punch because it never came true. I have to live out some daydreams between walks or they lose their reality.

I walked off the main road and around Christiana – a large gathering of bungalows with nice gardens – before joining the road again. The black kids laughed and clapped, making me feel happy, but the white children sniggered and I felt self-conscious.

Throughout the day, after the repetitive questions in Kimberley, I came up with a list of questions you should never ask a walker:

Q: Why?
A: It's personal and you'll never be given the real reason.
Q: What do you wear on your feet?
A: Look down.
Q: What do you eat?
A: Look at my plate. A walker eats constantly.
Q: Which way are you going?
A: North.
Q: Are you alone?
A: Look around me, I'm never alone.
Q: Are you raising money for charity?
A: Look at my halo.

That night, as we listened to the World Service Africa, we heard our story: 'Ffyona Campbell is approaching Botswana,' said the announcer and Oli got excited. I thought about all the people tuning into the broadcast right across this massive continent. I wondered if they were willing me onwards. I wondered if they cared.

9

We would push hard over the next seven days to get to Gaborone early enough to have a three-day break.

I was trying not to build the place up too much but I needed a break and found myself daydreaming about having Tom Cruise mixing me cocktails at the bar, juggling the alcohol and ice and giving me that drop-dead sexy smile.

Another storm rumbled through in the afternoon, creeping up quickly against an opaque sky. I wore Gerry's rainproof jacket for a while and then gave it back, preferring to get wet. All afternoon, cars honked their horns and sped by and I felt like screaming. It's incredibly miserable and frightening.

We camped in a layby, out of the southerly wind and underneath gums. This wasn't wise. Soon a gust had snapped a heavy branch and sent it crashing to earth only feet from my tent.

The Land Rover had been christened Stormin' Norman and was beginning to look like it had truly been through a military campaign. Most of the damage, however, was testament to our drunken revelry and rough camping. There were red wine stains all over the bonnet and slithers of grease from one of Gerry's steaks now congealed with dust. We decided to leave it dirty until we reached Gaborone. The dust was almost a badge of honour.

There were a lot of people on the road, many of them well dressed, including one in a blazer and white pants who was dancing with a radio pressed to his ear. I laughed and jigged along with him.

A cool breeze sent from heaven pushed us onwards and I felt better as we passed the last of the cornfields. Picnicking under a tree for lunch, we were visited by an old black man in tattered clothes held together by pieces of string. He motioned for goods and I gave him an orange. He blew me a kiss.

*

There were cold tailwinds in the mornings. Winter was catching up with us and I wondered how far north I would have to go to escape it. It was thirty-four kilometres to Zeerust, the last major town before the border.

Few cars were on the road and I hammered through the morning, my thighs feeling powerful on the undulations. A few hours later the hills were steeper and my energy level began to fall. At least there was a tin chalet waiting in Zeerust and a hot shower.

Stormin' Norman wasn't feeling well the next day – the front right wheel was out of alignment and leaking oil. Gerry and Oli found a garage in town while I made some sandwiches and set off alone to walk a full day without them.

Soon I passed through a village that didn't warrant a name or mark on the map, and waved to locals walking barefoot with plastic buckets of water balanced on their heads.

A wrecked container truck lay contorted and twisted by the side of the road, burnt out, but still the slogan of the company was visible: 'We Deliver Dreams.' Down the hill I trudged toward a plain that stretched out far, far away to a range of purple mountains.

A car pulled up beside me and out stepped a man with a florid face, wearing a shirt and tie. Almost immediately I knew it was Nick Byers, the De Beers contact from Gaborone. We shook hands and he kissed my cheek. Nick walked with me for half an hour and explained that he'd made all the arrangements for the border crossing the next day and had brought a bunch of documents. Until then, I'd only ever spoken to him on the telephone from London – when it had seemed impossible that I would ever get this far.

When he left I still had several hours to walk. The boys arrived late, having spent nearly six hours in Zeerust pulling the Land Rover apart. They had found the problem, but had no time to fix it.

My face was burnt and lips cracked despite the cream. The wrinkles were coming fast and I told the boys I grew them as they did their beards. In Winston Churchill fashion they replied that the difference was that they could shave their beards off. It was our last night in South Africa and we laughed with relief and high hopes for the morning.

Oli woke me at 3a.m. and I drank coffee in the damp dewy darkness. When we began walking an hour later, my head torch cast a bouncing beam over the hard shoulder of the road. Gerry packed up camp and ran over the shortwave radio which had been left beside the wheel.

De Beers has a relationship with the Botswana government which is probably the most successful in Africa. They are equal partners in the diamond mines, putting in equal amounts of investment and getting equal returns. It's a very orderly country: not much corruption in the government and the revenue from the mines is put straight back into the infrastructure.

The plan was to reach the border by 10 o'clock. It was more than a plan. Dignitaries and officials from Botswana were going to greet us there, people who don't like being kept waiting.

'Wouldn't it be wonderful if we'd got our sums wrong and it's actually closer than we thought?' I said to Gerry, feeling the thorns sting my bottom.

I took off my underwear to ease the chafing.

Oli went ahead to check the distance to the border. He came back an hour later.

'Bad news,' he said. 'It's not sixteen kilometres, it's another twenty-eight.'

'I don't believe it!' I screamed. 'Why are we getting this wrong?'

It was the third time the map, kilometre markers and Land Rover hadn't tallied. Turning away I put my head in my hands and tried to calm down. I could have cried.

I calculated we'd be two hours late and told Oli and Gerry to drive to the border and call Nick to delay his departure and those of the officials. I pushed ahead, singing 'God Save the Queen', 'Rule Britannia' and 'Onward Christian Soldiers' – all amazingly badly but it lifted my spirits. On the top of a plateau I looked down at the flat land below, thinking of Ayers Rock in Australia. I felt the steep downward slope tug at my calves and I broke into a run, thud-thudding down the road until all of me wobbled and my lungs cried out.

A couple of very well-spoken guys pulled up and asked if I was walking to Cairo. One of them was a reporter from Zambia, based in Jo'burg. He'd seen the story written up in Zambia.

'I read you are doing this to prove something to your father,' he said.

My heart skipped a beat. If my story had been published in the north it would mean that people in those countries knew I'd started my walk in Cape Town. All my efforts to disguise this part of the walk by keeping my passport clean of stamps could be in vain.

The first break came at 6.30a.m., the time we would normally be
setting off. It was 100 metres before a police check point which Nick
had told me about the previous day. Two policemen huddled in
great-coats, puffing cigarette smoke into the cold air.

Nick Byers looked dashing in a blazer, flannels and De Beers tie
when he met us with four suited officials in tow. In tourist countries
they require a currency declaration to be filled out when you enter
and leave. It's a way of preventing money exchange on the black
market. You declare how much you have when you go in and provide
receipts from banks when you leave to show you've changed the
difference legally. We were whisked into the packed immigration
office where a special kiosk was opened especially for us, which
didn't impress the gob-smacked, sweaty queue.

Our passports weren't touched. Nick had arranged to get the entry
stamp in Gaborone so it would look as if we'd flown in directly
from London and gone nowhere near South Africa. No mean feat.

Flanked by a police escort, I walked into Botswana on a red sandy
carpet. As we passed out of South Africa, I turned back to her and
whispered 'Thank you'. It had taken forty-three days and I'd covered
1,590.6 kilometres.

10

We spent three days in Gaborone luxuriating at the De Beers guest house for visiting directors. There was a huge sitting room with a fully stocked bar at the end, a games room with pool table and fully stocked bar, a swimming pool, and more staff than you could shake a swizzle stick at. All our laundry was done; we had use of the telephone and there was a large Quality Street tin, with contents, next to the TV and pile of videos. It was a daydream come true.

I telephoned Shuna. Raymond had phoned her saying he was worried about me. I tried to explain that I had found a sense of freedom, that Raymond connected me to a way of life I had left and wanted to sever all links with. I had a journey to make, I had to make it alone and I didn't want him to wait for me to return.

'Hadn't you better tell him that?' she said.

She was right, as always.

I telephoned Raymond.

He didn't believe me when I said I didn't love him any more. We had a long chat and I poured out my heart. I tried not to be cruel, but simply to tell him how I felt. What I wanted from Raymond was someone loving me back in the UK and sending me letters, but I didn't want him to come to Africa. Nor did I want to marry him. I was caught in a quandary. He was good and kind and secure, but here, despite everything, I was free.

We ended by agreeing to talk again.

I had my hair trimmed and washed until it felt silky and fresh and almost foreign to me. The boys had their hair cut, too. Thank God Gerry's was reparable after the knife and fork job I had given him in the beginning.

Hung over and heavy-headed, I had barely an hour's sleep on the night before we left Gaborone. Hauling myself into the shower I tried to motivate myself for the day ahead. When I arrived at the Land Rover I found the boys had been waiting twenty minutes for me and were not impressed.

When I told Gerry he didn't have to walk with me, he snapped, 'Good!'

Walking with a hangover is wonderful. My body just swayed forward beneath the pounding head without any effort. Within two hours my bottom was rubbing and I'd discovered that the blade-sharp grasses are as vindictive and vicious as in South Africa. The mosquitoes were out in force, a fact which worried me because for the three days in Kimberley we'd forgotten to take our malaria pills. Without exception, we were supposed to take two Paludrine capsules each day and two Nivaquine twice a week.

The road ran almost due north towards Francistown, over gentle hills and past traditional thatched mud huts surrounded by stick fences. Mothers clearing the earthen yards with hand brooms drew themselves upright and shielded their eyes from the glare as I approached, and then lifted their hands in salute. Hens scratched in the dirt at their ankles.

Although the road was quiet, I had already passed an overturned truck and discovered that local drivers paid little heed to the niceties of any highway code. In the early afternoon, two convoys of trucks overtook each other, slewing sideways onto the soft shoulder and nearly wiping me out in the process.

The road north from Gaborone to the turn off for Serowe was unpainted tarmac and virtually dead straight. I made good progress up the map but it was incredibly boring. The boys bought some dumb bells and announced they were on a health kick as far as Victoria Falls because Gerry wanted to run the infamous gorge. What was more, there would be no more alcohol: a team decision, said Oli. First I'd heard of it.

They walked beside me pumping iron for about three days, but gave up. Our mutual aggravation simmered gently. The boys even seemed to resent me writing letters at day's end even though they'd had several hours during the day to write theirs. I think they would have resented anything I did by then – just as I resented them.

I knew I was expecting a lot of them to fall in with this life and tempo. I'd always imagined that a driver's life was cushy, having so much time off. I hadn't realized that they didn't want free time. Yet when they had something to do at day's end they criticized me for not helping when I was very tired and it was the first time I'd sat down.

I was angry about losing our nightly contact with BBC World Service but even angrier that Gerry had taken so long to own up about the radio. I could no longer snuggle up and listen to a calm, conservative BBC voice tell me that the earth was still spinning; wars still being fought, politicians spouting rhetoric and Britain moored where she will always be.

I slept well, waking to find my tent heavy with dew and my fingers numb with the cold.

The President of Botswana, Quett Masire, passed by in the morning, somewhere behind tinted glass windows in a Merc flanked by police cars. I wondered what he made of his people when he watched them from airconditioned comfort. Did he ever feel the dust between his toes; taste it at the back of his throat; smell the exhaust fumes and the animal carcasses? I'd been told he was one of the least corrupt presidents in Africa, and was doing good things for his people.

Further along the road I came across another truck smash. It had been carrying cows and bulls, penned off behind metal barriers that were now twisted inwards. A couple had been crushed, as had the driver's arm. He had failed to avoid a cow on the road after swerving and never regaining control. That hapless animal lay dead by the roadside – food for the flies.

There are five times as many cattle as people in Botswana, although a few years ago the difference had been eight-fold until disease took its toll. Foot-and-mouth barriers had been erected to stop the spread of the disease. Thousands of heads of game died as they walked hundreds of miles around them to get to water holes. It was a disaster.

There is a 'Day 50 Syndrome' on any walk which is like the pain barrier that long-distance runners must crash through during a marathon. It's a boredom barrier. All novelty has worn off, the systems have run smoothly for a bit and then the realization sets in: this is it, day after day, week after week for a year. To cope with it, I have to change down a gear in my mind; the world gets smaller so that I'm anticipating nothing beyond what's in focus and the day-dreams slow down so that I turn everything over carefully and savour each sensation. I had started the walk by decorating a whole house in just one quarter. By Day 50, I was spending the whole day deciding on a lamp shade. I carried this state of mind into camp.

There is no cure. When it settles in – for however long – you can either drink yourself into oblivion for the duration, or work harder to take your mind off the sadness and lethargy. Since we were now a 'dry zone', the latter was the only option.

Gerry grew maudlin, missing his girlfriend and dreaming of going kayaking again. Oli's hand had become infected after he fell into a thorn bush and I spent an hour picking out the barbs. His fingers were swollen and throbbing. He had taken to breaking periods of silence with the words, 'I think I'm about ready to go home.' For my part, I was trying hard to resolve myself to losing both of them while finding that every ache and strain was multiplied.

I took no comfort from the cool flat land, or from the breeze at my back. Every kilometre seemed like five; every scent curled my nostrils. Not even the musical laughter of the people whom I passed on the road, or the sound of cow bells clanging across the bush, could lift my spirits.

Nick Byers arrived that night, bringing half a dozen letters for each of us. We all huddled in silence, Gerry on the bonnet of the Land Rover, Oli sitting on the tailgate and me lying in my tent, reading news from home. Occasionally paper rustled and somebody giggled.

The infamous 50th day dawned and I'd soiled the bed. That's a polite way of saying that a dose of diarrhoea hit so suddenly during the night that I had no time to unzip the tent before it exploded.

Much later than intended, I set off alone, carrying a day pack. After eight kilometres I crossed the Tropic of Capricorn – halfway between the South Pole and the Equator, according to Gerry. The soil was red and littered with melon vines and scrubby trees that provided good shade for lunch.

Gerry put a dead snake under one of the chairs. It was meant for me, but Oli sat down first.

'Don't move,' whispered Gerry.

Oli took one look and laughed.

The snake was about a foot long, finger thin with a tan-and-black diamond pattern on top and white belly. Gerry had found it in a tree, minus its head.

A long, tedious, upward slope took all afternoon and most of my energy. I was suckling the water bottle like a baby to a bosom and feeling my eyelids grow heavy with fatigue. I longed to finish and read my letters again and write a few back. It was the first time since Kimberley that we'd received mail.

I snapped at Gerry and Oli, particularly when the twenty-minute gap between 'pit stops' for water became sixty: they were driving ahead, parking the Land Rover and taking out tables and chairs so that they could write theirs.

That night I apologized for being such a shit and promised to mellow out. I wished to God we were drinking again.

Since we'd left Gaborone each day had blended into the next, offering little change of scenery. I had to persevere.

A tortoise stirred in the undergrowth and as I bent to pick him up he shot off at remarkable speed. He reminded me of me. I was a tortoise, crossing Africa slowly.

Just short of Mahalapye, the second largest village in Botswana, we discovered that Rajiv Ghandi had been assassinated in India. A woman with a bomb strapped to her body was handing him a bunch of flowers as he visited his mother's grave.

The days had grown hot again – 30°C – but at night it fell to 10°C. And the light was fading at 5.30p.m., giving us only about ninety minutes to set up camp after each day's walk. After the meal was made, eaten and washed up we each drifted off to our books and letters.

I had a shin splint that needed massaging and felt grubby after five days without a shower. The red sandy soil stuck fast to perspiring skin, making my legs look sunburnt, and I was worried that flies were laying their eggs in my hair since I'd found some busily burying themselves in my scalp. African women wisely avoid the problem by having their hair cut very short or braiding it into tight tails.

Oli saw the snake first. We'd found some shade for lunch away from the overloaded trucks that occasionally roared past. Oli sat on a chair, munching a sandwich when a puff adder slithered within inches of his feet.

'Shit me!' he bellowed. 'I'm outa here.'

He had every right to jump. The puff adder accounts for most of the snake fatalities in Africa because it is the laziest snake in the bush and won't move when it senses you coming. After retiring to a safe distance, Gerry's hunting instincts took over. The snake had disappeared beneath the Land Rover, making it dangerous for any of us to approach. There are accounts of snakes actually climbing up beneath cars and travelling hundreds of miles with them.

The tent poles were quickly unhooked from the roofrack and the boys nervously began searching for the killer. Oli leapt behind the wheel and reversed the Land Rover, hoping to flush it out. Sure enough, the snake slithered clear, straight for me.

Gerry whacked it with the pole, jumping back after each blow, while Oli spun the Land Rover and drove over the top, pinning the wriggling body into the dirt. The tail was still flapping when Gerry plunged the spike of the tent pole through its head and held it aloft. The fangs were dripping venom.

By nightfall, the details of this hunt had been debated and inflated beyond all recognition by the boys. Gerry said that I had screamed through the whole thing – quite stupid since I spent eight hours a day walking alone through the bush, saw many snakes and was far more vulnerable than either of the drivers.

11

T here were some interesting people on the road, either walking or waiting for the buses. One girl had scars on her cheeks and I asked her what had happened. When she was little she had bleeding eyes so they cut her cheeks and mixed the blood into her eyes to make her well.

'Good medicine,' she said.

I pointed to my fox-tooth necklace. 'Good medicine.'

She nodded and smiled. 'Keep you well.'

Further along the road I saw an albino negro whose red hair and freckles made him look almost Scottish. He would have been right at home in a bar at Palapye that night, where four Scotsmen burst into song and grew misty-eyed as the drink flowed. Their companion was crashed out in a chair and I thought he was drunk until somebody whispered that he was sitting there dying of cancer.

The alcohol went to work quickly. The barman kept pouring me doubles and the leading Scotsman, wearing a tartan beret, directed the dancing. Gerry bellowed at some innocent, calling him a 'fucking English bastard'. The guy was Irish and within seconds fists were flying and chairs connecting with skulls. I got caught in the middle until Gerry was pulled away and pinned against the bar. He was angry about something and angling for a fight.

Gerry disappeared into the village and stumbled back in the early hours, feeling hung over and sheepish. I tried to pull him into line, but he was in no mood to be lectured.

'When you realize this isn't Ffyona Campbell's glamorous walk through Africa . . .' he started, but he didn't finish.

I shouted him down, telling him in no uncertain terms how hard I'd slogged to get the money together and how nobody was going to put that at risk.

'You think I'm soft? You think I've never experienced hardship in my life? Well, you're wrong. I'm still going to be here when the going gets tough. Where will you be?'

We gave each other blistering looks and he backed off.

Although I had incredible respect for Gerry, I could easily have grown to hate him. It wasn't my fault that South Africa and Botswana were so easy.

We were now on the edge of the Kalahari. The road north to Letlakane would be mundane before the adventure, for there we would straddle the salt pans where big game roamed and suntans deepened.

I no longer walked on the tarmac, preferring instead to scuff along on the red dirt tracks where the donkey-drawn jigs trundled past and the boy regimented his cattle, tapping them lightly in the dust clouds that they kicked up with their cloven hoofs.

So far I'd managed to cover approximately 1,880 kilometres in fifty-four days, having had two stints of three days off. This was roughly 1,000 kilometres a month, putting the actual duration of the walk at about fifteen months. The days were rolling forward easily enough but I was miserable when I thought of Oli leaving at Victoria Falls, fifteen days hence, and Gerry in Lusaka another two weeks later.

The journey from Serowe didn't begin well when my drunken attempts at packing the previous night on the roof of the Land Rover resulted in us losing a tent and two sleeping bags. Turning back, we managed to find Oli's bag but Gerry's had disappeared. It had served him well during many trips and he wasn't best pleased. I tried to appease him by giving him my spare one, but as with all favourite things, they aren't easily replaced.

The Kalahari was salt bush, like Australia, sandy but no dunes. The mornings were freezing cold. Birds with new songs hovered in the wind. I kept up a steady pace on flat land. The fences had disappeared; now there was a greater sense of space.

I walked through a village that smelt like the inside of a butter bean pod – that succulent green smell of young vegetation that manages to find water in the desert. Surrounding it, the vegetation was low and scrubby, with a texture that reminded me of the wrinkled old men in the village whose faces were like bark.

My stomach had been dodgy since Gaborone, which meant stopping more often and thrashing the bushes with my snake stick before I dared squat down. An age-old cure for diarrhoea was simply to fast for forty-eight hours but I needed to eat for energy.

Helicopter insects hovered past, thrumming their iridescent wings, and the flaxen fluff from seed balls drifted on in the gentle breeze. At times I thought I was in the middle of a documentary. I could hear the soundtrack playing and see the camera zoom in on a Mrs Tigglewinkle-type black mumma in a field picking maize with a little naked boy clutching the ragged hem of her floral dress. Cows grazed with soft brown eyes and ears cut like blanket fingers.

The nights were growing cold. Gerry had a go at lighting the fire using my firebow and the yellow grass as a tinder bundle. After much blowing and cursing, using raw power to make up for lack of skill, a small coal began to collect in the hearth stick and glow. Very gently, I tipped it out using my knife into a tinder bundle, careful to keep it away from the sweat dripping off Gerry's face. I held it up to catch the wind and blew very gently, squeezing the tinder behind the breath to give the coal some food. But it wouldn't catch. The grass wasn't yellow because it was dry and dead – it's always that colour. A second attempt using the cotton padding of seed pods proved more successful. Fairies with fire in their hair danced among the embers, playing charades with the timbers, and the boys huddled close as the ground grew damp with dew. I felt guilty about them sleeping in the open without a tent. It was my fault and they made their accusations clear with silences.

We were four days from Orapa, where an important decision had to be made. I could save time by crossing the salt pans on the edge of the Kalahari, but the problem was being able to carry enough water to get us through. There were no roads or tracks; it was just a question of following the line of vegetation which ran virtually due north. We also needed a good map and some advice from the De Beers contacts in Orapa about hidden dangers.

I'd already worked out that we needed as much as thirty litres a day of drinking water between us, including a five-litre contingency. The Land Rover had five jerry cans for water and two for fuel. This would last us about three and a half days on the salt pans if we used none for bathing except a small amount for handwashing and teeth. It would take four days to cross if all went well.

Gerry and Oli were keen to give it a go too, perhaps sensing the chance for a new adventure. Oli had an Achilles tendon strain and chose to stay off his feet for several days. This was the end of them walking. I walked by myself, enjoying daydreams and smelling the woodsmoke in my hair. I was dirty, not having showered since Serowe, but there is something deliciously satisfying about cleaning nails full of brown earth using a Swiss army knife. Again there were niggling worries. My wisdom teeth were pushing through and keeping me awake at night; I had lumps on my scalp that itched and by day's end my bottom was chafing and I walked into camp with buttocks clenched and teeth gritted.

A truck load of dynamite workers reversed back past us and leapt out throwing stones at something. Gerry ran towards them and I watched from the top of the Land Rover as they stoned a six-foot grey-and-silver snake. One of them forked two fingers and indicated how deadly it could be.

Without our shortwave radio, we had taken to listening to the local Gaborone station on the Land Rover set. The music was surprisingly good but it was interrupted by a bizarre telethon. How on earth did they expect to raise any money in a country with virtually no telephones?

That night a howling gale blew up, driving sand off the desert. From my tent I listened to it flap the fabric and called out to the boys, 'For God's sake get out of the wind in here and get some sleep.' They stuck it out and woke with their hair and faces covered in sand. They did it on purpose, as martyrs. As my father would have told them: any fool can be uncomfortable.

A week later we reached Letlakane and stopped walking to drive into Orapa at the end of a road. It is a closed town, just for the diamond miners, but we were expected and were allowed in. The men on the security gate were wearing coats, gloves and woolly hats.

I spoke to Luly to organize the exchange of drivers, which was getting rather complicated because Blake Rose, who was born in South Africa, had to get his passport changed and Bill Preston was having another operation on his hands – he'd been shot in Pakistan the previous year.

My back-up team schedule was being rewritten on an almost daily basis and I began feeling like the donkeys I'd often seen by the road with their front legs tied together to prevent them from going anywhere. But when I rang to give Charlie a blast about the mix-up in team changes, I discovered he'd gone paragliding in Scotland and there was no point in abusing anybody else. I suggested sending Blake down to meet us at Victoria Falls, but his vaccinations weren't up to date.

Another complication was the news that a journalist and photo-grapher from *You* magazine in London were coming out to find us the following week. As major sponsors I couldn't tell them no, but I'd learned to be wary of reporters. I know what they do for a living and it doesn't always equate with printing the truth. The boys were surprisingly upbeat about the arrival.

'We're gonna piss on 'em,' said Gerry, full of conviction. 'We'll tell 'em there'll be no more glamour. We'll show them what it's really like.'

I agreed and we laughed. Suddenly we felt like a team again.

That afternoon we scored showers at the De Beers guest lodge and ate lobster thermidor that tasted like cauliflower cheese at a thatched, whitewashed restaurant with timber roof beams and wicker chairs. On the walls there were paintings of bushmen and animals.

We arranged a briefing from Noel, the president of the Off Road Club, about crossing the salt pans that lay to the north. Once the site of an ancient lake laid bare by primeval earth shifts, the pans are the largest in the world. The two biggest, Ntwetwe and Sowa, constitute the area of Makgadikgadi and are separated by a narrow peninsula of grassland. This is where the lost city of Kuba island was excavated and found to have been inhabited up to 2,000 years ago. Pottery shards littered the inner slopes and on the southern boundary, a crescent-shaped stone wall has led to speculation that it was once a cattle kraal, market place or work of some forgotten tribal significance. 'Kubu' is Tswanan for hippo, suggesting they lived here, or perhaps the nearby rock shapes are reminiscent of their form.

Noel lent us a tent and explained the alternatives to us. The boys could drive the pans, but if the Land Rover strayed off the hard crust it could sink ankle-deep, leaving us stranded. I could cross on the grass peninsula between the main pans, or keep to the edge of the pan and the peninsula. Whichever, I desperately wanted to cross them; I was starved of adventure. Crossing a desert by road I sometimes felt as if not quite part of it. The road was only three metres wide and the desert thousands of miles across, but still it set me apart. The endless stretch of concrete road which had been acceptable across America and Oz certainly wasn't so here, not when I knew there was so much wilderness out there. The next morning I bumbled roughly north on a dirt track that led out of Orapa.

From high ground I could pick out the escarpment where geologists have discovered beaches of rolled quartz pebbles that mark the fluctuating perimeter of the ancient lake. Water once lapped twenty metres above the bone-dry pan.

I could smell bush lavender and occasionally see springboks skeltering off like wind-blown leaves. Ostriches bounced past like musical notes in staccato rhythm; baobab trees, liverish in colour, reflected and absorbed every ray of sunshine; Kori bustards, the largest flying bird in the world, soared high in the sky while black korhaars exploded noisily out of the grass.

It's always where you need water most – in hot places – that it tastes so foul. We'd filled the jerry cans in Orapa but the water was so saline I felt more thirsty after a drink than if I hadn't had one.

The morning was bright, throwing stark shadows dotted with steams of light. I wore a filthy purple dress and padded through scrub whose leaves had begun to turn. In a mud hut village I found a page from a mail order catalogue crumpled in a pile of donkey droppings.

After forty minutes the track turned almost southeast and showed no signs of correcting itself and going north. I was going the wrong way and toyed for a while about what I should do. The sensible option was to sit down and wait for the boys, who shouldn't be far behind.

Marking the place with a sock, we drove back to the village where a woman in a towel and blazer pointed out the right road – a very indistinct powder track. I'd wasted six kilometres but found my footprints and joined them north.

It was hard work ploughing through six-inch-deep cotton dust that exploded like talc under each step. I grew frustrated at how it slowed me down and almost ran when I found patches of bare track.

That night we rough-camped around a fire. Oli was quiet and blamed his silence on the knowledge that we were in for a tough few days. True to form, Gerry made light of it all, climbing a tree to watch the sunset and then dancing around the flames until he'd singed his leg hair. I was loving this!

When I stepped out on the salt pan, a shimmering white carpet stretched out from my toes to the horizon, blurred by a heat haze that so easily deceived the eye into believing that there was, indeed, water out there. The only life I could see before me was a solitary butterfly.

As I walked, islands of yellow grass emerged and the odd black spartan tree. Puffs of talc sand burst under my feet. Taking off my shirt and tucking it into my pants, I walked bare-breasted across the pans, feeling the breeze and the enormous sense of freedom that so much open space can generate. It felt great to be alive and I didn't want the day to end.

I pinned my red-and-white spotted hat on the pan with a stick to mark my stopping point and sat on the bonnet of the Land Rover as we crossed the smooth lake bed inland to the Lost City, an island floating above the mirrored heat. Clambering to the highest rock, I sat down for a cigarette and looked out, north and east, over mile upon mile of crystalized salt.

I looked down upon a lone baobab tree with a trunk big enough to hide a hippo. When the sun began to set, the sky seemed to hold on to every last ray of light, embracing night and day for longer than I've ever seen.

In the orange glow of the embers, we debated whether a whirlpool crossing the equator would immediately change direction. What would it look like? And how many times does a scorpion turn when surrounded by fire before it stings itself to death?

12

The dawn was perfect, glowing red over the island which looked like a ship marooned by the outgoing tide. There were tracks of springbok and cattle in the salt, but no elephant. John, the administration manager at Orapa, had told us there was plenty of game on the pans, including sixty elephant, but unfortunately they were a good 100 kilometres to the west of us.

When the temperature rose, I took off my shirt again, elated at last to have my feet in contact with true wilderness. I crossed the thirteen kilometres to our previous night's campsite and then headed north, as directly as the crow flies, ignoring any tracks. The Land Rover followed a rough path on firmer ground to the east.

It would have been a lovely place for a day off, but the boys wanted to push on for Nata. Oli drove out to check on me, edging the Land Rover forward with his eyes peeled for weaknesses in the crust. I suddenly realized that if I continued in a straight line I would reach the middle of the pan bay and there was no way they could risk driving out to me. So I turned tail and came back to tell them to stay put.

Throughout the morning, still revelling in my surroundings, I tried to keep in visual contact with the Land Rover, but as we neared the middle of the pan I began to slither and sink as the crust turned to mud. Globs of it clung to my boots as I pressed on for another hour. But I was in heaven: flat land, gentle breeze, the sounds of the wilderness without trucks and the sun bouncing off every available surface.

By lunchtime my legs ached and the only signs of life were highly insistent flies that bugged the hell out of me. I started asking the boys for time checks.

Almost without warning the mud stopped and I was walking again on salt. The crust was like a great white popadom. Clouds of salt dust circled and lifted in a wind I couldn't detect.

There was a high-pitched whistle and I looked back. The Land Rover was well and truly stuck. They'd been cruising at eighty kilometres per hour and begun to sink, but even changing down hadn't helped. The back wheels disappeared.

We unloaded all the gear to lose some weight and Gerry and Oli dug deep beneath the wheels and put down sand mats. Then we collected grass and lay it across the mud to give extra traction, along with chairs, the tarp, the table and anything else we could lay our hands on. Under the crust of salt lies a quagmire of saline mud that absorbs the heavy dew. It stinks, and we were covered with it.

For two hours Oli and I pushed from behind but Stormin' Norman refused to budge. With no winch, it was beginning to look hopeless.

Gerry gave it a go, oh so gently at first in case he spun the wheels and dug them in deeper, yet ready to gun it at first bite. There was a great surge and then the chairs, mats, tarps and table shot out behind as the wheels won traction and the Land Rover shot forward. It hit softer mud and began to sink but the tyres must have gripped on something hard, and it charged on again. I picked up an armful of kit, lugging it across to the grassy bank where the Land Rover had stopped some way in the distance. I hadn't gone far when I heard their triumphant howls as they came tearing across the pans.

'Drop the bags,' yelled Gerry and he hugged me.

That night I filled two bowls with our precious water, topping one up with disinfectant and the other with soap. I cleaned their cut hands and feet and then dressed them.

We weren't really talking, so we hadn't made a plan for the next day. I set off along the edge of the pan the next morning while they were still getting up; after the events of yesterday, it would have been madness to walk back out onto the pan. However, that's exactly what the boys thought I was doing.

Hugging the edge, I headed for a peninsula on the other side. I judged the distance to be four kilometres, but had gone no more than half that when a dust storm appeared from nowhere. I could barely see my hand in front of my face but kept the weak glint of the sun in the corner of my glasses and pressed forward with a handkerchief over my nose and mouth.

The Land Rover was nowhere to be seen. When it failed to arrive for the next break, I presumed the boys were bogged again. But what should I do? Sit and wait? Retrace my steps? Push on for Nata to get help? My water had run out, there was no shade and they could be as much as six hours' walk behind me. If I turned back I might miss them completely. I knew they wouldn't be tracking me, because they hadn't before. Visibility out on the pans was far less than on the bush escarpment, so I reasoned that I should stay put. Surely they wouldn't think I was actually out on the pan after yesterday?

My emotions flipped between down-to-earth logistics, anger that they hadn't left with me, anger at myself for not having a plan – and fear. I climbed to the highest point on the escarpment, no more than a metre above the pan, and used the technique Raymond had taught me for detecting even the smallest movement. I stared straight ahead and looked into the peripherals of my eyes like a rabbit. What if they had already passed me? But they knew how far I walked in the time that had elapsed; they must be behind. How long do I leave it before I retrace my steps, find their tracks and follow them? We could be going round in circles for days. And I had no water.

I decided to stay where I was, conserve my energy until early evening, then walk to Nata using the stars to guide me due north. Even if my navigation skills weren't spot on, I knew I'd hit the east–west road which would lead me to Nata. The boys would search for me until their water ran out, then head for Nata to get help.

Then, by sheer chance, I saw the Land Rover way out across the salt pan and savannah grasses. I waved my sweatshirt. They were turning away from me. I began running at full pelt, galloping across ankle-turning clumps of salt grass and waving my shirt. The Land Rover was growing smaller as it drove away.

Somehow, at that moment, Oli cast the binoculars in my direction and saw a dot in the distance. They'd been looking for two hours in low gear, zig-zagging from pan to escarpment. It was all down to a lack of communication, but I was angry that they'd assumed I wouldn't take the logistical problems into consideration.

Setting off wearily across more salt and grass we decided to keep a two-kilometre check on our relative positions. The boys headed off northeast, while I tried to push due north. I picked out a particular tree in a line of them I could see in the distance and headed directly for it, regardless of what lay in between.

Eventually the boys met me and we decided that they would go ahead to give me some idea how far it was to the Nata road. I continued north, occasionally met by ragged looking cattle. My first acacia tree appeared out of the haze and suddenly it really looked and felt like Africa.

A gemsbock head with hair and ears and eyes and flies lay in the dust, but there was no sign of the body. As I headed for the acacia tree, I suddenly wondered if there would be a lion sitting beneath it, dozing. The shade was empty and there was no sign of the Land Rover, which had been gone for more than an hour. I thought of climbing the tree to get a better look, but as I reached for the first hand hold, I realized the dark bark was moving. It was thick with ants.

I didn't have long to wait. The boys arrived with the news that the road was twenty-one kilometres further and not five as I imagined. My shoulders slumped forward and suddenly I felt exhausted. I sat on the bumper with the map and tried to decide whether to stop for the day or push onwards. I was too tired even to rationalize the problem and we decided to stop and make camp.

Next morning it was freezing when I woke. My cold sores had gone but the muscles in my legs ached and my left hip felt bruised and tender.

I reached the road – no more than a track – before midday. Lavender grew beside the dusty white strip and I picked leaves and squeezed them between my fingers, rubbing the juice under my arms to get rid of the smell.

The first sign of Nata was a windsock and a dirt landing strip. The boys were delayed by a flat tyre – even Stormin' Norman was angling for a rest. The town itself was a pleasant surprise, with painted houses, neat thatched huts and palm trees lining the streets.

We headed for a bar and ordered a half-dozen cold beers, consumed in the darkest room I'd seen for days. My lips and eyes were sore and I dreamt of being clean, but I had to complete the week or the sense of achievement wouldn't come. I left them in the bar and pushed on for another two and a half hours on the road north.

At dinner, Gerry said we couldn't afford steaks so I suggested Chicken Kiev, the cheapest dish on the menu. Oli proceeded to order rump steak, so I followed suit. I looked at Gerry and said, 'Sod it, we've just crossed the pans.'

We were staying at the Nata Lodge camp ground, under palm trees and surrounded by tropical flowers. There was a ragbag mix of residents, including hippies in a combi van, a couple of gays and a rather tired young guy who'd spent three months working for Operation Raleigh building a fence across the pans. The time had come for me to make some decisions over the walk's direction. Four days alone on the pans was a hard task but it had given me a huge sense of fulfilment, and it made me wonder.

The fundamental problem for all of us was boredom. They were bored with making tea at 5a.m., sarnies and fruit every two and a half hours, washing it up, giving me water and waiting on my every whim. Gerry had been the boss on all his ten years of expeditions and was used to giving orders not taking them. He was a far too highly qualified and experienced professional adventurer to be reduced to a butler-cum-scivvy. Oli went along with Gerry but must also have been stagnating mentally under the absence of problems to solve, since he was fresh out of university. I had been guilty of satisfying my need for stimulation by focusing on the developing relationships between us, but they got nothing back from me. I realized we had become very noisy and inward-looking, and blind to what we were passing.

I needed more than this. I toyed with the idea of jettisoning the Land Rover either for a few weeks or the whole walk, in favour of a donkey. The first problem would be foot-and-mouth disease, which had run riot here for five years, reducing the ratio of head of cattle to people from 8 : 1 to 2 : 1. They'd put up control barriers every 200 kilometres to prevent the movement of livestock, so I would have to keep changing donkeys or wait a couple of weeks each time for quarantine. Then, of course, was the question of food and water. I knew that the idea was a bit crazy, but the very fact that I had been thinking about it for so long indicated my need for independence. I simply could not continue with things as they were.

A cloudy sky, cool breezes and an easy stride on the quiet, unmarked road. But I was out of the wilderness and a huge part of me felt dead and robbed.

A hunter from Tasmania with sun-blotched skin and a down-trodden wife told us of an aging lioness who had been attacked by a pack of hyenas. They had harried and nipped her until she sought protection in the glow of a campfire. Self-preservation creates strange bedfellows. I told him a story Robin Hanbury-Tenison had told me about his parents. Robin's father, Major Gerald, was a big game hunter, and his mother a naturalist. While in Botswana they went on safari across the Makgadikgadi Salt Pans and the major wounded a lion and went after it. The lion hid behind a bush and ambushed them. The gun bearer fled up a tree, Mrs Tenison played dead and was sniffed at and Gerald ended up with his arm in the lion's jaws, which did a very passable impression of a waste-disposal unit.

Robin visited the Kalahari many years later and went to the small town of Maun to see if anyone remembered the epic tale of the Englishman the lion chewed. The old garage mechanic claimed to recall the fabulous Chevrolet which Major Gerald had driven.

'But what of the lion attack?' Robin asked. 'Do you remember that?'

'Oh yes,' the mechanic said, 'I remember the major with one leg.'

Some time later, he went on, the Englishman had returned with a new car. Strapped to the roof were several spare tin legs.

'What are those for?' the locals asked.

'Well, I've come back to get the bugger and I've brought a few spares with me in case he gets the other.'

Robin said it was a good story, but he could have sworn it was his father's arm that was chewed, not his leg. But then, as he said, he didn't know his father that well.

Walking in the open, I was sharing the same space as the big cats. This was lion country, and I'd begun wearing my neck knife. There were also quite of lot of snakes about. That afternoon I'd passed a coiled up black mamba and we were forever hearing of deaths in local villages. Gerry took to sleeping in his tent with the fire extinguisher beside him.

I was sitting at the table by the fire painting a card for Gerry's birthday. I'd banished him to the cab so he wouldn't spoil his surprise. We both heard the heavy, rustling footsteps at the same time. They came from the darkness across the road.

'It's a jackal,' said Gerry.

'Too heavy for a jackal,' I replied. 'Could be an elephant. There's a water hole somewhere near here.'

Gerry made his stifled snigger just loud enough for me to hear.

As he reached for the halogen spotlight, Oli suggested a cow. He swung the beam into the night and locked it on the amazingly serene figure of a bull elephant less than 30 metres away, munching on foliage. He seemed to fill the entire beam of light. For a long while we watched him contentedly eating trees, until he was joined by a cow and calf and they moved quietly away.

It made me realize how much I was missing. I was travelling through a tunnel, keeping reality beyond the firelight. I was walking through the countryside and villages without ever really communicating or learning about how these people lived. I didn't know how they built their huts, or made their food, or what stories they told their children at night.

This was what I saw each day: some of their huts were neatly thatched and others shaggy. The better ones had blue paint over the bricks; other were russet brown or grey like the changing termite hills. Some had doors and even a lattice window. There were picket fences made from straight lengths of wood and no wire. The yards were swept with hand brooms and women tended chickens and goats while carrying their babies on their backs in colourful slings.

But I never looked behind the walls. I walked within a tunnel and each night I slept in a tent, listened to western music on the cassette player, wrote letters to a far-off country. All these were barriers which drowned out the real song of Africa.

Although I crossed this continent slowly – slowly enough to smell its air and feel its undulations beneath my feet – I was walking to the beat of a different drum.

As we drove to my mark next morning, we passed three elephants feeding by the roadside. One of them flapped his ears in annoyance, obviously resenting us interrupting his meal.

I would have loved to have walked with them but we decided the Land Rover should trail me at all times, at least till we reached Padamatanga. Throughout the day it crawled in my wake, startling a baboon who came to investigate. The only people we saw were some village men humping logs and wearing gloves against the snakes. No chance of integrating with the world beside me with the Land Rover grumbling along behind, but it was safer that way.

Now that we were cooking on an open fire, we collected firewood during the day and tied it to the front bumper of the Land Rover. Some days it was so plentiful that the boys could hardly see through the windscreen. Elephant spoor occasionally dotted the roadside. Grey anthills pushed up between the trees like worn gravestones. Oli described how the insects carved out man-size caverns beneath the ground which acted like an airconditioning system to keep the nests cool during the heat of the day. Apparently the whole eco-system of the Okavango Delta to the west of us was based on the termites. They begin countless food chains.

My energy level was low, probably because of my period, and my two big toe joints had begun to ache. In the high humidity I had no appetite and had to force myself to eat sweetcorn for lunch when I really just wanted to find a fridge and put my head inside.

The rusting shells of old cars lay beside the road, many having been abandoned more than thirty years earlier – an era when crossing Africa by car was itself an epic journey.

An elephant appeared at the side of the road and I waved the boys closer. I wanted a photograph, but Gerry was more concerned with what might happen if the bull decided to charge. I stayed close to the Land Rover, ready to jump in if things became dangerous. After a little ear-flapping for the camera, he turned and strode into the bush.

Two days out of Nata the crew from *You* magazine arrived in a hire car, looking relieved to have found us before they perished in the wilderness. Pearson Phillips had interviewed me before I left London. John Evans was with him, loaded down with camera gear. They planned to stay with us for five days till we reached the Zambian border and Victoria Falls.

Pearson is a grandfather and looks like a weather-worn gnome. He uses his avuncular style to get interviewees to open up and I could see his eyes sparkle when he jotted down a good quote. Gerry, Oli and I had made a pact to present a united front and not reveal any of the friction within the team.

Now I had a two-car convoy behind me.

Pearson walked with me a quarter a day for several days, although became annoyed when the sixteen-kilometre stretch was over and the Land Rover wasn't waiting up ahead. I told him that it was a game of the mind. I didn't like to rest, I walked to cover the distance. In the morning he would charge ahead while I ambled, refusing to alter my pace. By quarter's end, I had left him well behind.

Both he and John had trouble coming to terms with the slowness of the pace, having come straight from London, but they were eager and receptive. I worried that Gerry would dominate with his easy charm and wit; that they would go back to London with an awful impression of me and thinking how fabulous the boys were by comparison. My insecurity and lack of confidence started to surface with a vengeance.

On the second morning, Pearson was interrupted in mid-sentence when an elephant crashed into the open nearby with a youngster swaggering in her shadow. These are the wildest elephants in the world – they don't live on a reserve and wander back and forth from Zimbabwe to Botswana to avoid the culling season.

The villagers had also warned us about nearby lion. When the men went to cut thatching grass for their huts, they often had to spend the night camped in the open and would build a fire to keep the predators away. If the fire burned down, the lion would strike. We, too, made sure our fire burned brightly all night.

It was eerie looking out across vast acres of yellow grass, interrupted by the occasional tree. This was truly lion country, with enough cover to make them almost invisible yet open enough for them to scent and out-sprint their prey. I was nervous and it showed on one stretch, when a bush rustled near me and I reached immediately for my neck knife. Out sprang an antelope and I breathed again. In the cars following behind, Pearson and the boys saw me jump. They realized at that moment how vulnerable I was, alone on the road. If it had been a lion there was nothing they could have done to save me.

I was told that 'Panda matenga' means 'pick up your load and go'. It's a throwback to the days of epic journeys made by white explorers, who took sole credit for taming a wilderness and gave scant mention of the 300 native bearers who invariably lugged the European comforts of home on their backs.

We had few luxuries, save for cigarettes and the occasional glass of wine or bottle of beer. We managed, however, to pick up a bottle of whisky and on Gerry's birthday, Day 69, I woke him up with a mug of tea, his present and the card I'd made him.

'Happy 27th,' I said. 'Make sure you drink it when I'm around.'

He was thrilled and in his best mood for weeks.

I was walking alone again with a convoy behind. Occasionally we had to stop and look for the cement kilometre markers. The verge cutters, in their stupidity, would cut them down and we found one stuck in a nearby tree.

The road workers are funded by the government and the World Bank. Gerry befriended a couple who took our dirty washing away to be cleaned and brought us food for lunch. I also met a deliriously handsome South African called Alex who was taking a truckload of bulls to Zaire. He stopped for a chat and told me that his brother worked in Chobe and could take us to the watering holes.

I had one last quarter to walk before we could relax for five days at the Victoria Falls Hotel. I should have been on a high, but instead felt nervous. My period didn't help, but I was more worried about

money and the fact that each day we spent resting was another added
to the overall journey.

The previous night's camping had been tense and Pearson had
shown himself to be quite disappointed. I knew he was tired, but so
was everybody else. Instead of providing him with a story packed
with glamour or a sense of danger, we were just shattered. The boys
looked rough in beards, bare feet and inside-out T-shirts. A button
on Oli's shorts had popped. As he and Gerry arrived in Chobe I felt
they were ready to give up. If I could have, then, I might have done
too.

We drove the two hours to Victoria Falls in Zimbabwe. Given
our mood, it was a rather ironic place to end the first leg of my
adventure; the point where four countries converge at one of the
great natural wonders of the world.

13

The thundering wall of water disappeared off the edge of the plateau like an ocean off the edge of the world. I could sit and watch it for hours, picking out the colours of the rainbows that formed in every shaft of sunlight.

Until we'd stopped for several days, I didn't realize how much I enjoyed sleeping in a proper bed, showering twice a day and sitting down to eat dinner without worrying about flies or campfire smoke or poisonous snakes.

For the five days at Victoria Falls, Gerry was our pied piper. He had many friends among the white water rafters and knew from past experience the best places to eat and drink. During the day he disappeared to raft the Zambezi and Oli, too, found his own amusements. After more than seventy days together we needed to be apart.

Unfortunately, I still had work to do. John wanted more photographs and hauled me out of bed at 6a.m. shouting orders for me to walk backwards into snake territory or to stand still. I didn't appreciate having upped my daily distance from forty to forty-eight kilometres over two months to give myself time for a week's holiday and then spending five days of it performing for a camera.

Luly had faxed me at the hotel with the name of a contact who ran a safari lodge on the Zambian shore of the Zambezi. I left it late to call, but when I heard the welcome sound of an English accent, I couldn't refuse an offer to spend a few days with the owners, Will and Ben.

Will was tall with greying hair lying flat back on his head and a large lower lip as though he'd played a trumpet all his life. Ben was smaller and darker skinned, with the eyes of the Duke of Westminster and a thin upper lip that protruded into an over-bite when he talked. He'd been micro-lighting around Africa when he discovered the beauty of the Zambezi. He contacted Will in England and they went into partnership to buy title deeds and set up a safari/hunting lodge on the banks of the river.

The lodge faced across the water, which turned gun-metal grey as darkness fell, and a party of us sat in wicker chairs at a long table set on stone floors, being served black bean soup and fish pie with vegetables.

After roughing it for so long, the luxury was difficult to get used to. There were mahogany lavatory seats and real loo paper and that night I snuggled in a warm cot in a khaki tent with a mosquito net draped over me and the soft glow of electric hurricane lamps throwing shadows on the canvas.

I fell asleep reading Wilbur Smith's *The Leopard Hunts in Darkness.*

Will convinced me to delay my departure for a morning, so he could take me micro-lighting over Victoria Falls. Strapped in the narrow seat, shouting to be heard above the high pitched roar of the engine, I had slight second thoughts. I'd flown in light aircraft since I was a kid, but this thing was just a go-kart with wings.

Will gave me a grin and a thumbs up.

The fragile-looking craft, held together by a few struts and rivets, began rocking as we taxied and then accelerated along the runway. Then we were airborne and the noise left behind.

This was real flying. The sense of altitude and speed is all the greater for having little more than a plastic seat between you and oblivion. The adrenaline surges with every bump and air pocket.

Within minutes I could see the spray of the falls, but as we prepared to sweep low over it, the engine stalled. We were gliding in silence with the wind rushing past, and slowly turning back.

'What's wrong?' I screamed, hoping this was all part of the ride.

Will held a hand to his throat and mimicked choking. Then he tried to restart the engine while I scanned the ground, looking for a likely place to be obliterated.

Suddenly the engine coughed, spluttered, hacked and roared back to life. Within seconds it died again but in that brief time, Will managed to lift the micro-light a few hundred feet higher and give us the altitude to glide home.

Taxiing in, the engine backfired. It sounded to me as if it was running too rich. After changing the plugs and checking that he had been supplied the right petrol we took off again, but had to abort after ten minutes. For me, to have missed going over Victoria Falls was a bummer; for Will, it was a disaster. He wasn't a mechanic, in a country where good ones are gold dust and his only escape from the slog of his job was now grounded.

That afternoon I met up with the boys at the Falls and we crossed the border back into Botswana. As I walked onto the metal car ferry I found myself imagining a blue ribbon high behind me on a map of Africa with a drawing pin holding it down. Another border crossed.

There were no hassles with immigration and within two hours I was walking north on good tarmac road flanked by thick bush. That evening we set up camp at Tongabezi with Will and Ben and watched as the sun set, a red orb fading behind the pastel grey clouds above the Zambezi. The hippos grunted like failing micro-light engines and fish eagles plummeted towards the water and their evening meal.

It was a quiet evening in the wake of one we'd spent in Chobe with Dennis, a white hunter who looked like the lion in *The Wizard of Oz*, and Keith, a wild and eccentric artist who couldn't paint without a full crate of beer beneath his bum which he slowly consumed.

Dennis told us about the unwanted side-effects of darting animals with tranquillizers so that rich tourists could get their 'great white hunter' photographs. He explained, 'Some of the animals have become so addicted to the morphine that when they see the aircraft coming they bound towards us and present their rumps.'

For the first three days I eased back into the rhythm of walking. After such a long break, it was like going back to boarding school.

Although it added extra time to the walk, I'd chosen a route through the bush to avoid hassles from police and military who operate on the main road to Lusaka. Expats had warned me about the practice of stopping vehicles and demanding a full search. Everything is thrown out and stripped down until it's impossible to keep an eye on things. If the police or soldiers don't steal from you directly, they simply inform their criminal 'brothers' of what spoils are available and the search is soon followed by theft at gunpoint. Suspicion of espionage is another favourite 'offence'. Even more disturbing is the constant threat of mugging and rape.

The tarmac to Mulabezi was so broken and pitted it was virtually a dirt track. You can always tell who's drunk at the wheel, because they drive straight while the sober ones weave and swerve to avoid a broken axle.

The villages were also different from those in Botswana. The

square huts were supported by sticks embedded in mud with thick
thatched roofs with fringes cut as straight as a ruler, and each had a
small enclosure where children played, dressed in the remnants of
western clothes.

The poverty was also far more apparent than where I'd been. The
average monthly wage in Zambia is about 1,500 kwacha. One bag of
mealie meal costs 300 kwacha, yet it won't feed a large family for
more than a few weeks. Shirts cost 2,000 and shoes much more,
which is why the locals poach to have meat or fish on the table.

The obvious question is why Kenneth Kaunda, who has ruled this
country for nearly thirty years, is one of the richest men in the world?

Most Zambians speak English and the women wear traditional
three-piece wraps of thin cotton with beautiful patterns in red, yellow
and blue. They reacted to me cautiously, waving without warmth, yet
I felt more comfortable around them than I had in Botswana.

I'd already been told to dress conservatively, covering my thighs
and shoulders so as not to offend. However, I stuck to dressing like
a man. The witch doctors in Zambia claim to have discovered the
cure for Aids – sleeping with a white woman. And when receiving
something, I was to hold out my right hand cupped and put my left
on the crook of my right elbow. Never say 'thank you' – this is
reserved for expensive or extraordinary gifts. To use it for lesser gifts
would infer that one thought the giver mean-spirited.

On our second night in Zambia we were woken by gunshots.
Animal poachers were nearby, either hunting, or being hunted by
government troops. As the shots echoed in the moonlight, we quietly
packed up and covered the Land Rover with a groundsheet, trying
unsuccessfully to camouflage it.

The sounds came from across a nearby river. The poachers were
probably after elephant. Most Zambians are too poor to own firearms;
they poach fresh meat with traps. These hunters were after far bigger
game and profits. They'd also kill to avoid capture.

We were in a quandary. If we moved the Land Rover we could
easily be mistaken for poachers or game wardens. If we stayed put,
the same was true. Eventually we covered the moon side of the Land
Rover with the tarp as camouflage and slept with one ear open.

For five days I'd suffered bad stomach cramps. My bowels were
bloated and tight; I seemed to walk with the smell of sewage. An
infection such as this can spread quickly and we began washing our
hands in Dettol before each meal. Similarly, dishes were 'flap dried'

instead of towelled. This must have seemed a bizarre ritual to passing villagers, who tried to comprehend why three white people would eat, wash and then stand in a clearing waving plastic plates like aircraft landing paddles.

Each day I zig-zagged along the track, trying to find a firm base rather than trudging through soft sand. A trapped nerve in my back was sending shooting pains down my leg, but I was cheered up when I was joined by a gaggle of small children trotting to school. Wearing remnants of smart western clothes, they took an obvious delight in being around me and touching my hair. Walking on, I daydreamed of pulling the legs off croissants and of cold toast cut thinly and spread with *foie gras*.

A woman in a pink dress and wrap walked beside me, asking maternal questions and looking concerned. She told me her people were afraid of me but before she could explain, she hurried off, obviously afraid to be seen with me. Soon afterwards I noticed that there were no footprints on the track. Where did the villagers walk? I left the road and 100 metres to the right, through thick bush, found a small track beside the remains of a railway. In places the metal line had been contorted by trees.

Where the path had been worn to soft sand, the locals had hacked another one, giving themselves firm footing for at least another few years. Woodsmoke hung like mist around the trees and the light streaming through made me feel safe. It was too thick to be made by cooking fires and there was no sign of life until I heard the distant beat of drums.

I tried to walk to the beat, but found it impossible. Instead my feet beat time with the throb of cicadas until I entered a beautiful village decorated with vines and brilliant red flowers that grew up the bamboo and brick-walled huts.

I had barely left the village outskirts when a swarm of flies attacked from nowhere. Swatting frantically and cursing, I wanted to run and hurl myself into water – anything to be free of them.

At lunchtime I arrived at the Land Rover and tore off my socks and shoes. They were covered with grass seeds that tore at my ankles and shins like rusty needle points. I didn't know what felt worse, the flies or the seeds.

I couldn't get away from either. Swatting frantically at the flies and cursing loudly, we made lunch in short time and consumed it in the sauna of the cab. While Oli danced around outside with first his rugby shirt over his head and then my mosquito net, Gerry lay beneath his net looking forlorn. Yet worse was to come.

The following evening, the flies were replaced by bees. A swarm descended before dusk as if defending their territory against inter-lopers. These insects were unusual. About half the size of a housefly, they don't sting, but swarm towards any moisture, whether it be the leaking lid of a jerry can or the perspiration on exposed skin. They dive into ears, mouths, and noses, crawling under shirt collars and cuffs and generally making life hell.

African bees get very dehydrated and crave water. We found the only way to distract them from the camp that night was by placing a washing-up bowl of water off in the bush. The swarm emptied it within a few hours.

For three days we were plagued by flies and moisture bees – driving me to the point of madness. During the wait for me, Oli and Gerry would cover up in mosquito nets, doubled over for extra protection, but still the bees would find a way through. The heat made it difficult to cover up against them. It was 38°C and felt like the inside of a laundromat tumble drier.

On our second-last night together before Lusaka, where Oli and Gerry were due to make their 'escape', we camped in a small village with a thirty-four-year-old local mechanic called Stanley who was named after the explorer. Stanley lived with his mother and grand-parents and had spied the Land Rover and then later me and assumed it was a lover's tiff which caused me to be walking.

We sat up late talking about the history and politics of Zambia. Stanley said it was hard for Zambians to feel any sense of nationalism because the borders of his country didn't correspond to any tribal or linguistic area: they had simply been imposed by the British. The region was called Northern Rhodesia until, after eleven years of fighting, they finally gained independence in 1964. But by this time much of Zambia's mineral wealth, mostly copper, had been mined and the money spent in Southern Rhodesia. It left the country in poverty. The diversity of the tribes was one reason why Dr Kaunda had formed a single, democratically elected, one-party government system. He used it to keep control and, since he was also the head of the armed forces, he effectively operated as a dictator. Much of Zambia's GNP was spent on supporting the anti-white terrorist parties in four neighbouring countries in their fight for independence, leaving the citizens not only poor but also highly suspicious of foreigners, who were seen as saboteurs or spies.

Stanley's grandmother moved a log further into the fire and settled back into the shadows. The smoke drew upwards and into the floor of the maize store above us where it dried the cobs, out of reach from rats. She'd heard Kaunda's name in conversation with these white strangers but she had faith in her grandson to protect her family.

Stanley told us of the forthcoming elections, where the villagers would have a chance to vote for a multi-party system. He, an educated man, didn't know what to believe, but, 'Anything is better than this.'

'Sounds familiar,' I said.

Stanley would make a point of voting but thousands of other villagers couldn't get to the polling stations. They had to work on their farms; they wouldn't walk for days to make their mark on a piece of paper which they didn't understand – and besides, what good would it do them? All they wanted was the freedom to live as they'd always done, but who cared enough to give them back their rights to hunt?

Stanley described how he had to hunt illegally – on his own land – using traps because they made no sound. He'd cut up the animal in the bush and bring back the meat, but he had to leave the skins, the bones, the sinews: everything, in fact, that was useful in case they were found in his village. They had to rely on commercial goods from larger village markets to replace those they could have made.

The following morning, Gerry and Oli sorted through their kit and gave Stanley his first pair of shoes. His mother got a sweatshirt and his grandparents had a pair of my sunglasses and couple of pairs of socks. We shared our coffee and carried on our way.

The villages looked deserted as I walked through them, but I'd turn some way down the track and see the villagers standing there, watching me suspiciously. They'd return my wave, but almost as a spontaneous gesture before they realized what they were doing. Then I saw the Land Rover ahead, waiting for me and I thought, it will be better next time.

Oli had torn a dozen pages from his notebook and laid them in a line in the dirt, counting out my last steps to the Land Rover. He'd written a sign and pinned it to a tree: 'THE END. Lots of love from the boys. Good luck on the next stage.'

There was another message, which I wasn't allowed to read. I had to tell them what was written when I next saw them, hopefully in

London, as proof that I'd returned to exactly that place to restart my walk. As if proof was ever needed.

Stanley told us about the Kafue Game Reserve and suggested we stay there the following night rather than drive into Lusaka after dark. Whites moving at night are regarded with suspicion.

The lodge was on a small island in the middle of the Kafue River, surrounded by hippos. We reached it by rowing boat as the sun began to set and discovered the park was as empty of tourists as it was of game. All that was left were a rotting group of white huts built on stilts with leaking thatch and the musty air of past greatness. On the bamboo walls of the bar were bleached photographs of 1960s tourists and dignitaries, among them Kaunda, who once used the park as his private hunting ground.

A poster at the bar said 'Cage the Poacher' and the shelves held mementos of bygone parties, bottles of Glenfiddich long since empty and photographs of mini-skirted women posing in front of rhino.

At least the beer was cold.

14

26 June 1991. Lusaka.

At Lusaka airport, I waited for Bill Preston and Blake Rose to arrive on the flight from London. Oli had already sorted out his travel plans and was continuing to travel in Africa before flying home to start a job in the city. Gerry was due to leave the following night.

We had arrived into Lusaka on the very last dregs of diesel and our contact Mike Davies, who works for Anglo American, a sister company of De Beers, had agreed to put us up for a couple of days until I changed drivers. His housemaid washed our clothes in the bath instead of the washing machines because, she said, 'Machine not know where the dirty spots are.'

While we waited for the luggage to be unloaded I got talking to a Peace Corps volunteer called Amy who worked in central Zaire and was returning from a holiday in the US. We got out a map and located her village, but decided it was unlikely that we'd ever get close enough to visit her – not unless Zaire turned into a massive bog.

It was quite a shock to see Bill and Blake. Both were pale after weeks in London and Bill had a large pot belly that hung over the belt of his jeans. Although only thirty-four, he looked older, perhaps because of thinning brown hair and turned-out feet.

I'm always nervous about meeting new people and I didn't quite know what to say when Bill gave me a big grin, shone his twinkling blue eyes and said: 'G'day, call me Bill. Don't call me dickhead.'

The accent was pure, unadulterated Australian, cut from the cane fields of Queensland where he grew up. He was rough, brash and 'took shit from no one', but from all reports was the best off-road driver and bush mechanic I could possibly have been given.

Blake Rose, twenty-six, was entirely different. For one thing, he

had shaved his head. Blue-eyed with a heart-shaped face, he had the
clipped consonants and rounded vowels of an English public school.

Blake had grown up in Zambia with his younger brother and still
had a tremendous love for the place. Not the arrogant memories of
an expatriate but a genuine fondness for African people, their customs
and traditions. More importantly, he had gleaned from his experience
the vital quality you need in dealing with them – patience.

I was shy around them. Somehow, I felt like a freak. I felt they
were watching me, trying to work out whether they fancied spending the next few months of their lives pursuing someone else's
dream.

Bill took the lead and tried to make conversation.

'I managed to get the money through without declaring all of it.
Those bastards at customs would have pocketed a bribe but we beat
them this time.'

He was jovial and laid back but I couldn't help thinking how old
and tired he looked.

Gerry and Bill had known each other in Kathmandu, where Gerry
ran the white water rafting trips for Encounter Overland and Bill
was ferrying punters back to London across the Middle East and
through Europe. They greeted each other with hugs and slaps and
disappeared to swap stories. I was worried that Gerry would put Bill
off the journey.

Blake was the odd one out, but it gave me something to observe –
how a person walks into a difficult situation and holds his own.

Gerry had headhunted Bill, but I wanted to know how Blake had
been chosen.

'I heard through a friend that you needed a photographer for a
three-month trip in Africa, all expenses paid. Luly gave me a copy
of your Australian book and told me to read it and come back to
her if I was interested.'

'So you called her?'

'No. She called me. She was desperate.'

'Would you have called her?'

'No.'

'Then why the fuck are you on my trip?'

'I lived in Zambia when I was a kid and always wanted to come
back here.'

I suppose everybody's got their reasons, but still I worried that I
was being lumbered with a back-up driver who had no desire to help
me.

Bill, on the other hand, had been an Encounter Overland driver for three years and I knew he wouldn't mind the slow pace. He'd been recovering from a shooting in Pakistan when Charlie asked him to come. Bill's truck was stopped by bandits at a road block. He got out of the cab to talk them out of it, but spent some time with a gun at his head. He was allowed to get back into the cab, but the bastard opened fire and shot him through the door. The bullets mushroomed and passed through both arms. One lodged in his thigh. It took twelve hours' drive to get him to a hospital, where he was pumped with drugs for several months until he was fit enough to survive the flight home.

His motivation was simple. The route we were taking through Zaire hadn't been traversed by anyone he knew and this was his challenge. Although he was 'working class' and he called Blake a 'nob', they both immediately liked each other and merged into a team.

For Oli and Gerry the job was over. As Oli handed me the keys to the Land Rover, I kept my sunglasses on so he wouldn't see my tears. We hugged and I thanked him for his help. I felt relief for both of us.

Gerry signed my witness book, confirming that I had walked every step of the way.

After saying goodbye, Bill, Blake and I went shopping, stocking up for the next three months. Bill changed money and came back with several carrier bags full of kwacha. The highest denomination is worth about two pounds and at the checkout, the girls have to count wads for even a few items.

I wanted to stay another day at Mike's house but the boys were keen to get started. I liked their enthusiasm and that afternoon we drove back to the place where I'd stopped. The sign was still on the tree.

It said: 'If you're gonna get wasted, go out in style.'

That evening we had a team talk around the fire. It's the only time during the day when we're all relaxed, the work and walking have been done, the plates washed and packed away, the sleeping kit laid out and tidy.

I didn't know what Gerry had told Bill, but I had the feeling he was big enough and ugly enough to make up his own mind. I wanted to bring them into the walk, to make them feel their hard work had a value.

'Sixteen kilometres and you meet me for breakfast. Eight kilometres

later for water. Eight kilometres after that, for lunch. Then another
eight for water and eight to the night camp.'

The excitement of having a new team also meant training them. I
faced the same anxiety that they wouldn't turn up and I'd be left
alone on the road.

Eight kilometres after breakfast I found another camp set up with
food and·tea ready for me. Bill and Blake had worked at lightning
speed to pack up and get there in only an hour and twenty minutes.
They stood there waiting for me beside this unexpected meal and I
started giggling. I didn't want to hurt their feelings because they'd
worked so hard, but I explained that I didn't need to eat till lunch.

It was a short period of adjustment. Soon they knew the score
and I was back in a routine walking along sandy tracks through dry
woodland.

We had chosen to take a route through Kafue because the main
road north was patrolled by the police and military whose chief sport
was to waylay travellers and order full-scale searches of their vehicles.
Incriminating evidence was always found which meant bribes had to
be paid. If we stuck to the bush tracks, this could be avoided,
although we still faced the constant threat of suspicion.

Bill set up two alarm devices on the Land Rover – small battery
operated boxes that detected movement. We were woken in the early
hours by the high-pitched howl. Bolting upright, I watched Bill and
Blake desperately struggling to get out of their sleeping bags and
tent, certain we were under attack. By the time they emerged, I was
rolling with laughter.

Our trespasser had seen one of the black boxes sitting on the
bonnet and picked it up. A few paces down the road it went off and
in total shock he dived head first into the bush. God knows what
he told his fellow villagers about the strong medicine of the black
box.

I soon grew spoilt walking in the coolness of the tree canopy and
the sunshine would sometimes hit me like a wall. The soft sand
beneath my feet tugged at my calves and sent me weaving from side
to side looking for firmer ground.

I was on the path one morning, squatting over stomach cramps,
when I felt my cheeks flush with embarrassment. At that moment I
looked through the trees and spied a lone cyclist winding his way
towards me. Hurriedly pulling up my pants, I dashed into the bush,
hoping he would slip past. Instead he stopped, waiting for me. He

was joined by a giggling group of women carrying sticks, dried fish, nuts and berries to market in large baskets balanced on their heads or hips. So much for privacy.

We hit the tarmac road and turned right towards Lusaka before joining another bush track north. I came down a slope into the Luampa Valley, watching the river stretch wide beneath me, green with rushes and water lilies. Longhorn cattle drank at its edges and a man punted a dugout through the sun-dappled water. Cooking fires blurred the air.

For the next few days I crossed the Luampa River delta. The villages were built on slopes with the white earth swept antiseptically clean around their stick huts with not even a leaf allowed to settle. These people knew exactly where to position their houses under trees with canopies so thick the twigs were hidden. Banana fronds waved in the breeze casting a brilliant green amidst the red spiky flowers. These villages look like tropical resorts, although the inhabitants wore ragged clothes. I saw one master builder resplendent in a dark suit that must have been retrieved from the rubbish bins of a dozen former owners.

At Kaoma, I turned north along a dirt track that would take us 150 kilometres along the edge of Kafue National Park. Kaoma was a surprise. It had a few 'western' style shops – rectangular boxes with a stone porch and flat high square display front. The signs advertised fashions for men and women, linen and shoes, yet the shops sold nothing but cobwebs and broken glass. Everybody just sat on the street, watching other people sitting in the street.

I had to ask directions many times at the dirt crossroads trying to discover which route would take me to Kasempa, 220 kilometres to the north. Although trying to be helpful, they erupted in a fierce debate while I joked and giggled with the kids, scaring them with a growl until they saw me smile and ran back for more.

It was good to be heading directly north again, making ground. The stomach cramps had grown worse and I sensed something serious was coming. I even asked Blake about witchdoctors and thought about the logistics of driving back to Lusaka.

Water had become a constant worry, for we needed fresh supplies regularly. It was the dry season and many watering holes had a stagnant stench about them. Bill asked one village chief for water and was offered a cup of it.

The road to Kasempa was once tarmac but had been reduced to

a deeply scarred and pitted track, narrow and precarious, but at least dry. At one village a man came running after me shouting, 'Kasempa is a long way, are you going footing?'

'Yes,' I laughed. 'But I have a car.'

'OK. We were worried for you.'

Bill was fighting the pace and looking nervously at the changing bushland. His time in Africa had taught him to recognize different terrain and its associated problems. Although he rarely voiced his fears, I knew something worried him.

The following afternoon I discovered what it was. Out of nowhere the flies arrived. They attacked me over the last eight kilometres, biting me relentlessly on exposed skin and through my T-shirt until I screamed in frustration and thrashed wildly with tree branches. Within minutes I was covered in large painful lumps.

Ahead, in the Land Rover, the boys were doing their own dance, sitting in the cab with the windows rolled up. Still the flies were getting in, crawling through the air vents and engine. The swarm was so heavy, neither could get out. Bill spent his time cutting off their proboscis with scissors and letting them go so they'd die a slow death of starvation.

Blake hurled opened the door screaming at me to get inside.

'What the fuck are they?'

I looked at Bill's pink legs protruding from his shorts and saw a hard disc the size of a saucer swelling on his thigh. He had taken an antihistamine tablet but it didn't help against the itching, swelling or pain.

'Tsetse,' he said. 'Forget sleeping sickness, these bastards'll maul you to death.'

That evening at camp, we got our things together and decided how to protect ourselves.

'You have to cover everything,' explained Bill. 'They come in swarms and will stay with you for a mile or so at a time.'

I had three zoot suits provided by Survival Aids, who assured me they had been tested in the jungles of Belize and were the best way to keep cool and covered up.

Bill lent me his hat, which I covered with my mosquito head net. My hands would be covered by pulling down the arms of my zoot suit and clutching the elasticated wrist band in my palm and the legs would be held down under my socks.

My suit was light blue and the boys had black, which was unfortunate because tsetse are attracted to light colours. I should have also realized that these insects have a proboscis that is designed to penetrate hippo hide. The double layer of silk in my zoot suit was no protection at all.

The next morning, the tsetse were on me before sun-up. I thrashed at them with branches but they grew in number until my dance grew wilder and the bites more frequent. One got under the head net and I tore at it frantically – face to face with a blood-sucking tsetse there wasn't room in there for the both of us. Another slipped under the ankle grips and bit my thigh. I couldn't run or hide and without limited protection would have collapsed within minutes like a buffalo brought down by hyena.

As the sun got higher, the tsetse grew more vicious. The zoot suit was so hot I thought I was going to dehydrate and die all neatly wrapped up in my own designer body bag.

Going to the loo became a nightmare. Exposing my privates and fiddling with a tampax, it might have been comical if it hadn't been so terrifying.

When I reached the Land Rover for breakfast, I found Blake cooking pancakes. He was under attack and should have been inside but had chosen to make me breakfast. He was doing it for me and for morale. It was a major turning point in my feelings for Blake and my relationship with both of them. The tsetse were drawing us together.

The next quarter was the same. For mile after mile, the tsetse flies were buzzing around me like hurdy-gurdies. I drew the hood cord tight around my neck so that no skin was exposed on my face, but I grew lightheaded trying to breath and my glasses steamed up until I could see no further than the sand at my feet.

Cutting a switch I lashed at them, the hungry, blood-sucking, crazy bastards. I had bites around my neck, hands and ankles but couldn't scratch. The itch was unbearable, but if I scratched, I was doomed. A large white lump appears surrounded by redness and the itch grows even worse.

Even with the netting I was kissing tsetse as it leant against my face in the God-sent breezes under the first cloud for weeks. My right eyelid was bitten almost closed and it was difficult to see.

Sweating increased and I drank through the mozzie netting keeping my hands covered inside my sleeves and dancing a little jig because standing still made them bite my ankles.

At lunch the boys darted out to put up a mozzie net and chair for me and opened tinned veggies and made tea. I sat watching them dance in their suits. They refused to come inside, saying it was better out there. They were right, but I had to take a load off. Bill lit a fire on the track to try to smoke them away but they soon went of their own accord as a swarm of dehydrated bees arrived heading for a leaking jerry can of water behind my head.

Bill's smudge fire was burning the wrong wood and he promptly vomited from the poisonous fumes given off by the burning sap. The bees didn't notice and darkened the sky around us.

We packed up quickly and I reassured them I was OK. They drove ahead to day's end, but the tsetse followed me.

Nobody could tell us what was in the Kafue National Park which ran beside us because there were no longer any patrols or park rangers to keep count. An old man going hunting had told us that a lone male lion had been seen two days earlier. Lone males are often most dangerous because they're usually old, injured and cast out from a pride by younger competitors. With no females to hunt for them, they will attack only the weakest prey.

I looked anxiously about me, knowing that I came high on that list. Through the netting of my hat, my vision was limited and I knew that an attack would come from behind. When the woodland grew thick, I should have been able to use the noise of monkeys and cicadas as warning signals but the noise of the tsetse drowned out everything but my cursing. A lion could smell blood over a distance of thirty kilometres and I was burying my tampax deep in the soil, expecting attack at any moment.

I kept turning around, shouting like I was many people. My knife hung from its cord around my neck and I imagined what I would do if I saw the lion. I unsheathed it and carried it in my hand. Fat chance of being able to live through an attack but it made me feel better.

There were bushfires beside the road with flames blowing over the track. By now I didn't care what I burned, anything was better than this. I ran through the smoke and flames, thrashing off the tsetse.

I marched down the track and rounded the bend to see the Land Rover waiting. I had never felt such relief. In my head, I started my weekly countdown, 'quarter's end, day's end, week's end'.

Blake was looking out for me and saw I was covered in tsetse. He ran towards me with a can of insect repellent, spraying me down and tearing off the sodden mozzie net and silk 'body bag'. My face was swollen and right eye completely shut.

'Good onya, cock,' Bill said. 'There aren't more than four people who live on this stretch because of the flies and you're the first person I know who's ever walked through a tsetse belt.'

'But the hell ain't over yet,' I called back as I rummaged in the first-aid kit for antihistamines. 'Don't forget who's cooking tonight.' They didn't know how bad it could get until they'd tasted my 'one pan wonder'.

It was my night to take care of them, something I hadn't done for Gerry and Oli very often, but these guys deserved a break and it felt good to give them one. I gathered the wood, built the fire and cooked them supper. At last we'd all had something tangible to fight against, instead of each other, and we'd pulled together.

Blake was painfully coming to terms with the reality of Africa, somehow blurred over the years by his memory which recalled only the romance and the roots. Now he saw the neglected villages, the swindling, the corruption.

At Kasempa, the first village after the Kafue National Park, a wide grit street divided the shops, and towering above was a water tower where the boys hoped to fill up. This, however, was only second on their list of priorities. They'd heard that the town had a bottle shop and, since the camp had been dry since Kaoma, where we picked up two bottles of whisky and consumed them with a luxurious mix of sweetened condensed milk, they drove ahead in search of cold beers.

At lunch, Bill burst into song, 'Ain't got no milk 'n' alcohol', and I cut his hair in readiness for a possible night on the town. After the tsetse and the bees we deserved a break.

Rule number 1 of walking: never build your hopes up too high.

When they arrived at the shop they found it padlocked and having hammered on surrounding doors discovered that the manager had been arrested for embezzlement that morning and was now in prison with the keys in his pocket. There was no beer and no Coke. Only Fanta.

Instead I met them at day's end at a small cluster of mud huts and asked the chief if we could stay. Around us the families prepared their evening meals, children laughed and chickens scratched out scraps. Their main crop was sorghum, which is pounded and mixed with water and then cooked. We drank tea and ate fudge with the chief and he told us of a man who'd shot himself when attacked by tsetse. That I could easily believe.

Setting off for Solwezi, the track was soft sand, sucking my feet down and making me stumble forward when I hit an unexpected hard patch. Around me the bush changed every few hundred yards from autumnal trees with russet leaves and burnt charcoal undergrowth from recent bushfires to lush green canopies with an abundance of vibrant undergrowth.

A man in grey flannels and a pinstriped shirt was lugging a cumbersome bag and perspiring heavily when I passed him. He was a village school teacher and walking very slowly. The boys gave him a lift but when they arrived at the school an elderly man rushed up and explained that his daughter-in-law needed a doctor. She'd been in labour for four days and still hadn't produced. The local doctor had gone to Ndola for more supplies.

Lying her across the back, Bill took off for the hospital in Solwezi, four hours north, while Blake stayed behind to meet me at the lunch break. Her mother and husband squeezed into the front passenger seat, trying hard to keep her comfortable when the potholes threw the Land Rover from side to side. We found out later that she'd had a caesarian just in time and was now the proud mother of a baby girl.

As I hit the tarmac to Solwezi, I found the boys waiting for me under the shade of a tree encased by an anthill. Nearby was a rundown hut with a sign that said 'Bar', but again there was nothing to drink. A bus pulled up, spewing out passengers who adjusted piles of mealie meal on the roof.

Eight kilometres further, as I stumbled down hills and thrashed up the other side, I came across three plump little girls chewing sugar cane. Their under-developed breasts bounced beneath white cotton shirts that hung loose above their navy skirts after a day at school. They ran hard to keep up with me, kicking dust up with their flat black shoes.

From between the little family plots of sorghum, ragged boys streamed onto the road around me with such torn clothing they looked like extras from *Oliver Twist*. I felt like the pied piper leading them out of town.

A young man about my height, with thin lips and a face like a

Mutant Ninja Turtle joined me, asking questions. I told him I'd walked from Livingstone. He was astounded and unbelieving. When I looked back the whole road teemed with dancing children, laughing, clapping, shouting questions. I felt self-conscious after three weeks of solitude in the bush. They wanted to look in my pack so I showed them my water bottle and they seemed satisfied.

'How long are you going to be with me? My husband is up ahead and I know he'd thank you for escorting me.'

'We're just following you,' the young man said. 'Why don't you slow down and let people see your face?'

'My husband is waiting for me, they should run and keep up with us.'

'What political party do you support?'

'Neither, I don't know about them,' I replied.

Neither did he, it seemed. He was wearing a UNIP T-shirt but making multi-party signs with his fist. He slowed me down with his pace, constantly smiling while his eyes furtively looked behind us. Although he asked many questions, I knew he wasn't listening to my answers.

A truck going the opposite direction stopped on the road behind me. A tall, muscled man in shorts jumped from the back, strode towards me, pushing his way through the kids. He grabbed me by the arm and pulled me towards the truck.

'Hang on, what are you doing?' I demanded.

Suddenly the atmosphere changed. The laughing kids were howling like Red Indians, shouting, spitting, shoving me.

A young woman in a head scarf screamed in my face: 'This is Zambia, you can't walk alone in Zambia.' She grabbed my neck knife 'What's this for?'

'For cutting food ...' I couldn't think quickly enough.

From behind, somebody suddenly grabbed my hair and yanked my head back. Another unsheathed my knife. I felt it pressed into my windpipe. Desperately trying to stay on my feet, I was being dragged sideways with my head held back facing the sky. Adrenaline rushed in, whirring my mind into action. *This is pretty serious, be calm, talk quietly* – everything I'd ever been told came rushing back.

I spoke softly: 'I'm just going for a walk in your beautiful country, my husband is not far away.'

Suddenly aware of the appalling smell of their excited bodies, I wanted to vomit.

The woman screamed 'Spy!'

It electrified the crowd. I was almost lifted off my feet and dumped at the truck.

The driver hung out of the window, trying to make sense of the commotion. I told him that I needed a lift. He was frightened. He shook his head. I pleaded with him until I heard the military Land Rover pull up. The sight of that uniform frightened me more. In Zambia the militia rape, rob and murder. I'd walked for three weeks through an uninhabited game reserve to avoid them. But now I had no choice but to plead my case.

I shook hands with the officer. 'My husband is not far away, please take me to him. I've just been for a walk in your beautiful country ...' My words sounded hollow.

He listened to the crowd. He considered me with the knife held to my throat and looked away. With a slight tilt of his head, he indicated the back of the truck. I took back my knife roughly, and climbed awkwardly over the side on top of a bamboo bundle.

I looked away from the jeering crowd, now out of their reach, and shouted: 'Stupid paranoid fucks!'

We drove for a few miles. All the way I strained to catch sight of the Land Rover parked in the bush for evening camp, frightened that if I missed them I wouldn't be believed.

The boys always made sure they were out of sight of the track in case of trouble but their marker for me wouldn't have been placed yet: they weren't expecting me for another hour.

Luckily they were still on the roadside, but also under arrest. The local chief had seen Bill walk into the bush to find a campsite and sent two men after him. He accused him of planting a surface to air missile to bring down President Kaunda's plane.

As I got off the truck, I rushed to 'my husband'. Bill was very calm and explained to the army officer exactly what we were doing. My hands were shaking as I lit a cigarette.

Flatly and with no grounds for discussion, we were ordered to follow them to Solwezi, where our authorization would be checked at the police station.

The station courtyard was full of rotting Land Cruisers and the little shade was taken by officers in khaki shirts with braided cord on their left sleeves. Their marine-style belts had double buckles and held up dark brown trousers. Inside, the counter was like a kitchen table, except underneath were stacks of cartridges for their multitude of guns.

Slowly we began explaining what we were doing. Blake hunted

around for evidence, but the book jacket of *Feet of Clay* couldn't be found. Although in control, I could see Bill nervously eyeing the guns that were being twiddled absentmindedly around fingers. After the Pakistan shooting, I knew his heart must have been thumping.

After much to-ing and fro-ing I found the address of Marion Grove, a VSO worker whose name I'd been given when we stayed at the Tongabezi safari camp on the Zambezi. Marion was running the accounts for a government organization in Solwezi. Instead of spending the night at the station, Bill asked them if we could stay with our friend. The police all knew her and after some negotiation, escorted us to her house. I guess it wasn't such a surprise for this young woman to find three whites arriving at her house after dark with a police escort asking for refuge.

Marion greeted us warmly. She was older than I expected but romantically in awe of native Zambia. When she heard Blake's accent, she didn't give him a chance, using aggressive, emotive arguments about welfare and state responsibility. Diplomatic and stoic as ever, Blake wouldn't let her get away with it and stayed up till the wee hours defending the right to private education.

At 8 o'clock the next morning we had to be back at the police station. Bill negotiated again for our release but grew frustrated because there was no way of knowing exactly who was in charge. It was as if they were just waiting for the whole thing to blow over by itself.

Several hours passed before we eventually saw the head honcho. He gave us a letter which sanctioned my walk and would hopefully appease any more village chiefs who thought we were spying. Life in Africa is a series of deals. Everything is negotiable.

We drove back to the point where we'd all been arrested and then drove another fourteen kilometres further back. It was past my point but I couldn't remember it, so better to walk an extra five kilometres than miss any out. I didn't even see the Chief as I walked through the village but the atmosphere was tense – Dr Kaunda had been canvassing for votes and everyone was very confused.

That night we slept on Marion's veranda under her snake-loving vines and her black puppy with big ears and small feet slept with me under the duvet. I mulled over what we had heard at the bar that night: that we were heading into a virtual war zone. Thieves from Zaire were crossing the border with guns, hijacking cars and taking them back into Zaire. A handful of people had died in the past fortnight.

The next morning we asked at the police station yet we were told nothing had happened for at least three months. That same day, bandits hijacked a bus load of people and took all their clothes and provisions. They arrived naked at the police station in Solwezi, their clothes gone, along with the bags of mealie maize.

The Zaire robbers are military. The soldiers aren't paid regularly so they supplement their income by stealing cars and food from Zambia. Sometimes they would take the drivers with them to build bridges and break secret trails through the bush. The Zambian Government tried to counter the robbers by placing paramilitary along the border, hidden in the bushland with orders to shoot bandits on sight.

Solwezi was only thirty kilometres south of the Zaire border but the actual road ran due east, parallel to the border for 115 kilometres before turning north to cross into Zaire. Then it doubled back on the far side. Bill and I checked the map closely, wondering if there was some way I could cut straight to the border and avoid the extra distance. A small track ran due north from Solwezi and then appeared to continue over the border into Zaire. If I could get through, it would save me at least six days walking and avoid the bandit country.

I decided to try. We would head due north for the border and I could mark my crossing point with a cairn of stones. Then we would drive the road into Zaire and I would return to the stones from the Zairois side.

There was only one problem: the track I wanted to walk was in a military zone and I needed permission to enter. It was almost impossible to explain what we proposed, but eventually the chief of police understood the route and gave us two policemen as guards.

Our first attempt was abandoned when the guide proved he had no idea where he was going and kept directing us along the main road. We returned to Solwezi after six wasted hours of walking. No point in blowing your top, though Bill and I had trouble in containing ourselves. We tried again and this time found the track which took us through the military training ground. A charismatic commando escorted us, sitting on the Land Rover bonnet fondling the curved magazine of a loaded Kalashnikov. Although only twenty-three, he claimed to have killed at least eight Zairois car robbers.

The camp commander gave us a letter of authorization to walk the ten kilometres to the border through autumnal bush along an overgrown track consisting of two tyre ruts.

We reached a junction of tracks where a rusted signpost marked the border with two arrows ← ZAMBIA/ZAIRE →. There were no fences or observation towers or dog patrols. I stepped over into Zaire and Blake took a photograph to mark the occasion.

Driving back to Solwezi, we congratulated ourselves. The rainy season was fast approaching and any time saved was increasingly valuable.

The Nkana Hotel in Kitwe is a dump. We had driven a long day to get there, hoping finally to find a decent shower. Having negotiated an exorbitant price for a good, basic room, I discovered the plumbing didn't work. I put my foot down and after much hassle was given a perfectly good one with a working shower. For the first time in weeks I put on a dress and some make-up and we went for a slap-up meal. Within hours I was vomiting and continued doing so all night before collapsing on the bed in total exhaustion.

Bill woke me and I explained what had happened. I went down with him for breakfast and drank only tea but as we left and walked through a lovely courtyard to the car park, I vomited again. It sprayed the walls and was so violent I felt like it was alive.

Blake took me to their room so that we didn't have to pay for mine for another day. I tried to contact De Beers in Botswana to ask Nick Byers to send our box of extra supplies on to Lubumbashi in Zaire. The city had no phones, even though it was the second largest in the country. Rumour had it that the minister of communications had banked his budget in a Swiss account.

On day 106, I lay in the back of the Land Rover as we crossed the border into Zaire. This is one of the most corrupt borders in the world, yet we sailed through customs and immigration without a question being asked. I suddenly realized why. We were all wearing white polo shirts with the Hi-Tec logo that had been given to me before I left London. Initially I had dyed a batch of the shirts khaki but they were a dud lot and had shrunk. The store replaced them immediately but with no time to try again, I left with white shirts.

Now the Zaire officials waved us through, convinced that we were a party of missionaries.

'Can I have a book, please Father?' Bill was asked.

He shrugged.

'Bless you, sister,' said another.

*

Once through the Zaire side, we needed to change money. It's not a good idea to do it at the border because the rate on the black market is so poor and there is a risk the marketeers are in cahoots with the border officials.

The last time Bill was in Zaire two years earlier the rate had been 2,000 zaire to $1. He was offered ten times this on the street in Lubumbashi and did a deal. Then we found a shabby hotel and asked for rooms.

'How much?' asked Blake.

'500,000 zaire.'

'Are you crazy?'

'No. This is good price,' said the manager.

It was a grotty, run-down flea pit and they wanted the equivalent of about £200 a night. Then we realized what had happened. We'd been horrendously ripped off on the exchange rate. We got 125,000 zaires for our £100 instead of 1,250,000. An expatriate explained our mistake and then led us to a guest house.

Lubumbashi has the antiquated, crumbling ambience of past greatness. There is a sense of old expatriates gathering each evening behind screens, drinking coffee and gin while they played cards with monopoly money – their own riches having long since disappeared.

The guest house was a run down little dive but it wasn't a brothel. It stank. The eating area was full of grey, haggard men sat around playing board games over small cups of espresso, their eyes watery and yellowing in blackened sockets – more dead than alive.

The lavatory wasn't working, so I threw up in a bucket. All night I woke up burping. And when Bill came in the next morning and smelt my breath he gave me a cuddle. 'Giardias, mate.' It's a stomach parasite which can be distinguished from dysentery or amoebas because it makes your burps smell like farts (and taste a lot worse), but it can be cured by a heavy dose of Flagyl.

I spent the next day hovering around, unable to lie in the pit of a bed, unable to eat or drink, unable to wash because there was no water until evening. At least there was merchandise in the shops – toothpaste, shades, mosquito spray and knick-knacks nobody ever wants. There were bright Fanta kiosks on the corners in front of fading chain stores, banks and fashion shops. Little selling is done inside. Everything is bought from the back door.

Lubumbashi had once been a highly prosperous city. During the 1970s copper boom, it was the backbone of Zaire's wealth. There are many other more valuable minerals but Mobutu hasn't found the

country or company who will pay his price for mining them – except
De Beers, and the infrastructure just doesn't exist. Zaire was the
Belgian Congo until Independence in 1960; Mobutu rose to power
then by putting an end to the horrific tribal fighting.

What he has offered ever since is peace at all costs and openly
admits that he has raped his country's wealth in return. His seat in
Kinshasa is a long way from Shaba Province – the copper belt. So
every so often, his secret police garrotte a few civilians in the street
to ensure his power is still felt. There were four known garrottings
in the few days we spent there.

There had been around 250,000 Belgians living in Lubumbashi up
to the previous year; now there were fewer than 10,000. A female
student had been found spying and her fellow students threw her in
a pit and burned her alive. She happened to be the daughter of the
head of the secret police and he slaughtered scores of students in
retaliation. Belgium issued a warning to Mobutu to sort things out.
He didn't, so they broke off diplomatic relations. It didn't seem to
make much difference.

There's a greyness about expats in these far-flung, ruined colonial
towns – grey as Paludrine, the daily malaria prophylactic we took,
which seems to prevent a tan.

Bill made repairs to the Land Rover and was helped by the Belgian
expat who ran a parts store. He met a couple of travellers who had
driven south on the same route we would take going north. They'd
managed only fifty kilometres in a day. Fine for me and also for
Bill – he knew there was a heck of a challenge waiting for him.

Blake and I tried to find the box De Beers had sent. We went to
seven places: import–export, railway station, storage depots etc, but
found nothing. Months later I found out it had turned up in Zurich.

When we left Lubumbashi, we drove for eight hours on dirt track
that worsened to a deeply pitted, crevassed river bed in the wet
season and slowed us to less than walking pace.

That night we stopped at a mission and private boarding school
and camped in the yard, setting off early next morning to reach the
Zambian border. Having got through one military gathering we got
to Mumena and found another group of militia sitting on cushioned
chairs under a tree looking as much in control as the Nazis in
occupied France.

A drunk, superannuated old relic with two teeth garbled that the
border was two kilometres south and, yes, if we took an escort we

could walk down to it. Bill and I set off guarded by two men carrying Kalashnikovs and after four and a half kilometres arrived at a concrete pillar which marked the border. It was not the place I'd walked to on the other side. Fortunately Blake arrived. His French was better than mine, and he soon discovered that we were seven kilometres north of the mark. The Zambians had led us, the Zairois said, to the wrong place. If we wanted to walk to it, we had to get permission from the military in Lubumbashi to cross the border into Zambia, plus Zambian permission to prevent us getting shot if we did so.

Nobody screamed, nobody wrung anyone's neck, even though we'd just wasted over a week and now had to go back to Zambia. This was a disaster.

We were out by only seven kilometres yet had to spend two days driving back to Lubumbashi, cross one of the most difficult borders in Africa through twelve check points, any of which had the right to search the Land Rover; drive another day to Solwezi, battle for two days to get permission and an armed escort and then walk three days through bandit country before crossing the border again. That paltry seven kilometres in forbidden territory would cost me sixteen days. The only good news was that our visas were multiple entry.

A guide book had mentioned there was a friendly American mission at Kitwe and it was after dark by the time we found it.

The typical missionary family is large and this one had five sons and a daughter. They were very American – warm and inviting. We ate popcorn on the sofa and watched a ball game on video. They made pancakes with homemade maple syrup and gave us a tin of baking powder for our own.

Yet they were probably the worst kind of missionary. Their function was to teach religion. We suspected they also had a hand in other things since this area was of political importance to the USA. Mobutu had learned the powerful game of playing off the super powers.

Missionaries are focussed and determined people but I've seen some of the results of their blind determination to spread the word of the 'one true God'. Religion and rituals give strength and a sense of belonging. But what makes my blood boil is the condescending attitude of those who regard their own beliefs as absolutely right and everybody else's as pagan.

These missionaries spent every penny they were sent, bred like rabbits and expected the church back home to pay for their kids to eat bread, hotdog sausages and Aunt Jemima's pancake mix shipped in from Maine. They were a long way from those who lived in African villages, shared their poverty, healed the sick and taught farmers how to dig wells and grow more produce. I sometimes felt that these guys should be heading for London and New York to teach us how to lead more contented lives.

Back we went into Zambia and Solwezi; back to the police compound and the rusting Land Cruisers. The police commander shrugged when we told him what had happened.

'Oh yes, there is seven kilometres that you are not allowed to walk.'

No point in arguing over logic. They couldn't be expected to understand the rules of a walk. The damage was done. It was getting late and I had to walk fifty kilometres that day so that we didn't have to camp on a bandit stretch more than two nights.

The Land Rover followed me for three days, never losing sight on the narrow and hard-packed red clay. In the passenger seat our escort policeman rested his AK 47 out the window. The gun was cocked and he forgot there was a bullet in the chamber. It went off, flying past Blake's ear and out the window. He was more frightened of the bandits than we were – if they saw his uniform, they'd pick him off first. He was there to explain to the paramilitary that we had permission to walk through but, when a soldier leapt from the bush with his gun at the ready no more than three metres from me, our buddy buried himself deep in the passenger footwell, shaking.

My worries that the boys would despair at going through this all again were unfounded. Bill and Blake didn't question my decision. Blake sat on the roof or bonnet and read *Silence of the Lambs* to me. I loved it. The psycho stuff appealed to my curiosity, and I loved the depiction of Clarice Starling, the young FBI agent with the tormented past.

Blake was enthralled by it, too, and it led to some pretty heavy discussions about our childhoods. Sometimes I walked beside the open car window and Bill played me a Vangelis tune on the tape deck, over and over. When he found the BBC World Service I heard the words 'This is London', and thought they sounded cold and remote. It made me shudder and remember how far away we were.

At Kipushi on the Zambia/Zaire border, we camped with a drunken bunch of anti-bandit paramilitary who slept in Iraqi-made tents, shot

Russian made AK 47s and drove recommissioned 1940 East German trucks to the VD clinics manned by Cuban doctors.

Bill showed the officer in charge our black box alarm system and explained that if anybody walked past in the night they would go off. Later he overheard him explain this to his men. 'Okay. Listen good. If you walk past the Land Rover, the black boxes will shoot you.'

The next day I crossed the Zaire border again at a different border post from our first crossing. We had avoided the bandits in the bush and now had to handle the bandits behind desks.

I had reached Zaire and not missed a step. I never doubted that I could do it. If I had, the little niggles would have turned into insurmountable obstacles.

No one could accuse me of not taking this seriously. I'd lost sixteen days for the sake of seven kilometres. I was going to walk every step from the Cape to the Mediterranean.

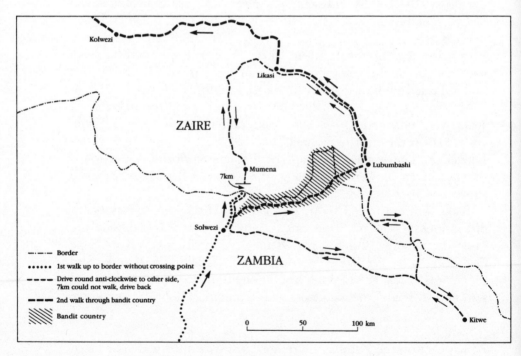

Sixteen days to walk seven kilometres.

15

We pulled off the tarmac for the first break out of Lub-umbashi. Africa can be very quiet — we make the noise. But here it was so quiet we could hear ourselves breathe.

'Where are the birds?' I said.

'Locals ate them all,' Blake said. 'Like they ate the donkeys, so now they have to pull their own carts.'

'Notice how the drivers hoot their horns just to show they've got them — and they work?' Bill said. He cocked his head. 'There's a vehicle now.'

Blake said he couldn't hear anything. Nor could I.

Bill said quietly, 'That's the sound of a Land Rover reversing.'

Sure enough, two or three minutes later, a Land Rover appeared over the brow of the hill — going backwards.

Out stepped the front cover of *Vogue*, a tall, elegant white woman in her forties, with an intelligent face and a shoulder bob of thick grey hair tied back with an Alice band. In sharp contrast with us bush bums she looked a picture of casual sophistication in her black slacks, thin grey sweater and half-moon glasses.

'Good morning,' she beamed. 'I'm the American ambassador to Zaire.'

She was checking out Shaba on her first tour of the country, she said, having taken up her appointment only recently. I hated the way she stood too close to tell me this, but I liked the vivacious way she spoke. I asked if she had any news about Algeria after the so-called coup.

'Stable again,' she said. 'You must come and stay with me when you get to Kinshasa.'

After breakfasting with us she climbed back into the Land Rover and with a cheery elegant wave, resumed her tour of Zaire.

Blake was sold a bottle of rather dodgy whisky by a Belgian who warned him not to drink much of it in one go. But – you forget these things. Bill was feeling a bit crook so he went to bed; Blake and I huddled round the campfire and sank the bottle between us.

I set off early, wonderfully hung over, the miles slipping by as I watched the sun rise as a dull orange orb through the grey dust. That was how central African sunsets and sunrises always were; the spectacular ones are only found in travel agents' handouts.

We had several unpleasant breaks in moisture bee country, made all the worse for Blake because he was nursing his hangover. We draped towels over our heads to keep the crazed creatures out of our ears and cut down the noise: with a hangover they sounded like fingernails scraping down a blackboard. And they couldn't be switched off.

At one stop we parked next to a bunch of freshly dead mice, strung up with a noose around their necks and hanging from a stick. No one was sure if they were lures for catching birds, deterrents to ward off other vermin, or – most likely – for sale as food.

The hills in the distance reminded me of a Van Gogh painting: conical mounds that didn't have tops, too perfectly shaped to be natural, draped with the remains of bushfires and dregs of dried vegetation in the shadow of power pylons nobody could be bothered to disguise. I wanted to take a picture but didn't dare for fear of arrest.

As I got closer I saw they were slag heaps. The houses clutching the side of the mining valley were built from bricks of baked earth and straw; they reminded me of Israel. To complete the illusion, the horizon was a war zone ablaze with black woodsmoke.

Carved wooden pots stood end to end at the approach to the villages, like some kind of talisman at the roadside. The houses had tiny windows that were bricked up against the winter cold.

Clouds gathered, the first I had seen since our last rest day.

We reached Likazi for the second time and met the other missionary family. They also had five sons and a daughter, and we were invited for dinner. We had an unspoken rule that when we stayed with missionaries we didn't swear, blaspheme, or talk about religion, but with this family we seemed to lurch from boo-boo to boo-boo.

Christine asked me if we'd like some lemons from her tree and I said, 'Oh, we only use lemons for gin and tonic, and we have neither.'

'That's a good thing,' she replied.

A lovely meal was laid out before us and Bill set to with gusto. A few seconds later, the missionary said grace.

The food was so delicious that Blake gasped, 'Oh God, this is good!' and saw one of the little boys gape, open-mouthed, at his big sister.

After dinner, this girl told me that she wanted to be a missionary doctor and travel the world. I recalled that Chris, the eldest son of the other family we had stayed with on the first visit to Likazi, had been head over heels in love with this girl for many months. He had wanted to 'study' with her but the parents forbade it until she was sixteen, which was five months away. Longer than eternity, when you're sixteen years old. He therefore decided he wasn't serious and began writing to a couple of girls in Zambia. I stopped myself from saying, 'Never mind, there are plenty more pebbles on the beach.' Out here, not only were there not any more pebbles for this poor girl, there wasn't even a beach.

I'd set up the roof tent and was just about to turn in when I was arrested by Christine with the words: 'Where do you think you will go when you die?'

I was stuck. A three-hour tirade on their branch of Christianity later, I hit the pillow.

They all came out and walked with me the next day, keeping up well and having a good time. They also taught me my first words of Swahili: the greetings. It was to be how I remembered Zaire most, walking through a village shouting: 'Jambo!' (Hello) and waiting for the echo: 'Jambo-sana!' (Hello very much).

The black women taught their children that if they were bad the white man would come and get them. They took great delight in handing a youngster to me while the child's back was turned, and then, when it screamed at the realization, they'd howl with laughter and refuse to take it back. They also told me not to mention Mobutu's name, nor write it in my notebook. A couple of years before, a nursing missionary had been accused of spying when the secret police had found her notes, couldn't read English, but saw Mobutu's name. They killed her. 'We refer to him as Uncle Mo,' I was told.

On through ugly mineworks and their dusty shanty towns. Up and over hills that were trashed – yellow ochre, scrubby dead trees, charcoaled earth, power pylons. But it was good to be on dirt, up above the noise and people. I'd been too long away from it; it was a joyous and refreshing return.

High on a ridge, I looked beyond and below at Zaire – undulating hills in regular layers till they merged into blues, and their fuzzy texture of dry trees faded into the gun-metal haze of forest fires. It was a primeval place, where few whites had gazed.

The hard slog to reach the summit was repaid by four kilometres of downhill bliss that worked other muscles and turned my attention to the strength of the old women who were labouring up the slope with 50 or 100kg bags of mealie meal or sweet potatoes on their heads. The heaviest woman I saw couldn't have weighed more than sixty kilograms. There would be no applause for them at the top, but a drunken husband with an empty gourd of local spirits in one hand and a painful slap in the other. Wife beating, we had been told, was commonplace.

I wore my new 'hat', the skull-cap cut from a Hi-Tec baseball cap to leave a visor, but my eyes were still closing against the brightness of the land.

It was the season of fresh fruit and vegetables. We feasted on avocados the size of melons, tomatoes that tasted like succulent fruits, pineapples so luscious and refreshing no American food inventor could create such a sensation. Fresh food made me feel good, physically and emotionally.

I hit a market. Clothes on the stalls were donated by US Aid and clearly marked 'Not for Re-sale'. Lots of men wore glasses; again, donated from the West. The villages were much more run down than those in Zambia but there was a new sense of vitality about them. My waves and greetings were returned by open-faced people with ready smiles who joined me on the road. Little boys displayed their prowess with their homemade, but quite deadly, stick and rubber catapults and little girls played a game of 'dare' to see who would get the closest to me. I'd hear a brave one sneak up behind and turn on her, growling and waving my fingers as claws. They'd scatter but, looking back from a safe distance, they saw my laughter and came running back for more. After a quick snatch at my hand by another bold youngster and she was still alive, she took my hand and walked proudly down the track, displaying her bravery.

My shits returned; my bowel felt like an Alka Seltzer was dissolving in there and sounded like a squeaky rocking chair. Giardias is tough to kill. I got over the worst and felt good having shed a lot of weight, but it continued to plague me every few days. When out walking, I'd skip off the track to go to the loo. Most locals would politely move on, but when a white woman dashes behind a bush and makes a noise as though she's murdering a goat, they take a look.

The road was long, open, unshaded, gently uphill, without respite from the heavy dust explosions coming from overloaded trucks whose guts made noises worse than mine. It was hard to get any sort of momentum going. The land felt so big with flat horizons and I felt so small, battling to gain any ground.

Bliss came at day's end after a shower from the electric pump, sitting in my dressing gown by the fire with a beer in my hand and my feet soaking in the washing-up bowl. Blake sat beside me, soaking his in potassium permanganate. We felt like an old couple.

Though the whites of their eyes were very white from the protein of the plentiful fish and the balanced diet of lush vegetables irrigated by the lake, the villagers by the Zaire river's first lake were not as healthy as they seemed. The mosquitoes were a tell-tale green – from the malaria they carried, said Bill – and the edges of the lake were thick with the green grasses fancied by bilharzia snails.

We had driven there to find a camping spot for the rest day. Everywhere I looked the word incongruous stuck in my mind. People in clashing, donated clothes, wearing shower caps for berets. Ducks with chickens' beaks and feathers. And trees that looked like metal filings in an experiment with magnetic fields. Totally congruous, however, were the men's bodies – exceptionally magnificent and flawless, solid and square with well-defined muscles and no body hair.

Kolwezi, once a former mining town of considerable wealth, was now in total stench and decay. Colonial homes and businesses, once with bougainvillea trellises in streets lined with pale purple flowering trees, had been taken from their owners and given to the Zairois overnight by Uncle Mo after independence. But these weren't their homes or their businesses, so they ran them the way they wanted. People say that Africans are hopeless at maintenance, but that's maintenance of Western things. I've seen them working feverishly to rebuild their roofs before the rains but not everything from the bush has such a long life span as machine-made things, so they replace, not repair. Hardly surprising that they didn't pour a lot of energy into the ornate gardens of the colonials – that kind of time on your hands is a luxury.

Their gardens contain useful plants for medicines, poisons and keeping off bugs.

The Fina sign at the filling station was rusty and squeaking. The small building was typical of the hideous, flat-faced concrete architecture of the 1960s.

'Diesel?' Bill asked the attendant in French.

'Sold out. All sold out, but I know where you can buy some.'

'Where's that?' Bill asked cynically, knowing full well what the answer was going to be.

'Round the back.'

Extortionate rates a speciality.

The boys had met a young Belgian guy who said we could spend the night at his sister's house. We weren't sure if he'd told his sister about this, but expectations were high. It was amusing to watch the boys go through the rituals of grooming; I even trimmed their hair. That night, as we drove to her house, the excitement and competition between them was hilarious. As we honked at the gate they both blurted out their wish: 'Oh please God, let her be pretty!'

But – no Coke, only Fanta.

Staying with her was a menagerie of rescued animals and a highly disturbed African prostitute. Whatever disappointment the boys might have felt, Isabella was exactly what I needed – another woman to have a good natter with. But, my French not being too good, we had to use body language. Between the same sex, it's easy. She introduced us to her animals in her garden: the chained-up chimps, the fish eagle, and she was just taking us to meet the dik-diks when she noticed that one was missing and rushed over to the pool. It was lying on the bottom. The water level was down, and it must have tried to drink but had fallen in. Isabella handed me her glasses and jumped in fully clothed. She retrieved it, but it was dead. It was hard to know what to say – if you don't speak their language, how do you comfort someone whose dik-dik has just drowned in a swimming pool?

The whole evening was bizarre. In the bathroom shaving, Blake looked up at the mirror and saw the reflection of a civet cat beside him. There was a mongoose in the bed and the prostitute was having a life crisis on the kitchen table. We went out for supper and then on to a night club with her and her friends. Isabella paid for our burgers and bought me five malachite ashtrays for 10,000Z the lot. Off doing their own deal, the boys paid 60,000Z for three much smaller pieces.

I wanted to explore and went off with a South African guy on an amazing shopping trip around the back streets. Unfortunately it took rather longer than I expected and the boys got so worried about me they sent out a search party. I got back to the house with my little parcels to find Blake sitting in the garden composing a letter of explanation to my parents. They were furious with worry. I apologized to both of them, but it highlighted the problem of wanting to have my cake and eat it: I wanted to be free but I also needed to have a safety net in case anything happened. There is no emergency button to press in Africa − or if there is, it doesn't work.

16

The missionaries in Likazi had warned us of troubles ahead. Football supporters walking home after a match had been shot by soldiers who mistook celebration for demonstration. The families of the dead later retaliated with bows and arrows and killed a good number of military. We decided to give the area a miss and diverted to Kanzenze.

We stayed near a leper colony at a monastery that was used as a training school for monks and priests. I wondered if the novices about to be ordained as priests thought I had been put there as the last temptation: after eight years of study, with twenty-two days to go, they were faced with a blonde running round in a singlet and shorts, albeit one with the squits.

We set off again and were immediately harassed by moisture bees that got into our ears. It was unbearably hot under the awning with netting at breaks and we became irritable, dirty and hung over. I shat my pants again in the night; with no control the muscles couldn't restrict the liquid. I left the sheet in a bowl of water to soak next morning but by midday a swarm of bees had drunk the water and the camp was enveloped in a swarm of bees and a stench of diarrhoea. I knew I had to move it. The boys hadn't had much luck by nudging it with a tent pole, so I picked it up and walked a couple of hundred metres into the bush. Gently, I brushed the bees off my body and helped them out of my hair.

My stomach cramps hadn't gone since Kitwe and after the all-night drinking session with Blake I never recovered. My period would come in two days and I knew I couldn't walk with double the pain. We turned back to the monastery.

The doctor, a tiny, elderly missionary lady with a hunchback, came to check me over. I told her I had vomiting, diarrhoea and stomach cramps: only in Africa can you present these symptoms and be told you have tonsillitis. It would, however, account for the severe earache

I had kept quiet about, not wanting to sound too much of a hypochondriac to the boys. Bill had already cracked enough jokes that a pommie sheila's delicate stomach couldn't hack Africa.

I was relieved to be told that something tangible was wrong; all this disease and infection was unusual for me. Now at least I could rest – in the bush I'd wandered around hot, dizzy and lightheaded. The doctor prescribed antibiotics, and told me that when a local went to the doctor complaining of a headache and was given a pill, the doctor made sure he swallowed it or else he'd take it home and put it on his pillow and sleep with it. He couldn't understand why, if the pain was in the head, you put something in your stomach instead of on the wound. The logic was hard to refute.

While I crashed out, the boys spring-cleaned the back of the Land Rover. We had two large metal trunks, one for the cooking kit, the other for supplies we had brought from the UK to see us through the more desolate areas. Bill and Blake now opened it for the first time in many weeks to check the contents. I was waiting for the sound of two hungry men finding twelve bars of chocolate, but there was just silence. I crawled out of the tent and leant over the rail.

'You stuffing your faces already?'

'Na, mate,' said Bill as he kicked the lid closed. 'The washing up liquid's leaked. Everything's fucked.'

I walked for the next couple of weeks through dry woodland that reminded me of an English autumn: thin trees with few leaves, leading onto occasional open flat areas that were blackened by fire and dewy in the morning light like Devon.

It was along this stretch that both Bill and I kept getting sick. I didn't know my 'African body' well enough to know the difference between being sick and able to push on, and being sick and in need of rest. It was several days before I succumbed to the boys' pleas to take a break. I was taking antibiotics and was overdoing it; I stopped at lunch one day and simply couldn't get up and walk on. I tried to rest in the roof tent, slithering around in my own sweat, slapping myself to kill the insects. That night I felt better and let Bill sleep in the roof tent because he had gone down with a severe head cold and needed a good night's sleep. I slept with Blake in the dome tent.

As Bill climbed up there he kept calling down to us how good it was. There was silence for a while, and then he said, 'Ah, but there's one thing I can do up here that you can't, Fi.'

There was another pause, and then the sound of pissing.

'Bastard!' I said to Blake.

It was a very special night for Blake and me. Very tentatively, we put our arms around each other and relaxed. We slept in an embrace, and in the morning he got up to light the breakfast fire. I drank tea with him before I set off, and all through that day I was skipping, dancing, laughing, feeling as if I was ten feet tall. I wasn't sick any more; the cuddles had been incredibly therapeutic.

I was so full of energy that when I got into day's end camp I said 'Thank God' that little had been done because they both felt crook. I had to burn off the energy somehow so I dug the fire pit, cooked, washed up, did my laundry, put up the tents, washed my body and hair and administered hot rum toddies to Bill, who was still suffering from his cold. Then I sat down and still felt raring to go.

The terrain was changing gradually from savannah to tropical and getting noticeably more humid. My stomach cramps continued despite the antibiotics and Flagyl and I was often doubled over with pain. They didn't stop for three weeks, then got unbearable. I felt fuzzy and spaced out; my movements were those of a badly worked marionette. My head was heavy and lolled between a string and an unsupporting neck. I couldn't judge distance, couldn't even feel I was walking. I bumped into things. I nearly blacked out at one stage and had to lie down for an hour on the roof. I used thermorests and sleeping bags to keep off the moisture bees, with the result that I started to cook. Hot, sweaty and irritable, I got up and walked on. At the end of the second quarter I collapsed and slept until dark.

Strong winds fanned a bush fire and turned up the thermostat even more. I staggered through pristine villages that were oddly divided by numbered plot signs. I said nothing but waved feebly, never looking up. Whenever I tried to lift my head to make eye contact I felt my skull would burst. But sick as I was, the deep pink bougainvillea looked beautiful against the deep red of the anthills, and the vibrant green of the odd palm was perfect against a dusty backdrop of dry season green.

Bats sewed the night sky, possibly attracted by the insects around the fire. In the darkness, the forest spoke in crackles and creaks which could be people, animals or ant-riddled wood. One particularly beautiful night, Blake remarked how lovely it would be to follow our camp fires one day, years after the walk was done, and remember the warm and good atmosphere that was left in the half-burnt wood and ashes from Cape Town to the Med.

*

We listened to *Africa Watch* on BBC World Service. The National Conference was officially opened, but not many of the 300 representatives had turned up. It was therefore delayed until they did, which could be some time, considering their communication lines had all been cut thirteen years before. The opposition candidate for the Zambia election against Kenneth Kaunda had also stood down, saying he thought his presence would divide the party's chances. The reality was probably that his life had been threatened. We'd got good at reading between the lines.

I had been walking downhill for at least a week and it felt good. Even better was the news that John McCarthy had been released and that Terry Waite was still alive and might be released in the coming days. I felt an overwhelming sense of relief and cried.

I walked down a hard-caked, deeply-rutted red track and knew a village would appear, for in the far distance, on the other side of the valley, was the pale haze of a forested bank. All valleys here had rivers in them, and all rivers had people. Gaily I waved and 'Jambo'd' down the hill till the children set up calls ahead and the villagers massed on the track before me. Calls that sounded like the Red Indian war cry rang shrilly and summoned the people, till they kicked up the dirt as they ran higgledy piggledy down the hill. Boys overtook me, the older ones aggressively asking questions in a language they could see I didn't understand. I remembered how easily the atmosphere could change; it suddenly seemed that all the individual things which had bugged us during the walk were beginning to come together in Zaire: mozzies, flies, bees, and intimidating people.

The forest was lush and scented with the aroma of freshly shelled peas. Swarms of butterflies covered the shallowest puddles like Sir Walter Raleigh's cloak before his Queen. Curling spirals of slender green vines entwined in lacy embraces with the heavily laden trees, and pads like water lilies sat high in the branches amid purple-headed flowers like foxgloves.

The people seemed to use whatever they had been given, and would walk miles in an old pair of wellies just because they had them – they ruined their magnificent feet. The women were very beautiful, with copper clear complexions and bodies finely toned by labour. They went to the fields as if they were going to the larder, gathering what they needed for the day and restocking by planting. In their head basins they carried leaves and cassava, peeled and ready to be soaked for a week, dried then crushed and the fibres separated to dry on the track before pounding into flour and mixed with water. Little girls played at being grown-ups by balancing anything they could find on their heads. A couple of inches taller and they would be balancing full buckets of water up there over miles of rough track – without spilling a drop.

I saw few men. The remains of trappers' fires were evident in the bush, but the men melted into the woods as I passed. One group returning from a hunting party showed itself, displaying a skinned carcass on a pole. Their guns were homemade and it could only be by chance that they didn't blow themselves away; perhaps this accounted for the lack of young men in the villages. The kids still used bow and arrows and I watched them practise like miniature Robin Hoods – they'd roll a soft round piece of wood fast across the track and each would fire an arrow into the centre. Frighteningly accurate!

The freak is never afforded privacy. A woman with a baby persisted in following me and I kept getting annoyed that she wanted something. Nobody was sure if I was male or female and they followed me because they didn't get a chance to look at white people when they came in a car. The woman followed me for the whole morning. She kept shouting at me but I didn't know why. I eventually found a man who spoke her language: 'She was asking you to slow down because she's frightened of the forest and wants to walk with you.'

We gave her food, sugary coffee, and milk for the baby, plus our only orange and a can of tomatoes we had been saving. She showed them to the baby and said, 'Santé' – health. The baby's head was the same size as hers. I wondered what chance it had. A fly got stuck on her mouth while she was eating the orange. She licked it in and ate it.

Flies landed on my face as though they had been sucked there, then pinged off. My stomach gurgled and rattled like a coin in a charity box tumbling down the runners. We had little triangles of Laughing Cow cheese for our breaks, and were down to pasta and sugar for main meals. In our minds we built up the town of Kamina because we'd heard there was a US military base there; we were pinning our hopes on it for morale-boosting helpings of steak, alcohol and the opposite sex.

We reached Kamina two weeks after leaving civilization in Kitwe. The town, as always here, had seen better days. We sank a few beers at the only bar, surveying the rusty signs for 'Imports and the Rural Development of Kamina' and other mouldy remnants of colonialism. The proprietor knew nothing about a US base but told us of white missionaries in town.

Blake went to find them. They were very suspicious of him, but eventually agreed to let us use the guest house at the back of their property. We had a rest there, taking our meals with them and talking of our route north.

I walked on across flat, open plains of succulent green shrubs and yellow grass, towards a far distant horizon where lines of tropical rain forest marked the course of small rivers. Bushfires lit the skyline like distant volcanoes.

As I watched a pair of black hawks drift on the thermals over the plains, a woman up ahead with firewood on her head was so scared of the Land Rover as it overtook me after a break that she started running with her load falling all around her; finally she dropped it altogether and pelted away at top speed. I'd been told that some Africans, especially the children, think that whites eat blacks. Yet one morning I came across a message written for me in charcoal on the track – 'Good morning sister.'

In one village the drums beat fast and rhythmically as I approached, then the beat changed to keep time with my footsteps. I stopped to see if the sound was the chopping of logs, but the drums stopped too and resumed as I walked on, Pink Panther style. It was somebody taking the piss.

Four days out of Kamina, we reached Kabango and were directed to the house of a Swiss nurse, Vreni. She wasn't at home, but we found her at the clinic. She came running out to meet us, looking drawn and pale: she had given too much of her own blood that morning to help a mother during a caesarian.

There was no 'hello', just a desperate call: 'My materials! Have you brought my materials?'

I thought she meant fabric and since I'd bought some in Kamina to make us new shorts I said I hadn't but she was welcome to mine. When she realized we had stayed with the missionaries in Kamina, she was on the verge of cracking up. All her medicines, staff wages and battery acid for her radio were being held there awaiting collection, and they hadn't said a word to us about them.

She gave us a tour of her 'hospital', complete with goat shit and pee in the corridors, and premature babies lying in boxes like newborn puppies. There were cooking facilities and washing machines, sterilizers and boilers, but not a single piece of equipment worked because the locals had stolen the fittings and the water pumps. There was no water; families had to bring it from the river to wash the patient. The staff had not been paid for months, and there were virtually no dressings or medicines left. No wonder she was upset at the missionaries' behaviour.

We all helped her cook supper and supplemented her ingredients with our own stores. I was fuming. Nobody had come to visit her for months on end, she had no car and her radio was on its last legs without more acid. Her obese 'neighbours' had full communications, two cars and an aeroplane and they couldn't be bothered to send on her supplies – in fact they'd probably been so busy making popcorn and watching videos that they'd forgotten all about them.

Vreni was the kind of missionary who knew what was really needed and just got on with it. She didn't preach, she was a living example of the power of faith: she got through each day because of it.

Vreni told us more about jiggers, a small insect in the dust which burrows into the skin and lays eggs. The eggs feed on your flesh until they're big enough to leave and find another foot.

'I've got one under me nail,' Bill said.

Vreni fetched her magnifying glass and tweezers and took a look at his foot. He looked so smug, fluffing himself up because he hadn't mentioned it.

Then Vreni looked up and said: 'It's OK, you're lucky, it's only a splinter.'

Poor old Bill had to stomach a round of abuse while Vreni dug it out.

'He's well 'ard pal, out cuttin' the cane before he could walk.'

'Yo Bill, ya pink, fluffy pommie sheila!'

I went out to get something from the Land Rover and locked the keys inside. The window was open a fraction and Bill was able to pull the lock button up with a coat hanger from Vreni. He then rigged up a system with a cord to open it when the window was shut. This system came in handy when the door key broke.

We set off the next morning and when I shook her hand, I asked Vreni the meaning of the word 'awapi', which all the locals used to call out to me.

She smiled and said, 'Oh, it means "silly".'

At the first break, a four-wheel-drive vehicle approached down the narrow track and stopped beside us. Out jumped Amy, the Peace Corps volunteer we'd given a lift to at Lusaka airport. We hugged like old friends. It appeared that due to our route changes we were now in PCV country for the next week. She invited us to stay and gave us directions to her house in a village a day's walk ahead.

For the blacks in Amy's village, the novelty of watching whites had worn off. It gave me a chance to watch them for a change. They had great charisma, and spent their days having fun. Much like a bunch of marines on a march, they chanted in rhythm with their footsteps to alleviate the burden while they did their work. The women spent their days pounding cassava together or working together in the 'gardens' – which were a long way from the houses but still called gardens. The men, too, worked together, though their labours were sporadic in time with the seasons. The kids played together in their own groups, not divided by age but by development. Everyone had peers, nobody lived a solitary life. It was easy to understand why Africans don't work well in the western way of the city: they don't want to work for seven hours a day and then play for two in the evening; they want to have fun all day and then go raging in the evening. I could relate to that.

The following day we dropped in for breakfast with Rob, another PCV, who'd got the villagers running around doing everything from building his house, to doing his laundry and cooking his meals. And at week's end we spent the rest day with Gena, the penultimate stop-over on the PCV run. Her house was a mess because she poured all her energy into her fish farms, which were spectacular.

Blake cut my hair because it was mouldy, and we learned that the locals burn their locks to prevent anyone making a voodoo doll out of the clippings. I picked up fleas because I'd hung my clothes under the eaves of the thatch to dry. Bill got on well with Gena and I felt like calling another rest day so that they could get to the point of bonking, but we heard a booming sound in the distance: our first thunder. We had to push on.

Within a week, I got sick again, vomiting violently during the night. After several episodes of climbing down and throwing up beside the Land Rover, I only had enough energy left to throw up from the roof tent. God knows what the villagers thought we were doing when they heard the sounds of my retching and moaning. Bill and Blake thought I was a shit – they couldn't get any sleep either. In the morning I was exhausted and called a rest day, and we drove ahead a bit to get to the last PCV in the village of Kakuyu. Gail helped us find more diesel on the black market, which entailed a lot of whispers down a lot of dark alleys.

We drove back and carried on walking the next day. Walking after being ill is fabulous: it gives a high, like fasting. Along the way we came to a river and decided to wash. I came out, dried myself off and immediately started to shake. All the sensitive skin on my body – my eyelids, lips, crotch, the inside of my nose – swelled up in lumps and I began tearing at my face to scratch them.

'Stop it!' Blake shouted. 'I've had this before when I was a kid in Zambia – it's an allergy to a water parasite.'

He told me not to scratch, in a few hours it would die down. HOURS! He even drew me a sketch of what they looked like.

I took a couple of Piriton and sat quietly, waiting for the rage to subside. When it eventually did, Blake confessed that he had never had the allergy before, but figured it would help if he said he did.

We called in at Gail's house again that night and had a proper dinner with her and some guests. Hers was the last village before the forest began officially. At various villages over the past weeks, we had been intimidated by the locals but we hadn't known why they were so unwelcoming. Bill and Blake often saw women running away at full pelt, as the woman with the firewood had done, losing their loads when they saw the Land Rover.

'They think you're evil spirits,' Gail said.

Papaya were always there, producing just a few fruit each day for breakfast. Now mangoes were coming out on the trees, small green baubles hanging on a stem, and we began to hit patches of rainforest interspersed with burnt woodland.

Over the next few weeks, through areas where whites had rarely been seen, the villagers became more and more frightened and hostile. At spear point they accused the boys of being slave merchants: why else would they have parked there, waiting? And the villagers accused me of cannibalism: why else would I be walking?

The rejection and fear took their toll on me. I was used to having a good time with the women, but now they were running away or demanding an explanation. The kids stoned me out of villages and the men intimidated me. I'd find pieces of fruit in a neat pile beside the track but no sign of the people, bar their tracks. They screamed a new word at me in the villages: 'Mamawata!' There were new kinds of images drawn in charcoal on their huts too – mermaids with long flowing hair and fishes' tails. But they weren't beautiful. I found out many months later that these people thought of the slave merchants as a mermaid spirit – strangers who came from the water and took their young men. People still take advantage of this fear by travelling through the villages demanding money and food in protection against the Mamawata. If they don't appease her, they lose their sexual prowess. I wish I'd known that then, we'd have lived like kings!

The stress on the boys, too, was considerable, as they waited for me to arrive at each break, never knowing whether this would be the day I wouldn't show up, having to keep tempers in check when surrounded by villagers intent on harassing them. If they didn't disperse the tension with the locals and there was a fight, they could drive away but I would have to walk through it. If things got bad, they could drive back, get me and drive on. But they knew I would insist on going back and walking. This put a lot of pressure on both of them. Bill's command of French wasn't much more than 'Bonjour' and 'Adios Amigos!' so Blake had to calm them alone. He never lost his temper with them which – forget racism – is easy to do. His job was to deal with people who had a different logic and a different rationale, and try to make them understand what we were doing. It's hard enough in Africa just buying the right plane ticket at a branch of British Airways, but he had to explain that a woman was walking for fun to a group of suspicious people who barely spoke French and who thought he was a slave merchant. If you fail to buy your ticket, you go somewhere else, but Blake could not fail or my life could be in danger.

Yet despite what was happening around us, we were able to keep things in perspective by taking the piss out of each other. I went hunting for jiggers in their feet each night and took on the role of bush nurse when I found some. It was a particularly unpleasant operation to perform while sitting still with mozzies biting ya bum through the chairs. I'd learned to identify them by their black heads on a white spot. I'd pick a hole out of the top, spear the jigger with a needle, then squeeze the white silken sac containing the eggs until it came out. It was a bummer if it burst because the eggs would spew all over the place. Blake got the most, and would usually soak his feet afterwards to cure a rather unpleasant fungal infection by dissolving a few purple tablets. Unfortunately, he had to give that up when we realized it was potassium permanganate and we'd lost ours for the veg.

One night, as I was hunched over his foot with a couple of socks as a bandanna to stop the sweat running into my eyes, our quiet chatter about the day was punctuated by a stifled scream.

'Oh what was that?' I said with the needle poised. 'Did "Blake, you can call me Stoic, Rose" say something there?'

I looked up and saw Bill pissing himself laughing while trying to knead bread by the fire. It suddenly dawned on me that we'd cracked it – in the most hostile and unpleasant place I'd walked, the three of us were having a seriously good time.

When it was bad out walking, I'd look forward to getting a break for safety. There'd be silence while I got in and was handed a cup of tea, then they'd resume their conversation. It was an anti-climax because I'd been so scared and was so relieved to see my own kind. They too were scared and relieved to see me each time I rounded a corner, bang on time. One day, I got to breakfast and again wasn't spoken to. I went around to the front of the Land Rover, sat quietly on the spare wheel, and cried. I just had to let it out. Bill gave me a cup of tea when I went back and sat with him while Blake was off on his lunchtime bush walk – somehow the guy kept regular.

As he rubbed my back, about the only place without any sores, he said, 'Sometimes we don't know who you'll be when you get in to camp, eh? Sometimes you're on good form and won't get wound up if we take the piss. Other times you'll come in and have a go just for the hell of it. We're just giving ya some space here to calm down.'

We hadn't had a relaxing rest day for two months – in fact, not since leaving Mike Taylor's house in Lusaka – and that wasn't even a rest day. After a week of primitive forest, we decided to spend our rest day in Kongolo. The map indicated some waterfalls, Les Portes d'Enfer – the Gates of Hell. It had always been a dream of mine to camp beside a waterfall: a good place for a shower, washing rocks for the laundry, and time for swimming and sunning ourselves and places to explore.

The villagers said there were many whites there – plenty of steak and cold beer. We drove for several hours and arrived in Kongolo after dark. Like all Zairois towns, we had arrived there forty years too late. The remnants of a thriving colonial Belgian town lay derelict in squalor. An Agatha Christie hotel with balconies and bougainvillea trellises had to be entered with a flashlight: there were no rooms, the hotel was a squat. A rusting *African Queen* paddle steamer decayed in exile on the bank. It had been sunk by rebels when expats tried to leave at the height of the fight for independence. Some survived, others, like a group of nuns, were herded to the edge of the river bank and fed to the crocs.

We got pissed in a bar and decided to think about camping later. When the bar closed we drove out of town and across a bridge. It was made of metal girders and one of the tyres got nipped between two of them and burst. We pulled up in the village on the other side, got as far as opening the doors, then fell asleep.

Bill declared the next morning that this was one puncture he couldn't fix. He changed the wheel and had a quick look around Kongolo for a replacement but without success. We still needed a rest day, so headed for the falls. When the track petered out we asked for directions. The map wasn't quite accurate: Les Portes d'Enfer were four hours' walk away. No chance!

We remembered seeing a white in town and went looking for him to ask about a spare tyre. A local gave us directions to a compound on the outskirts of town which we thought at first was a military base. In fact, it was a cotton refinery. The manager, Robert, greeted us and, for a fee, offered the use of one of the several vacant expat houses. He introduced us to the house boy, who went off to market to buy us a chicken for supper.

It was one of the very few times I had ever trusted myself to take an extra rest day because we really needed it and not because I was being lazy. For the most part, the fear of the 'slippery slope' prevented me from taking into consideration what the drivers needed and I would push on for my own sake. If I didn't keep a tight rein on my routine, I wouldn't get through.

We spent the next day on the compound, with the house boy doing all the laundry and cooking our meals. The house was a virtual ruin, the walls were mouldy, the bath was rusty, the taps chugged out reddish brown water and the beds were damp – a house you wouldn't even walk into in Britain. But it was more perfect than any of our daydreams, for the simple reason that it was private. For the first time in I didn't know how long there weren't twenty noses pressed against the 'bathroom window' when I washed or went to the loo.

Robert sold us a brand new spare and his mechanics fitted it. About five minutes later they'd punctured it. Bill supervised from then on and set to work tinkering with the engine. It seemed to be very therapeutic for Bill to tinker – he'd fix anyone's bike or motorbike on the road and never seemed to tire of cleaning the unleaded Coleman stove.

Robert entertained us that night with wild stories about the corruption and stupidity of some Zairois.

'Mobutu'd got some brand new MIG 15s and a couple of them were flying to Kinshasa airfield to land when they were told to divert due to fog. They flew out to sea and ejected.'

Bill came back with: 'And did ya hear about the two guys up in CAR who'd planned a coup? It was all set, eh, got the gear, set the time and place, but they didn't show up. One of 'em was climbing a wall and shot himself in the foot and the other had to stay home and babysit.'

We left early the next morning to drive back to the start point. The small rains had started and it rained every other day. Once the big rains came, it would pour down every afternoon. My shoes aquaplaned on the wet mud, which was uncomfortable, but driving on it was downright dangerous. The tracks we were on were the major roads in Zaire: they are a continuous line of bogs and deep ravines which the water has carved out over hundreds of years. The mud was thick, sticky clay without any rocks for tyres to grip on. Slithering off the top and into a ravine, or misjudging the strength of a sodden log of wood on a 'bridge', meant hours of digging, heaving and pushing to get the Land Rover out. With a winch fixed to a tree, the Land Rover could have been hauled out by hydraulics. But we didn't have a winch; Charlie had bought one but had never got around to fitting it. It suggested to me a lack of interest in our safety and in his vehicle, and I hoped it didn't mean he wouldn't be there for us if we needed him.

We walked for several days until we reached Samba. All along that stretch we were continuously attacked on suspicion of being slave traders. I could do nothing to alleviate the harassment in the villages as they rejected even my smiles, the universal white flag. In their own environment, Africans are not desperate and despondent people as TV programmes often portray, they are courageous and they fight if they're scared. The Belgians were the worst of the colonials and they treated the Africans appallingly. The locals had long memories. If I had been French or Belgian I might not have got through. I kept my accent English and my grammar pidgin, which admittedly wasn't that difficult.

'Don't be frightened Fi, you're only going for a walk.' Camps Bay, Cape Town. (*Charles Norwood*)

Inset Easy walking in South Africa. (*Charles Norwood*)

Above Gerry and Oli after a hard day of boredom. South Africa. (*Ffyona Campbell*)

Below Sharing a women's joke in Boputhatswana. (*Gerry Moffat*)

Bill. (*Ffyona Campbell*)

Blake having a go with the pen knife. (*Bill Preston*)

Below A typical break in moisture bee country. Zambia. (*Bill Preston*)

Left Military escort to cross bandit country. Zambia. (*Blake Rose*)

Below left This man-hunting party pose for a photo once they realise that Bill and Blake are not slave merchants. Zaire. (*Bill Preston*)

Below right Accused of cannibalism – this would have led to a stoning if Blake hadn't been there. Zaire. (*Blake Rose*)

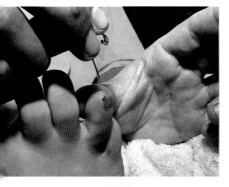

Above Picking jiggers eggs out of Blake's feet. Zaire. (*Bill Preston*)

Above If it wasn't rebuilt right, we'd lose the Land Rover. Zaire. (*Ffyona Campbell*)

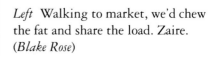

Left Walking to market, we'd chew the fat and share the load. Zaire. (*Blake Rose*)

Above left Pushing the cart with two years to go. Central African Republic. (*Raymond Mears*)

Above right Cooking monkey with a family in Gambo. Central African Republic. (*Raymond Mears*)

Left The fire plough being lit for the first time in years as Raymond unearths the old ways. Zaire. (*Raymond Mears*)

Below Raymond learning new medicines from the pygmie women. (*Ffyona Campbell*)

Above 'Indiana' Johann.
(*Raymond Mears*)

Above I got my walk back. Zaire.
(*Raymond Mears*)

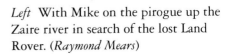

Left With Mike on the pirogue up the
Zaire river in search of the lost Land
Rover. (*Raymond Mears*)

Above Looking ahead to Central African Republic, nervous about what we would find after several months of being out of contact with the outside world. (*Raymond Mears*)

Right Tim. (*Ffyona Campbell*)

Below Tropical ulcers. (*Raymond Mears*)

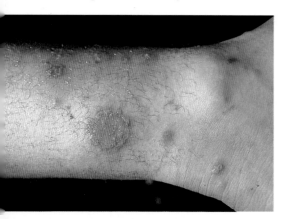

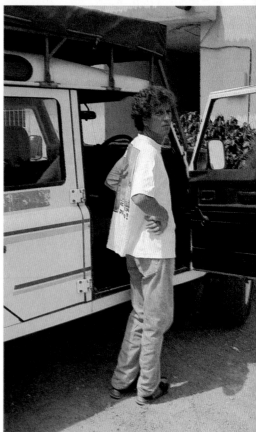

I was the constant focus of their attention. The boys went ahead through one village and I passed along ten minutes later to find the people still standing together in the centre staring after them. I came behind them, a white, undefended, feeling like a beetle walking into a dawn patrol of ants. An old man broke the silence with a barrage of shrill words. The crowd broke and re-formed around me, their shrill whooping getting louder and louder until it was a throbbing wall of sound. I daren't turn. I walked out of the village and I waved goodbye. Ten minutes later the hill behind was teeming with bands of children, whooping and hollering, their demands growing louder and louder. The tension needed relieving so I turned and smiled. They closed around me, getting excited. The ringleader grabbed at my necklace, demanding to know what it was.

'It is a present from my husband,' I said. 'Thank you for escorting me to him – he is waiting ahead.' And luckily both of them were.

Getting into camp was a relief not just because it meant I was safe but because I was not the only thing they were baiting any more.

A couple of boys would arrive first to watch the camp from a distance. Then more would come, just standing a small distance away. As the group grew, they merged into a crowd and become cocky. They were kids who'd found a new toy, and they loved to bait, to mess with it to see what it would do. They did this to me on the road – imitating me, shouting at me, and then a stone would be thrown. Blake had to defuse this in camp; I had to defuse this on the road. In camp, we could usually get them to leave in the early stages by picking out one and staring at him – this made them very self-conscious and they'd turn and leave.

On the road, I would turn around suddenly and growl with my hands out like claws. The children would scatter like impala changing direction. Some would take a look back at a distance and when they saw me laughing, they would laugh too and run back to hold my hand and dance along. But, after a short while, they wanted to do it again – as kids do – and the group would be gradually replaced as I walked through a long village, kids getting bored with it and falling back, to be replaced by new ones who started the baiting again.

The young teenage girls were the worst – they imitated my gait and would not respond to my games or return my smiles; they just sniggered. Teenage girls are the same the world over. There were times when I couldn't get the kids to laugh, possibly because I wasn't exuding the right presence. Then the stoning would be vicious. It is humiliating to be stoned, to be physically and symbolically chased out. I couldn't run; I couldn't stop them by stoning them back; I couldn't reason with them; I couldn't often get the adults to help. I was crying inside. Sometimes they hollered like Red Indians, a disorientating sound that made me feel like a hunted animal. I wondered if it was, indeed, a form of hunting. I hummed a Vangelis tune to make me feel like I wasn't actually there, just watching myself in a movie.

They read body language far better than us. They have grown up in a group and have learned to communicate more effectively without words – I think there are fewer misunderstandings. If I had been stoned in the last village and then saw different trees up ahead and knew there was another village coming, I would tense up. But I had to relax or face another stoning. I'd mull over something funny to make me laugh and relax my face muscles. I hated that first shrill call that signalled I'd been spotted, and mentally throttled the woman who'd made it.

I'd reply quickly in Swahili: 'Jambo Mama!' and walk over and shake her hand, clapping first.

The right hand is extended, the left is put on the crook of the right elbow. As a sign of respect to the elders, I would hold out my hand as a fist for my *wrist* to be shaken: this meant that I considered my hand too dirty to be shaken. When my fist was met by another fist for the first time, I was tempted to go into the scissor game. You rub them together.

I would tell them I was walking for sport, that my husband was not far ahead. I always wore a wedding ring, a piece of advice given to me by Christina Dodwell, one of the greatest female explorers of our time. Sometimes they were very concerned for me, thinking I had been left behind by the Land Rover. Sometimes they pointed to my tits and didn't believe that I was married. Sometimes I'd connect with a woman and stay for a chat – in body language. If they came with me to camp and saw that I had two husbands and that they were doing women's work, they pissed themselves laughing and looked at me with awe!

Even in the easy-going villages I couldn't stop to ask about the things which caught my interest because Bill and Blake were watching the clock – if I was more than ten minutes late, they'd come back for me. I couldn't let them go through all that anxiety because I was discussing the benefits of brain tanning with a hunter over a glass of palm wine in the shade. I just had to walk with them – the men slinking off to the palm tree they'd tap for wine while calling back to the women that they were off hunting. The boys couldn't enjoy Africa either – both of them wanted time to explore but they were tied to the Land Rover, unable to leave just one on guard because he would be severely intimidated.

In Samba we found another expat, Jean-Paul, who was also in the cotton business.

I went to bed early because the stomach cramps were exhausting me, and agreed to go to a doctor the next day. At 7.30p.m. an officious immigration guy rocked up to look at our passports. Once he'd seen my name he remembered a telex he'd received from the Zaire Ambassador in Lusaka to look out for us and take care of us. He saw that I was sick and suggested showing us the way to the doctor, a good five hours' drive to the east.

We set off, but during the drive I got delirious and confused.

'Why are we going on safari?' I screamed, hit by a sudden surge of anxiety.

Cerebral malaria is often confused with gastroenteritis because of the severe stomach cramps, but Bill knew I had malaria. At one point, when he had stopped to assess the strength of a bridge, I got out and walked back the way we had come because I was convinced they weren't taking me to a doctor. Bill didn't even look up, just said quietly to Blake, 'Go fetch her will ya, mate?' I knew I was behaving strangely and it scared the shit out of all of us.

We reached the Zaire river. All ferries are free in Zaire but you have to give them diesel to operate, and this one was on the other side of the river. The policeman took a jerry across in a pirogue (log dugout) and the ferry came over for us. People waiting to cross were delighted because now they wouldn't have to pay a dugout to take them. There were little stalls selling fresh fried sweet potatoes; we had some and I threw up. The convulsions wrenched my already cramping stomach. The last thing I remembered thinking before I passed out again was that I must remind myself never to have a baby: if labour is the worst pain a body can endure, there was no way I could go through worse than this!

The doctor diagnosed malaria and prescribed a whole bunch of drugs from our medicine box to kill pretty much everything. We carried Halfan, a new malaria cure which was much easier to take – two tablets, three times a day at exactly six-hour intervals for one day, followed by another course two weeks later. He sold us some Buscopan to stop the cramps. I took all the pills in a handful and went to sleep for a few minutes in the Land Rover. I then threw them all up.

During the drive back and all through that night I threw up. There was nothing coming out but stomach juices. I knew I had to get the pills down soon or I would be in big trouble. Blake took care of me that night at the expat's house in Samba. I was staring at the ceiling, a grid of white wooden struts with a gecko in the corner. He came in and gave me some clear soup as a base before trying the pills again. A few minutes later he looked up from his cooking to hear me vomiting. He came in with a glass of water to swill around my mouth. I vomited again. Several hours later he tried me on water again. I threw that up. The cramps continued and I tried using the labour breathing methods I'd seen on TV, panting and relaxing, but I was too exhausted. In the end I gave up; I didn't care if I died.

A decision was made in the next room to drive back to Kongolo, where Jean-Paul had said there was an airstrip; if I couldn't take the pills during the drive, the boys decided I would have to be evacuated. Besides if there was to be a long wait for my recovery, there was no point staying in Samba – we'd drunk the last three beers.

Blake tried again with water in the early hours and this time I kept it down. He gave me the pills a little later and I kept them down, too. They made a bed for me in the back of the Land Rover by leaving some kit at the house and we drove for seven hours to Kongolo.

Robert wasn't in the least surprised to see us again. We stayed with him for three days; I took my pills regularly and was herded back to bed whenever I got up. Blake was attentive; he was probably just assigned to the job while Bill went drinking with Robert, but I wasn't complaining. He massaged my back to help me relax.

My relationship with Bill and Blake was perfect because we were affectionate at times, we took the piss out of each other and we were attracted to each other but it never went further. I entertained thoughts of it but my dreams warned me to keep it like it was.

I was having a lot of violent dreams around that time – usually tearing someone apart with my hands! They were brutal and gory, but I woke up feeling refreshed. These were recurring dreams which I often had when I was on a hostile stretch.

It had rained while we were in Kongolo and the drive back using a different bush route suggested by a priest was the worst driving Bill had ever experienced. It wasn't a case of going into a slide or a spin and coming out of it onto hard ground after some moments: the sliding went on for over an hour as he fought to keep it upright. Several times he shouted, 'BRACE!' but he gained control in time. At one point I looked behind me and saw Blake with his back on the roof and his arms and legs dangling down like a weightless astronaut. We reached hard ground after an hour and Bill got out and fell over.

Several hours later we slithered to a halt.

Blake said, 'I think we've got a puncture.'

Bill got out and said, 'We've lost a wheel, mate.'

The nuts hadn't been tightened by the mechanics and the wheel was back down the track. Fortunately we were in mud so no damage was done to the metal hub. But: we had no nuts. We took one from each wheel until Bill realized there were six on the back fixing the spare wheel on. Blake and I screwed them on; Bill had lost much of the dexterity in his hands after they'd been shot. They jacked it up but the jack was sinking in the mud. We needed a flat base. I brought out the iron frying pan and it did the trick.

Some time later we ran aground. No amount of jacking, digging, pushing or levering got us out. Blake and I had been running down the track dragging logs from a ditch. A cyclist who came by must have had an horrendous journey himself. Without a word, he put down his bike and lifted a log which was too heavy for both of us and ran with it on his shoulder to the Land Rover. Africans will often help without asking when they can see exactly what's needed. We gave the cyclist a note to take to the expat in Samba to tell him we were bogged down and to ask if we could borrow his winch.

We made camp and hoped it wouldn't rain. It did. We rigged up a tarp over some of my roof tent because it wasn't waterproof and Blake and I slept in there while Bill slept in the cab. Lying there, waiting for the mozzies to find a way in with the torment of their high pitched whine was horrendous. OK, you buggers, I thought, I'll lie still so you can bite me. But these guys were like a bunch of football supporters on a pub crawl.

The Land Rover came out quite easily the next morning after the mud had dried a bit, and we reached Samba. Jean-Paul laughed – yes he had a winch, but it had been sent without a cable. An hour later, the cyclist turned up with the note. There was very little food around and we didn't dally. We set off the next day on a long and continuous stretch to hit the tarmac: sixteen days straight to Lubutu at the beginning of the tarmac road, then five days' walk to Kisangani. I was still weak after the malaria attack, but there was no chance of us getting through together if the rains came. We made a contingency plan in case the Land Rover could not make it: if the strike was off, Bill would go by train and boat to Kisangani and buy a winch, then return to drive the Land Rover out. Blake and I would walk. It would be difficult because there was so little food around and we, like the villagers, were living mostly from our stores – in our case, a sack of muesli that I'd kept back for just such a possibility.

From Samba to Kindu was a straight line due north, running parallel with the Zaire River, but we had been warned that it was a stretch of broken bridges. As always, the Land Rover was ahead of me, but I frequently reached it before a break. The bridges would once have taken a vehicle but as there was no need for them because there was no traffic, the maintenance had just kept them serviceable for pedestrians. Bill's construction experience enabled them to rebuild the bridges using what was available; Blake would drive while Bill directed him over.

I arrived at one to find the Land Rover hanging from the far edge with its front wheels taking the weight. At another, Blake was directing Bill. Halfway across Blake screamed at him to stop.

'Why?'

'The bridge is breaking!'

Bill gunned it across at top speed and only just made it.

They were working very hard and I cooked them good meals each evening during that stretch. We became very clever at making something out of nothing, but we were all losing weight – Bill more than the other two of us because he had more to lose. Blake and I both suddenly noticed the loss of his belly.

We cooked manioc leaves by removing the stalks, soaking them quickly in boiling water to get rid of the acetic acid, pummelling them to a pulp, then boiling them for an hour with pounded peanuts and palm oil. They tasted like oily spinach and I loved them. Where there were no bridges to build, Bill would begin the cooking at first break – boiling beans which take several hours, then packing up and putting them on again at the next break. One day, I found a bag of dehydrated veggie burger mix in the depths of the Land Rover. For three hours we worked on a superb meal – Bill sifted the flour, picking out the weevils, and baked six buns while Blake and I made manioc chips, onion rings, fried the burgers and sliced up the tomatoes. All the ingredients were laid out on the table to be assembled. A leg collapsed and it fell in the dirt.

We found a ruined mission made of red brick and camped there a night. I rubbed some vaseline on a spot on Bill's shoulder and watched to see if it moved.

'Yep, gotta putse worm in there.'

I picked out a hole then extracted the worm by winding it around a Q tip. We got them by leaving our clothes out to dry; the putse fly would lay eggs in them. It's one reason why the villagers' clothes are so well pressed – you kill them by ironing. Blake went and chatted to an old man who slept in an archway, and who told him he was the caretaker and had fought in the Second World War. He'd probably been left there twenty years before and had never deserted his post.

After a week we reached Kindu. We went drinking that night but I went to bed early not feeling well. We decided to postpone the rest day as the rains would be coming in a week. We had a long breakfast the next morning then crossed the river by ferry. While we were waiting, we met a conservationist who was studying the small forest elephant, some distance away. I asked if he was working with an Aid agency.

'Why should we take advice from whites about conservation? You don't know anything about it, you had wolves in Britain but you killed them all.' He had a point.

A Swahili word for problem is 'arabi' – perhaps meaning that the Arabs are the problem. We were expecting an arabi with the ferry, but luckily the queue was long enough to warrant a crossing and the vessel had turned up.

The road felt different on the other side. For two days there was a stretch of tarmac, narrow and new, cutting a clean swathe through the tall rainforest on either side. I'd heard that forest people have a problem with perspective, and it was easy to see why. The cleared areas were giant caves littered with massive carcasses, and although the forest edge was much further away every green leaf could be seen in vivid detail.

The villages, too, were different – longer, and built higher than the road on balconies that were carved out of the hard-packed, pale orange dirt. As I walked, hornbills with pterodactyl beaks flew overhead, their wings whirring like fans in an airconditioning system gathering speed. Their beauty made me feel happy, but that feeling was lost as soon as I began to encounter the local men. They hung around in twos and threes, leering as they mentally stripped me of my skirts, sniggering to each other or calling me with a predatory 'tsss tsss'. One of them tried to block my path but I kept my eyes down and kept walking. I guessed that whites must have been there recently.

Bill walked with me for a quarter when I told him about the unpleasantness – some guys riding on bikes had shouted at me as they passed me, then turned and did it on the way back, up and down several times. It wasn't life-threatening or anything, it was just a change in atmosphere and an unpleasantness I had to find new ways to deal with.

That night, we had to drive over twenty kilometres off the tarmac up an ochre dirt track to find a place to camp away from villagers. I was desperate to stop and take stock of the day's injuries: my ankles had been badly bitten again; they were raging and burning so intensely that I couldn't concentrate on anything until calamine lotion, mozzie gel and a calming sit on the Land Rover bonnet had been administered.

In temperatures of 35°C and very high humidity, my upper lip was wet and my clothes sodden before breakfast. Sweat ran down my chest like rain down a window. But there was no breeze to evaporate it and I overheated many times. Little bugs crawled all over my body. They especially seemed to like wriggling in the wetness where my hair grew on my temples and in the sweat on my neck. I couldn't sit still yet was too weary to walk around and shake them off.

I began to feel the edge, the frustration edge, the one where I could go crazy. The rains would begin in a week, but I did not feel ready for the push: I needed a rest day but I couldn't take one because of the impending rains – another eight days' walk to the next rest day in Lubutu just had to be a continuation of the last eight days. Jeff Crowther, author of *Shoestring*, had said this was the worst stretch of the worst road he had ever experienced. I wanted to sort out my clothes first and clean myself up; I hadn't had a shower for two days; if I scratched myself, my nails were left thick with black sweaty crud. It was frightening to wake in the night and find I'd been hacking the hell out of the infected sores with dirty nails. I'd thrash around, trying to find a comfortable position where my legs didn't throb from the poison but if I lay still, I could feel dozens of other things which were still on the move – all over my body. The boys washed in rivers where I couldn't because of gawkers – I just couldn't stand naked in front of people who intimidated me. I'd take a couple of bowls behind the Land Rover

after dark instead, or have a hose down under the water purifier if
we had enough.

I amused myself by adding to my list of the rules of
walking:

Rule 2:   It is always further than you think
Rule 3:   It is never as bad as people make out
Rule 4:   It is always prettier the other route
Rule 5:   There's always a logistical reason why you can't go the
pretty route
Rule 6:   Never say never
Rule 7:   There is always a village at the top of a hill
Rule 8:   There are no rules

It was going to be a testing week. I told myself to take each day
as it came, to remember that time never passes more quickly than
when forgetting to measure it. Dissolve into your rhythm, Fi, I said
to myself, feel excitement about where you are, not about where you
will be.

I set off, but bites had swollen my right calf and the outside of my
right thigh, restricting the movement of the muscles and making it
painful to walk. Worse than the bites themselves, however, was the
knowledge that I would be bitten there again during the day. It was
not like other illnesses, where at least you know you will get over it.
This, having set in, was continuous.

The locals saved up their money for Saturday nights and we heard
them dancing and drumming all night. A lone cyclist with a shotgun
came past in the night, contradicting what we'd been told about the
dangerous animals here.

'There may or may not be leopards and elephant,' he said.

He cycled by again at dawn having partied all night. He wasn't
tired, he said, because he'd eaten.

We came to a village with a market. Rule Number 9 of walking:
the only non-morning market in the region will be the one you arrive
at in the morning. It will be an evening market.

We reached a tin-mining town in time to see the raising of the flag
and hear the national anthem. Then, as I walked through the town,
herds of kids began to congregate around me, screaming and running.
Behind me I heard the booming, angry voice of an irritated man. I
turned, but instead of being confronted by someone demanding to

know what I was doing, I saw that he was hitting the kids with a stout stick. Good man. It did the trick – for a while. Further on they gathered again and three thickset mine workers in overalls put a stop to it.

The sky was overcast as I approached a new set of hills. They were steep and short, and often afforded me a glimpse of the horizon – undulating lines, heavily clad in rainforest, white trunks prominent amongst the dark green foliage.

The road had been graded with loose red gravel which was a bugger to grip on. Again, a new road surface seemed to produce new people. They were more confident here – perhaps better fed – and in turn more provocative.

The town had electricity and many outside lights still shone after dawn. There was a dam about twenty kilometres away on the river with a hydroelectric plant providing the whole village with electricity.

The women were all trussed up in ruffles and tight bodices. People are people wherever you go, and women are women. What we will endure for the sake of fashion and capturing men!

They delighted in our confusion and not understanding their French. The white is stupid, they said, and pumped themselves up with self-importance by confusing us more by speaking rapidly and more aggressively.

'Donnez-moi cigarrette,' they demanded.

We camped by a wild avocado tree and Bill thrashed some down with a long spiky branch to lay on the dashboard to ripen. It brought back memories of the Australian walk.

During the day, hornbills sounded overhead like the thrashing of a cane through the air. At night, fire-flies blinked around the tents and mosquitoes droned in for the attack. All of us, but especially me, had bites of varying stages on our legs – some new and white with red swelling around them, others with crystal tips, others cracked and open, others bleeding from bites on bites. We pushed on. In the areas that had been cleared for planting cassava, a tree or two had been left in the middle, almost as homage to the forest.

Outside one village a man loped down the hill with his wife, and in his hand flopped the biggest dead rat I've ever seen. Drunk as a skunk he showed it to us, then asked us for a bra for his wife. I kicked Blake before he launched into why I didn't have one.

The people were driving me insane. They didn't have phones, so they shouted at each other from one end of the village to the other.

They made as much noise as possible, chasing me, shouting: 'Madame! Madame! Madame!'

I rounded a corner and saw the Land Rover at lunch break. There were three other Land Rovers beside it; I realized immediately that they were overlanders. After the initial rush of excitement, I felt embarrassed and awkward – I wasn't sure how to deal with them. I hoped Bill and Blake would do all the talking. It turned out they were British and on separate, private trips, but had joined up to try this route south. There were queues of trucks bogged on all other routes due to the rain. It would take many weeks to get them out and moving. So, this was the only way out of Kisangani by road.

When the vehicles had stopped alongside our Land Rover they saw the lunch set up and the empty chair with an umbrella over it. Bill had rigged this up a couple of times when there was no shade and the sun was overhead.

One of the girls had looked at it and asked, 'What are you doing?'

Bill replied, 'We're just waiting for her, she'll be round for lunch in a minute.'

The girl thought Bill had lost it and was waiting for some fantasy blonde to walk into his life.

They had read an article about my journey before I left and had bought a roof tent modelled on mine – but they had the sense to get a waterproof/mozzie proof one.

Blake walked the last few kilometres to Lubutu with me. We could see the tarmac at the top of a hill and we looked around to see a truck catching us up. Out of principle I had to reach the tarmac before them, so we ran. It started as a jog but ended as a race between Blake and me up the hill. Yes! We hit the tarmac! We beat the rains! Five days to Kisangani!

We got pissed at a bar and were talking about the routine for our arrival in Kisangani. The boys were now within a morning's drive of the end: it must have been very hard for them to keep steady. They said they'd go ahead to Kisangani on the last day and meet me at the Olympia Hotel. I said I thought it would be good if we all arrived together.

Bill said, 'What's the point?'

'Out of respect for me and this walk,' I said. 'I think we should arrive together and drink that first beer together.'

Bill leaned forward and said, 'I don't give a fuck about your walk.'

I just stared at him for a moment, the realization of what he had said slowly sinking in. I had no comeback. I got up and left.

I walked down the dark street to the mission and had to wake the priest up to let me into the courtyard. I was very confused, and felt sick. Bill came into my tent the next morning to get some privacy from the workers in the courtyard – he desperately needed more sleep.

'Look mate,' he said as he tried to get comfortable, 'there's a pretty hot head on those shoulders. You need one mate to stand this shit, but you wind up pretty good, eh?'

It took a long time before I understood what Bill had said: a very painful realization of how selfish I had been.

17

Clouds had been gathering all day. By early afternoon the sky was ominously dark; at nightfall the moon and stars were blocked out altogether. We camped in inky blackness.

As I sat in the flickering oasis of light produced by Bill's cooking fire I tried anxiously to tune to the BBC World Service for an update on the riots. No luck: the interference was unusually bad, and most of it, a missionary had told us, was deliberate. President Mobutu knew a thing or two when it came to handling a rebellion.

An almighty clap of thunder boomed in the distance and moved fast towards us. Lightning cracked and sizzled, electrifying the rainforest with brilliant blue light.

The radio came to life and amongst the hish I caught the words: '... the British Embassy advises its subjects ...' The rest was lost when the sky was lit by another colossal lightbulb with a loose connection. Blake, sitting on a chair in the middle of the flat, red gravel pit where we were camped, was lit stroboscopically as he moved a cigarette up to his mouth.

'Advises what?' he said.

'God knows,' I said. 'Stay put? Drive out? Head to the nearest airport? I guess we'd better start making plans.'

Zaire was a powder-keg. Since the pre-election talks broke down on 20 September, the country had suffered its worst riots since the struggle for independence in 1960. Bus fares were doubled overnight so that Mobutu could pay the military their wages. In retaliation, the public burned all the buses. Shops, factories and office blocks in Kinshasa had been looted and set on fire.

But had the unrest hit Kisangani, I was desperate to know, just three days' walk to our north? The town was pivotal to my plans: Bill and Blake were scheduled to be flying home from there, and I was to take a month's rest until the new back-up arrived. I needed it: to beat the rains I'd just walked 625 kilometres in thirteen days without fully recovering from malaria and without a break; I was exhausted and injured.

A raw cry resonated across the treetops; then silence, as if the jungle was holding its breath. A strong gust of wind buffeted the camp, blowing a flurry of embers into the air like a firework.

The rain came suddenly, cold and heavy.

Blake jumped up from his chair and we ran towards the tent. Bill, with three mugs of Sainsbury's chicken and sweetcorn soup in his hand, was close behind.

The inside of the tent was clammy and it stank. I sat at the opening, my chin resting on my knees as I watched the rain boil in orangey-red puddles. I could already feel a freshness in the air, replacing the cloying humidity of the last few days. It had been overpoweringly hot and I had been walking through thick walls of hundred per cent humidity. My skin was rubbed raw from the friction of wet clothes; my face was sore from constant towelling. Mud stuck to the open ulcers on my legs, and many of the bites on my arms and other parts of my body were infected and pussy. Flies fed on them tenaciously.

I had been close to tears at one stage from the sheer lonely push and frustration of it. Dizzy and nauseous from the heat, I was no longer daydreaming of food, just of being dry. I hammered up the hills, keeping a good pace, but when I entered a village and faces stared at me incredulously, my own head felt too heavy for me to turn and reassure them with a wave or even a smiled 'hello'.

Hitting the tarmac had been a palpable relief. We'd beaten the rains! To celebrate, we stopped at a shack by the roadside that served beer and sat outside under the gathering clouds, drinking huge amounts of cold Primus and reminiscing. In our three months together we had covered 2,806 kilometres of road and track. The boys' challenge was done, and I knew I would not have made it this far with anyone less experienced.

A statuesque woman served us chicken and bananas. As we ate, a spider expertly wove my shoulder to the chair back. The woman's husband came over and began an aggressive outburst about what a thief the President was. There was a line across his nose between his eyes which deepened the more he blethered and I didn't feel comfortable being involved in a loud anti-Mobutu tirade; though the military had been disarmed when the General thought they'd turn against him, his secret police were everywhere. I was scared of anything that stood between me and Kisangani. It really mattered to me that I got there on time: a six-month journey through the Third World dead on schedule would be a remarkable achievement for all of us.

A warning shot was fired across my bows, however, when we learnt that 10,000 French and Belgian expats were standing by for evacuation to Brazzaville in the Congo, and that troops were being sent to cover their withdrawal. The American Embassy had called for the evacuation of all its subjects as well. Then we heard that most of Kinshasa was destroyed. There were no food stocks or medicine. Lubumbashi, too, had seen serious rioting.

I had been on the road for three days. The rain pounded down on the tent and I wondered if it would keep the Zairois off the streets and give them time to cool down. While we waited for the next news on the World Service I dug three jiggers out of one of Blake's toes. The eggs spewed, well-defined, over my hands and I held them outside the tent and washed them carefully in the downpour before they had a chance to burrow under my finger nails.

When we finally caught the news, it wasn't good. Europeans were now being evacuated by boat – the air evacuation had been called off when rescue aircraft were fired at.

Nothing, however, about Kisangani.

'So, what do we do?' I said.

'Let's not forget the local who told us about the missionary in Kissie broadcasting updates,' Blake said. 'There's been trouble, but nothing involving whites. It's just between the Zairois.'

Bill looked doubtful. 'France and Belgium backed Uncle Mo during the revolution of '60–'62 – and since. If the Foreign Legion has a run-in now against the military that could change. It could become an anti-white thing overnight and we'll be very exposed out here in the bush.'

'Have you noticed something eerie?' Blake said. 'It's just hit me: we haven't seen a single bit of traffic the last couple of days. It must all be bottle-necked in the towns. It can't be a good sign.'

'What if we're actually advised to leave?' I said. 'There's only a handful of planes in the whole of Zaire, so not much chance of one being in Kisangani. Maybe we could fill up with diesel and drive the thousand Ks to Bangui? Diesel and food will be in short supply as everyone panic buys. Should we use the water jerries for diesel and buy it now?'

We talked over our options until three in the morning, eventually deciding that since we didn't know what I would be walking into, the boys would drive into Kisangani early the next morning and check the lie of the land. Every instinct in me hated the thought of going with them; it meant reaching a long sought-after goal by car – and worse, crossing the Equator on wheels instead of on foot. Even though I was religious about starting from the very spot where I'd finished the night before, and so would return to our camp site if all was well in Kisangani, the joy by then would have been taken out of it. But I reluctantly had to agree that I couldn't stay behind. If the boys were arrested or shot, or couldn't get back out of town, I'd be stranded.

'Sunday best tomorrow then,' I said. 'No rips in the jeans when we're meeting officials. We'll see what the British consul says first, and take it from there. If we have to go, we've got £1,600 collectively that'll get us out, then we can use plastic to buy further tickets in Kenya or wherever we fetch up.'

'We ought to buy some fruit on the way into Kisie,' Blake said. 'Food stocks are bound to be low.'

I wondered if we should also buy a small lump of gold that we could conceal if we were robbed.

'Let's just play it by ear,' Bill said. 'I reckon our main worry tomorrow will be villagers attacking us again as spies.'

At 7a.m. we packed camp. I memorized the campsite for our return and we logged the distance into Kisangani on the milometer: 178.4 kilometres. We drove on tarmac through thick rainforest without encountering a single person or vehicle.

'It's quiet, Carruthers,' Bill said. 'Too damned quiet.'

His joke was greeted by strained smiles.

The Equator was marked at the roadside by a stone plaque with a metal arrow. We stopped and took photos, a bizarrely touristy thing to be doing in the circumstances.

At long last, we spotted a truck – the only vehicle we'd seen since the riots began. We both stopped. The African driver beamed from his cab and told us, 'Pas de problème, Kisangani. Pas de problème, ça va.' Then he waved cheerily and drove off. There was a problem though: it was that, out of politeness, Africans seldom tell you what they think you don't want to hear. We debated whether just to drive back to the gravel pit and walk in as if nothing had happened.

'Maybe the reason we haven't seen any vehicles is because the military have requisitioned them,' Blake said.

'Let's stick to the plan,' Bill said. 'If we hit difficulties in Kisangani the Land Rover might be our best means of escape.'

The bottom line was this: driving in to find that everything was fine meant the loss of joy; walking in to find ourselves in the middle of a war zone meant the loss of a whole lot more. Logistics overruled emotions.

We drove past the signpost to Stanley Falls without stopping, and as we approached the town we saw columns of smoke on the skyline.

Bill had been to Kisangani before and knew the way to the Olympia Hotel, an overlanders' hangout with security, showers, camping facilities and cheap rooms. We drove through deserted streets. Thousands of empty medical supplies boxes lay strewn on the pavements. Shops and houses were smouldering. Every car we saw was a burnt-out shell. Most frightening of all was the sight of dried blood smeared on broken windows. There were rebellious slogans sprayed everywhere, one of which said, 'Salut Mobutu – merci pour les fêtes!' – 'Hey Mobutu, thanks for the party.'

The Olympia Hotel was a one-storey, whitewashed box with bougainvillea and other well-established vines obscuring the front. It, too, looked deserted; there was no way of telling if anyone inside was still alive. We waited in the Land Rover outside the black double doors and hooted once for the guard.

A wary security man appeared and opened the gates. We parked under a corrugated iron awning in the yard next to a pink overland truck belonging to Tracks. The driver, Jeff Roy, and about ten of his passengers were drinking Coke in the open café area, along with a couple of hitch-hikers. They looked drawn but in good humour.

'You must have witnessed everything,' I said.

'Yep, from the safety of our ten-foot high walls,' Jeff said.

At 8.30a.m. on Tuesday 24 September they'd heard spasmodic firing from the other side of the river. The hitch-hikers were in the riverside patisserie, enjoying exactly the breakfast we'd been dreaming of for months. The owners told them to get back to their hotel quickly: the military were firing in the air as they crossed the river by ferry. They took the patisserie first: sod's law.

By 10a.m. the firing had increased, and soldiers, most of them boys in their late teens, were smashing up shops and looting. Red Cross ambulances were commandeered and used to transport stolen goods. Then they took over the premises of Cediza which had a radiophone – the communications base I had been offered by De Beers – and smashed it up. Firing continued through the night and by the morning the whole town was alight. Scores of people were dead; there was widespread panic. The looting and shooting had continued until mid afternoon on Wednesday and only stopped because there was nothing left to smash or burn. Thereafter, it had been quiet.

Bill and I drove to the residence of the British and French consul. The compound was unscathed, the gardens were still a mass of pretty flowers and green lawns. The housemaid let us in. I felt an instant rush of cold, airconditioned air – our first for months. We were shown into a sitting room, where everything was clean and there were ornaments, polished wood and light-coloured sofas. After so long on the road I was almost breathless at the sight of such civilization.

The consul's wife was finishing a conversation on the radiophone about evacuation. We explained the walk, and she immediately said I would be in grave danger if I went back to the camp site and attempted to walk into town. Kisangani was quiet now, but she was awaiting instructions on evacuation for all expats – and that should include us.

'The riots could start again at any moment,' she said. 'No food has got in for the last two weeks due to the halt of river traffic and road closures from rains. That alone is enough to spark off fresh trouble.'

She was interrupted by the radiophone.

'I can't predict what will happen,' were her parting words as she picked up the receiver. 'If you want to join the evacuation you must write down the nationality and passport numbers of everyone in your party.'

As we sat on the sofa we tossed around the scenarios. First, we could leave the Land Rover at the Olympia and all fly out, and I would return with a new team when things were back to normal. Second, Bill and Blake could fly home as planned, and I could stay to guard the Land Rover – but this would mean I'd be without communications, and unable to arrange the arrival of the new back-up team. Thirdly, we could drive the Land Rover out to the Central African Republic or Uganda – but all roads were impassable due to rain and we would have to wait for looted fuel to filter back to market. Or, fourthly, Bill and Blake could fly out, I'd leave the Land Rover at the hotel and walk out alone – but it was six weeks' walk to the Central African Republic, and the villagers we'd encountered so far had been absolutely paranoid about spies. What was more, there were rebel militia in the bush and if the Belgian and French troops turned against the Zairois military it would become an issue of black versus white and I'd be toast.

We returned to the Olympia, and Bill and Jeff Roy left to have a look at the town. Blake and I went to Cediza to see if there was a message for me from De Beers in Kinshasa. The front doors were boarded up but the door to the backyard was hanging off. Several men were moving furniture down the fire escape stairs. Inside, an American woman was directing her house staff to clean up, pack and hide items. She was in a state of deep shock.

'Your lives are in danger if you stay!' she screamed. 'They ransacked my house in front of me.'

She repeated over and over that they had even taken the light switches. And that an armed soldier had been in the process of helping himself to the contents of her safe when his partner came in and said, 'Leave some for me!' The soldier shot him dead at point blank range.

We returned to the hotel and drank a Coke. At least one daydream had been fulfilled: it was cold! But scarcely had the glass touched my lips when someone ran in and told us the call had come to evacuate. All of us were to be at the airport in two hours' time, with only one small piece of luggage each.

We hurriedly cleared the Land Rover of perishable foods, aired the wet bedding and tents, then packed everything away and taped up the windows from the inside. I stuffed my rucksack with witness books, notebooks, a few of my least tattered clothes and the five malachite ashtrays Isabella had bought for me in Kitwe. When I got back to the UK they would represent my entire worldly wealth.

With no time to find anywhere more secure, we left the Land Rover at the hotel and hitched a lift the rest of the way on Jeff Roy's truck. He would be staying behind; he had enough diesel and promised to park up the Land Rover as a favour to his old mate Charlie. He dropped us off in the airport parking lot, which was packed with expensive four-wheel drive vehicles that had been abandoned.

Inside, we were divided into nationalities. I spotted large contingents of Greek and Pakistani shopkeepers, all that remained of their worlds contained in a few pathetic carrier bags. There was an overpowering smell of baby wipes and blocked loos. Men were giving women a break, deftly juggling babies. Everybody was being very British; nobody was talking about what had happened. I still couldn't

quite believe this was for real, and clung to the hope that the call to
the airport was a false alarm and we'd be returning to the bush in a
few hours' time.

But then I watched as a massive Hercules transport plane landed
on the runway and disgorged Foreign Legion troops. They looked
very businesslike as they secured the airfield and buildings. As they
swarmed into the main terminal, I struck up a conversation with a
young officer. He explained that each man was carrying full kit and
had enough food for a week. The situation was, he said, 'très sérieuse.'

I elbowed my way back through the crowd and found the British
group. There was no point in kidding myself any longer. Kisangani
was in ruins. So, it appeared, was my walk.

'Add two Brits and an Aussie to your list,' I said.

I stayed with Shuna in her rented room in a flat in Battersea, concentrating for the first couple of days on fulfilling as many of my food daydreams as possible. But I wanted my walk back.

I called the Foreign Office, Zaire Desk, for news. They told me everyone had been evacuated, including the British Consul (which was a blatant lie) and that Zaire was extremely unstable and would be for the foreseeable future. I was tempted to tell them some things.

After a week of this, I called *The Guinness Book of Records* and asked them if I could overfly the trouble zone, begin the walk from the nearest point of safety and return to cover the missed-out stretch when it was open. No problem, they said; the two men who had walked around the world before me had come across exactly the same situation and had done just that.

My big problem was my support vehicle. There had been no news from Jeff Roy, and I assumed the worst – that Stormin' Norman was unlikely to have survived further rioting. I tried to find out if it was still at the Olympia by phoning De Beers in Kinshasa, hoping to get word to anyone still in Kisangani. No joy; nobody was going in.

I started phoning round for a spare Land Rover, or one that might be out there and need returning to the UK. My calls stopped fairly abruptly when I was admitted to the Hospital for Tropical Diseases with suspected malaria.

I'd hardly begun the tests when John Blashford-Snell left a message. I'd met him and Dr Richard Leaky a year before at the première of a film on poaching in Kenya. He was on the trail of money for a replacement Land Rover. A multi-millionaire friend had called him for an 'escort' to dine with a group of businessmen that night at Annabel's. His friend was broke, Blashers said, but one of the others around the table might get excited about the prospect of sponsorship.

Shuna brought me some clothes, I discharged myself from hospital, tore off my plastic medical identification bracelet and took a cab to

Mayfair. I discovered more or less immediately that champagne doesn't mix well with quinine, but stuck with it. It seemed no time at all before I was totally smashed, in the millionaire's flat, trying to squeeze £15,000 out of him before the next fever attack. Unfortunately I wasn't the only one doing the squeezing. He told me he was getting very excited indeed – but walking was about the furthest thing from his mind.

I headed straight back to the hospital that night and crashed out for forty-eight hours. When I was officially discharged, I felt I couldn't overstay my welcome with Shuna so I moved in with Jonathan Shalit, a friend of hers. I slept under the dining-room table.

In my heart of hearts I knew it might take months, even years, for Zaire to open up. I did the rounds of my previous sponsors but couldn't convince them – nor anyone else – to put in more money. I imagined they thought I was home because I couldn't hack it.

I decided to go back to CAR unsupported and keep walking until things got easier in Zaire. Then I'd go back, try to find the Land Rover and someone to drive it, and walk out.

The morning of 14 October, two weeks after my return to London, I called Raymond. I didn't beat about the bush.

'Do you want to come to Africa with me and walk unsupported?'

He didn't hesitate, even before I told him I'd pay for everything.

During the walk from Cape Town to Kisangani, I'd fallen out of love with Raymond. I'd been blunt with him about it at the time, but he hadn't accepted it.

'I'll be there for you when you "come down",' he'd said.

Now, I had often been accused of using people to get what I wanted. I'd always been aware of the thinness of the line between accepting people's hospitality, kindness and generosity, and taking advantage of it. I hadn't always got it right, but I'd never wasted what I had been given, nor taken it for granted. I was asking Raymond to come to Africa with me now for the simple reason that he was the best person I knew for the job. He was experienced in bushcraft, a good photographer, and committed to my walk. I also knew him very well and got on with him. We'd lived together for six months before the start of the walk; I'd been in love with him. If he could get through that, I thought, Africa was no problem.

I explained that our relationship was over; it might start up again on the road, but I didn't think so.

'I can't go into it like that,' he said. 'Either we are lovers from the outset or never again.'

He went away for a weekend with a friend, and got me out of his system.

During the month between agreeing to go and actually leaving, a whole new expedition had to be put together: equipment had to be bought and tested, vaccinations and visas had to be arranged, flights booked, and insurance brokered with Campbell-Irvine. The list was endless, and the last of my money was disappearing fast: £2,000 on travellers' cheques; £1,500 on kit and tickets; £500 to cover six weeks living in London.

At times it felt like six weeks on another planet. I'd exchanged humidity, mud and sores for a world of chintz, push-button cooking and communications. I washed my hair, dressed in business suits, travelled by hire car and got more exhausted and despondent than I ever did on the road. I was like a super-charged version of the expatriate who doesn't feel entirely settled abroad and yet becomes increasingly ill at ease back home. I also discovered, not for the first time, that whilst the walk was a kind of solitary confinement, it gave me greater freedom than the life I had between journeys.

Perhaps the isolation I often feel when surrounded by people is wilful; perhaps I need to feel in battle to keep alive. But I don't think I imagined the lack of enthusiasm I started to perceive then, even in those closest to the expedition. Apart from my family, two very strong friends stood by me as ever, Mark Lucas and Max Arthur.

I don't have an endless supply of energy, and what I have is put into my walks. But the walking itself is only half the deal; getting to the starting line is almost a tougher task. Every room I walked into seemed to be full of people shaking their heads. With every shake I got more determined. I went to see Robin Hanbury-Tenison to ask if he would be my patron. His enthusiasm just blew me away, but there was more to him than gung-ho bravado, as I learned when he brought out a gift for me. 'This was given to me by a Tuareg warrior,' he said as he fondled a flat, square piece of brass on a cord necklace. 'It contains verses of the Koran and will protect you as it protected me. So, if they find you dead in the sand, I assure you that if you wear this around your neck, you won't have died from "snake bite or thrust of sword".'

I picked Bangassou as the starting point because it was the closest place in CAR to Kisangani – it's on the Ubangui River, which marks the border between the two countries. It's also 750 kilometres east

of Bangui, where we'd land. We'd figure out how to get there once
we did so.

I had to buy return air fares in order to get our CAR visas. To
fly direct would have cost £1,000 each; I cut this in half by flying
via Lagos, Nigeria, and then on to Bangui with a stopover in
Cameroun. It meant we had an overnight in Nigeria, but there was
no time to get Nigerian visas, so we figured we'd just hang out at
the airport. Time was very much against me – I had the Sahara to
cross and I didn't want to do it in summer. Raymond had agreed to
be with me till April, when he had to return to launch his second
book. I wanted to be in Kano by then; I'd figure out how to cross
the desert when I came to it.

On the eve of the 14 November 1991 I walked up the hill in Kenley
that led to Raymond's house. My kit was already there. I walked very
slowly, savouring the lightness of my footsteps, aware I was not
going to be alone for a very long time. But I knew enough about
Africa to realize my slim chances of getting through were greatly
improved by doing it this way.

Raymond's parents drove us to the station. Even though he had
trained many people for expeditions across almost every type of
terrain, he himself had never been on something like this before.

'We'll be fine,' I smiled as we got on the train for Victoria.

I saw from the strained look on his mother's face that she didn't
believe me.

From Victoria we headed to Gatwick. It was the first time we had
carried our packs fully laden and even without food and water I
knew they were far too heavy. We spent a night at a Holiday Inn in
Paris. It was the only airport hotel with vacancies and I took the
opportunity to savour our last moments of civilization. I sank into a
deep bubble bath with a glass of champagne and tried not to think
of how we would get anywhere at all with the kind of payload only
the SAS could smile through. I don't usually behave like this, so it
must have given Raymond a sense of what was to come.

An early morning flight to Lagos got us in late that night. Plan A
bit the dust as the Head of Security told us cheerfully that the airport
was about to close; there was no possibility of staying. Two stranded
whites must have seemed like a nice opportunity to make some extra
cash for the weekend. He had the authority to issue us with temporary
visas – for a small consideration. Well, not that small.

I slipped him what he thought was a $50 note (it was, in fact, a neatly folded $1 note), took the paperwork and asked for a taxi driver he could vouch for. We were driven to an hotel nearby and stayed there till the next morning. Raymond spent the night sitting on the loo with a bucket in front of him after eating something bad for dinner. Whatever he'd picked up stayed with him for a week. It was about the only thing that did. Not a good way to start an expedition.

A President of Nigeria had been to Frankfurt airport and been amazed by it to such an extent that, in Remington fashion, he wanted one exactly the same in Lagos. They built it, complete with four snowploughs.

Our flight to Bangui wasn't announced in any way; Lagos airport might look good but it doesn't work. What was more, there are often no seat allocations, and they don't mean much even when there are. It boils down to a mad dash across the tarmac, and when you're talking first come, first served, the African granny has nothing to learn from her British counterpart.

When we realized we ought to be on board, we hurtled down corridor after corridor. Passport control, customs, and a whole series of other officials who wouldn't settle for one form when three would do just as well stood in our way. They knew we were in a hurry.

'What have you brought for me?' was the traditional greeting, our passport held just out of reach.

It happens at every check point on the road, but Lagos was outrageous. In anticipation, however, I'd brought some miniature bottles of duty free whisky back in France. We handed them out liberally and got through to the plane. As I gazed unenthusiastically across the carpet of yellow dust beside the runway, I hoped that the pilot would get going before the boys back at the desk started to party. Raymond and I had drunk the contents of the whisky bottles whilst crossing the Mediterranean and refilled them with urine.

During the flight to Bangui, I figured out a solution to our weight problem. I'd often seen Africans pushing small carts. I hadn't seen once since southern Zaire but it wouldn't take much to have one made. I sat back in my seat and almost relaxed.

De Beers had come up with a contact in Bangui, a diamond trader who very kindly agreed to meet us at the airport and put us up for a night on our way to Bangassou. Getting off the plane, I was struck by the familiar old greenhouse humidity and smell. It was Raymond's first time in the tropics, however, and he recoiled.

My last time in Bangui had been at the evacuation. Then, getting through immigration and customs was easy; this time, we were highly conspicuous and an easy target.

The immigration guys tried one on us, the usual intimidation bullshit which just takes patience to defuse.

'If there's a problem,' I said, 'I'd like to see the boss.'

You then stand and wait for the boss, who of course never comes because the charges are trumped up. You must then give them an opportunity to save face, and resist the temptation to rub their noses in it.

We got out into a den of thieves who were reading our body language and toying with us for a while until they made their move. I realized for the first time just how vulnerable we were – there was no vehicle to act as a buffer, and everything we owned which would make or break this trip was propped up against a lamp post and defended by two people against scores of experienced opportunists who had nothing to lose.

Our contact, Vassos, was nowhere to be seen. I borrowed a coin from a security guy and tried calling his number, but there was no answer.

'OK,' I said to Raymond, 'we'll give him half an hour and then get a taxi into town to one of the hotels in the guide book.'

Just as the circling vultures were about to move in, a big warm Greek came running across the dimly lit car park and embraced me with hugs and apologies. Communication was a little difficult because my French was not just rusty, but pidgin.

Vassos took us to his apartment block in the centre of town, pointing out on the way the colossal stadium which had been built for Bokassa when he crowned himself Emperor of the Central African Empire – and which was never used again.

We were ushered into an apartment next to his which was furnished but unoccupied. He bid us goodnight as he had to get up early, and we closed the door on Africa and felt safe.

There was a Jacques Cousteau film on video which we watched while starting to design the cart. I drew what I remembered and Raymond made a few modifications. We were both quite anxious. Life's very different when plans become reality and your mind has to adapt to using the opportunities at hand rather than planning how you want them to be. I'd always maintained that in Africa you have to impose your own schedule when you are in control or nothing will get done, but be flexible enough to adapt to its pace when you need the input of Africans. There's no point in shouting that you're in a hurry, so kindly get the cart finished by sunset, and there's no point either in knocking off early from walking because you're hot, tired and flea-bitten. If I had walked to Africa's beat, I would still have been at Victoria Falls, seduced by a pace which was not conducive to walking the length of the continent. Perhaps that was the major difference between what I was doing, and travelling. I felt the seduction and let it into my daydreams, but I kept it at arm's length. We had a mission to complete here; it wasn't a case of wandering where we wanted or changing direction if things got too difficult. Every decision held far greater importance for us than it did for the happy-go-lucky traveller.

We breakfasted alone on bread and coffee brought in by Vassos's house boy and went to see our host who was poring over a pile of rough diamonds.

When I told him our plan to get to Bangassou, he sighed and said, 'There are no river boats to my knowledge, and certainly no buses.' In all seriousness, he suggested chartering a plane.

I said, 'Good one, but I think we'll just look around town to check out transport.'

'I won't hear of it!' he said. 'Bangassou is only a day's drive away. It would given me great pleasure to lend you my 4×4 and driver.'

Wow! In the meantime, the driver was at our disposal to drive us round town and pick up supplies.

I changed some travellers' cheques with Vassos and he gave me a wad of CFA, a currency used in central and west Africa, interchangeable and supported by the French franc to keep down inflation. In return for this, they sacrifice freedom of trade and must sell their raw materials to France and buy back manmade goods. The rate is always 50CFA to 1FF. It made budgeting easier for people like us because you always know how much you'll get; unfortunately, the price of everything is on a par with the west – something I hadn't realized when costing the walk.

Within the first thirty seconds of the shopping expedition I saw fifteen small carts, each exactly what we needed. I bought one with two small fat wheels and a metal box frame with three planks of wood in the bottom. It was open framed and could not be closed for security, so we bought some tarp fabric for the cover and a chain to lock the wheels at night. I also bought a twenty-litre plastic jerry can with a tap.

We caught sight of the Ubangui River and I told Raymond that the far shore was Zaire.

'I want to be there,' I said, but even I didn't realise how strongly I felt it.

We had lunch with Vassos and then a siesta. Everything was going well, but I still wasn't sure where to start from. I didn't want to waste footsteps, so if we did get back into Zaire and found the Land Rover and walked out, I would cross the river into CAR at Mobayi-Mbongo, which was 200 kilometres closer to Bangui than Bangassou.

There is a track through Zaire to Bangassou but I knew that the ferry marked on the map had sunk several years before. I really had to make a decision on this, not just to know where we were starting from and to feel comfortable with it, but because I felt a need to be clearcut. I had grown very indecisive, sometimes making a decision simply to get one made, not because it was the best. I tossed it around all through the night and finally stuck to Bangassou because it was the closest point to Kisangani, and if Zaire did not reopen, I wanted to miss out as little as possible.

We left before dawn to get there by nightfall. A few kilometres out of Bangui there was a check-point where, unknown to us, your passport had to be stamped with an exit permit. The driver took our passports to the officials and sorted everything out. I should have checked what was going on but I didn't; it was subsequently to cause us many problems when we tried to leave CAR. On the orders of the guards, we were obliged to take a couple of military guys along with us as they needed transport. They got in the back and squashed our packs. Diesel leaked from one of the jerries and seeped into our kit.

The roads in CAR are graded and in good condition, the result of them being closed when it rains to prevent the surface being churned up into bog holes. It rained and we had to wait. The driver sensed our urgency at getting to Bangassou before nightfall and got us through many of the rain barriers until we could go no further and were forced to wait several hours. Raymond had brought his harmonica and practised a variety of Christmas carols and songs which might help get us through. Like the Tudor years of changing religious feet, we decided to play along with both Muslim and Christian.

Because the ferry had sunk, there was no through traffic to Bangassou and the only two guest houses had closed. However, we found a semi-derelict auberge, took rooms for ourselves and the driver, and spent a jolly night listening to the sounds of rats rummaging around and people trying to get through the roof. We put up the tent on the bed to protect ourselves against the mozzies, but by morning we were exhausted.

As we said goodbye to the driver and watched the car disappear down the road, I felt an overwhelming sense of being marooned. The only way out, I said to myself, was to walk. It was a familiar enough feeling.

Raymond played with packing the cart to balance it while I went shopping in the market for basic food stuffs: flour, milk powder, sugar, dried beans and some fresh fruit and veg. I also spied a couple of umbrellas in the hardware store and bought them – like policemen, shade is never there in Africa when you need it.

We made our way back to the auberge; I said, 'Right, let's go!', and the walk was officially restarted.

The cart was going to take some getting used to. The T-shaped handle had to be pushed from a certain angle to get the wheels moving at all, but Raymond was six feet two and I was five feet five. We found it awkward to push together, so we took it in turns. It didn't take us long to discover that it was the wrong height for both of us. The cart had a life of its own on the cambers, and where the road was deeply corrugated and potholed because the locals had lifted the tarmac to sell, it would jump and pump and the kit began to shake loose. Things kept slipping down the sides and catching in the wheels.

Some way out of town we met the first real problem – a small incline. Halfway up it, heaving and pushing and in danger of slipping back down, we also met the solution – a pair of generous black hands got behind the cart and pushed it swiftly up the hill. All right!

Our friend left us at the top of the hill and we pushed alone until we met someone else on the track who said he needed money and would help us. We made quite a bit of distance; things were really looking up. That night we camped in a gravel pit as I'd done with the Land Rover, preferring the solitude away from the enquiring eyes of the villagers. We were exhausted, having pushed all afternoon. We hadn't sorted out our system. Like the first few days of any new stretch of the walk, getting into the system is hard work. Putting up the tent and the water filter system, getting the fire lit and rummaging around for food made us wearier still. We felt very vulnerable.

The next day we set off, legs swollen from insect bites – a small, black, virtually invisible insect which I called 'Bitey Bitey' gave a nasty little sting and when you scratched it the stinging got worse. Physical effort in such humidity was debilitating. We rested every few hours, as I'd done before, but this wasn't the same walk and I was imposing my rigid schedule without letting it find its own equilibrium.

That afternoon we crossed a long open plain without shelter. We hadn't urinated all day and began to feel the onset of heat exhaustion. Both of us fell silent, unable to speak. We stopped, put up the umbrellas and emptied our water bottles. During the next two and half kilometres we drank ten litres of water between us.

We got to the edge of the plain and found some shade at the top of a small hill. We sat there trying to galvanize ourselves to get up and move. Thinking that there might be a stream down below, the chance of a wash got us to our feet and tottering down the hill, heaving back on the cart to keep it under control. We took it in turns to wash in the dodgy-looking water and I immediately got a repeat of my allergic reaction.

The area around the stream was too damp and insect-ridden to camp in so I recce'd the route up the other side of the hill. I spotted a clear patch in the long grass, went back down and helped Raymond manhandle the cart to the top. When we reached the camp site we sank to our knees. I knew deep down that the game was up; the weight of the cart was just too much for us, possibly only because we weren't acclimatized, but it pared away at our morale.

That night was the worst night of any walk or any other time of my life. Raymond had difficulty in lighting the fire, and as a bushcraft expert this was pretty serious. Working on auto-pilot I put up the tent, laid out the bedding and fiddled around setting up the water filter. It dripped one small green drop at a time, so to filter ten litres for a day's water would take a week, not a few hours overnight as we'd planned. It was only very much later that we discovered they have to be washed to get the colour and dressing out. We used Chloromin T instead and filtered the dirt with our teeth. I went to look for wood but couldn't see any. I forced myself to take a deep breath, relax and look again. I discovered that I was surrounded by the stuff.

Raymond boiled some water and cooked up one of the six dehydrated meals we'd brought. It smelt delicious and comforting, filling my mind with the image of a joey in its mother's pouch.

Raymond's shits continued throughout the night and weakened him. It started to rain. I lay under my sleeping bag with a lump in my throat. I knew beyond all doubt that there was no way I could do this walk. Not even in the first days of walking eighty kilometres a day across Australia had I felt such a deep and certain knowledge of my inability to go on – not because of the physical hardship, but simply because I had no motive. I was faced with pushing this cart for at least a year to get to the Mediterranean, yet even if I got there I wouldn't be able to say I had walked the length of Africa. The 807 kilometre stretch I had missed out would forever be a skeleton in my cupboard. I had often hung onto the line: 'I have walked every step from the Cape, I will walk every step to the Med,' but now there was no line to grip. I couldn't believe that I hadn't anticipated it when planning the restart.

Raymond had pointed out many times since I'd known him that I tended to rush into things with great gusto but without thinking them through. Sure, I'd say, but if I looked before I leaped, I'd probably talk myself into staying on the diving board. This time, however, I had to concede that he was right.

'Raymond,' I said, 'I don't think I can do it.'

Christ, to hear those words!

He didn't understand what the fuss was about.

'So what if you can't get back into Zaire?' he asked. 'What's 800 kilometres compared with the length of Africa?'

'800km less than the full distance,' I replied.

I woke the next morning and the sense of despair came rushing back: *this is all wrong – what the hell am I doing here?* I got up and cooked some peanuts in palm oil and boiled water for Bovril for Raymond, who was suffering somewhere in the bush with his diarrhoea. The act of cooking – of doing something constructive – must have acted as a therapy, because I began to feel more and more hopeful. When Raymond reappeared, I had a flash of inspiration.

'It's OK!' I said. 'We'll be wanderers! We'll just walk from one village to the next, taking it slowly, throw the schedule out of the window till we find our own rhythm!'

I felt much better: yes, there was a way to get through. And as usual, I got very excited with the new plan, disregarding all practicalities. Little things like: Zaire was closed. But what option did I have?

As Raymond was washing in the stream, he met three men walking to Gambo, a small town about thirty kilometres west along our route. One of them, a slight man with a mouthful of yellow, peg-like teeth, was going to visit his sister who was in hospital. He said he needed the money and agreed to help us push to the next village, three kilometres away. We decided this would be our destination for the day and we set off under our umbrellas looking for all the world like a Victorian expedition.

In fact we covered around thirty kilometres that day. There turned out to be no shortage of pushers. Not everyone needed the money. They weren't rich, but if they didn't have some particular reason to work for payment, they didn't. But for those that did, there were few ways they could make money and we were providing them with employment if they needed it. At each village we were refreshed by offerings of oranges, bowls of water to wash in and shade.

An old woman came haring across the track brandishing a six-foot stick. She stopped the cart by standing in front of it and bracing herself for the blow in case we didn't pull up. Her face cracked by a wide, toothless smile, she pulled her panga from its woven sheath and quickly cut up the stick, slicing off the outer bark and leaving a short length to grip. She stood up – much straighter than I expected – and presented each of us with her gift. We clapped our appreciation and gnawed on the stick. It was sugar cane. I reached for a cigarette for her and handed her mine to light it. She held them in front of her, end to end and blew on the coal.

We were told there was a Peace Corps Volunteer in Gambo and sure enough, we soon began to see fish farms, the telltale signs of do-gooding ahead. However, the prospect of kicking back with some Americans and having a good evening pulled us on.

The doughy, yeasty aroma of drying manioc hung heavily in the village air. We were first shown to the American's house, then taken to a village meeting which he was holding. He turned out not to be a PCV at all, but a well-educated African who had returned to his village to bring the new farming developments to his people. Mr Guy was the chief's brother, and spoke to us in English. What a relief – my French was hard work for both parties! He cordially plied us with cold palm wine, then served us roasted fish flavoured with chilli and fufu (cassava porridge).

We took a rest day in Gambo and I did the laundry under gathering clouds. Mr Guy arrived with some of his farmers and we greeted each other good morning in Sango.

'By your questions,' he said to Raymond, 'you have shown great interest in our work here. I would like to take you on a tour of our fish farms.'

I'd been given a tour back in Zaire and knew what to expect: the farm system is exciting but he was in for a very long walk. Seven farms, four episodes of diarrhoea and fifteen kilometres in the hot sun later, Raymond just about made it to camp without collapsing.

Our betoothed pusher organized two young boys to help us get to the next village the following day. We woke with the villagers at 5a.m. and Raymond paid our man.

'You are a man of honour,' Raymond told him.

He was greatly touched.

It was impossible to gauge how far we had walked and how far it was to the next village or the next water supply. The African kilometre didn't appear to equate to our kilometre, or probably to any distance at all. We decided to work in terms of time, and figured that fifteen kilometres was about a day's walk to the locals. However, we wanted to do thirty kilometres a day.

Sometimes the people we hired would stop after two hours and say: 'That's thirty kilometres, pay us.' Of course, there was no means of proving them wrong. The chief's brother in Gambo had told us how much to pay them: 'There isn't really a standard rate,' he said. 'It depends on whether he needs the money or is just doing you a kindness.'

It got very hot and humid around the middle of the day. We'd often reach a small village and be offered sugar cane to munch on and invited into the 'da' – a thatched roof on stilts which acts as the day house for shade. There we'd be offered a kiri-pa (bamboo bed) to lie down on, oranges with the top cut off to suck out the juice and water to drink. This was the only thing we couldn't accept so we explained: 'There are things in the water which are alien to us...'

'Ah,' they'd say, 'you mean the microbes? We understand.'

We never had to ask for anything; they could tell we were hot, tired and hungry. We didn't have to explain the journey either, it was just accepted that we were going somewhere because we needed to. It hadn't been the same when I was walking alone; because I didn't have a pack, I had been asked many times what I was doing.

We learned a lot from our pushers. They thought our way of doing things very dirty, and would show us not only which fruit to eat along the way but also how to do it. Pineapple cut up on banana leaves was sensational. Their eyes were much keener than ours: they killed snakes in our path before we'd even seen them. Snakes are always killed in Africa, no matter how harmless they are.

One of our pushers, a young man named François, joined us with his dog. He wore a Bond 007 T-shirt and matching belt and took control of the cart up a pretty steep hill. He was doing fine until he stopped, saying something we couldn't understand. Thinking it was a pleasantry, we nodded and laughed.

But François shouted and this time we caught it: 'M'aidez! M'aidez!'

He was slipping backwards. We took the cart from him and pushed up the hill together while he fumbled in his pocket for a handkerchief. Two French letters fell out: one you could read, one you could wear. He picked them up, laughing shyly. The 'Panther' logo on the packets seems to have gone a fair way in curbing the Aids problem, but like many education systems, condoms had been greeted with suspicion – 'Another white man's plot to keep our numbers down.'

It was around the fourth or fifth day that Raymond came into his own. We were taken at day's end to the house of the chief, who was a relative of one of our pushers. Raymond struck up conversation with a hunter, swapping tracks in the sand, illuminated at the right angle by an oil lamp.

'In my country we have deer,' he said, pressing his fingers into the sand in a realistic shape. Robert, the chief's nephew, immediately caught on and drew an impala track. Raymond drew a fox, Robert drew a hyrax and so on. They made the prints in running formation and altered them for male and female.

'What about lion?' I asked.

Robert drew a hand-sized circle with five dots inside. It wasn't a track he had seen, but it was a representation of what to look for. It astonished Raymond because it was exactly the same method he used to teach tracking – it gave all the right information: the overall size and shape and the number of toes with or without retractable claws.

When Raymond asked about their traditional firelighting method, someone produced a box of matches.

'Show him this!' somebody else shouted from the crowd.

The man came forward with a small plant and used a mime which Raymond read to be the hand-drill. The plant was called nsaba, which turned out to be one of those rare and very important plants with many uses: the bark was used for making cord, the inner bark was dried and made into a yellow powder as a topical antiseptic which we had seen being used a lot on tropical ulcers; the leaves were used for loo paper and the inner stem was used for making fire. Some of their uses for plants must have taken years to work out, but the 'loo paper leaf' I worked out myself – it doesn't take long!

Raymond is probably the only person in Britain who can work the hand-drill to such a high standard that he can take the wood, cut it to shape and produce fire within minutes. He has made it his trade mark. He had mastered the bow drill used in North America and was looking for people who lit fire with the fire plough – a technique which up until then he had only read about.

He set up a demonstration and the villagers crowded round. Only the elders had done this before, the young ones had never seen it. They all took turns at whirring the stick between their palms down onto the hearth stick. Eventually, the blackened powder from the friction began to glow and held together as a burning coal which Raymond tipped into a tinder bundle and blew into flame. When the flames burst from the tinder bundle, a great roar of delight went up in the crowd. This white man knew the techniques of the elders; he hadn't come with new ideas developed around the conference tables of aid offices.

It was quite amazing to watch the effect Raymond had on people, bringing back traditions which had disappeared with western ways. They had been noted down by the early explorers, written in books which sat on dusty shelves in the archives of the British Museum. Raymond had read them, practised them for fifteen years until he had mastered them – often they weren't written down correctly because the explorers hadn't tried them. He'd become a caretaker of these traditions and was returning them to their rightful owners. In exchange, the chief gave us protection and hospitality for the night and lent us two of his sons for the next day's push. This went on from one night to the next in the same way, and as a token of our gratitude I always gave to the chief's wife a gift of one of the sewing needles I had bought specially for the purpose.

We spent one memorable night with a chief who had four wives, twenty-seven adult children and countless grandchildren who all lived with him. We didn't see much of him – he shuffled around from hut to hut looking very henpecked. It was here that, instead of eating with the family, we were given a room by ourselves. A candle was brought in and they gave us a huge pile of fufu and a sauce to dip it in. It was very dark in there and we couldn't see the sauce but they usually tasted so good that I took a big mouthful – and nearly threw up. It was mud-sucking catfish, slithering around in a soggy pulp. Four sewing needles, too – it was an expensive meal.

We bought cooked potatoes and other food in the markets. They have fast food for travellers – pidi-pidi was one of my favourites which is crushed peanuts and manioc, rolled into sausage shapes, fried in palm oil and covered with spices. Fufu is made into balls and fried; we called these dough balls. We lived off a lot of this food as well as fruit. Some fruits are just between-meal titbits like the soft flesh around the cocoa pips which you suck and then spit out. I didn't like cola nuts though – they are an appetite suppressant and stimulant like coffee. You bite a little bit and chew it, but they are bitter and make your mouth taste furry. I wondered if this was one of the causes of the peg-like, discoloured teeth. There was also a lot of peanut butter on offer but we didn't eat as much as we'd have liked because it's a good source of amoeba.

Taking the cue from the Africans, we ate fruit and fufu for energy during the day and protein in the evening: mostly peanuts, monkey and impala. It is the same system as I have always used on a walk; protein makes me tired so I leave it till the evening unless I want to sleep at midday.

We were shown that chewing papaya seeds and small pieces of leaf from the tree are good for belly ache. We drank a lot of palm wine (peke) when it was offered. The taste varies depending on when it was harvested and how old it is. The fresh stuff is almost fizzy, like young coconut milk; the older stuff has a fermented taste and often has ants in which need to be filtered through your teeth. Neither will get you very pissed but it is a very refreshing drink. As I had seen all through Africa, when the cup is finished, a small amount is left which you swill around and then chuck onto the earth. This cleans the mug but is also a sign of thanks, rather like my ritual of throwing a stone in every stream I crossed as thanks to my 'Road God of Thirst' for keeping the river full.

As we pushed on I came to the conclusion that where villages had more open areas, the people were more relaxed. In those that were crowded with other houses or forest, they were uptight; but wherever whites had been, be it in forest or savannah, the villagers were often suspicious and lazy.

We heard of an American mission and walked several kilometres off track to reach it. But, no Coke, only Fanta – the missionary had left the previous day and would be back a year later.

Raymond looked at me and said, 'Doesn't he know there's a walk on?'

We were passed on the road by whites in 4×4s but they didn't stop. One eventually did, an American who was going the other way. He invited us to stay with him once we reached his village. Some days later we reached a Swiss mission and virtually had to twist their arms to use their shower.

'We passed you in our car and were pretty sure you'd broken down,' they said.

So why didn't they stop? I grappled with the logic, but held my tongue.

There was something rather disgusting about this mission of four families – there were dozens of white kids and all the women were heavily pregnant. They told us that a good wage was 2,000 CFA a day. They paid their houseboy of thirty years' service 1,000 a day. However, we walked on cool floors and drank water from frosted glasses that dripped with condensation.

The reaction to us pushing the cart was completely different from having a vehicle – something rather shoddy and bludging about us I suppose. It was quite different from the villagers' reaction. They hadn't taken much of an interest in being hospitable to me with the Land Rover, but now that we were on our own, they welcomed us excitedly.

We kept ourselves extremely clean, washing our clothes and bodies every day. It kept our spirits up. We had decided to risk getting bilharzia, the small snail in slow moving or stagnant water which lays flukes that burrow into your body through your skin. They lay eggs in the host body until they're ready to get pissed out into the water and continue their cycle. The effects aren't noticed for months, however, and on balance it seemed madness to pass up the opportunity. It was only many months later that I learned what an unhealthy wash it had been: I noticed blood in my stools and bilharzia was diagnosed. I took a course of pills, and could only hope that there was no permanent damage to my liver and kidneys.

Some days later we reached the mission where the Americans were staying. We knocked on the door. It was another Swiss mission and we weren't invited in. It took some time to convince them that we were decent people; I had wrongly assumed that they might be interested in our journey. The Americans had been evacuated from Zaire at the same time as me and were refugees at this mission until they could re-enter Zaire.

The head of the team was in his thirties. Paul Noreu had lived in Zaire all his life and was a keen botanist and anthropologist. He and Raymond swapped information about the uses of plants and living skills. Improving farming techniques, not preaching, was his primary *raison d'être*. But I didn't hold much store by this either – the Africans must have developed their skills to be the best way in their environment, otherwise they'd be dead. They'd certainly got it down to a fine art so that the men had plenty of free time. My thinking was backed up by the Africans themselves: they adopt the new way until the whites leave and then continue with their own. They're very tolerant people!

Even whites who have lived in Zaire don't understand how well the locals live. They think they are virtually starving, living hand to mouth and just existing. The reality is quite the opposite – the order of the day is to have fun and to take the piss out of aid workers, missionaries and anyone else who comes along with freebies, bizarre ideas or hand carts.

Paul had been back into Zaire the previous week to check on his mission.

'It was fine,' he said, 'there was no trouble. But I can't convince the Embassy in Kinshasa to let us in. That evacuation was mandatory for all Americans and they're concerned that if we went back we could be used as pawns.'

Hearing him say that it was quiet in the north raised my hopes of getting back in, even though it was the middle of the country that I had to get back to.

Raymond was happy with this way of life, he was finding his people – he'd known no other in Africa – but I was not. Even though we were settling into the rhythm of the cart and enjoying such richness from the Africans, I wanted my walk back. What stretched ahead were months on end of this kind of effort which would amount to nothing. The sheer weight of what lay ahead formed a barrier of anxiety to push against.

We had to get back on the road because our visas were running out and so was the money. I calculated that we'd have to walk thirty kilometres a day for seventeen days to get to Bangui in time. We reached one village at the top of a hill and set up camp in the Chief's 'da'. A young missionary stopped and wandered down to join us. He couldn't have been with the mission very long because he still had colour in his skin.

'Coffee?' I offered, putting the billy on and placing a stool by the fire.

'I heard that you're walking. It's very dangerous in Central African Republic.'

Raymond and I looked at each other. Apart from the hostilities in larger towns where our cart had been seized by a gang of opportunist thugs and the corruption in Bangui, we had received nothing but kindness.

'You don't know of the Zargena bandits?' He took the coffee and looked uncomfortable. 'They come from Chad, like highwaymen to steal from the road.'

His limited English lent a kind of romantic drama to the situation, giving me visions of black-caped Zoro, but I listened intently.

'One of my brothers at the mission was taking a break with his fiancée to the north of here. They ran into a road block and the Zargenas shot him dead.'

'I'm so sorry,' I said. 'When did it happen?'

'Last Sunday.'

We gave him a note to send to Vassos giving him a new date for our arrival some weeks away, and to ask for his driver to meet us at the check point where we knew we stood a slim chance of getting through with all our kit. If we didn't turn up on time, at least Vassos would know of whom to ask questions.

When the young man left, Raymond reminded me of my father's parting words: 'Have you made a will? Does your insurance cover the repatriation of your remains, because I'm not forking out like Julie Ward's father.' And on an even heavier note: 'What innoculations do I need? If you disappear, I'll have to go in there and find you.'

'Better keep out of Zargena territory,' advised Raymond in a mock British general's voice. 'Don't want Captain Campbell and the old 45 Commando Unit looking for us, what?'

'You might be able to live it down, but I'd be slaughtered,' I said.

It had been the only time my father had ever interfered with anything I did. It was an unspoken rule between us that where I went, I went alone, even when I was sixteen and left home with a hamster, a £50 note and a head full of adventures. Straight after my first walk, I'd gone to Australia to travel around as a migrant fruit picker. After three months I got to the airport in Sydney to fly home. I was using a 'daughter of staff' standby ticket that entitled me to 90 per cent discount, but the flights were fully booked for ten days, by which time my visa would have expired along with my ticket. I couldn't convince the BA desk to give me an extension and, as always, I was down to my last packet of smokes and nothing else. I plucked up courage to call home and ask my father for another ticket which I would repay as soon as I got back. He and my mother were on safari in Kenya at the time but eventually got the message from my grandmother.

Speaking from a bamboo hut in the Serengeti, my father dictated the message: 'Don't give her any money, she knows the rules. She can get herself out.'

And I did – in style. On my seventeenth birthday I was flying back to Britain with a borrowed pair of shoes so I could be upgraded to First Class.

My father didn't spend much time with my sister and me, but he taught us good lessons, albeit from afar. I'd rather face the Zargenas than face life after a rescue attempt from my father.

The next day we picked up a pusher who agreed to be with us for three days. We set off, but around midday something happened which was to change the course of the whole walk. Out of the dust an overland truck came hurtling towards us. I identified it as an Exodus Expeditions truck by the writing across the top and waved madly for it to stop. It's just one of those things on the African trail, that you greet the overland trucks, share a beer, swap a few lies around the campfire. But it didn't stop. The driver later told me he saw two very clean whites under golfing umbrellas pushing a cart and thought, 'Where the hell do these people come from? I ain't gettin' involved!'

I shouted something after them and turned to see a Land Rover following. I waved for him to stop, and he did. It was one of those epic meetings.

'Wild Jack?' he presumed.

'No, I'm Raymond.'

'Hang on,' I said, 'd'you mean Wild Bill?'

'Yeah, that's it!'

It transpired that Kevin had driven through the desert and spent a night with some overlanders in Tamanghasset. The story of Bill had been told around the fire – his shooting accident in Pakistan was legendary and someone mentioned he was now with a woman walking through Africa. Just fifteen minutes before he saw us, Kevin had been calculating where we might be.

The Exodus truck had stopped and was reversing back. Johnnie Simpson climbed down from the cab and ambled over. He was driving down to Zaire, across the northern stretch to Burundi and out to Kenya – the first entry from the north by an overland truck since the riots. One had got through from the south within the last few days and had said it was dangerous, but possible. The biggest problem was the armed rebel militia who had taken over the breweries.

We explained why we were walking along with golfing umbrellas pushing a cart and that my support Land Rover was in Kisangani. Johnnie took his passengers aside and put it to them that he'd like to offer us a lift. He needed as much manpower as possible to get through the bogs; instead of the usual twenty passengers, there were only three left and a couple of hitch-hikers. The others had overflown because they felt it was too dangerous. They didn't object.

He turned back to us and said, 'D'you want to come down with us? We'll take you to the river, you'll have to find your own way to Kissie from there.'

Raymond and I looked at each other. No need to discuss it. Yes! I had a chance to get my walk back. We paid the pusher for the full three days, put the cart on the truck and climbed aboard.

Our minds raced with this new development. Even though we had Zaire visas, our CAR visas would expire and there wasn't a place in Zaire which would issue them because the country had collapsed. Vassos would be worried, because he'd be expecting us. We would have to give Johnnie a message to telex to Vassos once he reached Burundi.

This turn of events not only led to getting the walk back but also saved us from walking into a danger we had no idea about. During the colonial rule, and before that with the slave merchants, the Central Africans were used to transport goods and furniture up to Chad. For decades, a trail of slaves in chains pushed and pulled great weights across the country. We were about to walk into the tribe who remembered this very clearly. And we had been using the chain to pull the cart up the hills – it was very strong and worked well. Our pushers helped us: the sight of whites getting blacks to pull their goods with a chain would have had us in pretty hot water.

During that drive back over country we'd already walked, the Africans looked very different. When they saw the truck they slouched, looked like peasants, and threw stones. This was in complete contrast to the dignity and pride we had seen as we pushed. Women swept their front gardens every morning to make a clear patch where the day's work is done – it's an open-plan kitchen and living room and everyone is welcome. I adopted this idea: it's much nicer and more practical to sit down in a clean area than in leaf litter. As we walked through a village in the morning and called our greetings to the women, they'd straighten up and greet us with pride. Their mud houses are beautifully made and cool to sit in, their clothes are spotless and we were the ones who, despite our daily washing, felt shabby.

Sitting on the truck, looking out the open window we saw a very different Africa. This was not simply an observation, this was a hint at what is going wrong out there. I had seen a way of life that I wanted desperately – the community life with all its fun, easy communication, vitality and contentment, but I couldn't have it. They, in turn, were looking at things they wanted – the pretty goods, the wealth, the labour-saving devices, the diversity of foods they saw the overlanders cook at camps. These overland trucks, forever seeking out untouched wilderness to sell seats, are spreading discontentment, making people realize for the first time that they are poor.

The Africans don't realize yet that you can't keep your community and be a slave to greed. In the West we are beginning to realize the terrible selfishness of materialism and how it has raped and ruined the world – not only the natural world, but the harmony of people. Our ever-increasing need for raw materials has brought Africa into the market place and they are vulnerable because they haven't experienced the cycle – from bush to city to bush. If we have realized the harm we are doing but can't give it up, what chance do they have? There are many elders who understand what's going on and have backed off from western development. They are having to fight not only the greed of governments who take over their lands but also the tempestuous questioning of the young who have heard about the city and leave. So often, they can't return to the village because they haven't made it and would lose face. Instead, they turn to crime. That was why I had dedicated my walk to Survival International, an organization set up to lobby for the rights of threatened tribal peoples, to secure their lands and allow them to live in the way they choose.

We heard of a Catholic mission which was encouraging the use of the old traditions – without, of course, the 'pagan ceremonies' which go with them – which was a step in the right direction: as I saw with Raymond, it brought back pride. Nobody had been into those villages and swelled their self-respect about who they are, or who they were. These people have been told for several generations that there's something wrong with them, with their religion, with the way they do things.

It took days to reach the border with Zaire at Mobayi-Mbongo. We camped in a gravel pit outside a village but it seemed nobody had asked the chief for permission. The villagers gathered round to look at this curious thing. The overlanders and the villagers began to bait each other, and stones were thrown. The second driver ran after one kid and whacked him. The chief arrived with many of his men and demanded to speak to someone in Sango. I knew the greetings but I felt this was a mess caused by the overlanders and they would have to clean it up themselves. Johnnie sorted it out, in his gentle way, with humility. It was perhaps more hurtful to see their anger now that I had lived with them, not hurried past them. But Africa is a land of contradictions – what works in one place won't work in another.

Raymond and I set up our own cooking fire, the overlanders set up theirs and the hitch-hikers brought out their stove. This must have seemed odd to the Africans – as it did to us – why didn't we all share one fire, share our food and enjoy each other's company? I noticed how wasteful the overlanders were of wood – when you've had to look for it yourself, you learn to be economical. They made a virtual bonfire in front of the Africans who had sold them the fuel – luckily, at rip-off prices.

An African cooking fire is made of three logs set in a star shape. Small twigs and thatching grass are laid on top of the apex and lit from underneath. This heats up the ends of the logs as the fire is gaining heat. Three stones are put in the spaces between the logs on which the pot is rested over the apex. It's easy to fan the flames using the broad flat leaves of the teak tree (called teck-teck locally), it needs minimal maintenance – just pushing the logs in a little further when they are burning down – and the pot sits there, simmering away. This is a good fire for boiling beans and making fufu.

The woods change in different areas, they have different properties and I learned which ones burn hot and fast, or slow and long. We used Ngengeakikoumou (local name for the 'yellow wood' which was my name, the leaves of which are crushed in water and produce soap) in the forest for long and slow, and bamboo for hot and fast for making tea. The art of cooking fires is knowing the qualities of the wood and what temperature you need. When I developed baking much later, I learned by trial and error. If I was cooking quiche I hunted for the right wood to cook it on. There were different ones for baking bread, pies, croissants and cakes. Baking is not a traditional cooking method for the Africans, so I had to find out myself. I got a huge amount of satisfaction from cooking and decided I wouldn't want to use a stove ever again!

At the border we ran into the usual problems – our passports hadn't been stamped with an exit permit in Bangui so we faced going all the way back there and missing our ride or paying a small dash. We all bargained down the dash. It is very important to show patience at these times – it's great fun for them to see a white losing his temper and being rude and they'll play you along and wind you up on purpose. They also like their position to be respected so humility is important. While we were waiting we watched a bull being slaughtered. It died quickly after its throat was cut but its body continued to twitch and convulse for some time.

We took the ferry over the Ubangui river. Getting the truck off proved very dodgy because the bank was steep and muddy. It was time for Raymond and me to pay for the lift: we all got behind it and pushed. Johnnie was very gentle with his truck, he didn't gun the engine and let the wheels spin hoping they'd get a grip. He instructed us to dig, place logs under the wheels and rock it until he could drive it out. When you're the only mechanic, you take care of your truck.

We waited a long time for our paperwork to be cleared. Kevin's vaccination certificate was rejected by the officials because it was out of date. They had, in fact, changed the date themselves, rather clumsily, and demanded money. Fortunately ours had been date stamped not hand written. The certificate proves you've been vaccinated against cholera and yellow fever. The cholera vaccine is virtually worthless, and most people just get a fake certificate. Our vaccines had been given free of charge by British Airways which saved me a small fortune.

During the next couple of days we got a taste of what it was like sitting on an overland truck. Even though the back was virtually empty, the infighting was ridiculous. Africa passed boringly outside. They stopped in markets to buy food, but they didn't have the grace to go from one stall to another buying a little here and there – they just bought from one stall, which is insensitive. They stopped at nightfall to camp. They had a tighter schedule than us, to get across the whole of Africa in nine months. If all was working with the truck they had to gun it as far as they could each day to get ahead in case of breakdown.

Kevin drove his Land Rover ahead. He was an interesting guy in his early fifties. His daughter's boyfriend had been offered a job in Uganda and needed a Land Rover. He asked Kevin if he would drive it from the UK to Uganda with him. Over the desert, the Tuareg nomads and the Niger military had begun a battle. Basically, the military weren't being paid (a very common and very dangerous situation) so they demanded bribes from the trading nomads. This turned to robbing at gun point. In retaliation, the nomads stole trucks on the Trans-Saharan track so that they could fight the military on more equal terms rather than riding their camels into battle. The Tuareg do not kill people. They behaved with great dignity when offloading a tourist truck by taking them close to the border and pointing them in the right direction. Bandits jumped on the bandwagon – dressing up as Tuareg so that they'd get the blame. The bandits shot people. This is what closed the border. There was a story going around that one of the overland trucks which was taken was carrying £80,000 in cash for its operation in East Africa to buy a new truck. It was in the chassis!

When Kevin and his mate were driving across, they had a hunch that some bandits were over the next horizon. They drove up to take a look and were shot at. Kevin drove at full pelt and they got out alive. Then in Bangui they were set upon by thieves with machetes. They escaped again, but his young friend cracked up and flew home. Kevin stuck to his commitment to drive the vehicle to Uganda but he didn't know then if the guy would take the job: all this effort and it might be pointless. A long time later, I heard that he had arrived safely, the guy had taken the job, but a group of travellers he'd met in Bangui hadn't been so lucky. They couldn't get into Zaire so they tried going through Congo, shipping their Land Rover around the short Zaire coast to Angola. It all worked fine until they were ambushed in Angola and all but one shot dead. This happened while Raymond and I were in Zaire and hadn't been in communication with the UK for some months. Some stupid journalist ran a half-page story on us suggesting that, like the Brits in Angola, we were dead and our parents didn't expect to see us again. They made up quotes from my parents and of course worried the shit out of everyone who knew us.

Kevin seemed to be losing it too. He was driving on the edge and had that nervous hype about him that I've felt sometimes in the forest. When Raymond got out of the Land Rover after a stretch with him, his knuckles were white.

The two hitch-hikers shared our fire one night and we hatched a plan. Mike, an ex-US Marine, had his bike with him and was touring Africa. He'd met the overland truck in Bangui and decided to go with them because it would be too dangerous alone and too boggy to bike. Johann, a huge young Swede with masses of hair – eight inches of beard – was travelling around independently and had taken a lift on the truck out of the same fear of Zaire. They wanted to get out to Uganda but they didn't want to continue with the truck across the north east of Zaire – they wanted to go to Kisangani. We were to be dropped at Bumba on the Zaire River.

'Hey, we can get the ferry, I've always wanted to do that trip,' Johann suggested.

'Rock n' roll!' said Mike.

'I wouldn't count on it,' I said, hating to be the downer. 'I doubt anything's running, there won't have been any fuel getting through. But there might be pirogues for hire.'

When we reached Bumba, Mike, Johann, Raymond and I rented two rooms in a filthy hotel while the overlanders slept in the truck and we partied, big time. At one point Johann went missing, so I went out looking for him. He was crashed out in the yard among the chickens being mauled by mozzies but he couldn't move. I started up a song, clapping and moving like a gospel singer, and shuffled back to the room: 'I've found Johann, yeah Lord, I've found Johann, yeah Lord, he's looking at the stars and he won't come in.' Like a musical, Raymond and Mike joined in, bottle in hand and we chanted back out to the yard, shuffling in rhythm, belting out the song. I've never had such a good session as that night. We danced, improvised songs and played wild and hilarious practical jokes until dawn. The truck left the next morning and we went in search of a pirogue.

There was an atmosphere of intimidation around the town you could have cut with a panga. We were the first tourists since the riots; travellers were an important part of the local economy and all aid had been stopped and no supplies had come up the river. These were desperate people and they needed our cash. Several times we were told our lives were in danger and we should get out of Zaire.

20

We were on our guard all the time. In fact, Mike didn't trust sleeping in the hotel room so he put up his tent in the courtyard on the second night. Not a good move. His tent was slashed as he slept and his 'precious' bag snatched from under his head. He lost everything: passport, money, credit card, journals, camera, photographs.

In every town where the overlanders pass there is a network of Mr Fixits who can be hired to find fuel, permits, guides, change money. Some of them are very good but, like a horse, they can tell if you're new at the game. They collect letters of recommendation

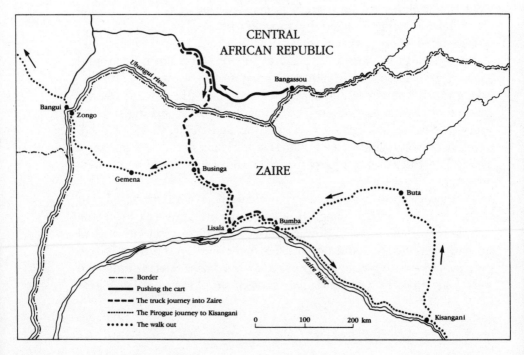

Two and a half months to walk three and a half days.

from overlanders. In these letters are certain hints as to just how good the guy is. Some of them have clearly been written by the Fixit on photocopied headed paper. Photocopiers are more common in Africa than condoms.

The man who approached us at the 'hotel' on the second day produced a card from Encounter Overland as his recommendation. The name of the EO driver was Bill Preston. It was my first experience of Mr Fixits and seeing Bill's name on his card, I took him on. It was only later that I found out that Bill's was an ace card, handed around the Fixits at a price!

We needed to hire a pirogue since there were no ferries or boats running the river and the roads were out. We were told there was only one pirogue with a motor in the town. This was bullshit. It took us a week to hire one and find the fuel. Mike and Johann had no option but to come with us but they didn't have much money so I picked up most of the tab.

All through that week, the Fixit tried to intimidate us, wear us down and screw more money out of us. He didn't but it came to a showdown on the dock the day of our departure where some bozo was waving a revolver around. They led us into a dockside house with the owner who had malaria and was also being intimidated so he wasn't fighting his corner well. They wanted us to pay for the hire of the pirogue up to Kisangani and for its return journey. We would only pay for a one way trip and one way fuel. We knew they could get return passengers because this was the only motorized vessel going up or down from Kisangani. They also wanted to put a load of goods on the pirogue but they wouldn't pay for part of the fuel.

They also said there would be six crew. No way, I said, two at the most – the others were clearly passengers. We stuck to our guns and the guy outside stuck to his. We climbed down into the pirogue, loaded on the cart and the bike and Johann's rucksack and started carrying off the sacks of goods and pushing the 'crew' towards the steps. We got all the unpaid-for baggage off bar one passenger who looked like a frog. He was later to prove his worth.

During that week, I'd got some clothes made for Raymond and me. We each needed another pair of trousers and a long sleeved top. They held together beautifully until we sat down. It's very tiring to have to stand over everyone who does anything for you to make sure they do it properly.

Our pirogue was in fact two lashed together with a petrol auxiliary engine on the back of one. They are made from one trunk of combo combo, which is like balsa wood (my name for it was the 'umbrella tree' because of the shape of its leaves). By burning and scraping, they hollow out the middle.

We set off up river on the four-day journey to Kisangani, and soon discovered that nobody travels first class in a pirogue. In the mornings we sailed through clouds of mozzies which sank down and bit our legs through our clothes. The weather was cold and damp or heavy and humid and storms whipped up suddenly and it poured. Tropical rain is cold. Out on the wide open river, the wind chill factor lowered the temperature.

We cooked on board using Mike's stove and stopped off at villages to buy produce, though there was little more than fried plantains and transparent, gummy tubes of pounded, cooked maize wrapped in leaves. We should have brought goods to trade if we'd thought about it. Even though we were the only motorized vessel, there were other pirogues being punted along the shallow waters near the bank, piled high with goods for market. It would take them over a week to get to Kisangani, so their goods weren't perishable. Several times our pirogue was boarded by opportunist passengers who, because they saw whites, reckoned they shouldn't have to pay. Sure they could get a ride, but they had to pay for it. The freeloader we called 'Frogface' turned to a particularly aggressive bunch and said, 'Get off the boat or I'll break your heads.' It did the trick.

We cooked ashore one night. The villagers gathered around Raymond and me as we cooked rice and pineapple with palm oil in their traditional way. We'd been taught this dish by a chief's wife in the cart-pushing days. From then on, I'd asked the chief's wife in each village for a demonstration, which they were delighted to do: we handed them enough ingredients for everyone, and it meant I didn't have to cook! They wash the rice, heat up three inches of palm oil until it's clear and runny, pour in the uncooked rice, leave it to cook for a while then pour in water which spits, put the lid on and leave it. We added pineapple and it was a heavy and filling meal. At the end of it, the women were clapping and shaking our hands – we'd been economical with wood, hadn't dropped a grain of rice and had cooked in their way. We shared our meal and downed some palm wine. It marked a very special stage in our learning. We had been vulnerable once and had relied on the Africans to take care of us, always on the receiving end of hospitality. But now we could hold our own and could give. Being thanked is a rare thing for travellers.

Back at the boat, a different kind of party was in full swing – the owner and skipper was in the thick of fever. They have their own medicines which are often based on the same plants we use in ours. I don't hand out drugs; I am not a doctor. Besides, we needed the drugs for ourselves. It came as a pretty stark reminder to us that they don't always work when we found the graves of two overlanders in Bumba.

It took the aid workers and missionaries a long time to convince the locals that white medicine is best even though many of them are based on the same plants. Many of the people we met were using their own medicine but wanted ours because they thought they worked better. This is all very well if you can continue to hand out drugs, but the aid workers had gone leaving them dissatisfied with their own medicines which might work better for them anyway. Their bodies are not used to such severe chemicals, they have been living off foods completely clean of pesticides and they build up their own immunities which our drugs are good at destroying. Malaria prophylactics have been seen to do this. If an aid worker has started them on a course as a kid to get through the first five years where there's an infant mortality of around 50 per cent, they have no immunity and must continue to take them for the rest of their lives. Aid workers come and go and these drugs are expensive so many people can't afford to continue with them. Malaria has adapted to combat prophylactics so in the very touristy areas of East Africa, the disease is far more likely to kill not just the tourist but the people who live there unprotected. It's yet another mess caused by well-meaning people who don't realize that nature is much smarter than they are. The moral issue should be based on long term thinking not just to satisfy some guilt complex – it is highly probable that you kill more people by leaving them dependent on prophylactics than if you leave them alone. The survival of the fittest is necessary in Africa – if ten out of ten kids survive through medicine but five of them are too weak to work in the fields, that's five extra mouths to feed without their labour. Nature has a balance, but we thought it wasn't fair.

Our gear was stacked in the left hull and we sat in the right. The crew sat at the back with a fully recovered skipper and a pet monkey I called Darwin, who was too young to have left its mother. With a lead tied around its waist, they tied it to the fish racks where it squeezed and scuttled to get out of the sun. I tended to her twice for a few hours each day. Her fur was matted with filthy residue so

I cleaned her up, washed her face with a finger dipped in water to simulate a loving tongue and fed her mushed-up pieces of ripe banana. She slept curled up in my folded arms with the comforting movement of my chest and I breathed deeply so she knew I was there. The men didn't know how to handle her – they loved to tease, waving food out of reach.

I sat with Darwin on my lap on the bow of the pirogue with my toes dipping into the water, breaking up the pollen crud that gathers on the surface, watching children swimming out to the boat, fishermen standing in their boats, patches of primary rainforest dwarfing the giant secondary forest, swarms of butterflies kissing the muddy banks. Papyrus plants nodded their fluffy heads like daffodil fairies.

One evening a storm blew up from the east. The skipper knew the pirogue wouldn't make it. He spied a bamboo house on stilts on the edge of the river and headed towards it. For several hundred feet back from the river, the bank was dense with long rushes, and the air heavy with mozzies; we heard their screams over the engine. Damp and swampy, this area was uninhabitable, but a fisherman had built his house there and for the first time I realized just what a house is: a place which is the opposite to everything outside. In this swamp, what he needed was a dry, mozzie free zone. So he built one.

We moored up under the house and climbed up into it. The owner was away but the skipper knew him. Inside was a platform of bamboo slats and a small enclosure of flour sack material. In that enclosure, no more than four feet square, was a dry, insect-free zone – and an empty Pepsi bottle! Perhaps it had fallen from an aircraft; in this area there was only Fanta.

Mike started up the limericks. Egged on by our reaction, he tried pretty hard to rock us off our perches and into the swamp.

'There once was a man from Kent, whose dick was so long that it bent; to save himself trouble, he put it in double and instead of coming he went.'

The on-board rules weren't explained to us – like what to do when you needed to go to the loo. We just assumed, having watched them piss in the river, that you did it from the boat, so when I needed to go the next day we set the umbrellas up lying on their sides to give me some privacy from the crew. They must have smelt it as it got clogged between the hulls. They sat there fuming and pulled over onto a bank.

During the journey, I read Mike's copy of *A Bend in the River* by

V. S. Naipaul. The novel was based in Kisangani and followed the fortunes and misfortunes of an Indian trader who lived there during some of the uprisings. 'This place keeps you tense. What a strain it is, picking your way through stupidity and aggressiveness and pride and hurt.' It gave me an idea of what I was going to experience in Kisangani after the rage had subsided and they were confronted by what they had destroyed and the realization that nobody was going to build it up for a long time. Kisangani has suffered a handful of these riots but it has always been rebuilt. It is the most important trading point in central Zaire. I was very nervous about our safety there – the last I'd seen of the town, it was in ruins. Since then no supplies had got through, we didn't even know if we could get diesel there. It was virtually a certainty that I wouldn't find the Land Rover – there had been more riots since I left and the Zairois knew that the whites might not come back. I mulled over what I would do if I saw someone driving it. If I couldn't get it back, Raymond and I would go back to the start point, three days south of Kisangani, and push the cart. I was faced with perhaps a year and a half's pushing to reach the Med. But hell, if that was what it took, I didn't mind – I'd have my walk back, intact.

The weather fronts came tumbling in – distinct bands of dense black cloud in an arc across the sky. It weighed heavily on my mind that Raymond's commitment to the walk had a limit. I had nothing to lose, he had little to gain. The experience of that second night pushing the cart when I felt beaten for the first time on a walk had shocked me. If I failed at this, I couldn't return to Britain. I had nothing except the walk – all my eggs were in one basket, and it became more fragile the further I got around the world.

We talked about this only once, when we were about a day from Kisangani. Raymond wanted my assurance that I would back out if it got too tough. I told him I wouldn't, but I wanted his assurance that he would go if he needed to and not try to persuade me to go with him. We understood each other.

In contrast to us, Mike and Johann were enjoying the trip. It didn't matter to them what happened at the end of the pirogue journey; in fact they probably wanted Kisangani to be bloody and wild. Nothing was riding on this except their lives, and as a traveller when you've got out of scrapes before, death becomes more distant. Mike was running from something which had given him a fright. He'd shacked up with a woman back home in the States who had a couple of kids. That was as much as he'd tell us until one night on the pirogue, when he and Raymond were telling us again about the witch doctor they had visited in Bumba to get Mike's bag back.

'Man that was some serious shit,' said Mike, adjusting his hat and leaning back on a rucksack. 'Especially when that woman was in a spin, out of it on dope and thrashing around with her fists.'

'And then that guy leans over and says, 'keep your knees apart.'

'I tell ya, man, you don't know the power of that shit.'

Mike crossed his legs. 'That woman I was involved with back home, she was into the occult. Scared the shit out of me. I figured it's all a load of crap, I was outa there, man. But you can't run from it, they'll find ya.'

Some strange coincidences and accidents had happened to Mike during his journey through Africa, and the further he was away from her, it seemed, the worse the accidents.

Johann, the Indiana Jones lookalike, was running too – from everything he hated back home. He never washed, never cut his hair and pigged out on chocolate powder and heavy metal. This irritated Raymond and me, possibly because we were under stress and it didn't affect him but also because we were being judged by the opportunists and the sight of unkempt whites made us easier targets.

We reached Kisangani on the afternoon of the fourth day. When we saw the first big house set back from the bank we packed everything away into our rucksacks and covered them with flour sacks so that nobody could see our possessions. Several large boats lay rusting on the banks, none of them fresh kills but it made us feel very small – this wooden boat, so low in the water we could trail our hands through the surface. Nothing much seemed to have changed but we saw a car and a handful of people and caught a glimpse of a white man on the dock. We landed in a washing area and pulled the pirogue high up the bank to unload.

We'd attracted a lot of attention and we had several items to keep an eye on. As we ferried the baggage up onto the harbour road, I saw another white.

'You're the eleventh to return in the two months since the riots,' he said. 'The rage has gone. Now people are trying to put their businesses together by buying back looted goods which are brought to them. The military are still in town, policing it, the very same people who started the riots. The storeowners don't mind them, they understand them.'

'What happened to the Olympia Hotel?' I asked with trepidation.

'It's open! It's no longer a hotel though.'

'What is it?'

'A brothel.'

I ran back and told the guys. Mike on his bike, Johann with his rucksack and Raymond and I pushing the cart, we walked through the town. There were no shops intact. We passed the Land Rover parts dealership and it was open. I walked inside to find a man behind the counter; if we found the Land Rover, we'd need him.

'We're open,' he said, 'but we don't have any parts.'

I'd seen this kind of loyalty at deserted missions, the guards continuing to stand at their posts for years.

I hadn't been feeling well because of the anticipation and was nauseous as we rounded the corner on the wide, dusty street and saw the Olympia. I was actually burping, about to be sick, as I ran up to the big black doors and rang the bell. The little old pygmy-sized guard opened it and greeted me warmly. I shook his hand and exchanged the greetings in Lingala. Then I ran into the courtyard. The flowers were still bright around the verandah tables and chairs where I had sat with the boys once before, but there was a large empty space where the Land Rover had been and no other trucks or signs of travellers. I threw up.

I heard the first few bars of a song, 'Forever Young' by Alphaville, coming from the open air bar. It had been the song of the walk; I'd played it over and over across the Karoo. I was convinced now that my Land Rover was in town.

I asked for the manageress, a big black mumma, but she was out. It could wait, we had some celebrating to do. I ordered a round of cold beer and we took a table in the shade and toasted each other. We were so excited to be there, so thankful that we'd made it after the tension of the pirogue journey and all the hype. It turned into an all-night session. At some point Mumma ambled in. In true form, she was as pissed as a fart. She overheard my conversation and called me over.

'Are you the one of the white Land Rover?'

'Yes! Where is it?'

'The Procure.'

'Where's the Procure?'

But she was too pissed to tell me. I'd have to wait till she sobered up. By the look of her, that would be late tomorrow.

I spent the night pacing the path around the hotel. I was like a cat on a hot tin roof, a child on Christmas Eve. The old guard was pacing it too with his bow and arrow. He knew I was pent up so he took both of my hands and held them in front of him, looked at me with his cheeky, shining eyes and started to shuffle his feet. He sang me a song, chirping and chattering like a little bird. I didn't understand the words but the message was unmistakable: 'It's going to be all right.'

I woke up at dawn. Bitten and sore, I felt sick again. I went to the desk and asked for the Mumma. She was still asleep. I wasn't going to wait for her to sleep off that kind of hangover so I asked about the Procure. I didn't know if it was a place in Uganda that Jeff might have driven the Land Rover to, a section of the military who had taken it, or just a term for dead vehicles.

'It's a Catholic Mission.'

'Where?'

They gave me directions out of town along the old airport road. The Mumma's driver said he'd take us but he had to find fuel. We had breakfast while he was searching the backstreets. I couldn't eat but drank coffee and wanted to punch Raymond to stop his running commentary on the importance of relaxation.

The driver arrived, we got in and I started to shake. Out along the dusty road, passing women carrying produce to market, I braced myself for the worst. We pulled up outside tall red brick walls that were topped with barbed wire. Thanking him, not thinking of asking him to wait in case it wasn't there, I got to the black metal gates and banged. The guard heaved one back and I peered through. Between the wrecked and burnt out cars, I immediately saw the blue tarp cover of my Land Rover. I started crying as I ran across the courtyard and between the cars and rammed myself against it. I backed off and let go, sobbing.

We went in search of the Father to thank him. He'd stayed through the riots and watched them destroy many of his vehicles. I had no carnet, no registration document or letter from the owner to show it was my vehicle, but my name was written across the Land Rover and I showed him my passport.

I used the metal wire Bill had set up through the top of the window to open the door when the key was broken and checked the contents. Everything was there. No damage except an ant's nest in the driver's footwell. I silently thanked Jeff for parking it up. I owed him a big one. The mission mechanic hot-wired the ignition and I put on Mike & The Mechanics.

Yeeha – we'd got my walk back!

*

Stormin' Norman needed a full service. There was a supply of filters inside as well as oil and various fluids. The mechanic was delighted to do the work. To improvise an ignition, he fitted up a couple of switches on the dashboard, tucked all the wires away and charged us £2.50. He was chuffed with the fifty pence tip.

We walked back to town and went straight to the Olympia bar to toast Jeff Roy and tell Mike and Johann. They had been investigating a lift out of town and had been told a beer truck was leaving in a couple of days for Uganda. We spent those days cleaning out the Land Rover, sorting, repairing and replacing kit, getting an iron tripod for the fire made and getting howling drunk. Mike and Johann packed to leave and we bade them farewell, vowing to keep in touch. Raymond and I turned back to our journey, just two weeks after meeting the overland truck. It felt good.

That night we woke up to a loud banging on the door. Both of us tensed. Raymond pulled on his trousers and opened the door.

Johann was standing in the darkness covered in blood.

'What the hell happened? Where's Mike?'

Johann went to the bathroom and threw up. We cleaned his wounds and spoke quietly to him. Eventually he sat on the bed, pulled himself together and told us what had happened.

'We were sitting on the top of the beer truck along with ten other passengers, piled up with goods, tyres, crates way up over the sides of the truck. It was going very fast, we had to cling on at each corner as the top-heavy goods heaved the truck to one side. We called down to the driver to take it easy, but he didn't slow down. As we rounded a corner, in one awful split second we knew the truck was going over.'

Half jumping, half thrown out, they landed amongst all the heavy goods as the truck toppled over at 100 kilometres an hour and bounced on its side. Mike's arm and leg had been dislocated, Johann was knocked unconscious. Mike screamed at him to get up. Under Mike's direction, he pulled his arm and leg sharply back into place and then fell over unconscious again.

One man's legs were amputated. A heavily pregnant woman lost the baby inside her: it had come out through her burst belly. Nearby villagers swarmed on the carnage, carting off the crates of beer. Somehow word got to a forestry guy, a Frenchman. He came to the scene and went straight to the whites, Mike and Johann. Mike shouted at him to take the most seriously hurt to Kisangani. The Frenchman loaded them all into his van and drove through the night to the hospital. But there wasn't much the doctors could do. There were no medicines; they'd all been looted.

Raymond and I took it in turns to keep a vigil on Johann during the rest of the night in case he vomited in his sleep. In the morning we went to the hospital and found Mike lying in filth. He was in good spirits but badly needed support for his leg. Raymond and one of the hospital staff searched the town in the Land Rover to track down looted plaster. They were successful and Mike's leg was set. We got him out of that stinking hole and into a restaurant – amazingly, almost perverse, this French restaurant was open and serving frogs' legs, snails and bite-sized pizza bits and wine on white table cloths. Mike nearly cried when he saw it.

For the next two days we made them comfortable, shopped for fruit and kept them clean. When we knew they'd be all right, we bought the last of our needs and drove back down the track, 178.4 kilometres to the start of the walk.

I knew the place but I had to be sure. If I could find our campsite eight kilometres further back down the track, I'd be convinced. But the rains had come and the landscape had changed – bamboo can grow a metre in a day. Something caught my eye and I asked Raymond to stop. I waded through thick vegetation into a gravel pit. I went to the far corner and looked for any evidence of our last night's camp. There, amongst the grasses, was a soggy scrap of paper – a Sainsbury's Chicken and Sweetcorn soup packet. Yes!

21

We shared the chores as usual at day's end but it was a lot more work than we'd been used to with only one driver and a new routine to get into. The Land Rover needed maintenance and there was a lot more kit to deal with than on the cart. Raymond, who had spent all his camping life squatting down for cooking, was now faced with everything on legs at different heights. It was alien to him.

On the road, people approached me with a blank expression – a bare canvas waiting for me to set the tone, hostile or happy. I wanted so much to be a good ambassador for my race and colour, to help mend the damage done by tourists. Raymond was getting harassed whenever he stopped to wait for me, shop or organize a break. He couldn't watch everything while he was setting up and the villagers realized this. They crowded round, thinking he was another aid worker coming to give them freebies and got indignant if he didn't hand out food.

'A situation builds up and you defuse it and think, phew, that was a close one, I hope it doesn't happen again,' he said. 'But it's happening at least three times a day. It's difficult to project a sense of calm when you know what's going to happen. But I can't allow tension to build up in my wake because you have to walk through them.'

'That's the major difference between us and the overlanders,' I said. 'They don't care what happens so long as they get through.'

We had to get another driver; this harassment could turn into something very nasty and it would only take one incident to blow everything – just because it hadn't happened yet, didn't mean it wouldn't. The old traveller's adage: safety is no accident.

I walked into Kisangani at last, right into the Olympia Hotel and hit the bar! It had effectively taken two and a half months to walk those three and a half days.

It was Christmas Eve and the hotel was full – all the rooms were reserved by the prostitutes – so we booked a suite at the Kisangani Hotel and sat down for a meal in the restaurant. The waiter came over with menus and stood beside the table with pen poised, adjusting the white napkin over his arm. Two long columns of food – it blew us away just looking at them.

'Two steaks with chips,' I said slowly in French, 'and a bottle of water, not opened, please.'

Half an hour later, we called the waiter over and asked for a progress report.

'It's coming, it's coming.'

He wandered back to the kitchen. Half an hour later, we called him over again.

'Where is our food?'

The waiter looked down at me with an expression of dull surprise.

'But there is no food at this hotel.'

We made a corned beef omelette in the yard and got hammered on Christmas Day with Johann and Mike and painted his plaster. It was one of the best Christmases I've ever had.

We stayed there a couple of days, getting things made and repaired now that we'd had time to test the vehicle and its systems.

'I'm going to wait in Kisangani until my leg is better then cycle out to Uganda,' Mike said.

Johann refused to go on another truck; there were no boats running, no planes, no way of getting out.

'Can I come with you?' he asked.

Raymond and I went into a huddle. We were concerned because Johann had been lazy, slovenly and selfish and we didn't think he would pull his weight.

'Let's give him a trial run to Buta,' Raymond said. 'If he proves to be a liability, we'll ask him to leave.'

Raymond was keen to get into the forest to find out more about fire-lighting techniques. Frenzy, our Mr Fixit, knew of a village further down river and hired a vessel for us.

Leaving Kisangani by wobbly, leaking pirogue, two punters took us down river an hour or so. They needed fish and pulled up alongside a group of fishermen. One, while debating the price, chopped the fins off his catch with a blunt machete. I watched intently, as the fish he handled was still alive. One of the fins flew into my eye. Squawking, I turned away, holding it shut. Amazingly, when Raymond had sorted out the medical kit to take for that day trip, he'd paused on the eye patch and thought – yes, better take that just in case. He wrapped up my eye but it made trekking through the bush quite tricky without a sense of perspective.

The villagers were highly suspicious of Raymond because there was a communications mast on the other side of the river and they thought he was a spy. This assumption was fuelled by Raymond's knowledge of the old ways because they didn't understand why a white man should need to know these things, and my use of Swahili only affirmed we were up to no good – tourists don't go into the forest nor speak the local tongue.

Frenzy, our crippled guide, battled on our behalf till two young men broke off from the dispute and led the way into the forest between two great clumps of bamboo. It was cool and clean under the cathedral archways of bamboo where no insects bit or buzzed. The floor was covered in a springy khaki carpet of dried bamboo leaves. If I lived here I would clear away all the undergrowth and use it for dancing.

A short way into the secondary forest, it was hard to hear the birds for the shouting of our guides; perhaps their loud chittering kept snakes away. Under a large tree in a clearing, we rested to drink raffia beer.

'Everybody who gathers from the forest must rest under this tree before returning to the village,' they said.

There was a practical reason behind the seeming mystique to this ritual – they had to clean up the things they'd brought from the forest to keep the village free from leaf litter, snakes and spiders.

As we went on, the old one pointed out different uses of trees and plants. He peeled the bark from one tree called temba and using a stout stick as a tool, rounded the end and cut notches down the side for about twenty-five centimetres. He laid out the bark and began to beat it with the notched end, stretching the bark with the other hand. Soon it doubled its size and became soft and silky like suede. This is what they had used to make clothes.

He pointed out the medicinal plants he knew, like Banbalumba for headaches, but indicated that these were known better by the women as were the edible plants – the men's job was the construction of things and hunting.

Raymond prompted him about the fire plough. He led us to a

fallen 'umbrella tree', cut a groove about forty-five centimetres long along the grain which would be the hearth, then took a dead branch and fashioned a stick from the dry centre about the same length. He shaped the end to fit snugly at an angle into the groove then straddled the trunk. He rubbed the stick forward and back along the groove. This is friction fire lighting, the same principle as the hand and bow drills – the hearth warms up, the dry wood dust from the scraping gets hot and as it's pushed together at one end, it will begin to glow into a coal. This is then lifted out with the point of a knife and tipped into a tinder bundle to be blown into flame. The old man didn't have the stamina any more and, as had happened in the villages in CAR, everyone took it in turns. The old man got impatient at the clumsiness of the youngsters and stuck the end of a match at the end – we didn't notice it until it flared into fire and the youngsters danced around thinking this was fabulous. Raymond lifted out the match and began again.

We returned to the village and drank palm wine with them then left before they got into yet another debate about espionage.

The walk restarted from the bar at the Olympia Hotel on 30 December 1991. The first stretch was to Buta, a distance of 321 kilometres – two weeks' walk through what some people call jungle, but is more correctly called rainforest. The locals just call it 'the forest'.

The villagers were in jovial mood because of the New Year. Greetings of 'Bonne Année!' rang in our ears. The people were getting more drunk; all day they demanded gifts. Reciprocating their 'Happy New Year' wishes only prompted them to ask for Bic pens to make their festive season happy.

We spent New Year's Eve with a chief in a village and sent out a message on the drum to all the villages within a twenty-kilometre radius that the white tourists sent their good wishes to all Zairois for a happy and peaceful New Year. I had been bet by Pippa Snook that I wouldn't be allowed to use the drum. It takes some years to learn the skill, so there was no meaning to my thumping – the drummer did it for us. The drum is a hollowed out combo combo trunk lying on its back with a slit about eight centimetres wide running down its length. It takes years for it to be mellow so they all have their different sound. We went to bed at about 10p.m. after a meal of chanterelles in a cream sauce made from thick powdered milk. It would have cost around £100 a head in London.

*

New Year's Day, 1992, and the air was filled with the smell of singeing monkey fur and the squeals of pigs being chased for the feast at midday. After that, a lot of drink is consumed. The whole of the former Belgian Congo was hung over. Screaming kids demanded: 'DONNEZ MOI!'

I closed my mind to their howling, trilling, raucous noise and wished this was an Indiana Jones movie and I had a pump action shot gun instead of a revolver. Vangelis played in my head. I hummed my favourite tune – keeping out the noise, keeping them at a distance, pretending this was just a film and I wasn't the centre of their attention. I thought about the next break and our latest bad habit – bananas dunked in chocolate Nesquik powder.

We met a witch doctor on the track, painted with white chalk and bedecked in charms and leopard skin. An African will commit suicide if the witch doctor tells him to – they have more power than anything we have in our society. They are a medium to keep the balance between good and evil. This dodgy brother, painted white with a bark loincloth over his shorts and an ocelot skin around his neck, kept us talking while he silently instructed his followers to surround the Land Rover. When we said our goodbyes, he casually halted us with his spear and said, 'Give me your car.'

We saw that we were surrounded and that they meant business. Somehow, I had to walk out of sight before the boys could gun it out of there, so we laughed and chatted and asked after his wife, whom he said was coming soon.

'I must go now,' I said, 'but the drivers will stay.'

I practically ran down that road to get over the horizon. The guys had a narrow escape.

The witch doctor's charms gave Raymond an idea to prevent the kids going into a frenzy: he carved a stick with a mask face and slipped it into a hanging case he'd made by plaiting split liana. Then he stuck owl feathers into it, because many Africans are frightened of owls. He'd wait till they were screaming through his window while waiting for me and stick it in their faces – there'd be a hushed silence until their eyes focussed on the face. Then they ran and didn't come back. A Peace Corps volunteer had another way of getting them to leave her alone: she caught one, tied him to her verandah pole and put kindling around his feet.

We crossed the Aruwimi River by ferry at Banalia. This river was Tarzan's home. The ferryman, something of a local historian, told me about Stanley's crossing of the same river in 1886. In June that year, Stanley's 650-man expedition for the relief of Emin Pasha split up. He left some of his men at the river and marched with 388 into the forest. They were the lucky ones. The sight of such a huge gathering of men on the riverbank must have been very frightening for the Zairois, who would have assumed it was a war party. They responded accordingly.

Johann had undergone a complete seachange. He looked up to Raymond and became fastidious, tenacious and competent. I had never seen a transformation quite like it. Instead of kicking him out at the first opportunity, we couldn't imagine anyone better suited to the job.

We got so good at organizing up day's end camp that we could have everything set up and be sitting down to eat within half an hour of our arrival. They wouldn't set up before I arrived because there were so few places to camp that we nearly always had to drive back to find one. As soon as the Land Rover stopped, I climbed on the roof and pulled down the sleeping kit while Raymond set off for firewood and Johann set up the table, chairs, pots and day box. Johann and I would put up his tent together while Raymond lit the fire. I'd unpack our sleeping things while Johann did his. All this was done in silence with a sense of knowing exactly what had to be done and by whom. A gelled team is a great feeling. No stress, no lost kit, nothing tripped over, nothing forgotten.

The terrain made me feel as if I had malaria – high humid heat in the sunlight, then plunging into the cold of the shadows. I walked through vast tunnels of bamboo, the leaves moving overhead like a croupier shuffling cards. Clearings were dappled with patches of pretty sunlight and butterflies. Despite the physical battle, here was tranquillity.

The fallen and jammed bones in my foot had caused the big toe joint to wear and swell. My foot was turning inwards – a classic shin splint problem. I worried that the strain on this area would aggravate the old hip injury and lower back ailment, which was suffering considerably from lax stomach muscles. Raymond noticed how my tracks changed during the day, that as I became tired, so my foot leant inwards. He studied my shoes and noticed a considerable wearing on the inner left sole. This side had been severely compressed; the rubber was not strong enough to support the fallen arch. We

Above The walk resumes when a border has opened but the months of waiting have put on pounds. Nigeria. (*Tom Metcalfe*)

Left Tom. (*Ffyona Campbell*)

Below G. (*Ffyona Campbell*)

Above A really good evening camp. Nigeria. (*Tom Metcalfe*)

Below With the most beautiful women in the world, the Fulani in Niger. (*Tom Metcalfe*)

Right Once I had perfected the bush oven, I could do something with the mangoes. (*Gordon Nicholson*)

Below Walking quietly through a village in Dolol country before I'm spotted. (*Tom Metcalfe*)

Above Gordon. (*Ffyona Campbell*)

Left Shuna, taking a break with us in return for running the logistical support from London. (*Gordon Nicholson*)

Below Jagga Jagga on a good day. (*Ffyona Campbell*)

Above My father joins me in Senegal. (*Tom Metcalfe*)

Below Stoned by kids on the Paris/Dakar car rally route. Senegal. (*Gordon Nicholson*)

Above Talking about babies, grocery prices and men. (*Tom Metcalfe*)

Right Crossing the desert before the knee injury. (*Tom Metcalfe*)

Below In a hurry, got to cross the border before it closes. Mauritania. (*Gordon Nicholson*)

Above left Pete. (*Ffyona Campbell*)
Above After 2,000km of sexual
harassment and attack, this was the final
straw – Pete had to trail me with a
Gendarme escort for the last 4 days. (*Peter Gray*)
Left Ffyona Campbell. (*Gordon Nicholson*)
Below The Sahara, like a graveyard.
(*Gordon Nicholson*)

Above Nearly there. (*Fiona Hanson* [PA])

Below It doesn't get much better than this.
(*Fiona Hanson* [PA])

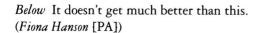

Above Journey's end. Tanger.
(*Fiona Hanson* [PA])

would try massaging it and perhaps improvise with inserting some denser rubber.

We set up camp 1.3 kilometres short of the end, because of the pain and because it was the only camp ground nearby. A guy told us there was a Belgian mission two kilometres up the road and the missionary was in. Though I was stretching in my tent, so relieved to be there, we packed up and walked on.

There was no Belgian, nor a mission, but a semi-ruined church still bedecked in the grass archways of Christmas decorations. We were surrounded by angry-looking locals, but it turned out that the head man knew Frenzy, and the guy I sold the cart to.

'I am not a good business woman to buy at 13,000 and sell at 4,000,' I said.

Camping by a water source on the rest day is very important because we needed a huge amount for our laundry, body washes and cleaning out the Land Rover. But there wasn't any at this gravel pit. It's a downer when this happens because you've got to walk another 300 kilometres to get to the next rest day which might not have water either.

A blue overland truck drove past. I ran out to flag it down and they camped with us. But, predictably, we didn't mix well. It's quite common, so I'm told, for people in small groups to stick together when meeting others so overlanders rarely shared our fire.

I looked at them and wondered: all you see is what Africa looks like, you don't know her secrets. All you smell is the dust and dirty clothes and bodies. Do you know the sweet scent of the white coffee blossom? Or hear the sound of a liana basket placed on the head? Or of a seed pod breaking open on the ground, or the whirr of the hornbill? Do you know the trail of the centipede or which way it curls up or which plant is ticklish, do you know which leaf to wipe your arse with? I hadn't known these things either when I'd walked with my eyes down, but now that I knew, I wanted everyone to know, especially since they were ambassadors too and we were about to trip over their past.

Over the next two weeks the flood gates opened as word spread that Zaire could be entered. One afternoon I saw four overland trucks and Land Rovers within three hours. It was like the M1. One of the first came haring through the forest, filling the track. It stopped and I went up to the window to say hello.

'S'truth,' said the driver. 'Where the heck did you come from?'

It was a Hann Overland truck which took old people across Africa. Each truck which passed told me more about the Tuareg problems in Niger. I didn't pay much attention; for them it was two weeks away, for me – four months. But each one told of yet another person who had been shot. It was only much later that we learned they were all telling me about the same person.

We had a good camp with a Dragoman Truck. The driver who introduced himself as 'Bad Man' shared our fire while his group were cooking supper. We had fried mashed potato patties with tomato paste; they were cooking salmon cakes and drinking cold beer. Bad Man shared his beer with us, but I still felt the pangs of animosity that I always felt when we camped with overlanders. They had so much food, and we had only what we could get in the markets. We got a sense of what the Africans must feel like when they see these camps.

One night we'd got a chicken. When making something spectacular for the evening meal, I'd plan it during the last quarter, working out all my movements so that I could do it quickly: get in, wash hands, over to cook box, get out small saucepan and two cups, bag of flour, oil, milk powder, eggs, onions, back to table, set ingredients in a line from left to right ... and so on until the whole thing was planned. Raymond had been planning the meal for a couple of hours so that it only took him an hour to kill, skin and gut the chicken, slice off the meat and prepare a fabulous sauce of wild mushrooms while I winnowed the rice. It's much easier to skin a chicken than pluck it – just take its jacket off, no mess, no feathers.

We had the joy of sharing it with a guest, a Japanese motor cyclist who arrived and camped with us. He was biking around the world and shared his bread with us – we hadn't had any for many days and we hadn't perfected our bucket oven yet. He didn't speak much English, but could mime everything.

At lunch one day another Japanese biker arrived with his wife. They were having great problems in the mud and sand. I fetched them a bowl of water to wash before eating. They were very thankful for it. Then a Land Rover arrived.

'Do you know where there's a good hotel where we can rest without mozzies?' they asked. 'One of our party has got hepatitis.'

They took him out of the Land Rover and laid him on the ground. And boy, he was more yellow than the Japs. We tried our best to get them to turn back – there were no such places in Zaire and they were two weeks' hard drive from Uganda with the tracks so bad.

They didn't understand. They had chocolate spread on bread for lunch; we had oranges. They didn't understand because they had chocolate spread – they'd come from civilization and had no concept of the hugeness of the forest in a fallen country. That guy was the closest thing to a corpse I'd seen.

By this time, we could only get four days' walking in before one of us fell sick and we had to stop. Johann got dysentery. All morning he got out of his tent and walked to the bush and back every half hour. Before afternoon he could hardly stand and by evening he just did it beside the tent and we covered it with the spade. As always, the kids watched. Raymond looked pretty bad and slept.

I asked Johann to take his temperature the next day and by the time I reached the Land Rover again, Johann said it was normal. I couldn't believe it, because he was burning up, so I took it myself.

'For Christ's sake, Johann, he's on 103!'

Johann worked in degrees centigrade and had done a quick conversion but got his maths wrong. I started Raymond on a course of Halfan for malaria and made him comfortable in the back. Johann drove the Land Rover.

He had never driven one before; in fact, he confessed, he'd never driven off road. I don't know how he got down those tracks. They were waterways in the wet season so the water carves out grooves. These grooves are about 1.5 metres deep leaving a ridge along the top. The ridge of course, is slimy wet mud. They don't run in nice even lines down the hill; they split up so the path you've picked can lead you to a dead end and reversing along a ridge is impossible, especially when you've never done it and the other guy's losing it on the back seat. I helped where I could by directing him, but he did most of it himself. Bill's driving was impressive; this was mind-blowing. Slip off one of those ridges and the Land Rover would topple. No winch, no villagers when you need them. I'd wait after a bad stretch or before a broken bridge to guide him over. But, we'd run into sand flies, or bitey-bitey, as I called them. They are virtually invisible and they sting. When you scratch them they sting even more, like there's a barb in there or something. In fact, the bastard blood suckers inject spirokete into the bite so that it won't heal. These attacked my ankles whenever I stopped. I got pretty good at the Highland Fling. At breaks I'd sit with a towel around my legs, listening to Johann curse in his heavy Swedish accent: 'I hate all these small animals in the air!'

Wearing trousers didn't make much difference because they'd get

under the hem and get stuck in there. And then there'd be the rubs
from the damp cloth on my skin and fungal infections. These bites
were the cause of the tropical ulcers.

In the forest and the desert, wounds don't heal easily. The bite
gets infected and spreads out through the flesh down to the bone in
a cone shape. The top crusts over, so you think it's healing. You
have to keep them wet so they spread upwards. We didn't go in for
antiseptic because it corrodes the good tissue too, so we washed
them with salt water, sprinkled them with antibiotic powder and
bandaged them. I had about thirty on my legs. It's a deep pain, worse
when standing for the first time after a break. Sometimes my legs
would shake from all the poison. It took about an hour each evening
to clean up and dress them. We'd use Johann's tent because it was
mozzie proof having sprayed and scanned it with the torch to make
sure it was free of insects.

Food was hard to come by. Sometimes the Zairois wouldn't sell us
anything. We were standing in a field of pineapples one day and
asked if we could buy one. The owner said no, probably because we
were white. We ate bananas and pineapple during the day and rice
with whatever we could buy – impala, eggs or something in the
evening. One time, Raymond found a tortoise for supper. We hadn't
had protein for quite a while. We were shown into a gravel pit near
a village by some hunters and they gathered to watch us. Raymond
hit the tortoise on the head with a hammer. It lay there with its
tongue sticking out. Minutes later, he looked up from the fire to see
the tortoise walking away in the direction he'd been going before.
Raymond knows how to kill an animal with the least amount of pain,
but no amount of coaxing would get the tortoise to stick his head
out so Raymond could chop it off. Not even a paracetamol. Raymond
has killed and eaten many animals; he has a great respect for them
and has never wasted anything of an animal. This is the Indian way
and I agree with it – there is nothing wrong with killing and eating
an animal if you need it, but to waste it is appalling. He thanked the
tortoise and then ripped its shell apart. It gave us food for three
days. The first night we had stew. I got the oesophagus – at least it
was better than the shell – and then it was another stew with
vegetables and then it was soup.

Impala was my favourite meat – tender and sweet. We'd tenderize
it in pineapple juice for about half an hour or cover it with papaya
slices. Any longer and it began to disintegrate.

Raymond and I took it in turns to cook and Johann always did the washing up. He didn't like cooking and enjoyed the praise we gave him for cleaning up. When it was all done, we'd relax by the fire, smoking and listening to music. Johann liked heavy metal, which was a bit hard going at the end of a noisy day so he listened to it during the day and played something more atmospheric at night. It was good that we gelled, because around the corner from Buta, we hit attacks – big time.

A woman had warned the boys that ahead lay people who were aggressive. She said they should stay close to me or – and she drew a line across her throat.

22

The worst of our troubles were the villagers between Buta and Gemena, a stretch of about 1,000 kilometres that was a tourist trail. It was a bottleneck of overlanders: Angola was at war, so was southern Sudan; there are no other routes. If you wanted to go to southern Africa, this was the way you went. We had experienced the change in attitude from pushing the cart to sitting on the truck – the villagers were incredibly hostile when they saw the truck. Hardly surprising, since not all overlanders have respect for the locals – they charge through the villages running over chickens, they buy up huge amounts of food in the markets, they're rude at camp and they've got a lot of pretty things in their trucks. The villagers don't know where they come from – they just see a truck passing through from left to right. Everything in the village can be replaced from the forest, so they think all our things can be, too. The kids see a truck and swarm, yelling, 'Donnez-moi le Bic', or 'Donnez-moi un cadeau' – give me a Bic (pen) or give me a present. They stone the trucks and if one gets bogged they have a field day. The passengers are irritable because of the forest humidity and sores and digging out the truck only to make a few kilometres before it bogs again. They fight back. The kids love to see whites losing their temper – like we all watched McEnroe.

So when they saw a white walking through the village alone, they had a riot. They'd stream down between the houses to the track and set up their hollering. I'd greet them and wave at the elders. But there was little chance of getting them to play any games – they wanted to beat the shit out of a white in retaliation for the last truck. It got so bad that the Land Rover had to keep me in sight, waiting at the end of a village or just before as I walked ahead. They attacked it, too. Climbing on the sides, some tried to slit the rubber around the windows, others getting their hands under the roof tarp, little hands darting into the cab to grab something before the drivers could stop them. Raymond would slam the brakes on hard and they'd crash into the back. That was the only way to get them off.

He told me what was going on behind me – men would hear the kids yelling and saw them surrounding me and they drew their pangas. Then they'd hear the Land Rover and sheepishly put them away. At the breaks there would be a gathering which wanted to get aggressive. The pressure was on to calm them, but they didn't want to be calmed – not like the ones down south, who'd never seen whites. At day's end camp, they'd set up the baiting. We'd ignore them after peace couldn't be made. But it gets like an itch which can't be scratched and won't abate. Raymond would try to chase them off, then the stones would start flying. They're good shots – I got one on the head which bled a bit. They get excited when they see blood. We'd get the chief. He'd send them home and leave a young man with us to chase them off. But then, as the kids grouped again, came that awful realization that he was one of them – like in a psycho movie when it suddenly dawns on you that your sidekick's an alien too.

One night we were woken from sleep by the shrill trilling of a bird in distress. We looked out of the tent at several dark figures clad in black feathers, moving around the camp in a dance. They saw us and started imitating animals, jerking their bodies, weaving their limbs, scuffing in the dust. They made noises which sent shivers all over my body. They had come to intimidate us, these boys, out in the bush to test everything they knew before their circumcision into the adult world. But they weren't sure how far they could go with us, not certain if we were the demon they should confront, afraid to turn away from us in case we were, in case we came from behind, in case they failed. How often did they see white people? What if the last time was in bad circumstances – even for just one of them? They left and we didn't sleep any more that night.

A thousand kilometres is about a month's walk. During that time we lost fifty kilograms between the three of us. We were hyped, exhausted and sick but the worse it got the more we were determined to get through. It came to a head, this pent-up aggression, when we hit Aketi. We'd been told by the other overlanders that a bunch of crooked immigration guys had set up a scam there. They'd stop a truck, demand to know everyone's occupation and ask them to prove it. If they couldn't they were arrested as spies. Like drawing a Monopoly card: pay $25 and get out of Jail. We didn't have that kind of money and we'd made a pact not to pay bribes when we had full rights and documents to travel.

Aketi was on the other side of a bridge which needed rebuilding – another scam. The villagers take the important planks and hide them; when a truck comes along they rent the planks and the labour. Aketi had the first market for several days – we really needed food having walked fifty kilometres each day on a third of a pineapple and a handful of bananas. I walked through first, hoping nobody would notice me – much like the troll under the bridge, I hoped they wouldn't hear me crossing. Then the Land Rover would hammer through. I'd asked them to buy some dough balls but they were caught as soon as they stopped.

A young guy halted them. He wore a kind of uniform but had no insignia.

'Passport,' he said.

Raymond refused unless he showed him some identification – he could be a thief. An armed soldier arrived on the scene and the crowd got very hostile. Johann got out to sort them out and got into a fight, punching the soldier in the solar plexus. Raymond charged after me in the Land Rover. He was chased by the first guy. When he got to me, there was a full-on battle. He snatched Raymond's passport and I ran after him, shouting 'Voleur!' The crowd ran with me but didn't touch me. I grabbed the guy and ripped his pockets to get at the passport – it had been handed on to someone in the crowd. Bloody hell. We now had to face the crooked officials. I rode back with Raymond to find Johann sitting calmly where he'd been left, smoking. We were taken to the immigration office some way into the village. The immigration chief sat like a big fat spider, waiting for victims to be brought.

We explained that the guy had no ID; they displayed mock horror that we should even think there were thieves in Zaire! Two lesser officials got into the conversation: one of them was hammering in my ear in French and the other was speaking English. We were just about getting somewhere, when I couldn't stand this aggressive shit any longer and wanting to shut him up so I could hear the other guy, I put my finger to my lips and said, 'Ssh!'

There was a pause of shock.

'Now!' said the chief. 'We stand ready to fight you!'

Hell was let loose. They refused to speak English, called me rude, bad and disrespectful. Apparently no woman in Africa can do that to a guy and get away with it. They arrested me and said I was going on a boat to Kisangani. All our passports were taken and the Land Rover was searched. Everything was taken out, flung around: all kit out of their bags, cutlery thrown out of its box, a whirring of black hands inside our Land Rover and many more to pick up stuff and run off with it. They were about to open my toiletries bag when Johann strode over, like Obelix to the Romans, and said, 'No, that is the lady's bag. If you want to look in there you ask the lady.' They backed off.

They took out our documents box and sifted through the contents. They confiscated the bow and arrow which the pygmy in Kisangani had made for Raymond as a Christmas present from Mike and Johann because it was spy equipment. They had a field day over the alarms and our knives. But when they got to a photo Raymond had sent me months before, we got into big trouble.

It was of a human skull in a pile of leaves. Raymond played a lot of practical jokes on the people on his courses and this one was his favourite, especially on women: he'd place the skull somewhere where they'd have to gather leaves. He called it 'Dead Head'. But the immigration guy looked at it as everyone gathered to look too and said very quietly, 'Did you kill this man in the forest?'

Try explaining it was a joke when you don't know the words in French and to people who don't share the same sense of humour. We were solemnly led into the office. The fat spider sat behind his desk, no doubt doing a bit of mental arithmetic on the going rate for a murder. It was time to scoff humble pie.

He lowered his voice and leant forward over the desk and said, 'The man has no insignia because we are undercover counter-espionage agents.'

'Ah, that would explain it then,' I said. 'You must have a terribly difficult job and must be so brave.'

I was unarrested.

'But,' he said when he'd let me 'go', 'you have given me a great headache. What are you going to do about it?'

'If you let me go out to the Land Rover, I'll get you some pills.'

This kind of crap went on for some time. Eventually he settled on an umbrella to keep the sun off his head and some bars of soap for the officers' uniforms, which had been messed up in the fight.

'We have heard from other overlanders that you are asking for money here,' I said.

'That is a dreadful lie,' he said.

'From now on, I shall tell all the overlanders that the immigration people are not asking for money if their occupation cannot be proven. They are honest men and have suffered the lies of other people. All they want to see are your passports to make sure all is in order. If they ask for money then they are not immigration officials.'

'Yes, that's correct,' he said, all fluffed up.

We packed up and drove to the place where I'd stopped. I got out and the same crowd began to gather as I walked through the village. Something went whizzing past and landed in front of me. Shit, I didn't have the patience for another stoning. I turned around to whack the hell out of whoever was closest, to find a group of eager young faces. One of them picked up the object and threw it again. It was a football and they wanted me to play.

Sometimes I walked with hunters or women going to market and we chatted, or laughed or just scuffed along together, chewing the fat, walking-style. But one day, a man who wasn't a hunter and didn't seem to have a purpose fell in beside me. He was pleasant enough in the bush but as soon as we approached other people or a village he started accusing me of something. The villagers came out and saw this and joined him. I got a good look at him one time when we had to stop for the barrage of people – it was a dodgy face. I took his hands and said, 'Thank you for escorting me to my husband, he's not far away and will be delighted to see you.'

Somehow this got him aroused. He pushed the crowd aside and said he wanted me to visit his mother. I explained my husband was waiting, but he grew more insistent and the accusations in company grew more aggressive. I took off my day pack and asked him if he wanted anything – it only had a banana in it, and some loo paper. The kids snatched both. He grabbed my arm and demanded I go with him to his house. I could see that his penis was erect – and that it's true what they say about Africans. I showed him my wedding ring and repeated that I was married. I was working out my moves to send my knee into his crotch when he ran off. Phew, OK, no problem. He'd seen the Land Rover before I had – Christ their eyesight is good; there was just a corner of the blue tarp showing through the vegetation some way off.

The boys had stopped to see if they could buy some eggs. When I got there I just cracked apart – not just that incident, but the whole heap of fear and stress from hundreds of kilometres of aggression, came pouring out. The guy who sold the eggs saw this and led us to his da and shooed away the kids. He heard what had happened and knew the guy. He was furious. He left us for a bit; when he came back he gave me two onions. To put this into perspective, the average yearly wage in Zaire is around £100, and an onion costs 40p.

You get humbled like that often in Africa. Another time, the Land Rover was ahead and a truck came up behind me. The track was so narrow I had to press myself into the forest so that it could pass. It leant over towards me as it went by. The passengers tried to grab my shades, and when the last guy couldn't get them, he thumped me on the head. Bang! Oh well, at least it was a different kind of pain.

I got a full-on pelt of rubbish thrown at me by another truck's passengers. The Land Rover was some way behind so couldn't chase it by the time I told them. They went ahead about five kilometres and parked up for lunch. A little old man passed them and stopped for a chat. He was wearing a Red Cross uniform and said he was a member. When he heard that a truck had pelted me he said, 'What? Where is she?' 'Back down the track.' 'Is she hurt?' and without stopping for a reply he went hurtling back to find me. They picked him up and explained I was OK.

We reached Bumba and had a rest day. We parked up in a garage courtyard and camped in a relatively oil-free corner where a dozen fat pigs rooted around in the sand.

Old Mr Fixit arrived with his henchmen who looked like their parents were closely related, and pretended he didn't know us – all whites look the same, too. We crossed a bridge on the track to Lisala and spent ages rebuilding it. A mission on the other side looked like a good place to pull in for the night but the Paludrine grey French jerk told us to go back to Bumba. It meant rebuilding the bridge because the locals had taken the planks again. You get a sense of where's a safe place to camp; Bill knew it and we knew it too. And this place stank. So back we went and met another group of overlanders.

Three days later we reached Lisala, Mobutu's country home town, and saw a sign for camping! We were met by the most charismatic, full-on good guy I'd ever met.

He greeted us with the words: 'What would you like for supper?'

As if that wasn't enough he then asked, 'Do you have any laundry for us?'

He showed us the shower and then asked what we'd like for breakfast. It just blew me away.

Through the next week the harassment continued, and so did the illnesses, the ulcers and the lack of food. We started trading for food – a plate for a bottle of palm oil, a fork for a pineapple. The local foods are chanterelles, snails, caterpillars, monkey and bat. I was offered a dead bat for supper for 5p. During one encounter with overlanders a girl mentioned the exact distance to Businga and the river. I broke the rule again by believing her. It was forty kilometres further – almost a full day's walk. But we had a fabulous rest day, swimming in the Mongala River and washing our clothes. Raymond put his trunks on for the first time and virtually disappeared when he turned sideways. Another month of wasting away and he'd have no immunity against the diseases.

He felt the Africans could see him so unnaturally thin and it worried him. All through the day, through every break and every quarter and every evening and all through the night, we were under attack. Mr Nice Guy didn't work at this pace on this tourist trail. We punched our way through northern Zaire but we were winning – every step was walked, food was always found, fires lit and laughter kept the spirits high. And on top of that, they protected the Land Rover and kit so well that nothing was stolen. That's the litmus test in a way. That's very rare on overland trucks, and they're professionals.

We were joined at the rest day by two Land Rovers. One of the drivers was a really good guy from Botswana. He asked if he could have some of our inner tubing to make a repair. We gave it to him; he then came back and asked if we needed help with the Land Rover. Neither Raymond nor Johann being mechanics, they were very relieved to have a full check over done. We ate goat and manioc chips and drank the bar dry of cold beer.

Two days later we reached Karowa, the mission run by the American refugee missionary we'd spent an evening with in CAR while pushing the cart. We went in to see if anyone was there. Two other missionaries had been given permission to return for two weeks to make sure everything was OK and do a more thorough packing-up job. They were so proud of their guards, who had kept people out during their absence. One lot of locals, though, had got in and had stolen some cheese. They ate it and were violently sick – it had been sitting out for two weeks. The doctor flew in after a day visiting outlying areas and came to meet us as we were being shown round by his wife. We talked of our ulcers, diseases and general malaise. He asked what we found to live off and we told him – fruit and rice. 'I know what you need,' he said as he walked into the mission.

He returned with a large bag of M&Ms! They were also in the process of defrosting their freezer, so we had arrived at the perfect moment and loaded up the cool box with chicken stew, minced meat, cheddar cheese and sliced white bread from Maine. They offered us their pump station to camp by because it had a crystal-clear pool and a guard. It was an amazing meal: cheeseburgers followed by chocolates.

The next morning, he took some blood tests from me because of my continuing kidney pains, but couldn't find anything wrong.

The next night, as we were cooking another delicious round of cheeseburgers quickly before it rained, a man came swaggering down the track with an empty palm wine container in his hand. He was trying to tell us something, pointing to the combo combo trees. We eventually worked out that they were about to fall on us – not obvious as they were alive and strong. But, we figured, being so porous, they'd swell in the rain. So we moved.

Two days later I walked into Gemena and saw my first EO truck. They were being hassled by an immigration guy who wanted some kind of document that they didn't have. I think our arrival distracted him, and the truck drove past us. It then stopped and the driver leant out the window and said, 'Bill told me to tell you that your carnet is waiting for you with the Greek guy in Bangui.' All right! It meant that Charlie had got the letter I'd given to the British consul in Kisangani saying the Land Rover had been found and I needed a driver, trip funds and the carnet.

I walked through the ruined old colonial town with its mouldy, crumbling walls and passed a statue of Zaire's symbol of independence – an arm holding a torch in flame. It looked to me like the embodiment of 'Not waving but drowning.'

We had heard there were missionaries in Gemena and went to look for them. They turned out to be two British middle-aged spinsters, linguists who were translating the Bible into Lingala, the language of northern Zaire. They showed us a place to camp round the back. One of them said, 'Perhaps you'd like to join us for tea and cake? 7p.m.?' That killed us.

We were all in a fluff over getting camp set up and ourselves groomed in time for 7p.m. We hadn't had a date for months and it would be really bad form to be late. We got it together and had chocolate cake with whipped cream made from powdered milk. It blew us away. Johann's stomach had shrunk more than he realized and he couldn't finish his piece.

The women had been at their task for about two years and it would take another two to get it done. One of them had translated the Bible into a language which had never before been written down, so she had to make an alphabet and spelling and work out the grammar, then teach people how to read. Some Christian concepts don't have words in other cultures, so she had to figure out a different way of explaining things – especially the resurrection. They were appalled to hear about the witch doctors we had come across and used.

We had a rest day with them, and Raymond went with one of their staff to his village while I did the washing and writing. Rest days were the only time I could make a place and get on top of everything. I didn't mind not going to the villages – I got an insight every day into how it all works. The boys didn't because they were in the Land Rover and greeted in a different way, just as we'd seen when pushing the cart. Raymond learnt that these were the Nbaka tribe who in 1964 had singlehandedly stopped the Simba rebels at Mobay-Mbongo. This was one of the major events in the war after independence. The Simba had so far beaten the military and the CIA mercenaries; the Nbaka were sent in to stop them. They did it with bows and arrows and their enemy didn't even know they were there. They hid in the trees in ambush, and their poisoned arrows were so sure and potent, the rebels were wiped out within minutes. A sort of Culloden in reverse.

Raymond's guide pointed out the bangbama (local name) tree, planted near most of the houses. Its bark is mixed with the latex sap from a vine to make the arrow poison. Another plant grown outside their houses was a fish poison – crushed in water, it kills the fish and they float on the surface.

'One leaf will send a man to sleep,' he said.

He pointed out several different medicines in front of most houses for women's problems – the sap of one was used as an internal wash after childbirth, another helped firm up the stomach muscles, others for stretch marks – a veritable fortune in the making for the Body Shop!

The guide also brought back a bread fruit and showed us the right way to choose one and how to cook it. It became our staple because it tastes so good, like soft, sweet chestnuts. Our other staple, rice, was an indicator that there was nothing else to eat.

We'd made a decision a long time back that we'd get off the tourist route at the first opportunity. There are two border crossings from

Zaire to CAR on this side – Mobay-Mbongo where we'd come in, and Zongo right opposite Bangui. It was reputed that Zongo was a den of thieves; in fact anyone who couldn't make money in a town headed there to learn the trade. One full-on day of hassle was worth going for rather than a week of daily attacks. So we headed for Zongo.

Then the forest broke – and there, for the first time, was open savannah.

And wind. It evaporated my sweat and it sifted through my hair. The villagers were different, too. Much more relaxed and welcoming, they hadn't seen many trucks and they weren't inside the forest. If it makes us irritable to be in there, it makes them irritable too. The change came at just the right time; much longer in the humidity and my sores were in danger of stopping me.

The week still had its attacks, though. Johann used bluff to get the people off the Land Rover and away from me, but in a small village one memorable day, someone called that bluff. Johann had run full pelt behind the Land Rover to scare off two thugs when one of them ducked into a hut and brought out a machete. He was running towards Johann too fast for him to get to the Land Rover. Raymond saw it and reversed up between them, Johann got in and thank God I was over the next hill so they could put their foot down and get the hell out.

That night we tried out the bread fruit. You put the whole thing on a fire with good embers and burning sticks till the nobbles are charred smooth, then you turn it over, short end down. This takes about twenty minutes. Next, you cut off the charred outer skin and the brown skin just below the surface – you need to have a bowl of cold water handy to dunk the fruit and hands in when it gets too hot. It smells so good at this stage that usually you can't wait for it to cool – but if you can, the correct method is then to cut it into longitudinal sections, cut off the grey furry core, and eat.

We added our own spin to the recipe by slicing it into triangle shapes and frying, Indonesian style. The result tastes like crisps with a gooey, bready centre.

I hate the build-up to a waypoint. We were now two and a half days from Bangui and I was nervous that it would not be as fabulous and restful as I needed it to be. I dreaded terrible anticlimax and disappointment. But a very much bigger worry was arriving at a border without carnet or visas, with very little bribing money, and with our Zaire visas expired – even though we had letters of extension.

As I walked on the grassy plains I looked to the side and saw the sky against the grass and felt the wind about me, and wished I could look again to the road and see England.

On our last night in Zaire we baked bread fruit, scarcely able to sit still for the excitement of getting to civilization the next day, and we voiced our fantasies.

Johann: 'Pizza restaurants with air conditioning and cold beers.'
Raymond: 'Showers, cool, clean, white sheets.'
Me: 'Privacy.'

Zaire had been cracked. We'd returned to Bangui with the Land Rover and ourselves alive – if not well.

When we had finished eating I wanted to remind them of something. We'd been out of contact with the outside world for nearly three months; we were in a state of innocence.

'We should chill out now and enjoy it,' I said. 'What we walk into tomorrow will put us in contact with the world and it might not be as we'd like it.'

We had dealt with life as it arrived in front of us; we had received no information about anything other than what affected us directly. We had complete direction over our lives: we must go find the Land Rover, we must get a pirogue, we must start from the right place, we must cover fifty kilometres a day – everything we did was for us and by us.

Sometimes you have to prepare for things that are going to happen which you might forget. By fast-flowing streams we had seen men stop and lay a flower on the bank before crossing – the flower itself didn't mean anything, they were told to do it to make them stop and consider the stream. We kicked back a while and watched the fire, mentally laying our flowers.

I walked into Zongo the next morning and Raymond and I went into the immigration and customs huts. We didn't have visas for CAR; we didn't have a carnet; our Zaire visas had run out and we didn't have any money for bribes. The immigration chief had passed me way back down the track and thought: this woman is crazy, if she can walk the length of Zaire, she can't be stopped. We got through the whole lot in an hour without any documentation and without paying any bribes.

We waited for the ferry on the sandy bank of the Ubangui River, looking over to the high rise buildings of Bangui, and thought of the day we had arrived there, in need of a cart, looking across at Zaire and wanting to be there. Our daydreams were cut short by the sound of someone trying to slash the rear tyre.

On the ferry, with the wind in our hair, the sunlight bouncing off the huge expanse of water, we punched the air – YEEEHA! The boys drove the Land Rover off the ferry and up onto the street to the immigration office and I walked off and met them. Raymond and I sorted out our visa problem – no problem; they were used to people arriving from Zaire without visas. They issued us with a temporary certificate and indicated where we could get a full one in town.

There was a yell from Johann at the Land Rover and a crash. We turned to see him chasing off a group of thieves, the back door of the vehicle open with kit half dragged out. The immigration guy shrugged.

We drove through the town to the post office and called home. I spoke to Luly: the funds were exhausted, there was no more money in London and Charles wanted his Land Rover back.

Then Johann called home. His nerves were just about shot any way, but when he put down the phone I could see that he was shaking.

'Bad news?' I said.

'My father is dying of a brain tumour. I must go home.'

23

High up in the Land Rover, looking out at the town, we felt in control as we drove to Vassos' apartment block. I jumped out at the front of the building while Raymond parked around the back by the swimming pool we'd dreamed of when pushing the cart. I ran along cool, airconditioned corridors to his office and found him standing in his sorting room, talking to a woman. I rushed past her and hugged him.

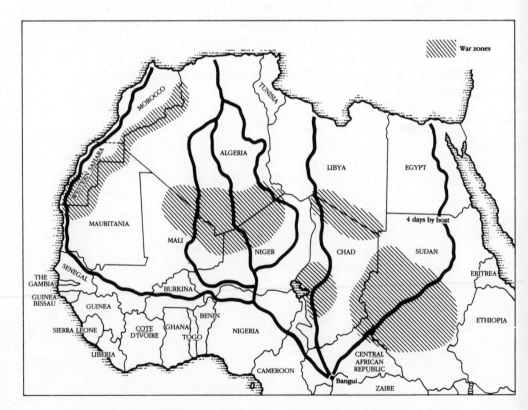

All routes north closed by wars.

Vassos was excited, surprised and relieved to see us. In hurried African French I explained what had happened. He had not received the telex from Uganda to say that we were going into Zaire, and had sent his driver to the checkpoint as per the previous message we'd sent via the missionary while pushing the cart. When we didn't show up for three days he was worried and sent his driver on a search, but none of the villagers had seen us. More concerned than ever for our safety, Vassos next sent word through the diamond network, which had an ear to the ground on most things, but they didn't come up with anything either. He feared that we had been intercepted by the Zargena bandits from Chad, who had murdered a missionary in the north while we were on the road.

Raymond strode through the door and pumped Vassos' hand. He introduced Johann. Then Vassos dumbfounded us all by saying, 'And may I introduce you to your new driver, Tim Kirkpatrick?'

I did a double take. The 'woman' I had charged past earlier was in fact a man, albeit a rather dainty one with blond permed hair and babyish big blue eyes.

He pushed a limp hand towards me and announced: 'I'm expedition leader.'

I nearly laughed. I couldn't quite grasp what was going on so I turned to Vassos for an explanation.

'Charles sent Tim down with the carnet in response to your letter,' he said.

There was a long pause.

The phone rang, and it was Charlie.

Very pleased with myself, I told him his Land Rover was with us and that Raymond and I were safe.

He didn't thank me for getting his lifeline out of Zaire. Instead, he said he wanted it back and that Tim was there to collect it and drive it back to London because the Niger/Algeria border was about to close.

Stung by his attitude, I said, 'Well I want reimbursement for the cost of getting it out and payment to Raymond and Johann at the normal driver rates for their work. And since I still have use of the Land Rover for another two months, I will keep it until the end of the hire period.'

Then I put the phone down.

There was another pause.

This time Vassos broke the silence by saying he would be delighted for us to stay with him for as long as we liked, but unfortunately his boss was returning in three days and would need to use the spare apartment. Until then, however, it was all ours. We went and got our day bags and took them up to the top floor, where we took badly needed showers.

Later, we assembled in the sitting room with its typically Belgian decor of cream-tiled floor, long sofas and dark polished wood bookcases with china ornaments on bits of lace. We stared at Tim like a committee of enquiry.

'Since you were two weeks overdue, I was sent down by Charles to look for you in Zaire,' he explained. 'I've been in Bangui for five days and was thinking of going into Zaire in the next few days to look for you if you didn't show up. I knew you would arrive though. I'm a bit of an old Africa hand – been up her three times, if you know what I mean.'

Johann had disappeared after his shower but now returned with a very large bar of chocolate for Raymond.

'Happy birthday,' he said.

Johann was very good at sussing things out and had also found a place where we could stay, the Peace Corps auberge. We went over to meet the owners.

Del and Jack Crain were American expats, of about retirement age. They'd come to CAR with the Bahai faith and had taken over the running of the auberge; Jack also worked at the American ambassador's residence as a handy man. They sat us down in their homely living room and brought out a large box of homemade chocolate cookies. They agreed to let us camp in the garden and have use of the showers and da. I told them we might be there for a couple of weeks and we struck a deal on a price per night.

We then went to a fabulous pizza restaurant to celebrate our arrival and Raymond's birthday.

A month after we arrived in Bangui we were still without answers or direction. Team morale had plummeted and rash decisions were made hastily by Raymond when he realized the consequences of time delays. Johann flew home at the height of his father's illness and Tim, who had arrived ill with hepatitis, seemed to have lost all confidence in himself and in Charles, and was drinking away his sorrows.

I was still physically ill with crippling stomach cramps, severe pains in my kidneys and urinary tract, and constant diarrhoea. Whatever my condition was, it could not have been helped by the build-up of potassium from bananas and acid from pineapple which my kidneys had been clogged with in Zaire. I had been eating four bananas and a third of a pineapple and walking forty-eight kilometres on it. However, even that seemed luxury now; on our meagre funds we had precious little to spend on good food and Raymond had lost twenty-two kilograms.

The dispute with Charles Norwood dragged on, debilitating me even further. I billed him £5,180 for the cost of support from 20 December (when we were in Kisangani) to 20 March, the end of the contract. He had injected £2,800 via Tim, and so I wanted the balance. This would cover the cost of Raymond's flight and wages, Johann's wages, and the diesel and vehicle parts when getting it out of Zaire.

His position was that he hadn't asked us to rescue his Land Rover and had been planning to recover it on his own. He would not accept that I had the right to use the Land Rover until the end of the contract and that I had already paid for it.

The logistics of phones and faxes were very difficult. Up till lunchtime I waited in the British consul's office for calls. In the evening, the local Bahai faith dentist allowed us to receive calls. If I wanted to make one, I had to take a cab into town with someone because the thieving was so bad, and call from the post office where I could also send faxes but not receive them: that had to be done from the British consul.

The head of French forces in North Africa tried to find us a route north but all were impassable: Sudan/Egypt was impassable due to the increasing spread of the Muslim/Christian war in Sudan; Chad/Libya was impassable due to the area of Tibetsi having been closed as a rebel militia stronghold at the border and the Lockerbie terrorists' trial would mean that, even if we did make it through the rebels, we'd probably be used as political pawns; Niger/Algeria had two routes, one of which was impassable because it had no water for a walking distance of one month and we could only carry enough for a maximum of ten days, and the other was closed due to the Tuareg nomad/Niger military conflict that had resulted in several white deaths and several stolen overland vehicles; Mali/Algeria was closed for the same reason and, even if it opened, we would be faced with another one-month stretch without water; Mauritania/Occupied Western Sahara had been closed for seventeen years due to the occupation of the Western Sahara by Morocco.

I decided to go up to the most recently closed border,

Niger/Algeria, which would take about two months. By then, fingers crossed, the problems might have been settled.

CAR, however, was a dangerous place. Bandits from Chad were raiding the road we intended to travel on – they'd robbed bus-loads of Africans of everything they had, including their clothes, and they had killed. It meant I would have to walk at night and we'd have to hide the vehicle during the day. It was hardly surprising that Raymond wouldn't go on the road with Tim, especially with Zaire still so fresh in our memories. There we had relied on each other every day to do the right thing in a crisis. Tim might well have driven the length of Africa three times, but it had been in a huge truck thundering along at seventy kilometres an hour, not in a Land Rover trundling along at six.

Raymond sent word via Luly to an ex-military friend, Dave Halton, to ask if he could come as a replacement. If he could, Tim would stay anyway, simply because it would be cheaper than sending him back. Dave said he'd give his answer after the weekend but he never got back to her. He was in a climbing accident and broke several bones as he landed in a tree, his jaw pinned shut by a branch.

During those six weeks of uncertainty, I was under incredible pressure to save the walk. Both Raymond and I felt like puppets: having gone into Zaire and got my walk back, we were now unable to control its destiny. We argued constantly, raging at each other over the most trivial points.

I spent one particularly distraught weekend mulling over my position. It was easy enough to summarize: I had no team, no money, no route north and a dispute over the Land Rover. Even if all this was sorted out, I still faced guns on all sides from the Zargena bandits. I should have found a way to pull everyone together, it was my walk after all, but I didn't have the skill.

Luly had been working on the walk for eight months without pay. Hardly surprising, then, that she didn't toss in everything and get on top of the money crisis – she had one of her own. She didn't appreciate my demanding tone either, but at £10 for three minutes, the pleasantries were short. After a month of waiting by the phone at the British consulate, badgering her to keep on at a marketing manager who was always away marketing, I finally spoke to Hi-Tec myself. I got my answer, but it wasn't the one I had been hoping to hear: they wouldn't give me the money, but they'd lend it to me. And they'd send out a press release stating how Hi-Tec had saved the TransAfrica Walk. More disappointing, they'd pay it in instalments, which would mean us having to drive untold kilometres to a bank each month and do battle with the bureaucracy, only to receive money in local currency that we'd lose a quarter on as soon as we had to exchange it.

I broke down in tears. I was over a barrel. I was trying to bargain from a position of weakness and it wouldn't work. I accepted. I had no choice.

Then we heard from Johann. His father had recovered and he agreed to come back and carry on. Maybe things were on the up.

We drove down to the far side of CAR over a weekend to meet a tribe of pygmies. Raymond and I left Tim at the camp and walked into the forest with the women who showed us many of their medicines. Louis Sarno, an American who was living with them, taught us about how they lived and how the aid agencies were messing up the careful balance of the relationship between the pygmies and the settled tribes. The pygmies spend several months in the forest then return to a tribe's village where they trade the medicines they have harvested and prepared for things they need which the villagers grow. They also work for them in their kitchen gardens; then they leave again for the forest. The Africans are frightened of the forest and will not go in there, and the pygmies play on this fear. The aid agencies had designated a camp for the pygmies away from the village. Louis couldn't understand why so many of the pygmies were coming to him with complaints of headaches and why they died within four days. He worked out that this area was rife with cerebral malaria, yet a couple of kilometres down the track the area was clear. He got them moved. They put the tourist camp on the site of the old pygmy camp and planted lemon grass to try to keep down the mosquitoes.

There are very few mozzies in the forest; they live at the edges. It was cool and clean in the forest as the women led us deeper inside. Their laughter was constant, they chattered like little birds and it lifted our spirits as nothing else could. We had lived day to day as they do during our journey through Zaire; we'd had control then over what we did and so do they.

We'd left it up to Tim to figure out the fuel needed for this journey. He got it wrong, which meant we had to drive to the Congo border in the hope that we'd find some smuggled diesel. We did, at astronomical prices. When filling up, a man was standing in front of him with his hand reaching up onto the rope of the roof cover. I had to tap Tim on the arm to draw his attention to it.

We had reached Muslim country in CAR. I spent much of those weeks of waiting making long dresses out of my sheets and duvet cover. I cut up my shorts and made a patchwork duvet cover. When Johann flew in soon afterwards with the first instalment of the Hi-Tec money, we were revitalized. We put in for our Cameroun visas, got the last of the kit sorted out as we wanted it, and prepared to restart the walk from the immigration hut on the Zaire river.

On the evening of 29 March 1992, I stood with Del, Jack and Raymond and watched the sun set. 'When it rises,' I said, 'I will be walking.'

We got up at 2.30 and stole through the dimly lit streets of Bangui and past the police checkpoint before the robbers could get their act together.

Even though the road to the Cameroun border was patrolled by French Foreign Legion trucks between the bases in Bangui and Bouar, the Zargena bandits seemed to be taking the piss by raiding travellers as closely to them as they could. There are various rivers and geographical ridges and valleys which run from Chad in the north to this road, which runs southeast to northwest. At the points where the features met, we would be very vulnerable. To avoid trouble on this two-week stretch, we had therefore worked out a new schedule to reduce our visibility in daylight hours. The bandits didn't attack at night because they liked to see what they were doing.

The routine was: 3a.m. start and walk a quarter to 5.30a.m. Then breakfast for half an hour, 6a.m. to 8.30a.m. walk the second quarter, then hide the Land Rover and the camp till 6p.m. when the last quarter was walked till 8.30p.m. We'd eat and be packed away by 11p.m., sleep for three and a half hours, then get up and do it again.

I'd sworn in Australia that I'd never night walk again because the daytime hours are too hot, too noisy, full of flies and herds of long-horned cattle with their nomadic herders having to yell and whoop to steer them around us on their way to water: no chance of sleep unless you're completely worn out. That kind of exhaustion is fine for a few weeks if it's then followed by some R&R, but not on a trip which goes on for months on end. Getting just three and a half hours' sleep at night was desperate, but there was no alternative.

Raymond would have to leave when we reached Cameroun to launch his second book *The Complete Outdoor Handbook*; then Johann, Tim and I would continue alone. We'd be out of the bandit area, but

Raymond wanted to have pulled the back-up together by then so that he felt I was well supported. Tim's attitude of, 'It doesn't matter to me if this walk succeeds or fails, I'll still get my pay cheque' had to be changed or we couldn't rely on him. One of the best ways to do that was to get them to walk with me for a quarter so that they got an insight into just how much effort was going into the walk. I couldn't help but walk at my own pace, however; if they lagged behind, which they did, that was their problem.

The team split in two – Raymond and me, and Tim and Johann. I thought that Johann had perked up under Raymond's influence, but now he found a new leader and he copied him.

And then, the mango rains began. These are the intermittent rains which come before the wet season, and are so called because it's the time when the trees bear fruit. It's also the time when there is nothing to eat except mangoes. They are sickly, slithery and taste like soap, and I hated them. However, Raymond perfected a way of cooking them into a pie and my opinion changed.

We were not really set up for rain; there simply wasn't enough room to carry all the extra equipment. So we trudged all night through the downpours and lightning that lit the sky like the veins on a cabbage leaf, only to get to a bedraggled camp of wet people, wet chairs, wet firewood and only one dry tent. We'd try to sleep in the storms, in a leaking tent, then get up in the wet dark and walk through till morning. It became humid and close as the sun dried the land and we'd brace ourselves for another onslaught, for this was the perfect weather for mozzies. It was impossible to sleep through their biting frenzy and high-pitched, whining torture.

The roads were corrugated like washboards, jarring our already tired backs. Men and kids came running up behind us, instilling the same fear we had known in Zaire, but all they wanted was to offer us a little monkey or a baby rabbit. Often they asked for cigarettes, but when Raymond told them that ours was a very long journey they apologized.

Raymond was diligent over cooking, the only comfort factor in our lives that we had any control over. We'd bought a cook book from the Peace Corps which was full of great recipes using local foods. Apart from the African dishes we knew well, there were American ones like quiche, cakes, breads and cookies. We'd worked out how to construct and operate a Dutch oven: a large iron pot with three small stones in the bottom on which a smaller pan stood. The pot was covered by a lid and set on an ember fire. Some delicious meals emerged from that oven and Raymond tried to coax Johann and Tim into using it – or at least the recipe book. But – no Coke, only pasta and tomato paste.

Up on the hill plateaux, the air was clean and the views out across the undulating green and blue bush made the villages look more friendly than the stagnant claustrophobia of Zaire. One day, losing the battle for sleep, Raymond went walking and found a ravine. He followed a stream down through layers of vegetation from savannah to subtropical to a tangle of jungle vines, until he came to a spectacular waterfall. He came back and fetched me and we had the power shower of our lives. I felt cleaner than I had for months, and washed my clothes.

We would have climbed to 1,000 metres by the time we hit Bouar. The road was one long hill, broken by flattish stretches where villages perched. They all looked grey from charcoal and smoke.

Raymond's feet had swollen as if with elephantiasis, the result, we both suspected, of the mud in the waterfall. He took Piriton but there was only a small reduction in the swelling. My 'ovarian cyst' was still plaguing me with severe, stitch-like pains.

For days we headed uphill until the land lurched upwards with Bouar on the top. We climbed around boulders as big as houses, below us a sea of mountain ranges worn smooth by the morning mists – a great strategic position for the French military base. I knew I was close to good food, which made the absence of an invitation to breakfast all the more frustrating. We parked amongst the mango litter and got a lecture on smoking from a black Jehovah's Witness who tried to convert us with a picture book – he was obviously taken with the drawings and had accepted the faith.

Unimpeded by doughy baguettes or any other delicacies, I came down from the summit to a flat valley which stretched to the far mountain range some sixty-five kilometres away. As the boys drove ahead in the last quarter the sky turned a mighty black behind me. I kept looking back at it, enchanted and totally innocent of what was brewing. Then I caught the full force of the wind and had to fight to keep my balance. The rain, glinting in the sun, hit my face and ears like silver bullets. My cheeks were bruised as battered and cold I sought shelter under a mango tree – something you're not supposed to do during the rains because the fruit are so heavy when they fall. I danced under the tree, not in joy, but to keep warm, for forty-five minutes.

The boys didn't come and I was faced with walking ten kilometres in a freezing cotton dress clinging to every contour of my goose-pimpled skin. The rain eased and I stepped out and walked through a deserted village, my thumbs under my dress straps to hide my nipples. When the Land Rover arrived I screamed: 'Why the fuck didn't you come for me?'

Johann and Tim said they'd been driving all the time.

What had actually happened, Raymond later told me, was that they'd found a campsite, realized for once that it was going to rain, and had started putting up the tents. Because I didn't have any waterproof clothing with me, they should have returned at once. Raymond was out of it: he had malaria again and was busy trying to put up his tent in the storm so he could sleep.

'They just hung around and watched me,' he said. 'I had to tell them to go back for you.'

His suggestion was at first met with blank expressions; then they shrugged and got back in the Land Rover. The attitude was frightening.

After two and a half really tough weeks we reached the Cameroun border. We crossed without problems and spent the night at a mission with rooms for rent at Garoua Boulai. It was good to be out of the rain.

Raymond sorted out his kit and we drove to Yaounde in time for 14 March, the due date of the next instalment from Hi-Tec. We'd pushed hard to get there on time and I looked forward to cashing the cheque and treating us all to a little something from the patisserie.

We had met the ambassador in Bangui and went now to the British Embassy to see if we could stay with him. We had very little money and city prices would drain our funds. He was away, but the deputy head of mission, Brian Donaldson, offered us his courtyard to camp in.

Tim collapsed with malaria. We made him comfortable in the roof tent and started a Halfan course while Raymond and I went into town to call Luly. The answering machine was on. We tried seven times that day but she wasn't in. We left Brian's number, asked her to call us, and went to the most expensive hotel in town and pitched them for free rooms for the night. They agreed.

With Tim settled in a five-star room, we called Luly again and left the number of the hotel.

The next morning, we called her again.

For three days we called.

Raymond needed a flight out and it was less expensive to fly direct from Douala, a few hours' drive away. Tim recovered enough for the journey and we got a room at a Catholic mission which rented out rooms to travellers. Geographically, Douala is the armpit of Africa. Well, not just geographically. Next Johann came down with malaria. It wasn't pleasant. He got delirious, and his forehead was so hot at one point that you could have fried an egg on it. Luckily, he responded quickly to Halfan.

There wasn't a flight for several days, so we stayed put and called Luly. Eventually, she answered. She'd been on holiday with her boyfriend and hadn't left a message to say when she'd be back.

'Actually, the money hasn't come through from Hi-Tec yet,' she said.

'Why not?' I demanded.

'It's slightly my fault,' she said. 'I haven't badgered them about it. But don't worry, I'll get on to them.'

I exploded. The cheque needed to be raised, sent to Luly's bank, cleared, then sent by telex transfer to a bank in Cameroun where we'd receive it in local currency. This meant at least another week's delay, on top of the four days we'd already spent there. It had cost us a month's walking money at £200 per week just to get to Douala, and was costing us £50 a day to stay there. I needed every penny of that money for the walk.

We couldn't wait in Douala any longer; I just didn't have the money.

Raymond got a flight and we all went to the airport to see him off. The two of us walked away for a moment.

'You did it,' I said. 'You got me my walk back.'

'I'll get on to the money situation as soon as I get in,' he promised.

I waved goodbye to a man of honour, and turned back to Johann and Tim. We drove back to Yaounde, where Brian welcomed us again and gave us bedrooms when he saw the condition of the drivers.

Raymond called from England. I told him the money hadn't arrived and I hadn't heard from Luly. He called her. She heard his voice and his request for an update on the situation and screamed: 'I'm sick of you people!' and slammed the phone down. He called her again and she did the same thing. He called me. Fuming, I asked him to get onto Hi-Tec himself. Luly called me, and I told her she'd have to apologize to Raymond and get the money transferred to us immediately. She borrowed £2,500 and wired it to us.

I went to the bank the next day, presented my passport and asked for a telex transfer from Standard Chartered in London for £2,500. The teller looked through her list and pointed to my Christian name, which had been spelt with an 'I'.

'So your money hasn't arrived,' she said.

'It's a spelling mistake!' I said.

She shook her head. 'No, it's not your money.'

'Don't you think it's slightly unlikely that there's another person with the same surname, the same Christian name and the same nationality, calling at the same branch for the same amount of money from the same branch in England? I mean, do you think that's logical?'

'It's not a question of logic,' she said, 'it's a question of doing things by the letter.'

I called the manager and eventually persuaded him that I was indeed this person.

That's the problem with Africans handling western bureaucracy: they've had the system hammered into them but they don't know what it means. It happens with everything: I'd get to a border and they'd see that my passport would expire in 2001, which, they thought, meant I couldn't use it until 2001. Coupled with that are the scams: a set of traffic lights in Yaounde was broken – they'd flicker on and off intermittently. A traffic cop had figured this out and plonked himself by the lights to nab any expensive car when the lights were out. He pulled Tim over and said he'd gone over a red light. He wanted to see his driving licence. As always, he pocketed it and said Tim could either appear at the bureau the following afternoon and pay a fine or pay something now. Tim said he'd collect it tomorrow and drove off; fortunately, he had two international driver's licences. The expats just shrug at this sort of thing and say 'WAWA' – West Africa Wins Again.

Now that the bandit problem was behind us, the old routine resumed, but the support was as slovenly as ever. They'd leave the water jerries in the sun and they'd park so that the shade fell on the road. I asked them repeatedly to get it together, but nothing changed.

I started to get hassled on the road. Two guys tried to reach inside my dress but I sidestepped in time and screamed at them.

'I am a stranger in your village and should be welcomed!'

They laughed – the bully-boy laugh known the world over when men assert their physical dominance over women and play on their natural fear. I resolved to start a charity called 'Bromide for Africa' to dump vast quantities of the stuff in all their water sources.

The villages were either of round huts with thatched roofs and plaited-grass walls around their compounds, or square mud houses with tin roofs and mud brick walls around their compounds. Whichever, they were full of the bovine smell of dried dung, and empty of laughter.

I was rarely greeted and the kids still demanded cadeaux. The grown-ups bullied their beefstock too – I saw one animal collapse under their beating and I told them to stop hitting it.

'It's exhausted,' I pointed out. 'It won't fetch a good price if you kill it now.'

My right hip felt as if a sharp splinter of bone was sticking into my buttock. My back was also very painful, my ovaries were hurting inside me like tugged stitches and the nausea made me light-headed and worried.

It became incredibly hot, around 50°C. The terrain changed from wooded savannah to bare green hills the shape of mangoes, then a landscape that was one big plain dotted with worn-down volcanoes and little else. The Fulani are a graceful and beautiful tribe, but they are quite shy. Contact with the locals had petered out, which was great on the one hand because I wasn't getting stoned or harassed, but it meant on the other that I missed walking with women to market. Until they weren't there, I hadn't noticed just how much I'd relied on their company during the long hours of solitude.

At the end of the next week we reached Ngoundere. The map indicated a waterfall – Les Chutes de Telo – about fifty kilometres through the bush from the town, which sounded to me like a perfect rest day campsite.

We got there after dark and quickly set up camp. The boys slept in late the next morning but I was up early and went in search of the falls. The river was little more than a stream and I found only a few rapids further up. Then I walked down the way and heard the sound of white water. I came to the edge and looked over. It was a stunningly beautiful sight: a great canyon where water tumbled several hundred feet below me into a still, green pool with a beach and a large rock that protruded into it. I went back and got my laundry, toiletries and bathing suit and climbed down.

I spent a glorious day washing my clothes on the red monolith and showering under the fall, exploring the cave behind it and sunbathing. I fell asleep and was woken by shrill squeals. I scanned the dark vegetation on the far bank for telltale black limbs, but saw nothing. Thinking the sounds could be those of the bird which whistles with a 'come here' call, I lay back.

Again I heard the shrieks over the thunderous sound of waterfall. I sat up, and there, flat against the rock, under the overhang behind the falls, was a line of small white children, perhaps twenty of them, holding hands and moving steadily across guided by a couple of adults. As they neared the edge they made their way down to the small shower fall and darted in and out, shrieking at the cold and ferocity. Lying on my rock, I watched them for a long time. I hadn't seen white children in bright summer clothes for many many months – perhaps a year. When the adult male looked at me, I waved and he waved back. Then I lay down again, feeling the cool as a cloud sailed between me and the sun.

The shrilling died away, and when I looked again there was no sign of them; I wondered if I had been looking at something which had happened long before, a ghostly scene of some terrible accident when Cameroun was under colonial rule.

The clouds thickened and I knew it would rain.

I climbed back up to camp where Tim and Johann were sitting in a mess of flies and cigarette stubs, music blaring, all the dirty contents of our lives spread out on the ground between pats of cattle dung. This wasn't a camp; I had to tidy it up. I had to pry them away to look at the falls.

I organized the camp when they were gone. They didn't mind living in the clutter, yet just a little organization and we wouldn't have to trip over everything; cooking things together, washing up bowls and jerries lined up nearby easy to use. When they cooked and ate they sat squashed up amongst the dirty pans and peelings, balancing and picking their way between the mess. You can tell the state of morale by the state of the camp.

They returned and didn't utter a word. Then Johann said, 'Yeah, the falls are all right I suppose. Nothing spectacular though, I've seen better.'

Nothing improved in the days that followed. I walked along the edge of the Benoue National Park and got a fright when attacked by buffalo fly. They're not as bad as tsetse but they torment.

I baked a cake to celebrate Day 400 but as I was preparing it I worked out the dates and realized the occasion had passed a week before.

Bows and arrows were back. Little boys practised between the maze of mud dwellings in a village; I pretended to shoot them with an imaginary bow and they joined in the game at a distance till I fell, mortally wounded. They were delighted.

The sound of chopping echoed around the great granite crags as I wove my way down the mountain range. Finally I spotted a woman just as the tree she'd been hacking fell with a great whoosh and a cloud of red dust. She stood back, slapped the dirt from her hands with pride and laughed as she heard me calling 'Bravo!'

We shook hands and I congratulated her.

The bush was just low scrub with the occasional thorn bush or neem tree – refreshing because it spits on you. The landscape had changed within a month's walk from thick, dense rainforest to dry savannah and semi-desert. The game was limited to gazelle, baboon and monkey but it was lovely to watch them and gave me some distraction from the gracelessness of the drivers.

The hot winds began to blow off the Sahara and I found myself overheating. I arrived at one break to find the boys had left the water in the sun and the back door open as they waited for me so they wouldn't have to do much when I arrived to refill my bottle. The sun had baked the water, but they didn't care.

Out walking, I'd duck under a wait-a-bit thorn bush when I felt that terrible pounding in the head of overheating. I'd use a little water to cool my face, then I'd stroke my skin with my finger tips which sent a slight tingle all over my body like shivering. I'd take off my sunglasses and talk to my reflection like an old friend. I wasn't walking with back-up now, they weren't a safety net. Time and again I'd get in late, but they didn't even notice. What was going to happen if I didn't arrive one day? Would they just pack up and drive home?

Another week and we crossed into Nigeria. The map didn't indicate there was a crossing at that point but everyone we met assured us there was. It was an old smugglers' route which had recently been found out and a post set up nearby. But the river which defined the border had no ferry or bridge. A bunch of opportunists hung out on the white sandy banks charging a ridiculous sum for pushing vehicles across. Dressed in renegade berets and leather flying jackets they offered their services for 50,000 Naira – (£100). If we declined and had a run and got stuck, the price would double. At that price you're either getting ripped off or it really is a dangerous crossing.

However, I asked the customs official and he said 2,000 Naira (£4) was more the mark. Tim waded the 500 metres across; the water came up to his knees and it was shingle bottom all the way. He came back, said he didn't need any helpers to push, but if he got stuck he'd pay 15,000. They agreed. He drove the Land Rover into the water and Johann and I walked behind to make sure they didn't leap on the back to drag it down. One guy got on the ladder but when Tim reached the far bank he gunned it at hell's pace across the sand, weaving from side to side to throw him off. When we met the vehicle at immigration the guy was still on and all the others demanded payment. Calmly we took our passports into the most relaxed immigration building I'd ever seen.

The officer lay on his mat in the grass hut wearing just a pair of trousers. He stamped everything that was put in front of him. When I left, the arseholes outside were still demanding payment for nothing so I walked out of sight into a line of baobab, Tim and Johann paid them a small something for showing us the way, then hit the accelerator.

Some kilometres later a checkpoint stopped me: Nigeria is one big police checkpoint with little bits of road in between. When the Land

Rover caught up they looked through our passports and sent Tim back to get them properly filled out; the laid-back official had failed to complete most of the stamping.

We only had CFA currency and needed to get Naira. I sent Tim and Johann ahead to Yola to change money, get some fuel, buy some more Halfan and stock up on food. It was a long way but if they were quick they could do it all in two and a half hours. It was around 45°C, there were no villages, so I carried as much water as I could; but the terrain was very hilly and I'd drunk most of it in the first hour.

I stopped after seventeen kilometres at the kilometre marker and waited for them. They arrived after four and a half hours, still with beer froth on their lips. They didn't apologize for being late and no, they hadn't bought any Halfan. And it went without saying that they hadn't bought me a beer.

I walked into Yola on a Friday afternoon and asked the guys to keep me in sight as I walked through town. Friday is not a good time to be out walking alone because Muslims do drink and after prayers they get rat-faced. Tim and Johann didn't fancy the hassle, so they didn't bother. The anti-Christian ravings got worse and worse as I moved through the village; by the time I reached the other side I was convinced I was going to be hanged.

A couple of days out of Yola, around ten kilometres from day's end, I saw a Range Rover pull over next to the Land Rover ahead. I prayed he was local and inviting us back to his airconditioned house with a cold shower and a swimming pool. It was so hot my nose had bled and my skin felt like parchment paper. The driver, the managing director of a vast cotton plantation, had indeed invited us to stay. And he did indeed have everything I had dreamed of – plus a video machine. We stayed for two nights and a whole rest day.

The next day out I got the shits. African shits are nasty. Over the next week I was hit by vomiting and diarrhoea that came on suddenly. I walked into one trading place, thronging with be-gowned merchants, and felt an urgent stabbing in my gut. With nowhere to hide, I leapt down a thorny embankment, ignoring greetings and queries, to relative shade. Sweating profusely until a herd of cattle and their curious herder had passed, I whipped up the back of my dress with one hand and steadied myself with the other. Bleating noises brought a crowd around me, all wanting to see what this strange white walker was doing that sounded like the killing of a sheep. When I felt I'd

convulsed my last, I kicked it over with dirt, responded weakly to
their enquiries as to my health and wellbeing, and with as much
dignity as I could muster set off on the open stretch of blazing
tarmac ahead. Dizzy and nauseous, I found the Land Rover two
kilometres later. It was one of the rare occasions on which I was
relieved to see it; Johann and Tim, of course, were having 'a nice
drink, lovey' in the shade.

The stomach cramps got progressively worse. I finally decided to
pack in the heroics and look for a doctor. I called in at a clinic and
it was diagnosed as amoebic dysentery. I took a course of Flagyl but
needed a couple of days' rest – I'd walked on Flagyl before and it
only made it worse.

We drove to Yankari Game Reserve to the Wiki Warm Springs
where Johann had been at Christmas. No overlanders had been there
for two months. I'd been looking forward to getting there since
Johann had mentioned it on the Exodus truck: there is a deep ravine
from the dry savannah where a natural spring forms a long narrow
lake of clear blue water with a white sandy bottom. Underground
water at 31.1°C seeps out from a great sandstone monolith at one
end and the pond becomes more shallow the further away from the
source. Sadly, the monolith was defaced, and a rusting pipe led into
a broken concrete shed stuck to the rock where they once used to
bottle Yankari water. It's now a lovers' bath and it was obvious from
the smell that people pissed in it. There was no life because of the
high mineral content, no decomposing vegetable matter on the pond
bed: just clear, clean, warm water that makes the skin prune to old
age. Fingers, swollen in the sun, shrink and rings fall off – one tourist
had collected 150 in the five weeks he'd been stuck there awaiting
the outcome of the Tuareg talks.

We spent two fabulous days there and then went back to the walk.
Tim got malaria again but I wouldn't give him the last of the Halfan,
starting him instead on a course of Fanzidar because he wasn't
allergic to it and I was.

Despite my medicine, my own symptoms weren't clearing up.
During the first quarter a few days later, I felt overwhelmingly tired.
I tried to gee myself up and shake it off, but I was falling asleep. I
got to camp forty minutes late and collapsed in a chair. The drivers
are supposed to keep a check on my time and come back if I'm
more than ten minutes late – this was the safety net and why they
were there. But Tim and Johann didn't bother. I took my temperature:
it was only 100 but I felt like death.

I said, 'Tim, I need to find a doctor. My head hurts. I feel very tired, I've got a temperature and there's a lymph node in my crotch which is hurting.'

As usual he made no visible sign that he'd even heard me, hesitating his standard thirty seconds before replying.

'Do you want us to pack up?'

'No, leave everything under the tree for the kids.'

Neither of them asked any questions about my condition; I just lay back and let them get on with it. They drove up and down and around and about without asking directions, until they eventually found the hospital in Darazo. Tim went to locate the doctor while I sat in the open-plan waiting room with benches for the sick and their entourage of cooks.

We were led behind a curtain into a doctor's consulting room, a dark, dirty and smelly place with a curtain to one side, behind which the consultation table creaked with its rippled plastic covered foam mattress. A good place to catch God knows what.

The doctor juggled patients, lab technicians, hospital finances and lift arrangements in English, Hausa, Fulani and local tribal languages and delivered the right tone of support or outrage with each. It reminded me of air traffic control at Heathrow airport. He examined me and found that *all* the lymph nodes in my neck, underarms, crotch, and backs of my knees were swollen. He instructed a male assistant to take blood.

The assistant had never done it before. The doctor did it instead and decided to make the operation an object lesson for all his staff. They gathered around and watched as he failed to find a vein, even though he'd plunged the needle its full length up a blue one.

'Don't worry,' he said, 'we don't reuse needles on expats.'

We sat around while they ran tests on the blood. I was restless and fidgety, rocking on my hands, getting hot and dizzy.

The results came back: double positive malaria, white blood count 5,000 – i.e. not a virus.

'That's good news,' he said.

But it still didn't account for the lymph nodes and he said he had no facilities for further testing; I'd have to go to Kano for that. He was about to detain us till the next day so I could have two shots of chloroquine but I suggested Halfan.

He agreed, then said, 'I must leave you now, I am needed in surgery,' and started running off to amputate a woman's gangrenous arm. Then he paused in the doorway and said, almost as an afterthought, 'You haven't been to Yankari and been bitten by buffalo fly, have you?'

'Yes I have,' I said.

'Then I don't want to frighten you but you should get to Kano very quickly.'

Tim and I went back to the Land Rover. Johann didn't ask how I'd got on; he didn't even turn to look at me.

I popped two Halfan and we sat in the Land Rover with Cokes. Tim didn't want to drive to Kano ahead of schedule and asked me if I couldn't just get myself sorted out when we got there a few days later.

Naturally I didn't want to break the walk, nor get to Kano before I'd walked there, but there was definitely something very wrong with me and it wasn't going away. He gave his gormless expression, which he called cool, before answering with a slight thrust forward of his lower jaw. While he was busy doing that I explained everything to Johann, who to his credit fired the ignition and started heading for Kano.

We drove for five hours, stopping four times for me to pee. On the last occasion it struck me how little they cared when they pulled over some way from a wall and suggested I get behind it. I could barely put one foot in front of the other and the wall was 200 metres behind us: the Land Rover could easily have reversed to it.

For five hours neither of them looked around or even asked a simple, 'How ya doin'?' I had to take my own temperature because neither of them knew how to read a thermometer – not what you'd expect from an ex-Exodus overland driver and self-styled expedition leader. I lay curled up on the back seat remembering all the care I had taken over both of them when they were sick.

We reached Kano, but instead of asking where the hospital was they drove around trying to outdo each other's directional memory and wasting time. Eventually we arrived, but not at the hospital. At the post office.

There I lay in the Land Rover with a temperature of 103.5 while Johann went to see if any mail had arrived for him. As the temperature inside the stationary vehicle began to rise I felt lightheadness creeping in and became more and more drowsy.

After some time, Johann came back complaining about African bureaucracy. It was Tim's turn to go in. Johann looked back at me for the first time in nearly six hours and saw my eyes staring unblinking, my mouth open, my breathing rapid and laboured. He gripped my hand, reassured me we'd get to hospital, then ran inside to get Tim. They took a while to come back out.

Tim told Johann to take my temperature, which was slightly closing the stable door after the horse had bolted, and he tried to stick the thermometer in my mouth. My mouth was open. It fell out. They bickered between themselves as to where the hospital was and ended up taking me to the eye hospital. By this time I had got myself wound up in confusion and anxiety and fought off Johann when he tried to get me out of the Land Rover. Aided by his restricting arms, I stumbled through the hospital grounds behind the nurse, between filthy outbuildings, going deeper into the degenerating decay of a once-functional hospital. My eyes were unable to focus and I roared odd exclamations at everybody.

The clinic was padlocked. The nurse indicated a bench outside and told us to wait. An African wait can take days. After half an hour a woman arrived, looked at the three of us and asked which one was sick. She unpadlocked the doors and led me through a filthy, damp waiting room into the consulting room. It smelt of stagnant piss; there was a cut-up foam mattress on a rusting bed; cockroaches fled to their hidey holes across a tray of needles in a dusty kidney dish.

Between bouts of hysteria and confusion, when Johann had more than three dimensions, I spoke fairly coherently to him, saying I refused to stay there.

The nurse returned.

'What's wrong?' she asked, bored and disinterested.

'I've got malaria.'

'I will take a blood sample.'

'Oh no you won't, it's already been diagnosed.'

Tim asked: 'Where's the doctor?'

'But the doctor is Egyptian.'

'I don't give a fuck what nationality he is,' I said, 'I need to see him.'

'You can't,' she said. 'He is in Egypt.'

My eyes felt on fire as we left. We drove to the International Clinic, where a clean doctor in a modern consulting room admitted us and didn't say much. I drowned out anything he might have said with my delirious rantings but I was still able to explain what the problem was.

He thought it was just malaria but wanted to run tests anyway, so

Johann led me upstairs. They gave me a private room with air conditioning, TV and fridge. It was dirty, dusty and full of mozzies, but private.

They took blood and shoved a drip in my vein. Nobody told me officially what was wrong with me but Johann heard one of the nurses mutter: 'Typhoid fever.'

The boys left to get Coke as I was very thirsty but didn't return for two and a half hours. The nurse wanted to give me a sleeping drug but I didn't want it till they came back. She kept asking me where they were. Eventually they reappeared: they'd gone for a pizza. They had, however, brought me some, which I devoured.

They then disappeared again, booking themselves into Kano's most expensive hotel and eating at Kano's most expensive restaurant. They had a leisurely breakfast the next morning, then rocked up at 10a.m. to bring me something to eat. I was starving and couldn't take my pills till I'd had food. Tim hadn't called Raymond, as I'd requested, to ask about my medical insurance because he said he knew I would get better.

The nurse gave me a very painful injection in the hand to make me sleep. It was painful because she had forgotten to dilute the solution. There were also bubbles in the drip which I was trying to flick out, and as I drifted into drug-induced sleep, I called out to Tim: 'Fucking make sure I wake up.' But I didn't get all the words out and I felt panic. I knew I couldn't rely on them to make sure I woke up.

After four days I moved out to the tourist camp. My kidneys started playing up again and I was urinating every twenty minutes. The room was oven-like, full of mozzies, and the loos were clogged up and overflowing into the shower area. There was only water for a couple of hours a day.

'Fuck this', I said, and I checked into the Central Hotel.

My room was full of flying ants. I called the manager. He wasn't in but whoever answered the phone said, 'Call back tomorrow.'

I called reception. I asked for another room and for the key to be sent up.

'De man is on break, he has de key' – the standard Nigerian response to everything.

'There must be somebody else?'

'No, you'll have to wait till he gets back from his dinner.'

And she slammed the phone down.

*

Tim went to the British consulate to ask their advice. He met Karen Blackburne, one half of the most knowledgeable, helpful and down-to-earth couples I'd met in Africa. She told me later that it took a while for her to get anything out of Tim because he just stood there. She directed us to the expat doctor, an Indian lady named Sanju, who ran more tests and treated me for a urinary tract infection.

Karen sent Tim to her husband, Harold, who managed Nigerian Oil Mills. He is an old Africa hand and had crossed the Sahara several times. He is also the British liaison officer in Kano and had set up a system for overlanders to post information at the tourist camp on the situation on all routes across the desert.

Harold was the man who got people out of trouble. If one of the expats was dying of a heart attack in the middle of the night when the airport was closed, Harold got him out. There was no bullshit about the guy; he was as straight as a die, modest and incredibly entertaining. He told Tim that all routes north were closed and that the danger zone now stretched down to Agadez, just two weeks' walk north of Kano. He hoped the situation would improve by September, in three months' time, but he couldn't be sure. He confirmed once again that there were no other means of crossing the Sahara overland. He then made Tim an offer which saved me a huge amount of money, not to mention anxiety: 'Park up at the workshops till it all blows over.'

So, I could walk up to Agadez but would then have to drive 2,000 kilometres to Niamey, the capital of Niger, to get re-entry visas for Nigeria, and then drive another 1,000 kilometres to Kano, park up the Land Rover and fly out. The extra week's wages spent getting visas and the cost of fuel for 3,000 kilometres wasn't worth the two weeks' walk up to Agadez because I hadn't a chance in hell of getting through.

I decided to walk up to the Nigeria/Niger border because when I returned I'd probably bring a Land Rover down from the UK and the carnet cost would be greatly reduced if I didn't have to enter Nigeria. We drove back to Darazo, where I'd stopped, and I 'swam' the 500 kilometres to the border on tranquillizers.

I reached the green-and-white striped barrier of the Nigerian border post and touched it. Then I took a walking stick one of the boys had left in the back of the Land Rover and planted it, saying to myself: 'Quarter's end, day's end, week's end, country's end, but this isn't walk's end. I'll be back.'

We drove back to Kano and camped at the tourist camp for the drivers' last night. We got blind drunk on some pretty foul whisky and I told Tim exactly what I thought of him. His response was to try to get me into bed. Christ, I would sooner have walked all the way back to Cape Town – on my hands.

Tim and Johann flew out the next day, having parked up the Land Rover at the Nigerian Oil Mills workshop. When Harold took the keys from Tim, he asked him what he would do next.

Tim's three word answer didn't surprise me.

'Retire from life,' he said.

My discounted air ticket to London was being sent by DHL, and Harold and Karen invited me to stay with them in their guest house for a week while I waited for it to arrive. I ended up going to the DHL office every day for a week.

'Do you have a parcel for Miss F. Campbell?' I asked on the seventh day.

'I am checking.'

He came back some time later.

'No, I don't have one.'

'Which name were you looking under?'

'Oh,' he said, 'I forgot it.'

You have to write these things down. I sent him back and sure enough, he had the ticket.

Walking back from the DHL office I had an inspired idea and went to the tourist camp. Just as I'd thought, the compound was littered with overland trucks and Land Rovers that had been parked up when the owners discovered that they couldn't cross the desert. It might be that in exchange for relocating it for the owner, I could borrow one to use as my support vehicle. I got a list of owners' names and addresses from the manager.

I was due to fly out from Lagos, getting a fare-paying flight down from Kano. The day before I left, Harold, Karen and their ten-year-old daughter, Cherina, took me out to their bush retreat. They had spent many years living in the forest when Harold was a tree engineer and even though Karen was very sophisticated, she had missed the bush life. So Harold had built a wooden hut by a stream with sunbathing rocks and a barbecue area with a table, and they went out there at weekends. I eyed the rocks, thinking how perfect they were for washing clothes. It struck me then, as Karen and I laid out our towels, that I must begin to look at things differently. I lay there and said goodbye to my way of life. Everything was going to change now: for me to go back to UK life was as traumatic as sticking a middle-aged PR executive in the middle of the rainforest and saying: 'Now walk out.'

I flew back to England at the end of June 1992 and parted company with Luly. I spent a couple of weeks traipsing round from one doctor to the next, one hospital for this test, one for that. My symptoms had got so severe that I was often crippled by the pain in my stomach. My parents secured me a place at the Royal Naval Hospital in Plymouth where they were used to testing for tropical diseases and hungry enough to spend a lot of time on me. I was in isolation for two weeks. They tested for everything but found nothing, so they figured it was Irritable Bowel Syndrome.

The papers ran a stupid story about how I'd left the walk because I was sick. It didn't help me to come to terms with what I had lost – this time was different from the first evacuation because there was no way of getting back there until the border reopened. I knew I couldn't miss out the war zone and walk on the other side because I remembered how I had felt when I tried that in CAR. And it was lucky that I didn't just hang out there waiting for an opportunity to cross because it wasn't until a year later that they started to let convoys through – and even then, travelling at eighty kilometres per hour.

I rang the Foreign Office every week for updates. I rang aid agencies, film crews and the overland companies but the news was always the same: nobody had got through anywhere across north Africa. Sudan/Egypt was ruled out from the start because of the military zone at the border. Everyone had to take a boat and I would have missed out four days' walk. No way. The border between Chad and Libya at Tibesti was a rebel militia stronghold and we wouldn't be welcome in Libya anyway because of the Lockerbie terrorists. The borders between Niger and Algeria and Mali and Algeria were closed due to the Tuareg conflict and the Mauritania/Occupied Western Sahara border had been closed for seventeen years because of Morocco's occupation of Western Sahara.

Raymond came to see me, but being alone was frightening – it brought back powerful memories of being trapped in Africa. It took over a year before we even felt safe enough to share a campfire in the woods.

A friend of my sister's offered me her flat in Brixton since she'd just had a baby and moved out. Although it was a sanctuary, away from the petty squabbles of flatsharing, it was damp, mouldy, dark and cold, and so, before long, was I. I tried to pick up the pieces and started on the book, but all my efforts went out of the window – quite literally – when the flat was burgled one night and they stole my computer and all my disks.

Two weeks later I was filling in as a carer for a friend of mine, Trevor Jones, who is paralysed from the neck down. I woke up to find a man climbing through the window. He fled when I screamed.

My life was falling apart. I couldn't get a job, I couldn't start anything new because I wanted my walk back and I didn't know when it would happen. I couldn't explain to anyone why I had left. To them it was the same old story. Friends would call and say, 'Fi! You're back! Did you make it?'

'No, all routes across the Sahara are closed due to ...'

Forget it.

I had never known such despair. I didn't have anything left. The weather got cold and miserable, I got pale and out of shape, my stomach cramps didn't go and I had no money. Like an Australian aborigine, I was in between two worlds – unable to go back to the bush where I belonged and unable to change to fit in with the western way. Like them, I curled up with a bottle and stared at the wall.

I went down to the Brixton dole office and was waiting to sign on when someone recognized me in the queue. She was a freelance journalist who had interviewed me in 1988 before I'd left England to walk across Australia.

'My God, Ffyona, you're the last person I expected to see here.'

I scuffed back to my damp little flat and called the overland companies, film crews, aid organizations and the Foreign Office all over again, but nothing had changed.

I needed to be with my people, people who had experienced another life. I called Mark Shand and met him for lunch, I spent several hours on the phone to a vicar, Geoff Howard, who'd pushed a wheelbarrow across the Sahara. And then I called Robert Swan. We spent two days together in Yorkshire, talking about everything from loneliness to how we are perceived. I didn't feel so isolated after that; both of us can be complete arseholes, but we cut the crap and it halved the burden.

After two months, I decided to go back and cross the desert with camels. It hadn't been a possibility before because of the seasons: nobody who knows the desert crosses in summer, when the temperatures reach 65°C in the shade (if there is any). For the plan to succeed, however, I would need an Arabic speaker to go with me. Trevor gave me the name of an old school friend, Alasdair Gordon-Gibson, an Arabist who was now working for the Red Cross in Ethiopia after seven years in Beirut at the height of the troubles and in Kurdistan. I sent him a letter asking if he'd like to join me. He wrote back saying yes.

Another friend, Anthony Willoughby, called to say he was in town from Japan and we went out for a drink. His diary was so booked he had to overlap on people, so I sat down with him and his first boss, Detmar Hackman, who'd given the young Willoughby a job as a copper bracelet salesman. I mentioned my fright with the guy coming through the window and we worked out that Detmar knew Trevor Jones too – in fact, they'd been to the same school, Gordonstoun.

Aha! So had my father and his cousin was the deputy headmaster. This opened up a very amusing conversation and we got round to what I was doing. I told them I wanted to try crossing the Sahara with camels. Anthony had run many camel trips himself through his company 'I Will Not Complain', which takes Japanese businessmen on expeditions to work on leadership skills. They have to sign a document saying they will not complain if they get eaten by mozzies, left behind, run over by a camel or whatever.

Detmar sounded very interested in what I was doing, largely because I had intended, at the time, to raise money for Trevor's charity trust on my Europe walk. The world got even smaller: Detmar was one of the trustees.

'I've taken on a PR company to handle my product promotions,' he said. 'I'll speak to them about sponsoring you – it might be a good idea. Perhaps we could meet next week?'

Perhaps the Pope is a Catholic?

He rang me a few days later to say his PR people did indeed want to meet me: they wanted to assess whether I had the charisma to carry it off. It was like a red rag to a bull. I gathered up an armful of feature articles and the videos of my best TV interviews (not the Wogan one, where I'd gone over the top on promoting sponsors – I wouldn't do that again), and blew them away. I wasn't so impressed by them, though. They didn't seem to have a grip on how big this thing could be, especially when they asked me to walk another 2,000 kilometres across the top of Africa so that I could do an interview with *Hello* magazine. When Detmar offered me the sponsorship of £15,000 I had a hard time stopping myself from putting in a condition that I'd take it as long as he changed his PR company.

Raymond put me in touch with a very good guy in Spain known in the expedition industry as Dr Diesel because of his skill as a bush mechanic. He'd run many camel trips and spoke Tamashik, Arabic and French. If he could be persuaded to come with me, I had a more experienced guy for this job than Alasdair.

I flew to Malaga to convince him to cross the desert with me. Jean Pierre was really excited about the project and we spent a couple of days poring over maps. But while I was there a fax came through from Harold in Kano. He said point blank that 'anything moving that smacks of a Tuareg is shot on sight'. What was more, all Tuareg were now restricted in their movements and the war zone had spread to the Nigerian border. It was another wasted trip.

I called Detmar when I got back.

'It's on hold until a border opens,' I said.

He said, 'Don't worry, Fi, the sponsorship is still on.'

Nicholas Duncan, the guy from Niagara Therapy who had heard me on the radio in Perth and got me some sponsorship happened to call a few days later and asked me to lunch while he was in London. Great, I get to eat today! He introduced me to the company's UK managing director who agreed to sponsor me in exchange for giving motivational talks to his salesmen. I could use this to top up the sponsorship money from Sabona if and when the project ever got off the ground.

It did. Life was suddenly breathed back into the walk in November when I got a phone call from a driver at EO to say that one of their trucks had managed to cross from Mauritania to the Occupied

Western Sahara. Sod's law again, however: it was the longest possible route from Kano to the Mediterranean, and would mean having to walk west for 4,000 kilometres before making an inch of progress northwards. But it was a way through!

The phone rang again with good news – *You* magazine had received a call from a man in the Middle East who had read my story and wanted to donate money towards my costs. Robin Allen became a kind of 'Daddy Long Legs' figure to me – he injected not only funds, but also a huge boost of confidence that I was on the right track. This contribution, along with Niagara's, would subsidize the sponsorship from Sabona, which only covered a three-month trip – and this would be at least six months. But with even the most carefully worked-out budgets, you just can't have a contingency for everything that Sod will throw at you.

I met Andy Sutcliff, the EO driver, for a drink and he talked me through the long chain of bureaucracy I would encounter when I got to Mauritania. The route itself was worse than I'd imagined – it meant crossing the Sahara without piste, which meant, in turn, that I would need back-up.

I wrote to Alasdair to ask if he would like to join the trip in a different form, as a back-up driver? I painted a pretty bleak and boring picture of the job, but finished the letter by saying: 'Really hope you can join me.' He wrote back saying he was sorry about the camel trip but he'd love to join me on the new one.

I still needed one more back-up driver and a few in reserve. I put ads in the Australian and New Zealand magazines and at the embassies. I wanted people who were already travelling because they wouldn't have masses of obligations to sort out to take six months off. Aussies and Kiwis are also more used to off-road driving, and I like their relaxed attitude and willingness to get stuck in.

I had about sixty calls and lined up meetings with the more promising-sounding ones. The interviews were to be packed in at the rate of one an hour for ten hours, for three days. On the eve of the first day I went drinking with a girlfriend, Anna Ginty. We tended to get into ridiculous scrapes together even though we hadn't known each other very long. That night I felt like climbing over a wall outside a pub but fell three metres and landed on my head – as you do. I took a cab to the hospital the next morning after being sick all night and bleeding a lot. They stitched me up and kept me in for observation.

For some reason my sister decided not to go to work that morning.

When the doorbell rang and my interviewees started to arrive without me being there, she phoned round all the hospitals. While she was bringing me a few things, Tom Metcalfe arrived at the flat for his 3p.m. interview. Getting no answer, he hung out at the pub on the corner for a couple of hours. When he tried again, Shuna was back and explained what had happened. She said I'd be in touch.

I discharged myself the next day, rearranged all the interviews and conducted them with a splitting headache. I'd also lost my sense of smell, but that didn't worry me. In Africa it would be a positive asset.

Shuna told me about Tom, saying: 'He struck me as a really decent guy.' After about thirty interviews I hired someone else.

Anna and I took him away for the day to get to know him. It turned out I'd made a big mistake: the guy was so sexually charged he was even sizing up the beer bottles. The first guy on the reserve list was Tom. He'd told me he wasn't a professional mechanic; he could improvise, he said, but if the Land Rover wasn't in good condition, he wouldn't be the right person. I called him and said I was going to France to get the lowdown on the Land Rover and if it was in good shape I'd like to offer him the job. He said he was going to Ireland for a visit and would be back in a week.

I'd called all the owners of the abandoned vehicles in Kano and now flew to Aix-en-Provence to meet the one guy who had said yes. His was a short-wheel-base diesel Land Rover in great condition – in fact, his friends took me aside and said not to worry about the engine, Laurent was very fastidious about engines. We agreed that I'd pay for the cost of bringing it back if he lent it to me for free for the duration of my walk. I gave him a deposit and £500 for a new carnet.

Tom called me from Ireland.

I said, 'D'you want to come to Africa with me?'

We booked our flights for 5 January, which left just three weeks to get our Nigerian visas, vaccinations and insurance, and for him to bone up on Land Rovers. I bought all the kit that I'd worked out we would need, and the right kinds of boxes to make the system modular.

I threw a couple of leaving parties and Tom came round the night before we left. I hadn't spoken to him much – there would be time enough when we got there and were our only company.

I'd put the cargo on an Air Nigeria flight the day before and

Trevor drove Tom, Shuna and me to the airport in his van. I kissed him goodbye and gave Shuna a big hug. I was relying on her now to organize all the logistics from London. Little did we know what a nightmare that was going to turn out to be.

W e flew Air Egypt because it was the cheapest, but the downside was that it entailed a night's stop over in Egypt. I figured we'd sleep at the airport to save money, or get a cheap room nearby. We arrived in Cairo to discover that the travel agent hadn't told us that Air Egypt would put us up in a four-star hotel with buffet dinner and breakfast and a tour of the pyramids and the Sphinx before the 9a.m. flight, all for an extra $10!

We checked into the Central Hotel in Kano and I called Harold to let him know we'd arrived. Then, full of anticipation, we went to check out our new Land Rover at the tourist camp just a short walk away.

It was in an appalling state: all the tyres were flat, the bodywork had been badly patched up and it wouldn't start. Tom had a go under the bonnet but this would be a long job – not just a case of recharging the battery. Harold sent a pick-up truck to tow it to his workshop.

Apart from replacing all the tyres at £100 a throw, it took two weeks to work out which part of the clutch needed replacing. The top can was replaced, then the bottom, and then came the awful realization that the problem lay with the clutch plate itself. The engine was a 1981 Land Rover 110 diesel dropped into the narrow space for the original Series III petrol engine. The fastidious Frenchman hadn't warned me about that little detail. The upshot was that access to many major parts was so limited the panels had to be removed and riveted back afterwards. I'd also lugged out all the wrong parts.

The state of the Land Rover was a considerable worry, a) because Tom was not an experienced mechanic, b) it was draining the trip funds and c) it was going to be our lifeline across the Sahara and by the look of it any number of things could start to go wrong. Harold came to our rescue by persuading his company to sponsor me with labour if I paid for the parts. It took his skilled mechanics a month of work to get it into shape.

The universal joint was replaced, the fuel system was cleaned out but at least the engine was firing on all cylinders. The electrics, however, were a dog's dinner, the result of patched-up, improvised repairs which didn't follow any logical pattern and dust getting in and causing short circuits. All the lights were replaced and the interior was gutted of its scraps of sheets pinned up across the roof and the windows, revealing great chunks of fibre matting. The previous owners had also overladen the roof rack, causing cracks down to the windows. These were braced, as well as the roof rack itself. By the end of it, the Nigerian mechanics had christened the vehicle Jagga Jagga, which sounded rather sweet, I thought, until I found out it was Hausa for 'junk'.

I bought an ex-military munitions trailer which Harold had found but it took weeks to find Land Rover wheels for it: they had to be interchangeable with the mother vehicle. We also carried two spares. A brake system was installed in the trailer to stop it crashing into the back of the Land Rover, an electrical hook-up was put in, a licence plate made and reflectors put on. To avoid paying import tax on it at every border (up to 200 per cent in some countries) it was then sprayed to match the Land Rover so that it looked like one unit. Laurent had lodged my bond with the French AA who issued the carnet – the log book, stamped at entry and exit of each country to prove that it is not being imported for sale – as an assurance that we weren't going to sell it.

The real value of the sponsorship was Harold's beady eye on the job and his wealth of knowledge of desert crossings. He put a huge amount of work into the project and gave us many of his own items of gear, including a trailer hook, snake bite kits, books, water bag and headlights. He also designed and had made the canvas awning of my dreams, as well as a cover for the trailer and a canvas envelope for the sleeping kit. The roof rack was still so weak that this was the only kit it could bear.

Harold and his mechanics had to fit this project in between their other commitments, so delays were inevitable. Each item had to be done in order, but as they worked on one part, they realized work had to be done on something else before continuing. Tom and Jamal, Harold's head mechanic, made many forays into the Sabongari market to find parts. Jamal's knowledge kept the 'white price' down but often a vital part which couldn't be found immediately halted everything. Then one of their own trucks would come in and need work and the whole project would be put on hold. I was sure that if Harold hadn't been overseeing the work it would have taken many more weeks, with tension mounting as the summer approached and the possibility of that very frail border crossing closing again ahead of us.

Harold lent me the services of his company's insurance man to get the 'brown card' which covers most west African countries. This went into the documents file with the carnet, the *carte grise* (French ownership document), a letter of authorization for me to use the Land Rover which Laurent got stamped by police in France and a translation of everything into English. I also carried a letter from Survival International saying what I was doing and why.

During all this time I felt irritable because there was very little I could do to help get the Land Rover on the road. I spent long hours getting the kit ready in one of Harold's warehouses and buying bits and pieces from the market. Laurent of Arabia and his fellow French explorers had told me the Land Rover contained all the camping kit we could possibly need – and then some. In line with their assessment on the state of the Land Rover, it was all junk. There wasn't enough space in the vehicle to carry theirs back so I gave it away.

Charles had collected Stormin' Norman, the first Land Rover, some weeks after I'd left and had driven it to east Africa. I'd left some of its kit with Harold, and Charles had asked me if he could use some of it because it would be useless for the camel trip. I'd agreed to lend him the fridge – which we never used anyway because it drained the battery – and sent Harold a list of things which I'd agreed to give back or lend to Charles.

Harold watched over him as he picked over the items.

'The medical box is mine,' Charles said.

And so it was, but not the contents. Half were mine, and I had paid £600 for them, but Harold wasn't to know that.

Then Charles said that the spade was his.

Harold said, 'Look, I'm not going to argue about a spade.'

Charles thought he was going to get it, but Harold simply shut the door and walked away.

Now that I knew so much more about kit, I'd brought down exactly what I wanted (see Appendix 2) and stored it all in boxes or bags that I'd made. Everything now had its own place: there was a wash box, a cook box, a day box, a camera box, a books box, and so on.

I'd bought several sleeping bag inners for making my dresses – the Egyptian cotton was so fine and soft it would reduce the rubbing. I cut out the fabric and sent them to my mother, who worked over Christmas sewing them up. I dyed them dark blue; it stands out well in all that khaki countryside and is the colour of the Tuareg, who must have worked out what was best. I sent them to Sabona for overprinting with their logo – not as a promotion on the road, but for the photos which would be taken during the journey.

The stickers for the Land Rover had been made up in the UK, and Detmar had given me a handful of gold-plated copper bracelets for gifts. Olympus supplied the OM4 camera and 50mm and 50–250mm lenses; Ian Dickens from Olympus had supported me since my walk across America, when he gave me a Pearlcorder dictaphone for my diaries. Unfortunately it was stolen along with all my tapes, diaries and negatives in San Francisco a few weeks after the walk finished, which was why I didn't write a book about that walk.

Tom and I spent two weeks staying at the Central. I then moved into Harold's guest house and Tom stayed with Harold's right-hand man, Zaven. He was an Armenian refugee who lavished us with hospitality. He took us racing in his buggy, showed us the town, and invited us into his circle of friends at the Kano Motor Club. They presented us with a trophy each, engraved with the words: 'TransAfrica Walk – Kano to Tanger'.

When the Land Rover was just about ready, bar a few small jobs, we drove down to Yankari to give it a test drive and to run through the camp systems. It took nine hours to get there over broken roads but it ran well. We nearly lost it though to a charging elephant: after two false charges the bull came on again and the guide told Tom to accelerate. Tom thought he meant drive away, but the guide meant rev your engine. Fortunately, the bull lost interest. The reserve was plagued by buffalo fly: now that I had the choice to get out of a swarm, I wanted to take it, but Tom hadn't experienced them before and didn't mind them. We were both viciously bitten. It was time to start taking our malaria prophylactics, bitter little pills which have to be chugged back with masses of water or your mouth retains the taste. But Tom didn't know that.

'You take two of these Paludrine tablets every day,' I said, holding them out to him. 'You've got to chew them very slowly and you mustn't drink water for at least twenty minutes afterwards.' He never forgave me.

Alasdair (nicknamed G) was due to arrive at the end of January and even before we met I was putting a lot of responsibility on his shoulders. Tom and I hadn't been getting on well; we disagreed about virtually everything and neither of us would back down. I hoped G would be able to soften the impact of these two motors wearing each other down. I liked Tom's feistiness, though; this wasn't the right territory for a yes-man.

We collected G at the airport after his flight from Addis Ababa, where he'd been working for the Red Cross for six months. My expectations were high, mainly because he'd cost as much as Tom and me together to insure and fly to Kano. As we drove back to the hotel, he told us that arrival on time from Ethiopia was thanks to my patron, Robin Hanbury-Tenison. G's application for a Nigerian visa had been plagued by delays and bribes. I'd sent him a letter of intent on my headed paper, with the name Robin Hanbury-Tenison OBE in bold across the bottom. The Nigerian official G was negotiating with sat upright as he read it, wiped his forehead and said most cordially: 'Ah, you will have no problem in the processing of your visa – your patron is a very important man in Nigeria, this Mr OBE.'

G brought a breath of fresh air. He was fun, he laughed a lot and I could see at once that he saw the bright side of life. But when I sat with him in his room at the Central, the first question he asked me was: 'How are we going to keep up morale?'

I thought it was an odd thing to ask, mainly because I didn't know what he was really asking. I didn't know then that G didn't want to be there.

The new route entailed walking due west to the coast through northern Nigeria, southern Niger, Burkina Faso, Mali, Senegal then north through Mauritania, Occupied Western Sahara and Morocco – a six-month journey if everything went smoothly.

The timing in terms of weather windows couldn't have been worse: I'd be walking through the Harmattan Wind which blows fine sand and mica off the desert and is bitterly cold for Africa, through the mango season when there's nothing to eat, and then across the Sahara in midsummer. I hoped that the coastal temperatures would be cooled by the Atlantic but I really had no idea how cold it was going to get. Anyway, I didn't have a choice – that border could close at any time: reports were coming in of tourists being caught trying to smuggle alcohol into the Islamic Republic of Mauritania. I was infuriated because this was the only route open to many overlanders and these idiots had jeopardized the chances for all of us just because they couldn't go without their beer.

G and Tom packed up the trailer and the Land Rover as quickly as they could but very carefully: the trailer had to be properly balanced because it carried all the water and diesel jerry cans along with the spares. Harold reminded them to take care on parking up and unhitching on flat ground: one overland driver had unhitched his trailer on a slope. The trailer lurched forward and popped his head.

Then, at last, on 5 February 1993, Jagga Jagga was ready to roll.

I started walking from the Central Hotel, which I had walked past on my way up north. It was 5 a.m., still dark and very cold from the Harmattan.

Zaven was there to see us off and take photos in the dark.

'Smile guys!'

I hate that feeling on the first morning of a walk; the week ahead would be hell. Settling in takes time, and it hurts – muscles stiffen, body sores develop from rubbing, blisters erupt on feet that have lost their condition; and on top of everything seethes the mental torment of training a new team. I had no rhythm and I'd be counting down the kilometres to a break: would they be there on time?

I'd replaced my usual baggage of western day pack and water bottle with local ones because I was sick of kids demanding them. I carried a Fulani shoulder bag woven from grass, a calabash for my water, and a broad-brimmed Fulani hat and wrap-around shades to keep some of the dust out of my eyes. G had bought an Arab scarf called a kaffiyeh for each of us from the market and taught us how to tie it. Mine soon replaced my hat because I could tie it across my nose and mouth as a dust barrier. It also caught the moisture in my breath and kept my face cool, and having something over my ears muffled the noise of the wind. But it wasn't enough to stop the nose bleeds from the dust.

Walking out of Kano along the old city wall, I passed a burnt-out truck lying in a ditch by a bridge – probably the loser in a game of 'chicken'. The religious slogan emblazoned across it just cracked me up: 'No condition is permanent.' I turned a corner and there was the Land Rover. The bonnet was up; it had broken down after just ten kilometres.

Tom's arms had disappeared into the guts of the engine like a vet delivering a calf. 'I think there's a short circuit,' he growled, 'which is causing the starter motor to kick in while the engine's running.

But this piece of shit's so wrecked, it could be anything.'

As I set off, Zaven passed them and offered to return to Nigerian Oil Mills to get a spare part. Tom improvised well, however, and soon had it fixed. It was going to be down to him to keep that vehicle on the road, and the responsibility weighed heavily. He knew as well as I did that although we had an offer from Harold to send a tow truck if we broke down anywhere in Nigeria, we wouldn't have that facility for the remaining 5,000 kilometres of the journey – and much of that was across desert.

Nigeria, as with most African countries, has kilometre markers every one or 5 kilometres. I reached the marker of thirty-four kilometres from Kano, which should have been the lunch break but the Land Rover wasn't there. Where the hell were they? Some time later it came trundling down the broken road out of the dusty Harmattan fog.

'We stopped at seventeen kilometres,' Tom said, 'another two kilometres up ahead.'

I insisted this was wrong. I know what seventeen kilometres feels like whether I'm fit or not.

When Zaven returned with the spare part, they drove seventeen kilometres on his clock and found that the Land Rover's gauge was 1.4 kilometres out. Seventeen kilometres would mean a reading of 15.6 kilometres. If Tom and I hadn't been engaged in a battle of wills, I'd have let it drop and got to Tanger that much quicker.

I had to cover fifty kilometres a day, six days a week, or I wouldn't finish on the money I had. The motivation to get up in the morning and go through it all over again was hard to muster, so I pretended that the walk was my employer: I had to get up to go to work. If left to my own devices, I'd lie in: that's my nature. If I met the target each day, the walk would take on its own momentum. Stopping early is unthinkable. I start out each day set on covering that fifty kilometres; if something happens and I don't, I have to try it again the next day. It's like dieting: each time you break it you lose a little bit more faith in yourself until you think, 'What's the point in starting – I'll never finish?'

The drivers had to be taught about the camp, but the trouble with Tom and G was that they wouldn't listen to my suggestions, they had to experiment and find out for themselves. I'm like that, too, but when their experiments failed, there were direct repercussions on me: I walked into an inefficient break. In those early weeks, I was battling to find my rhythm and I just didn't need a fight with back-up as well.

There were piles of cooking wood for sale by the roadside. It was the yellow wood used for long, slow cooking. Manioc and sorghum are their staple foods and they need this kind of heat. It's not right for boiling water quickly for tea – for that, you need small twigs which burn hot and fast. I told the boys this, but time and again I'd get into a break and find a star fire of yellow wood and a kettle that wouldn't boil even if I didn't sit and look at it for an hour. It wasn't just that I wanted these things on time and done right; it also helped them if they were doing things right, because then the chores became easy.

They had to put up the awning at breaks because there were so few trees for shelter from the wind and sun, and for privacy. It's impolite to eat in front of others without offering them what you have; we had a long journey ahead and could not afford to feed the local population three times a day. These were not starving people and they didn't live like us. We gave people hospitality when it was appropriate, but we didn't demean small courtesies by paying for them, as many overlanders do. They have left a trail of social pollution, where people demand payment now for help.

A farmer approached G and pointed to the sign on the Land Rover.

'You are from London?'

'Well, the boss is.'

Encouraged, he pulled out a card and showed it to G. 'Perhaps you can give me a tip on the football pools?'

The farmer didn't offer a cadeau for G's advice, but an overlander would have if he was an African.

The sun never really rose over the horizon, it just appeared above the dust around 10a.m. and at night disappeared like a fading orange light bulb into the dust clouds. The Harmattan blew from pre-dawn to just before dusk. At night the dust settled and the moon was clear – it was strange to see it after the sun had been so blurred.

I fell in time beside a young Fulani with a ghetto blaster playing Enigma. We chewed the fat for a while. I threw some of my bread to a few ducks but they moved off in fright – nobody had ever thrown them food before. Goats teetered on their tiny hooves along a rain worn ridge, donkeys brayed like Bob Dylan and neem and gum gave them shade on the edges of the dried-out sorghum fields where an old man was preparing the ground with a hoe. He looked up from his work as I asked my companion about the Harmattan season.

'We Fulani are cattle men, but he is Hausa, he can tell you about the fields.'

The men didn't know each other but my companion shook his hand, exchanged greetings and took his hoe while the old Hausa came to talk to me.

Part of the big dilemma of walking with back-up was that these little exchanges would be going on around me while I was alone, but as soon as I got to a break I'd step into a capsule of England. Then I had to protect my belongings, because I was suddenly seen as being like all other travellers – rude and rich.

This new team also experimented with day's end camp. They went through the same old criticism of me that I was being unnecessarily fastidious.

'The wash bowl goes here, the fire goes there, the day box ...'

But Tom would cut in with: 'Fuck's sake, Fi, you're so anally retentive.'

'If you won't learn the system stop whingeing about how much work you've got on.'

But experience had shown that if a camp is set up in the same way it means less work for them, because they know exactly what to do and in what order. They can see what's missing, what needs to be bought or repaired, and the locals who gather around can see that we are organized and that there aren't bits of kit lying around as easy pickings. Day's end camp is a home, and in all the unruly mess of the bush to have something clean and ordered is a delight. Like wearing a uniform, it gives you a sense of pride. What's more, camping on a dry, flat, clear patch of ground means fewer insects, it's easier to spot snakes and if you drop something it's much easier to find it.

But they continued to camp in grass and set up camp a completely different way each night. Tom did it on purpose, to assert some authority. We were engaged in a power struggle. Neither of us would back down and G had to be referee. It got to the point where we'd have a major league confrontation at each break, which was tiring for both of us and exhausting for G. We talked about it rationally when walking together for eight kilometres each week and vowed to resolve it. There's something very different between 'sitting down' talking and 'walking' talking – the latter is easier for me because it is done in rhythm and you don't have to keep looking at the person when you're not speaking. Tom cooked on the fourth night. After much preparation he produced a superb spaghetti bolognaise and handed us our plates with a flourish. One taste of it proved too hot to eat, but as a measure of our unease, it took a good ten minutes of eating before one of us passed comment. The Africans find it very rude to keep eye contact when talking; that signals confrontation. So I learnt to do as they do, and look down. I also learnt that staring is a means of communication, too – if we didn't stare back at the kids who gathered around us at breaks, they thought it was OK to be doing nothing but standing on one leg, gawping at us. But the act of staring back makes them self-conscious and suddenly visible in the crowd; we could pick them off one by one and they'd move on.

From Kano, I walked due west along the tarmac to Gwarzo then took the bush tracks beside granite boulders of Road Runner fame. Direction finding was sometimes a bit tricky because the villagers assumed I wanted to go to a place via the road. I had to insist that I wanted the old route. It took quite a while before the drivers realized that after a break it was better for them to pack up quickly and get to the next stop so that they could kick back and relax before I arrived. I put this to them as the incentive to be ahead since they didn't pay any attention to my request to get ahead of me in case they broke down and couldn't reach me. Tom picked up the Hausa language very quickly and was able to check the route and leave stone arrows for me at junctions in case their tracks were obliterated. His mind was alive, inquisitive and retentive. When not arguing, we had the most amazing conversations about everything from aid in Africa to who got the bigger half of mango pie.

Zaven came out to see us three times, his car brimming with fruit and Lebanese dishes which his father had specially prepared for us. Each time he came he commented on how much longer he'd had to drive, and that made me feel good about the progress we were making. He'd probably thought that a walker would be in his area for quite some time, but after four days I was already 200 kilometres away – a return car journey of eight hours.

The system finally clicked into place when Tom assumed leadership of the back-up. We reached Gusau, a small town that seemed to be populated entirely by patriots: every tree and bollard – indeed any vertical, inanimate object – was painted green, white and green in the national colours. We spent the rest day in a hotel; Nigeria is very cheap, so for once I could afford it.

The next day, G dropped me off at the start place and went back to collect Tom who was changing money to pay the bill. They didn't return for three and a half hours, during which time I ran out of water and the temperature soared. I sat in the shade of a tree and waited. The cotton season was over and the brown stalks were gathered in piles in the fields. I fell asleep. When I woke, I saw a camel caravan of about fifteen animals, the drivers all dressed in Tuareg blue with heavy head gear. The camels plodded along obediently, their loads packed in woven mats tied round with traditional sisal cordage which squeaked as it strained.

I joined the last camel and walked in its shade. A bleating sound came from behind us. We turned in unison then looked at each other and started laughing – like the children of Hamelin, all the goats and sheep were streaming from the fields and following us. The Tuareg were carrying salt from the mines in Bilma, as they have done for years. To protect their trade, trucks in Niger are forbidden to carry salt. I was very excited. The existence of a caravan meant that Tuareg were now on the move again. Did it mean there was a chance of crossing the desert by the original route? If there was, the best place to join a caravan would be Niamey, and I wouldn't get there for another month.

The Tuareg didn't mind me walking along beside them, nor did they ask me what I was doing there. I moved on up the line and walked in the shadow of the lead camel. After some time, I offered the driver my water bottle. There was only a small amount of liquid at the bottom – I never drain a bottle, it's psychological – but I reckoned that if I was thirsty, then so, probably, was he. The man took the bottle and looked inside. Then he signalled back to one of the others who unlashed a guerba, a waterbag made from a goat's stomach, and without stopping the caravan, poured some of the contents into a wooden bowl. The water was green and opaque but I didn't care. I didn't thank them, as that would have been considered very rude.

Some time later, we came to a village. The cameleer indicated to me that he was leaving the track here and waved goodbye. The Tuareg are not allowed to ride through villages because they can see the women over the walls of the homesteads. If they do, they are stoned.

At the end of the village, the Land Rover arrived. They were late because they'd had to change travellers' cheques to pay the bill, but the hotel wouldn't do it and the bank wanted a bribe to change them at the correct rate. I drank my fill and we carried on for a few kilometres even though we were well past the break: it's bad form to set up a break in a village. We stopped beside a grandfather baobab. There was a large hole inside and a human molar tooth embedded in the bark by the entrance.

'I guess it's there to scare off kids from going inside,' I said. 'It might be full of snakes.'

'Nah, I reckon it's just voodoo,' Tom said.

We argued about that too.

As we were sitting there, skirmishing and drinking tea, the camel caravan slowly approached down the track. I was delighted to see them again and called out a greeting. I pulled out a thirty-litre water jerry and motioned for them to refill all their guerbas. We also gave them oranges, and they gave us dried dates. This was the best way to thank them, and I felt so good for being able to repay them for their hospitality earlier. I walked with them for a bit and then overtook them, waving goodbye.

As Tom and G were setting up evening camp, a bunch of teenagers arrived, clearly bent on a fight. They said they wanted payment for camping where we were, which was totally out of line. G told them we were road workers and entitled to camp near our work!

Attracted by the rumpus, an older man approached from across the ploughed field and handed me three large eggs in a calabash bowl. I reached for my wallet, but he objected. With offers of food it's tricky to know when to pay and when to accept it as a gift. Later in the evening he came back with his children to let them see the new show in town.

Sometimes I'd reverse the spectacle when watching people down the track, waiting for their reaction at the moment they realized an alien was walking towards them. One would stop, look hard, then inform the others. They'd form a tight group and continue walking towards me. Fortunately for me, they don't spend hours in front of the TV absorbing sick images of what I might be. They are not so exposed to perverts as we are so the kids, and their parents, are more confident. And they don't make that dreadful wail like kids in the supermarket when their mother pushes on past the sweetie counter. G commented on it too – in all his years in the Third World he'd never heard that sound, never seen a kid throw a tantrum. He put it down to how they see themselves: they are not the centre of everyone's world in childhood.

The collar on the trailer braking system had fallen off, causing it to crash into the Land Rover whenever it braked. Then it had a puncture. The villagers indicated which way I had gone but wouldn't let the Land Rover follow me because the track was too bad. Instead the Chief mustered up a couple of bikes and G set off on the back to find me before nightfall.

Tom made an improvised repair with the help of the villagers and looked up from his work to see a truck, full of passengers, grinding up a hill. It stalled, and it had no brakes. The vehicle slid back down the hill at terrific speed, spilling women and children in all directions. Unbelievably, nobody was seriously injured.

The Land Rover engine fired, but then a banjo bolt, part of the fuel line to the engine, severed. Tom screwed it down with the last of the thread but we needed another. There was no alternative but to return to Gusau that afternoon to look for replacement parts. The problem was that Zaven was due to meet us that night.

'If we're quick,' Tom said, 'we could call Nigerian Oil Mills before he leaves and get him to bring those two parts with him.'

The nearest phone was in Gusau. Zaven had already set off, but Harold very kindly sent a driver out to us with a replacement bolt and collar. Zaven, too, managed to locate us by following the trail of loo paper we'd left on trees through the bush. We set up camp and he unloaded another stash of goodies from his car. He then proceeded to cook us a superb meal of kebabs and laid out the feast before us. We were blown away again by his hospitality but he swept all thanks aside with his usual command: 'Eat! Eat!' As we were eating, a cast-out lady came and sat by the fire. I gave her some food and water.

It had been very hot. Even a few minutes into a break, my heart still thumped in my ears. There was scant shade in the thorn bushes, and the fluffy-footed flies were out to snatch a walk on my upper lip. Each part of Africa has its peculiar aspect of discomfort; up here in the savannah, the grasses were the irritant. Burrowing grass stabs a needle-sharp root into the flesh when it senses moisture. Dry burrs stick to everything from socks to bedding. I often had to pull over under the shade of a thorn bush to pick them out of my pants. But the worst of them were star-shaped bastards the size of carpet tacks which worked their way into the Land Rover tyres and punctured the inner tube. Step on one while out for a pee in the night and nobody sleeps through the hollering.

At the end of that week, we reached Jega – population 10,000, most of whom were kids. Like Russian dolls, there was always an even smaller one. A river cut through the village, providing a good place to wash the sand and sweat out of our clothes. Tom found a new way to defuse the inevitable baiting when surrounded by kids. He climbed on top of the Land Rover as they watched below and sang 'Day O!' The echo came back 'Day O!' In true big brother fashion he managed to get them under control and massage his ego at the same time.

'Who's the leader of the gang?' he sang to the theme of the Mickey Mouse Club.

'*Who's de leader of de gang?*

'T-O-M'

'*T-O-M*'

'M-E-T'

'*M-E-T*'

'C-A-L-F-E.'

I'd seen several riot police driving round but didn't know what they were doing. The call for prayer the next morning began much earlier than on previous days and G didn't like the sound of what he was hearing: it certainly wasn't from the Koran. There had been a clash between Muslims and Christians in a town nearby, and several people had been killed. The aggressors, three Muslims, had come from Jega, and they were to be executed that day. We kept well out of the way and tuned in to the local radio station for updates.

That night, after the meal, as Tom and I sat sparring and drinking tea, G said: 'Either you two sort out your personality clash, or I'm leaving.'

I was shocked. In my book it's unthinkable to threaten to leave a trip just because you're not having a good time. Emotional flare-ups are all part of expedition life, and the first weeks are always the hardest.

I went to sleep planning to get rid of both of them: G would fly home, Tom would drive the Land Rover to Nouakchott, wait for me to cross the desert, and I would carry on with a donkey. It was a thoroughly impractical plan, because I had to get across the border quickly and walking with a donkey would take twice as long, and I didn't have the money – but it was a measure of how strongly I wanted out.

I asked Tom to walk with me the next morning. I told him we'd give it till Niamey, about two weeks away, and if we couldn't get along, he'd have to leave.

'Why me? Why should I go?'

'Because it would be a bit pointless if I did.'

I decided to rethink things. Tom was also finding it hard to work with G, although when things were going well they seemed really to enjoy each other's company with long discussions about history and traveller's tales. But G was a plodder. It's not a bad thing to have an expedition member who just puts his head down and gets on with the job, but G took slowness to its extreme, wandering off for an eternity in the markets. G's language skills were very useful but the important skill now was mechanics – better to be moving and unable to communicate than have a rip-roaring conversation and be stuck for months. It was clear to me that if one of them had to go, it would have to be G. That left me with Tom and, unless we could work out our differences, that was hardly ideal either.

We crossed into Niger at Gaya under a light covering of cloud and a gentle wind that nudged me from behind. After the farming land of Nigeria, the landscape was dry scrub forest and vast plains dotted with termite mounds. Parts of the area were lunar-like with bald patches of gravel, yet I walked on raised roads above luscious fields of kitchen gardens – literally named, because they grew calabashes to make pots and bowls.

We camped up a steep hill the first night. But by 2a.m. we were up and moving camp: a dodgy brother had been sniffing around, saying there were bandits in the area and we should move. Funny how those who warn us of danger are usually the ones who pose the greatest threat.

We followed the Niger river, a great, slow-moving body of water flowing west, and camped on its banks for the next rest day. The Scottish explorer, Mungo Park, had travelled this river in 1775 and proved that it flowed east. No doubt he passed the great-great-grandparents of those who punt the river today, plying backwards and forwards in their pirogues to the market town of Bumba on the Benin side.

Our kit and our bodies were a uniform khaki. Great to have a wash and discover you're much browner than you thought but the socks were tough going. I'd wear a clean pair every day and leave them till the rest day. I sat on a smooth rock and scoured them with a bristle brush and Omo soap powder. It gave my upper body a good workout.

Walking away from the river, the landscape changed to Dolol country, a name for the dried-out fertile old river valleys – pale yellow sand with small 'noisy palms' like giant green pineapples. Here I met many Fulani women, exquisitely colourful and poised. They are fine, elegant women bedecked in silver coins on their heads, with necklaces and bracelets. Their legs are shiny mahogany and do not wobble as they walk; even their calves are rigid. The Fulani are such a gentle people; in their presence you feel deeply relaxed, almost sleepy.

We camped beside a baobab tree and inevitably the local villagers arrived for a look at us. One of the young guys, an incredible acrobat, shinned up the tree, picked the hard fruit, and threw it down. Removing the outer shell, he exposed white flesh held together in dry, yellowy strings with a texture like popcorn. He took a bite then spat out the pips and covered them with dirt with his foot, motioning that they would grow into a tree. He left all the fruit for us. It was lemony and refreshing, but too much of it made you very thirsty. I took to eating it as I walked, dropping some into my water bottle if the water wasn't good.

After several days we hit the land of the 'touri bird' – my name for the noise kids make when the tourists have been in the area. You can kiss the fun goodbye – they won't make friends, just set up a demanding chant for presents. I'd get so pissed off with it because they could see I wasn't carrying anything but it was almost excusable in the kids – they used it as a greeting to whites. You couldn't even win by saying 'I'll give you a pen if you give me something' because they'd start taking off their shirt. But the adults do it too. Tom had spent an hour under the bonnet of a burnt-out motor trying to help the stranded passengers of a bush taxi. He managed to get the thing started for them but as he wiped the grease from his hand, one of the passengers ambled up to him and said: 'Donnez-moi un cadeau.'

There was a check point as we reached the tarmac road to Niamey. We handed over our passports, the carnet, the insurance and the carte grise and got one of them to sign my witness book.

'You are walking from Kano?'

'From Botswana' I said, never mentioning South Africa. 'I wanted to walk up to Algiers but the border is closed so I have to walk around the Sahara.'

'But the border is not closed now. Just yesterday an Italian came through in a Mercedes. I saw his carnet, it said he'd crossed at Assamakka from Tamanghasset.'

This was incredible news! It meant we could divert up there – a three-month journey instead of six months around the edge.

There was no time to waste: I wanted to find this guy before he moved on. They told us his name and that he was probably selling his Merc in Niamey before flying back to Italy. We drove in, trying not to get excited. At the check point outside the city, they told us where the guy was staying. We found him at a hotel and bought him a beer. It was my birthday and that beer was the best present I could have had – so cold it numbed the back of my eyeballs.

'Yes, it's possible to cross the border,' he said with a dismissive shrug. 'But you have to do it in convoy with the military.'

'How fast?'

'Maybe 80, 100 kilometres per hour. But then, there is no certainty that you get through. If you break down, they won't wait for you. It's not the Tuareg any more that have the trucks, it's the bandits or the military.'

But this could still work, the Land Rover could gun it through with the convoy and G and I could go with a camel caravan. A Mr Fixit brought various camelmen to see us but none of them would go further than Agadez on the southern edge of the war zone. They said I could find another caravan there to take me to Tamanghasset on the Algerian side, but I didn't believe them. It was not a traditional trading route and with the danger of ambush there was no way I could get them to cross that stretch: the bandits hung out at the wells and you couldn't cross the desert any other way.

Reluctantly, I had to let it go. This must have been a major let-down for G since it was the only chance of undertaking the camel crossing which he'd been picked to do. Now that we were in francophone countries, he had started to come into his own. At last, he had a role. However, the disappointment with the camels was too much for him on top of Tom's irritable behaviour, and he folded himself away even more.

We had to get out of Niamey quickly; there were controversial presidential elections and the whole town would be closed down from midnight for two days. We drove back to where we'd stopped and I started walking again, now towards the river. The Sahel savannah was getting quite wild and sparsely inhabited. When there were villages, the houses were made of mud with domed mud roofs and storage containers outside that looked like giant jugs, or rondavels with straw roofs, each with a braided top.

Tom and I took it in turns to do the evening meal, which helped to bond us. It was fun to channel our competitiveness into something useful. Even though I had the edge because I'd been bush cooking for so long, Tom managed to hold his own. In the mango season there's very little to eat except mangoes, which is fine if you like them for breakfast, lunch and supper. So I made green mango pie which tastes like apples or stewed the old ones with spices. We bought pulses in the markets and made curries or chilli and when we had eggs I made quiche – beautifully browned with slices of tomato on top. Tom never outdid me on that one. The warm smell of baking and the way it brings hungry people together was beginning to heal the rift between Tom and me. During the day, I found myself singing as I walked, something I hadn't felt inclined to do since the era of Bill and Blake.

But now G and Tom were not getting on. It got incredibly hot on that stretch and I fell into a mental void of no thought to get through. At breaks there'd sometimes be a few telltale signs of a dispute and the hunched figure of old G pumping away at the Katadyn water filter. I encouraged G to come and walk with me to get a break from Tom. G had a fantastic collection of stories – whether half of them had happened or not, he never said. But eight years in the Lebanon, and serving with the Red Cross as the only Brit in Iraq during the Gulf war, had given him a wonderful supply of tales. He taught me a poem, 'The Cremation of Sam McGee', giving me a verse each time, leaving me to mull over it till I got to camp and then I'd perform it. A good choice in the heat: gold prospectors on the Arctic trail.

We left the tarmac and headed southwest towards the Niger river again to cut off the noisy road to Niamey with all its dodgy roadside dwellers. A beaten-up old Peugeot trundled past and the driver leant out of the window shouting 'Bon courage!' The cocktail of dust and stones had barely settled before a brand new Land Cruiser came past. A row of white heads turned to look back at me. I waved to them, hoping they'd stop for a chat and share a cold beer. But they didn't even return my wave. Neither did the next three.

'French fucks!' I shouted at them: aid workers off for a weekend.

I turned to the little boy who was walking quietly beside me and explained that he'd just witnessed a good example of how rude westerners can be to each other. It wound me up till I couldn't be bothered to speak in French and just hammered on, demanding an explanation as to why, when they saw a lone white woman walking way out in the bush, they didn't stop to say hello. He kicked stones and looked up at me several times with a rather surprised, quizzical look but was happy to trot along with me despite my outbursts.

The clouds were gathering, great white cumulus, and I told him in French: 'If you walk north every day for three years, you'll come to a land that looks like the clouds.'

There was no bridge at the point where I wanted to cross the Niger river, so we drove round through Niamey, which gave Tom a chance to make more repairs. The silencer fell off in the carpark and had to be welded. (It promptly fell off again three weeks later.) Tom spent all his time on the repairs and didn't have much of a break. We had begun a banter which was just about bordering on flirting. It surprised me when I realized this after so many weeks of hating him and regretting my decision to hire him. What surprised me even more was my realization that I was growing to like him.

We had to take another day off when we crossed the river because I got sick – probably from something I'd eaten in town. Tom made a kite to cheer me up. The next couple of days were terrifically hot. It was harder for the drivers waiting for me because there was no breeze; even the slight breath of wind generated by me passing through still air when walking was enough to cool me down a little. But they had none of that and then had to light a fire in the heat for tea when I got in. Just before the border, we spotted a game reserve camp on the edge of the Parc National de W. Since the border wouldn't be open until the next morning, we drove over.

There was a swimming pool. One minute we had been virtually passing out from the heat and the next we were plunging into the clear blue water.

The first night across the Burkina Faso border, we camped beside a group of travelling circumcisers. They were a bunch of very jolly old men, having a good time. They had five youngsters in there with them and we snuck over to take a look. They welcomed us at the fire, but we realized that I, at least, shouldn't stay long. Four of the boys were covered in reddish paint and one in white chalk.

Tom heard a dog get run over on the road, and its terrible

whimpering. He took his knife and went out to finish the job but one of the men cautioned him; apparently it's unlucky to kill dogs.

That evening, Tom and I drove back to the town to buy some beer. It meant crossing a check point and then again on the way back, and we waited in a small room for the official to be free. A uniformed guy appeared and I explained in bad French that we were spending the night in the bush but had come back to get some provisions and would be crossing again. Would this be all right, so they wouldn't have to stop us again? He looked nervous but said that it was fine by him. Then he rushed off. I found out later that he wasn't a policeman at all, and that I had asked permission to cross the border from a forestry official.

It became much more humid. The mango rains had begun and the sky was heavy with cumulus. I learned to spot an approaching village by the vultures, spiralling above like an airport holding pattern. When they landed, heavy and ugly, I could see their ears, flat and round on bald heads and strong necks.

After some days, I got to a break to find a swarm of bees. Tom and G had had a massive argument over stopping there and Tom was still going through his histrionics. He was incredibly tired because he hadn't had a break in Niamey and he was under huge pressure from the responsibility to keep the Land Rover going.

Something had to be done, not only to show Tom that his rage was not acceptable, but to give him some R&R. I decided there and then to give him some money and told him to hitch into the capital, Ouagadougou, for a few days, get some sleep, get laid and forget about the walk. G and I would just have to manage without him for a few days. Tom was distraught.

'You'll fire me when I get back, won't you?'

'Just pack, Tom. And I don't expect to see you when I get to the next break.' Unless he came back refreshed, I added, we'd have to reassess the situation.

I set off and some time later the Land Rover caught up with me. Tom got out to say goodbye. He looked so forlorn and tired I wanted to hug him but didn't.

It was during his absence that G told me why he had come.

'I felt under pressure not to let Trevor down,' he said. 'I didn't have the time to take six months off but I felt obliged to.'

'I'd pretty much felt the same way,' I said. 'I thought you had handed in your notice to the Red Cross when we'd agreed to do the camel trip and that I couldn't let you down by not inviting you to join the Land Rover supported stretch. I had wanted to hire two drivers in UK so that I knew they'd get along.'

Tom and G had their separate jobs. G didn't know all of Tom's because he was quite possessive over them, but we muddled through. G seemed able to relax at last – he usually worked at a steady pace from dawn till dusk, pumping away at that bloody Katadyn filter. But now there seemed to be less work with just the two of us and we had some great storytelling sessions around the fire.

We were due for a rest day the day before Tom got back but decided to take it early in case we missed him. We had seen a sign for a safari camp and decided to spend it there. It was probably run down without water but we tried our luck. As we drove down the track, the camp emerged – whitewashed rondavels covered with bougainvillea, a swimming pool with Greek urns and fountains and a lion in a cage. This area of Burkina still has lion, and this place was still run as a hunting lodge. We could hardly contain our excitement at this find: I ran around chattering my delight to the bar staff, waiting for the manageress to book us two rooms.

'Look,' said G, 'I don't give a damn how much this place costs, I'll pay for my room.'

Considering he earned £50 a week, it was a very generous offer. A middle-aged French woman arrived and turned up her nose at this rough looking couple standing beside a clapped-out Land Rover which looked oh so forlorn beside their zebra-painted Toyotas.

'What do you want?'

There was a short pause as I thought what to ask for first – a round of cold beers for everyone present or two clean, fresh, private glorious rooms. I didn't get the chance to say anything.

'We're full, you can't stay here.'

'Could we camp and use your facilities?'

'No.'

'Could we just buy a beer?'

'No.'

There can be few tougher situations in life than seeing a cold, clean place in the middle of the dead heat and not be allowed in. The closest I could think of was coming across a hot chocolate and warm muffin bar with an open log fire in the Arctic and being turned away. We drove back into the bush, taking the piss out of her to keep our spirits up: 'Can we at least kiss your ass?'

There was no water nearby so we found the best place we could before dark. It started to rain and we put up our tents. There was a terrific storm that night and both of us got the feeling that a lion was in the camp. In the morning, G's tent had been pissed on quite high up and we didn't think it could have been cattle. He had another fright in store. When sitting by the fire the next day, he felt a tickle on his leg. A scorpion was hurrying through his hairs and heading for his crotch. Very, very gently, he brushed it off with a cloth.

While I did the laundry using water from the jerries, G went off on a bird watching walk, something he often did at day's end when Tom and I were cooking and he had finished his work.

He'd been off for a couple of hours and decided to turn back.

'I said to myself, "I'll just have a look over that ridge to see where that eagle went and then I'll head back."'

He stood on the ridge and looked over a plain and saw another Land Rover. He got very excited, thinking they might have cold beer and headed down the escarpment. Not far off, he saw the SABONA logo on the side and thought it was quite remarkable that they had sponsored another overland vehicle following exactly the same route. About 100 metres from the vehicle it dawned on him that this was his own camp. G was the first to admit to having no sense of direction, but this incident took the biscuit.

He came waltzing into camp, singing his old song:

'Indicate the way to my abode,
I'm fatigued and I wish to retire
I partook of a small beverage some thirty minutes ago
And it's gone right to my cranium.
No matter where I wander
Terra ferma, aqua or atmospheric pressure,
You will always hear me singing this little ditty
Indicate the way to my abode.'

My ideal rest day is to wash my clothes, clean out the Land Rover, wash myself and hair, make a cake for tea at 4p.m., and then sit down at the table with everything clean around me and write up my notes: it's sheer bliss. I played a Sarah McLaughlin tape – one of Tom's – and suddenly realized how much I missed him. I was quite shocked at myself, just as I had been in Niamey, but I was really looking forward to having him back. We had the same sense of humour and enjoyed the same music and our banter was fun as we teased and took the piss out of each other.

I covered full distances for the next couple of days, even though

it was pretty tough on G, who had to manage all his own work as
well as the jobs he wasn't familiar with.

The night before Tom was due in, he turned to me and said, 'I'm
sorry Fi, but I can't carry on with Tom. I know you need him
because he's a mechanic, so I'll go.'

I wouldn't talk him out of it but I was pretty sore – it had cost
me a huge amount to get him out there (as much as Tom and me
together) but, as per our agreement, he'd have to pay his own way
home if he left voluntarily. I'd have to get word to Shuna to find
another driver and we worked out the only place he could come out
was Bamako – one month hence.

Just out of the town of Fada the Land Rover broke down, and
there was no way that either G or I could get it started. We'd been
there about ten minutes when I looked round and saw Tom running
towards us. The timing was perfect.

I ran up and hugged him.

'We missed you,' I said.

'I missed you guys too,' he smiled and hugged me back.

He got right to work and discovered the same problem as they'd
had just out of Kano – the starter motor electrics had short circuited
with the dust and it was butting into the engine while it was running.
The starter motor was wrecked. While Tom and G tried to fix what
they could, I set about gathering wood for tea.

An old man arrived on a bike, realized he couldn't help with the
big problem of fixing the Land Rover, but saw what I was doing.
'Sanu!' he called, laying down his bike and helped gather wood. He
didn't ask if I needed a hand – he knew I did and he knew what to
do. I didn't thank him – that would have signified that I hadn't
expected him to help, that I'd thought he was a mean-spirited person.
When the fire was going, I simply made him a cup of tea, and that
was right.

A French aid worker passed without stopping to lend a hand, but
an American missionary stopped and invited us to stay with him.
Unfortunately, his house was sixty kilometres into the bush and at
that time we weren't moving anywhere.

Tom somehow got the engine going and we drove back to Fada,
parking up at a French missionary school. One of the main features
of Fada, we discovered, was that no one in the town stocked starter
motors. We'd have to go to Ouagadougou. However, the school
mechanic knew the garages and parts places and agreed to go there
with G and Tom to find one.

I wrote a fax to Shuna asking her to find me a new driver. Of the people I'd interviewed there was a list of ten possibles who had agreed to be on stand-by. It was a start. She'd have to get the guy picked, briefed, insured, vaccinated, visa'd and flown out, and she only had three weeks in which to do it. It had to be the right guy too, and he had to get his affairs in order. I also told her that my feet were incredibly blistered because I'd bought expensive shoes which didn't give. I knew the Hi-Tecs were made of cheap fabric which could mould to my feet, but Hi-Tec didn't make them any more. I suggested she contact South Africa to DHL three pairs to Ouaga. It was one hell of a request.

The boys sent the fax from Ouaga and were away for the whole of the next day. Meanwhile, I had some fun.

Jean-Pierre, a French school teacher, took the day off to show me around.

'Burkina is mostly Christian,' he told me, 'but they keep their own religion going. You want to see the sacred mountain?'

Does Dolly Parton sleep on her back?

We drove out of town with Claude, a man of the local Gormanche tribe who was delighted to answer all my questions. The women were bald and filed their teeth because, he said, it's a sign of beauty.

'And these insects?' I said as I brushed the moisture bees out of my ears, 'What d'you call them?'

He gave me a local name and translated it into French, which I translated into English – sweat bee!

It was a mountain by Burkina standards, rather like Hanging Rock in Oz – a collection of granite boulders alone on a flat plain. We parked up some way off and walked quietly through the bush and up the rubbly slopes till we came to a ledge.

'This is where the grandfather of the current chief of the Gormanche made his sacrifice for rain,' announced Claude. 'He was a very powerful man. He made a sacrifice to end a terrible drought and as his blade fell on the neck of the man, there was a boom of thunder and the sky split open and the rain fell in torrents.'

We had a look inside the small cave. A smooth rock plinth sat in the middle and a few chicken feathers were stuck to the sides with dried blood.

'Now the chief makes a sacrifice of chickens to stop the crocodiles from taking women in the pools beside Fada,' Claude explained and Jean-Pierre translated.

'How often does he make the sacrifice?' I asked.

'Oh, twice a year,' Jean-Pierre said, turning to Claude out of courtesy to check his facts.

'No!' said Claude in perfect French, 'he does it every Friday.'

We found our way to a 'dolo bar' in Fada, a refreshing, mildly alcoholic drink made from millet. The ambience was so rich; everybody greeted us without any shyness or sniggering. It was wonderful to be accepted so readily, and made me all the more curious about what they knew of people. There is so much substance in their communication – not just words or inflection, but a whole range of minutely subtle, uninhibited body language signs.

The bar was also the brewery. Four earthenware pots sat in a square. A fire was burning between them, cooking the potion. Once it was ready it was strained through a hanging basket made of grass, then cooled. It was served up in small gourd cups.

One man had added a medicine to his. He had been troubled by demons in his sleep. He kept his calabash bowl to himself, but there were four others going round for everyone to share. I didn't want to leave that gathering; it took a great effort to get up, not because I was pissed, but because I felt so accepted. Free from the tantrums of back-up, free from the desperate pull of the road with all its blinkers, free from being a freak.

Tom and G returned late that night having found only one source of a starter motor – it was brand new, and priced at £1,000. Burkina just didn't have Land Rovers.

After another severe drought in the 1970s, hundreds of aid agencies poured into the country using Japanese four-wheel drive cars. They were equipped with all the Gucci gear – even snorkels, for God's sake. If the country had enough water for diving in such conditions it wouldn't need aid agencies. The roads were good in Burkina, no need for such expensive equipment. The aid workers lived in fine houses with air conditioning and servants, living off the situation and playing along with Westerners' views on what Africa needed. We talked of this one night and G told us a story of a woman he'd met in Kurdistan.

'Don't think much of this washing powder,' she said as she scrubbed away at her clothes, 'It won't foam.'

G picked up the packet beside her and read the label: 'Instant mashed potato mix.'

The school's mechanic had given instructions to a garage to look for a second-hand starter motor over the next week, by which time

I would have walked to Ouaga. If one couldn't be found, it would be cheaper to fly to Gabon and pick up one there.

During that week, we had to push start the Land Rover each morning and leave it running at breaks which was noisy and wasted fuel. Push starting it on sand was really tough but we couldn't leave it on the tarmac or it would be smashed to kindling by morning. Tom discovered that G wasn't physically very strong, having spent six months in Ethiopia living on goat and rice. More tensions arose.

Tom was much refreshed when he got back but this responsibility was weighing heavily on him. He came out to walk with me one time and said he would stick with me to Tanger even if he had to carry the water jerries himself across the desert. He had commitment; I couldn't ask for anything more.

We were all pinning our hopes on Shuna finding a replacement for G, or he couldn't leave. Tom was especially concerned: a good mechanic would halve his responsibility.

I reached Ouaga and we went to the hotel where they'd sent the fax and had given that number for the reply. A fax was waiting for us: it was full of good news. Shuna was completely on top of everything, providing me with a list of guys she'd already contacted, indicating where the mail had been sent and telling me to go to the DHL office to pick up my shoes. We toasted her with cold Coke. We were all so relieved at her attitude – it makes a huge difference if you've got full-on, competent and enthusiastic support back home.

We stayed for three days at the tourist camp ground so that Tom could work on the starter motor. There we met a Scottish couple who had been cycling around west Africa. They worked for an aid organization in Glasgow and wanted to see the effects of their work. After six months, their opinion of aid in Africa had completely changed – they saw the waste and the wrong projects. They saw the joy in the African people and the richness of their lives which surprised them – they had believed the one-sided information they received in monthly bulletins, that Africans were despondent, down-trodden, starving and desperate.

What really impressed me about these two people was their journey along the route to Kayes on their bicycles. They could have put them on the railway line, their journey wasn't a pure cycling trip because they took lifts when they needed, but they soldiered on, anonymously. Bob had malaria and Susannah had raging cystitis, but they carried on. When I walked that track, I kept thinking of these two people and how incredible their tenacity had been. Walking is easy, cycling on rough ground and deep sand is hard core. They gave me inspiration.

Outside the post office we met an American traveller who said he was a journalist. He'd been up to Agadez to check out the Tuareg problem and had been arrested.

'But you didn't tell them you were a journalist did you?'

'Oh yes, and I spent eight hours being interrogated.'

A second-hand starter motor had been found for about £150 and was fitted.

Everything was going well until the Land Rover was broken into for the first time in the whole of the walk. So much for 'Burkino Faso' meaning 'land of honest men'.

The thieves took all the cameras, though not the film (thank God we kept it in the cool box), and both of G's bags. He lost everything – not just essential camping kit, but all his personal possessions from the years away from home. He was self-sufficient with them; he called them his 'gubbins' and his rucksack the Tardis. It was a major blow to him.

We went to the police station to report it and get a letter for the insurance company. It took two days just to get them to fill out one form. (And nine months to get the insurance company to pay up because they wanted more documentation from the police and couldn't understand why I didn't have it.)

We set off for Bamako, two weeks away, in high spirits that Shuna would be waiting for us there with a replacement driver. As a thank you to her for being my London support, I'd invited her to join us for a week in Mali. She'd tried to come out to see me at the end of my walk across America but had appendicitis the week before and had to cancel it. She'd also planned to come out for my month off in Kinshasa but had to cancel that too after the evacuation. This was the last time she'd be able to join me. She didn't know anything about expeditions or Africa but she had learned how to adapt and improvise from watching my mother over years of sudden house moves.

The two weeks from Ouaga to Bamako were among the happiest of my life. I'd been ragging Tom about being overweight, calling him Fat Boy, which really got under his skin. So he walked a quarter a day with me knowing that I hated walking in company. We chatted away as we walked, observing things, telling stories, falling in time with each other's footsteps. We'd have a conversation running for a couple of hours then resume it when I got into a break and then again in the evening. We produced fantastic meals each evening, and laughter returned to the camp as we flirted with each other. Out on the road alone, I laughed and sang and felt incredibly high. G sensed this too, and even though he had distanced himself from us, he looked visibly more relaxed.

We put on a play for the kids at one evening camp. To their delight, I played the bossy wife: 'How does he expect me to produce economical meals when he won't fix the oven? See? He whacked the hell out of that in a temper and now all my bakes won't brown ...'

We'd kick back on the roof, me and Tom, after everything had been done, and trip out on the stars, the cool breezes rustling the noisy palm and the drums in the distance, the pulsing hum of the cicadas and the warmth of peace time in camp. We were jolted alert one evening by a light moving along the track beside us.

After some shuffling in the bush, Tom called out: 'Pas de problème.'

There was no movement. 'Continuez s'il vous plait.'

Tom's voice was so calm and commanding in the silence it made me stiffen. After a pause, a voice called out that we could not camp there. This guy was bad news to come creeping up on us. We got down from the Land Rover and the tall visitor, dressed entirely in black, swept past us without shaking our hands and pointed to several large mounds.

'Les petits animaux?' I asked, forgetting the word for termites.

'Non!' he bent down, moving his hand over the low, hard-packed mounds.

A graveyard!

'Je m'excuse, monsieur.'

The man rode off on his bike, we woke G and moved the camp to the other side of the track.

Tom walked in open sandals and the stones got in, making him let out a sound like a wooky in pain as he stepped on one under a blister. He syringed his blisters each day but he carried on walking. This was pretty amazing stuff – none of the others had carried on with a blister.

His body became lean, muscular and tanned and his hair was wild and blond. Fat Boy had gone, but I kept up the ragging, 'Yo, Tom, you big bush man, get a hair cut.' I, too, was in great shape, my body was taut and shiny and deeply tanned. My hair had lightened and I felt so free of anxiety.

On the rest day by a river, we built a raft with the camp beds and a couple of plastic jerries. We played and laughed. It was such a simple life and it was running smoothly – nothing went wrong with the Land Rover so I could walk complete days every day. We were on a roll.

I warned myself out on the road that this flirting would have to calm down. I mustn't have an affair with him, this joy was too precious to be jeopardized by all the anxieties of having a lover and the stress it would cause on the team when G had gone.

But I was in love with Tom and it felt like he was in love with me too.

30

New shoes meant that I could exercise hard without the sting of pinched blisters making me gasp. It was far from being the worst sort of pain, but it kind of wore me down. Pain free, I became less demanding and more considerate.

Breaks were such fun now. Tom would put up the seat hammock for me and I'd sit in state with a cup of tea and a book, from time to time throwing out an observation for Tom and me to banter with.

Conversation had centred around the walk during the stretch with Raymond, and later with Tim and Johann. Even though we had a new radio, we seldom listened to it, except for the *Africa Watch* programme, to check on trouble zones ahead. But Tom was always looking for the interesting angle and like many New Zealanders he was a mine of information on practically any subject. Our minds wandered freely in and out of topics, perhaps in an act of compensation for our inability to wander physically. I wasn't used to talking during the quarters and I hadn't enjoyed walking with other drivers because I felt compelled to chat with them. But once Tom and I had sorted out the hierarchy between us, we clicked.

Along the narrow, dusty track, I watched two men walking ahead with a saunter, a water bottle and a table on their heads. Occasionally they stopped to pick resin burls from bark. They turned back to the track, eating their delicacy. And the table remained facing the front.

Crossing the border into Mali, the landscape changed from dry scrub forest to open farmland. We were in the area of Mali that feeds the whole of the rest of the country, most of which is Sahara. Every patch of land was cleanly cultivated in vast flat fields that ran right up to the walls of the Muslim villages. But it was gleaned land, and that made it difficult for us to find camp spots and wood.

The men here wouldn't return my wave, smiles or greetings, but the women would. They looked more negro than the men and as vain as women everywhere. They henna'd their hands, feet and nails in delicate patterns, they plaited their hair, inserted extensions, and their clothes were in all shapes and designs with one common theme – they had to be worn off the shoulder. Sometimes I'd pass a village where the women were plaiting each other's hair and they'd call out to me to join them. They took great delight in trying to do something with my blonde mess but the plaits never stayed in. Sometimes, however, the women would see me on the track and run to gather their children, grab them and dash into their houses.

Tom and I pondered what life would be like with the new driver in a week's time, just as G was no doubt pondering what life would be like when he was free. Instead of flying straight back to the UK, he'd decided to travel overland along our route and try to cross the Mauritania/OWS border.

We reached the village of Konseguela and Tom found some wine. We'd just set up camp beside a small copse of noisy palm when the chief arrived. He greeted us warmly and animatedly, explaining that he'd heard we had bought some alcohol.

'This is very serious,' he said to Tom and winked at me. 'It is forbidden for people to drink the wine without my permission.'

He asked for a mug: people were always asking for presents and I figured he wanted one in exchange for his permission. Considering he was such an amiable guy and we did have a couple of spares, I gave him one. He tipped it upside down, looked inside, and gave me a quizzical glance.

It suddenly dawned on me what his request had meant. Luckily, Africans don't harbour grudges; when there's been some confusion and the penny drops, they roar with laughter. He and his entourage drank only one mug each and then said their goodbyes.

This night was particularly bad for what I called 'racing spiders', which moved like lightning around the camp. G hated them and thought they were scorpions.

'No, they're not scorpions,' Tom said. '*That's* a scorpion.' He pointed to a creature that was at that moment crawling under G's camp bed.

The next day, Tom walked the last quarter with me. We crossed a tributary of the Niger which was on its way to Timbuktu; the wide, flat, sandy alluvial plain would make a perfect rest day spot to drive back to that night. As we charged up the dusty orange track and through a village on the hill, we were so wrapped up in laughter with each other that I had to gather all my strength and remind myself that this flirtation must not amount to anything. But it had reached fever pitch, and I knew it couldn't go on as it was – I felt anticlimactic every night and my whole life seemed to centre around having fun with him. I was bursting with happiness.

We had spoken about it in a roundabout way, when I had said I never have affairs with back-up drivers. I wanted to have fun with Tom without the possibility that it might change so I told him from the beginning it was a hands-off situation. But I was no longer sure I wanted to keep it that way. I'd devoted so many years of my life to celibacy for the sake of group dynamics, and each time I returned to the UK I was so wrapped up in my work that I had little time to develop relationships. Here, in my place, in my way of life, I was having a really good time. It took the edge off the hardships and made the walking easier. So why the heck shouldn't I?

I'd tossed this around most of the days I walked alone, and when walking with Tom I sensed him behind me. I'd look round and find his eyes fixed on my behind so I'd sway it a little more. One time he had massaged my back for me and then, because I asked him to, he did my legs. I thought he lingered but it was so slight I could have been mistaken. I didn't know what he felt and it made me deliciously crazy.

We drove back and had quite a hassle driving across the sandy flats to the edge of the river, having to dig out the Land Rover a couple of times. It hadn't rained for a few days, but if it did while we were there we'd have a hell of a job getting out. We set up camp some yards from the river. When it was all done, I grabbed my swimming costume and ran down to the water for a plunge. There was no vegetation on the banks or in the water, just cool, clear water, moving silently north to the desert. As I waded in my toes touched something hard. I reached down and pulled out a shellfish. There were hundreds of them, shaped like large whelks with mother-of-pearl shells, buried in the pure white sandy floor. I figured we'd cook some the next day because we had nothing much else to eat.

I called to Tom to come and check them out. We played in the water, splashing, chasing, diving, throwing each other around. He saw my body for the first time since Niamey.

'God, Fi, you look good,' he said.

We built a good fire up after supper and G went to bed. We took out the bottle of church wine and got irreligiously merry. Then we ran down to the river and swam in the moonlight. Afterwards we dried off by the fire. Tom and I had been used to touching. Now we sat shoulder to shoulder as we dried off, but I had got so pissed that I kept getting a head rush and the urge to run around the camp and get rid of it before plonking myself back down beside him. I fell over one time and lay with my head on his thigh. I was about to run again, but as I sat up, Tom kissed me on the mouth.

I pushed him off after a few seconds.

'No. We can't do that.'

'Yeah, yeah, sorry ...'

But I just couldn't take it any more. I kissed him, and we went into the tent. I was too drunk to remember what happened next. I just knew that I woke up beside him in the morning; his body looked incredibly good but the sun was rising and the tent got clammy and sweaty. I had a momentary sense of loss, that the fun had happened but I'd missed it all.

Then Tom woke up and we looked at each other.

'What's this emaciated man beside me?' I said. 'Get up and eat something.'

And we laughed.

Later that morning the two of us set off on a washing expedition down to the river with our laundry, figuring we'd let it soak while we found a good sandy place on the bank among the trees and really went to town on each other's body. But there was no privacy from cattle herders. Nor was there much time, because we had to do our laundry, get back to camp, relieve G for his bird walk, cook lunch, clean out the Land Rover, make the repairs. I realized that the logistics of this affair, if it carried on, were going to be very difficult.

I figured we'd cook up some of the shellfish, and gathered and cleaned a large bowlful. I rolled them in a simple flour and oil batter and put the oil on to heat up. It was then that G spotted a cattle man and asked him about the shellfish, using sign language. The reply was very graphic: if you put those things in your mouth you'll throw up.

Over the next three days to Bamako, Tom and I had to adjust to what had happened. I'd been so completely independent that I felt his affections were an invasion. I quickly realized that Tom wanted all my free time. But I refused to regret it; if we could build a relationship here then we'd have something very special. I talked to him about it and asked for space. He didn't say much. It was pretty shitty of me, but I hadn't thought that it would really happen and I wasn't prepared.

We had to get to Bamako by 8 April, in time to meet the new driver's plane. This had been arranged when we left Ouaga but there had been no contact since so it might not have happened. Because of the two days' delay in Ouagadougou getting the theft reported, we were about eighty kilometres short of the city by the evening of the 7th. We built a cairn of stones and drove in. It was G's last drive in the Land Rover and his burden seemed to lighten. That morning he'd pumped his last litre of water and gathered the few of his bits and pieces that hadn't been stolen. I looked at him and thought: G, with your flat hat, kaffiyeh around your neck and your overalls, your very Scottish ancestry and your storytelling, I haven't really got to know you at all.

We dropped him in town, planning to meet up again the next night at a club for a big blow out.

He said, 'I'll carry on, you know, if Shuna hasn't found another driver. Things have got much better, and I'm actually beginning to enjoy it.'

It must have taken a lot to make that offer.

I sent a fax to Shuna, asking when she was coming out and who the driver was. I didn't get a reply, which led me to think that she might be on the same plane. I knew she'd planned to take one the next day using a discount ticket as the daughter of a British Airways pilot but it was with an affiliated airline and sometimes these didn't work out.

We always built up these towns in our minds as being the venues for major blow outs and rests, but in fact they were full of running around trying to get kit repaired or replaced, money changed or telgraphed, faxes sent and received, and simply somewhere to stay. Tom and I checked into the Sofitel Hotel, one of a chain of French hotels throughout Africa. I'd seen them in the big towns and had longed to go in and get cleaned up, relax in privacy and eat good food, but I could never afford to. And part of me knew that it would have been difficult going back to the walk after being so clean. But this was a celebration: one stage of the walk was over and Tom and I were beginning another.

The car park was the domain of several Mr Fixits. We hired one and scored off several items on the long list: repairs to the canvas awning, chairs and tent, as well as doing the laundry and other mundane tasks. From another, I bought a very expensive free-standing mountain tent for £15 which would have cost over £200 in the UK. No doubt it was of dodgy origin, but – dog eat dog.

It was the first time I'd seen myself in a mirror for six weeks and I couldn't believe what I saw. My body was completely lean, the muscles were firm and shiny and I was tripping on it. I had a power shower, pulled on a pair of old 501s and a singlet I'd swapped with a guy in the bush and went down to the pool with Tom. He tried to throw me in but I kept a grip on him and we both went in. The moon was still full, the stars were out too and there was no one else in the pool or around it. We played. I think I was more happy then than I had ever been.

The next morning we savoured yet another power shower and went down for breakfast. It was the stuff daydreams are made of. The last buffet breakfast I'd had was at the Victoria Falls Hotel nearly two years before. The memory of pulling the legs off fresh croissants had stayed with me all through Africa and was the one item I would use to describe civilization. These croissants were so fresh the legs came off easily; I got a big bang out of it when the soft centre uncurled with the leg.

We cleaned out the Land Rover to make room for the new driver to sit in the front with us and drove to the airport. We had no idea who we were meeting, how we'd recognize each other, or what his impact on our lives would be. We also hadn't figured out whether we'd make our affair public or just keep it to ourselves. It was all so new: in just three days our lives had been completely restructured. After three months of an unchanging, strict daily routine and way of life, my system was still reeling.

Bamako airport was undergoing very necessary building work. The waiting area was a pile of rubble and the arriving passengers simply walked off the tarmac and over the piles of bricks and dust.

We bought a cold Coke and waited.

'Hey!' Tom exclaimed, 'there's your sister!'

We had to wait where we were for them to get through the barrier, but then – wham – that huge hug I had dreamed of for weeks. And beside her, six feet two and gangly, was our new driver. I wasn't sure if I had interviewed him but Shuna quickly made the introductions.

'This is Gordon Nicholson, he's a friend of Andrew's – one of the guys you interviewed. It's a very long story.'

We shook hands, I welcomed him on board with cold Cokes all round, and left him and Tom together to get the luggage while Shuna and I blurted out all the best bits in unfinished sentences about what we'd been doing for the past four months.

Shuna had worked her arse off to find the right guy and get him jabbed up, insured, visa'd, briefed, a contract written and signed, kit bought, flights arranged – in three weeks.

Following the instructions on my fax to her from Ouaga, Shuna had called Bill Preston. He was running the EO workshops, turning haggard trucks around after a trip and sending them out again. He had a network of drivers and suggested she try Peter Hickey, an ex-SAS guy. Peter had supper with Shuna and Raymond at her flat three weeks before the departure date. He was offered the job, and accepted. Shuna paid for his vaccinations and was working on his kit list and a further briefing when he called three days later to say he'd decided to go back to Australia.

Shuna started calling everyone on my reserve list. Peter Gray was at the top, but he had work commitments. Many of the others were untraceable – being travellers, their contact numbers were long out of date. She faxed me in Ouaga with details of two men, numbers 7 and 9 on my priority list of 10. Neither of them sounded appropriate. I urged her to track down Andrew, number 2 on the list. He was off doing something rugged in the wilds of Norway, but he would be ideal.

A week before the deadline, Shuna and Andrew met. He was highly enthusiastic, had all the right qualities and was offered the job. He accepted. They agreed to meet the following Saturday to firm up the details because 9a.m. on Monday was the deadline to get their passports over to Paris for the Malian visas. Andrew arrived with his girlfriend and a bottle of champagne – it was her birthday. They spent several hours going through all the nitty gritty and Shuna was convinced he was a first-class guy with a great attitude.

Right at the end of the conversation, Andrew said, 'Of course, I can't go without my girlfriend.'

Shuna wanted to throttle him. She knew it would be impossible, but she had nobody else in reserve. She called Raymond to ask for his advice. He said: 'Absolutely no way.' He explained that this was not a holiday, there would be no room in the Land Rover for another person and it would completely shake up the balance of a hard working team if a freeloader was tagging along. Shuna called Andrew on Sunday morning and explained the situation. He still refused to go without his girlfriend, so that was that. In the grand scheme of things perhaps it was for the best, because we later discovered that the one thing he hadn't told Shuna about himself was that he had multiple sclerosis.

Anna Ginty, one of my best friends, called from Paris to say that she'd met a perfect guy for the job but he didn't have various documents and there was no time to get them. At midnight on

Sunday, just nine hours before the deadline, she still had no driver. Andrew called, said he felt very bad about letting her down, and threw her a lifeline. He knew someone who could do it: Gordon Nicholson, his flat mate, an Australian who was free to go immediately. Gordon was a good mechanic and sportsman, he said, a bit quiet but very reliable. Andrew had talked it over with Gordon, who called Shuna at 1a.m. on Monday morning. Their conversation was brief; she offered him the job over the phone and he accepted. She then spent a sleepless night wondering if yet another person would let her down. Gordon, too, was having second thoughts – hardly surprising, because his whole life was about to change and he didn't have a clue what he was letting himself in for.

They agreed to meet at Shuna's office at 9a.m. to hand over his passport. He turned up on time but Shuna had serious doubts when she met him. He had all the right qualifications but no presence. 'Fi's going to bulldoze this guy,' she thought. But there was no other choice.

The Malian visas could only be issued in Paris. Shuna couldn't go through the Visa Shop because it would take seven to ten days and there was no guarantee that they would be ready in time to take the weekly Aeroflot flight. She had called round everyone she knew who could take three days off to fly to Paris and hand them in, but nobody was free. She called an old family friend, Katinka Wells, who lived in Paris and whom she hadn't spoken to for ten years. She asked a huge favour. No problem, Katinka said, courier me the passports and I'll do it myself.

By the skin of her teeth, Shuna had pulled it off – meanwhile, working full time at her job. Her employers pulled her up on the amount of time she was spending on the walk, but she pointed out that she'd told them at her interview she'd be working for me on the side. They put her on observation. Shuna knew that if anything like this happened again she'd have to forfeit her job – a job she'd spent six months hunting for.

The day after Shuna had hired Gordon and sent off the passports, Peter Gray called and said he could do it. He was twenty-four hours too late.

We took Shuna and Gordon back to the hotel to get cleaned up and then moved out into a cheaper place where we could all stay. Shuna and I shared a room and Gordon and Tom shared another. We then had the goodie box session. Shuna had brought out a video camera from Sabona for us to get some footage for the media. She'd also brought a whole load of paperwork from the sponsor's PR company, but we put that all aside as she pulled out the equipment we needed along with all sorts of extra goodies. Three boxes of chocolates from Anna Ginty disappeared very quickly; Tom and I felt sick as dogs with the sugar rush.

We met G that night in a club. He was in incredibly good form, alive, talkative, telling jokes – a very different G from the one we knew. He loved the music and had decided to stay for a few days to listen to the bands. But he promised to leave us messages at the poste restante in Nouakchott and Nouadibou in Mauritania about how he had got through.

Shuna and Gordon were tired and I wanted to take them back to the hotel. Tom and I had a huge argument over it, which must have been a bit disturbing for Shuna and Gordon to hear for the first time and a great relief for G to hear for the last.

'Arguing is just the way we communicate and let off steam,' I said to Shuna. 'It isn't taken personally.'

'I might come back,' I said to Tom, but I didn't. When my sister and I get together, we can't stop talking.

I'd promised Shuna that we'd take a few days off to go on safari in the Parc National de la Boucle, not far north of Bamako. I didn't want to walk all through her week-long stay or I wouldn't have time to talk to her. We got the necessary permissions the next day and headed north.

The rough tracks gave Gordon a chance to drive the Land Rover and he proved to be very good. Things were looking up! I warned them not to build up any expectations about this park: there was probably nothing there, the lodge would be run down, there wouldn't be any water. We hired a guide who escorted us on his moped. He had a puncture and spent an hour repairing it. Off we went again. He had another puncture, we lost another hour, then off we went again and the same thing happened. We took directions from him and drove to the lodge; he could catch us up later.

It had taken us a whole day's drive to cover fifty kilometres, we were tired, we needed to make camp before dark. Despite my pessimism to prevent a major let down, the camp was worse than I'd ever imagined – it was completely uninhabitable. The only sections of the walls which were still standing were covered in spray-canned graffiti, the concrete courtyard had cracked into rubble along with broken window panes, the water pump was broken and the stream was dry. A few rusty beer cans were the only visible signs that anyone had camped here in decades.

The guide arrived and Tom let rip.

We eventually decided to head back to Bamako and spend some time at the 'Oyster River', the site of our last rest day. We camped on the way back and Shuna went a bit over the top in expressing her amazement at how well it was set up. She saw me in my element, and she loved my way of life. She had only seen me between walks, despondent and ill at ease in London, looking for money and planning the next trip. Now she was in my place and I didn't hold back on subtly showing her how phoney city life was in comparison.

We arrived the next afternoon at the river and went for a therapeutic swim. The next day was largely spent going over the PR paperwork. They wanted me to do a live telephoned interview in two weeks' time with some radio station nobody had heard of. By that time we'd be way out in the bush. Once again, Shuna was going to have to play pig in the middle.

In the middle of our last night, it rained. Or rather, it poured. There was mad panic as we scrambled for our clothes, packed up the kit and tried to drive off the sand before getting bogged. We had to use the sand mats and dig out all the way to hard ground. There, an hour later, we put up the tents and fell into an exhausted sleep.

We drove back to the start place and I walked into Bamako. Shuna came and walked with me for about five kilometres: I was disappointed that she hadn't seen the walk on a roll – just the hotch-potch of driving here and there trying to find a good place. But she loved it. She and Gordon made supper on the last night in the bush; it was very good and Gordon looked like he knew what he was doing in the outdoors.

We drove back to the airport to put her on a flight. I had enjoyed having another woman around, but I was looking forward to getting on with my walk: too long in a place and you lose the edge. Tom looked as though he felt the same – it had been a long push to Bamako but it wasn't the end; we had to prepare for the next stretch, two weeks of unused tracks to the Senegal border, where my father would meet us for ten days.

We applied for our Mauritanian visas in Bamako. They spent days over it, saying the guy in charge was not in. Gordon nearly lost his passport by giving a Mr Fixit permission to collect it when the visa had been issued. It was a bit green, but his travels in South America would have done nothing to prepare him for such African incidents as being escorted by riot police to their headquarters for failing to bribe a traffic cop.

A message was left for us at the guest house from one of the American Embassy staff we'd met in Bangui. He had been posted to Bamako and heard we were in town. I called in at the Embassy and Mel, a big, all-American guy, invited us all to stay with him. It gave Tom and Gordon a secure place to work on the Land Rover, while I went shopping for food and odd things and had a good time in the markets, hanging out with the artisans who carved with their Walkmans on. During one of these forays I found the answer to our water and fuel container problems for the desert stretch – two 44-gallon drums which could sit upright in the trailer, lashed down with ropes. Like buying jerry cans in Kano, I couldn't pick the two we wanted because I couldn't smell. I also bought some tubing for siphoning, and marked the drums with paint to tell them apart.

We had another chance meeting with the American traveller who had been arrested in Agadez after announcing himself to be a journalist. He'd been travelling down south and thus far had managed to keep out of trouble.

We set off on 18 April. The first two days were fairly OK, the track was pretty churned up and our load was heavy, but between them Gordon and Tom handled the Land Rover with skill. If I closed my eyes, it could have been Bill driving. We reached a village where part of the roof rack was rewelded and they were given information on the road ahead.

'It is very bad,' they were told.

Tom shrugged it off.

'We've driven from Bamako,' he said. 'We know how bad it is.'

Someone stepped forward to say, 'Sorry, the road from Bamako is good. It gets much worse after this.'

And it did. A railway line took all the cars and goods between Mali and Senegal; this road hadn't been used in years. Boulders the size of tables partially hid deep ravines, tracks led off in all directions but didn't come back together, villages on the map had never existed and it got hotter and hotter with a wind like a hair-drier coming from the desert. For me, the walking was incredibly good – there was no traffic, no people, no tarmac, just hopping from one rock to another, charging along hard-packed orange dirt and checking out the tracks of small animals. It was wilderness: I was home.

It rained a couple of times, flooding the camp and bringing the mozzies out. By the end of the week we reached a tributary of the Senegal. After much searching we found a waterfall, an excellent place to stop, we thought, for a couple of days while work was done on the Land Rover after the rough crossing.

The waterfall was virtually dry but the riverbed had water in. Tom and I blew up a couple of inner tubes as rubber rings and climbed down through the smooth rocks to reach the water. The rock was catacombed with holes, funnels and chambers. We floated through these on the still water and into caverns where the light bounced off the walls and our splashes echoed back at us.

Out in the main stream, I saw a heavy splash.

'Hey, Tom,' I shouted, 'better get going, there's a croc in the water.'

I doubted there was one but if you're going to be frightened it's much better to scare someone else and take the piss. It gave me a bang to watch him try to climb the sheer face of the cliff like a spider in a bath. We made our way out to a bank where there was a stone jetty – perfect washing rocks. On the far side, a grassy bank was littered with baboons. Not the arrogant, irritable beasts like those at Yankari; these animals were completely natural, they had probably seen very few people. The whole place reverberated with a clean, fresh gentleness and a pace which somehow said, 'This is how it's always been.' I'd never encountered that anywhere else – a deep, certain knowledge that nature ruled here.

Tom and I made love on that rock then fell into the clear water to cool off from the hot sun. The little fish nibbled at our toes. When we got too cold, we'd clamber out and sunbathe on the rock until we got hot again.

This was our way of life, it wasn't a holiday; we worked during the day and came home in the evening. If I had treated it like a journey, I would have been battling to get somewhere instead of enjoying what was around me. Our affair hadn't altered our friendship. We agreed that if we gave it a go and it didn't work, we'd just go back to how we were. Sometimes we said we weren't old enough to be a couple, other times we just felt incredibly happy and complete. This was where Africa's magic began for me – when I could stop and wait for the dust to settle after my footsteps and listen to the animals returning.

But what was driving me onwards instead of staying still, was a need to free myself of this ambition and the only way to do that was to complete Africa and then Europe. Tom and I clashed – we both

had the same amount of conviction and instead of having a relationship based on one motor and one rudder we were two motors and
we wore each other down. I liked to argue – it's exercise for a
dormant mind – and he couldn't let go of the bait. Nor could he let
go of the responsibility over the Land Rover and share it with
Gordon; even though Gordon did much of the work because he was
a better mechanic, Tom still felt possessive over it. It tired him out.

There is a point when dusk falls and the camp hasn't been set up
nor the wood collected when you get a sudden anxiety rush that
you've been caught out. The North American Indians call it the
'Mischief Maker'. Tom and I reached camp after the long walk back
from the water, lightheaded from dehydration, and there was nothing
to eat or drink immediately. Odd bits of kit littered the campsite
without any sense of order, the water jerries baked in the hot sun,
the fire was cold and there was no wood.

Tom picked up a piece of clothing and flung it into the bush. He
kicked the pan by the fire and screamed: 'I hate this fucking shit!' as
he scanned the mess, looking for something choice to break.

I gathered some wood, lit the fire, poured out water into the kettle
and put it on for tea. I took the table around the other side into the
shade, wiped it with a cloth in the wash bowl, set out the tea things,
scrubbed the fly-blown plates and sliced up some mango pie from
the night before. While the kettle was on, I retrieved the bedding
from various bushes where it had aired, made a brush of small sticks
and swept the camp clean. I washed my hands and face.

'Tea time guys!'

Tom thudded back to camp, sat down, took the hot cup of tea
and the clean plate and almost burst into tears. The Mischief Maker
can get such a hold on you, like that blind panic I'd had when I
couldn't get away from the insects in my ears for thousands of
kilometres; but the turning point had been when I took hold, realized
I could do something about it and just did it – walked out, with two
friends beside me.

'Hey, Fi,' he reached out and took my hand, 'thanks, I'm sorry.'

'Tom, this is what you do for me every day.'

We put on 'Eric Clapton Unplugged' as night drew in and lay
back on the roof. I wanted to show him that he didn't have to carry
all the responsibility on himself, that it was OK for all of us to lean
on each other – Gordon for mechanics and me for emotional
support, and it didn't mean handing it over or that he was weak.

'You're still in control,' I said, 'just use the crutches that are there.'

31

I reached a village where everyone was on a roof mending job to prepare for the rains. The thatching grass is at its prime just before the rains: sod's law doesn't seem to apply in nature. They took me hand in hand to meet the chief and ask the way; the track had split and the Land Rover was still behind me packing up lunch. He lent me his son, who took me down to the dry riverbed and pointed left along the bank. I thanked him, crossed the grey stony bed and turned left along the sand.

On the rest day I take out the map and have a look at the route for the next week because sometimes we have to work round a logistical problem. I'd pointed out this feature but I wasn't sure if it had sunk in. The Land Rover was always ahead of me, usually having overtaken me about half an hour after packing up the break. I would then follow their tracks, and was used to picking them out amongst any others – but they weren't used to tracking me. By looking at tracks I know when a village is coming when I see children's footprints. I can tell the men from the women, roughly when they passed by, and I see where they stopped for a chat and where their dogs met. But I hadn't seen these before – larger than my palm, no claw marks, five toe prints and a round pad. Lion. I looked closer and worked out that this was a lioness and her cubs – so fresh that there were no other tracks over them.

Fuck!

I shot up a tree and figured I'd just wait there till the Land Rover came along. After a while I got bored and wondered if I was overreacting. It was midday; hopefully they were dozing under a tree.

I climbed down and carried on. I didn't have the same sense of being followed as that time in Kafue in Zambia, but the tracks continued and they were very fresh. It got pretty hot and I was dehydrating fast. I'd expected to see the Land Rover after no more than forty-five minutes so I'd virtually finished my water.

I squatted for a pee every few minutes. I had bad cystitis, and the last few times I'd peed I'd noticed I was passing blood. Now I had two problems. Not only did I need water, but I was leaving a trail of blood.

An hour and a half went by and I was desperately thirsty. Then, so unbelievably that I thought I must be hallucinating, I saw a water pump standing alone in the bush. There hadn't been any villages or people since I left the village by the river. I worked the handle, and the first thing to appear was a swarm of dehydrated bees that must have flown up the spout in search of moisture. I swiped them off my face as the water chugged out. I couldn't smell it, but it looked OK. I knew I shouldn't drink it but after weeks of being slightly dehydrated I no longer cared. I later found out that this sight is quite common – villagers pack up and leave when cholera is in the water.

I carried on. I had assumed that the Land Rover must have been slowed by the track, but now I was worried. However, I had passed the point of no return: night was coming and behind me were lions. Better to keep going. Just before dusk I climbed a baobab, strapped myself to a branch with my bum bag belt and settled down for what could be a very cold and scary night. It was only much later that I also found out that lions do climb trees. Naïvety is bliss.

I heard the Land Rover in the distance, gunning it over the rough ground, making a terrible noise. Two very weary men pulled up and hugged me. They'd gone straight over the riverbed and instead of turning left had carried on to another dry riverbed. It had taken them two hours to get across – the boulders were the size of bungalows. The chief's son had run after them all the way from the village. When they were almost on the far shore – cursing me no doubt – the boy had caught up with them and said that madam was back down the track and along the river. There was no way they could reverse or turn round with the full trailer on the back until they'd reached the far shore. Then, they faced another two hours getting back across with the ever-growing fear that we were separated by quite some distance. The chief had told them there were lions in the area. They dented the steering arm on the way back over the boulders, which slowed them down on the eighteen kilometres of rough track that lay between us. Tom drove like a madman – he guessed I'd be furious.

But I wasn't. I was just relieved they were safe and the Land Rover was still going. We kept the fire in all night.

*

The days got so hot it was all the boys could do to sit still and sweat without passing out. I wasn't in so much danger because of the small breeze I produced with walking but I recognized the signs of overheating – my breath would be short and sharp, my face would get hot. I'd pour a little water into a palm and wet my face then turn into whatever breeze I could feel. If I had enough water, I'd soak my kaffiyeh and wet my head.

My cystitis had reached a worrying pitch. The best cure is to drink water, but I was consuming ten litres a day. I was pissing blood, and there was blood and mucus in my stools. I knew the latter could be a multitude of different things which we could cure, but the medicine would lay me up for a day or so. I couldn't afford the time; I had to reach the Senegal border quickly because my father would be waiting there. I looked forward to seeing him, but I was nervous about it, too. There was so much bottled up inside me that I had decided to tell him.

The heat came belching off the desert and I could feel my skin contracting under it. I walked early and spent three hours waiting out the worst at midday. But camp was a killer; past the stage of irritability, we all felt nauseous.

Cone-shaped volcanoes littered the landscape like giant pawns on a chess board. There were more monkey footprints than human and the tracks split up like an unbraided rope. As usual, the best walking was the worst for the back-up; I was having a great time but they couldn't even overtake me. I kept them within earshot, and had to run back a few kilometres when the Land Rover and trailer jack-knifed on an eroded dirt slope. It took three of us half an afternoon to dig it out with shovels, sand-mats and piles of rocks.

I'd often ask the locals if it would rain that night but they always said no, even if it did. These were still the mango rains – the big rain would come in a few weeks. I noticed small tufts of wild dog hair on a thong around the children's necks and in the hair of the girls and asked a chief's son what it was for.

'It keeps them safe from disease.'

He indicated spots in the skin and added, 'The medicine is not scientific, it is African.'

The dust and high temperatures started a fire under the dashboard, killing the electrics for a few days. The same night the boys put a hole in the radiator by driving into a tree while trying to find a campsite in the bush without headlights. As if that wasn't enough, we then realized it was going to rain but discovered that one of

Tom's tent poles had been lost. There was a point when we thought the clouds might blow over and save this being one of the most stressful days of the trip, but it was not to be.

Next day, the oil sump cracked. It was losing around a litre of oil every twenty kilometres, and since it had already drunk the reserves we carried, simple arithmetic said we didn't have enough to get to the next town. The map indicated there were no villages between us and Kayes, another 150 kilometres away. If the worst happened, I could walk in and get some but I was still pissing blood. Our map, the Michelin 953, unfolded to something two metres long and we were moving along it by the width of a small fingernail a day. It was very good as maps of Africa went, but it had been a while since any mapmaker had visited some of these places and the information was about twenty years out of date. Towns of thousands of people had sprung up, others had disappeared without trace.

We came to a railway bridge over the Bakoye River which also served as a motor and pedestrian bridge. Some officious guy in civilian clothes demanded payment for our crossing. We refused, and even though he was running a scam, he got highly excited.

Mahina was the first town we'd seen for two weeks. But – no oil, only Fanta.

We decided to risk driving to Kayes. The situation got pretty serious, but we managed to buy a few precious litres from a cement factory to get us into town. After a good hunt through the Land Rover, I found the pills which Susannah had given me in Ouaga for cystitis. They turned my pee a brilliant red/orange – not quite the colour of blood but just as frightening. We also checked out the railway to Senegal – we didn't expect the Land Rover to make it, and it didn't matter if it went by train. Unfortunately, the next train was in five days' time, so we drove back.

As I walked into Kayes, I stopped at the outskirts to check out the ruins of a French military post beside a glassy smooth river – the kind of surface which must have the same effect on swimmers as a fresh slab of clean white cartridge paper does on an artist.

We were two, maybe three days to the Senegal border – the map indicated there was a forty-five kilometre stretch of no-man's land between the border posts but this seemed very odd to me.

A couple of French guys in a car coming from Senegal stopped to tell the drivers that my father was at the border and very worried. It infuriated me that I couldn't get word to him because there was no traffic going in that direction – it all went by rail to another border post.

This actually made me cry. Although my father had been a Royal Marine and was used to showing initiative, I was concerned for him: he'd been there for four days without word from us and I hated to think that he was worried. I could handle the stress of the Land Rover breakdowns, the heat, the dehydration and the cystitis, but putting something emotive in there made me lose control.

On the second day out of Kayes, I asked the drivers to go ahead to the border where Tom could cross alone, get a bus across no-man's land to the Senegal side and meet my father before he went home.

I walked alone through a baobab forest – weird undisciplined trees where nothing else will grow. I was gunning it at full pelt to cover sixty-eight kilometres that day to reach the border. Through a small village, a young man held up a glass – the sign for a water break. I thanked him and ducked under the thatch, my eyes adjusting to the sudden darkness. I was too thirsty to care about the water and drank several glasses full.

'Are you hungry?' my host asked.

I wasn't, because of the heat, but I just felt like some company and sat on my haunches, as they did. Four men, all spotlessly clean in their white robes, even their sandals were clean of dust. A woman brought in a large calabash bowl of rice stew and a fork in a bowl of water. I declined the fork, motioning with my fingers that I would like to eat like them. We washed our hands, skimming off water from the surface so as not to mess the rest of it – a practice we had adopted in camp. The bowl sat in the middle on a brightly coloured plastic woven mat and we scooped up the rice, moving it on the side to cool before wiping it into our mouths.

'Mmmm, good.'

'You like?'

'Very much.'

I washed my hands when I had finished and told them about my journey and that my husband was waiting for me. We shook hands and I ducked out again into the brilliant light.

Gordon returned with a gendarme who said, 'You cannot walk on this stretch.'

'Oh yeah?'

This pathetic little trumped-up bobby thinks he has the power to stop me after 10,000 kilometres?

'Why the hell not?'

'Because there are bandits. A Frenchman walked this way two weeks ago and was dead after three days. And there is no water.'

'I have water, I have a back-up vehicle,' I said. 'Why don't you follow me?'

And I turned back to the road and carried on. Gordon drove the Land Rover at crawling pace some distance behind me but after about five minutes it drew up beside me. The gendarme didn't want to drive thirty-five kilometres to the post at this pace so Gordon drove him ahead to the border.

I reached the border village and met the Land Rover.

'Did Tom get across?'

'No, he didn't want to.'

I couldn't believe it. Tom knew how much this mattered to me, he knew how much I wanted to see my father, yet he'd chosen this moment to wind me up. We reached the thatched wall of the immigration office as I gave Gordon shit about not making Tom go – or even going across himself – and was getting very heated. I walked into the hut and my eyes hit on Tom. Then I saw who he was talking to. Everyone cheered as we hugged and they explained what had happened.

My father had waited on the Senegal side for two days, asking everyone who came across if they had seen us. Nobody had. He crossed the bridge to the Mali border post to ask them, but they hadn't either. Each day, he walked across and finally they gave him permission to get a train to Kayes with a temporary visa. If we hadn't shown up today, he'd have taken the train. He had just been walking over the bridge when he saw the Land Rover trundling towards him. There was a lot of 'Captain Campbell, I presume?' and they rode back together to wait for me.

My father's wait had not been entirely without incident. Arriving at the Senegal border post late at night, he had been taken by a young girl to what he thought was a guest house. When she led him into a room and started stripping off, he had to do some pretty swift talking to get a room by himself.

We walked together over the bridge, my father and me, keeping a good pace, waving at the fishermen below as they cheered that the white man had found his daughter.

'How's my cat?' I asked after a rundown of family and friends.

'Oh!' he laughed in his clean, western clothes and funny straw hat, 'he's just fine. Got into another fight with a fox and came in looking pretty pissed off, wanting some food.'

Driftwood was more than a stray cat I'd nurtured back to health: he was the way my father and I could communicate affection for each other.

We reached the end of the bridge and went through the formalities.

'Campbell?' asked the clerk. 'The Campbells are coming!'

It was time for a rest day. Quite apart from anything else, there was a lot of work to be done on the Land Rover after the rough crossing of the last two weeks.

We drove to the Senegal river and parked up for two days. It gave my father a chance to empty his rucksack of goodies and for us to play with them. Like Mary Poppins' carpet bag, there never seemed an end to the fine display of gifts, from cheese sauce mix to gear oil.

'... and a wee something for the evenings!' he said, pulling out a bottle of Glenfiddich. Things were really looking up.

The camp was dry of wood – at least to our eyes. My father brought back armfuls of thorn but they wouldn't burn. We bought some from passing wood salesmen but even then it wasn't enough. This area was Sahel; I was told by a teacher that twenty years ago it was teeming with game, but because of overgrazing there was nothing left now but sand. My father and Gordon got on well while tinkering with the Land Rover. It gave Tom and me a chance to be alone and we went down to the river to swim and wash and listen to the birds hitting the water like muffled dynamite. Our arguments were wearing us both down but our relationship had always been like this whether we were having an affair or not.

My father had been in training for months to come and walk with me.

'I didn't want to slow you down,' he said.

He kept up well and walked a quarter every day – usually the first one, because the temperature wasn't so hot.

A truck came trundling past.

'Watch what they do,' I said.

And, as always, a limp wrist was flipped out the window in a gesture of 'Why?' as the truck sped on.

'Well, it all began ... Hey, come back here!'

My father and I hadn't spent any time together on our own since I was thirteen and we'd sailed a yacht down the Caledonian canal from

Inverness to the west coast of Scotland. Now he was in my place. I was the boss and he had agreed not to criticize nor offer advice unless asked to – those were my conditions. One of my problems with him had been a sense that he was always looking over my shoulder and finding fault with what I did. It made me self-conscious to the point of not being able to do anything right. That was why I had planned and executed all my walks in my way and strictly without any input from him.

We had a tenuous respect for each other and kept it at arm's length, never speaking much. Out on the road in the hot sun, however, I told him there were a lot of things I wanted to tell him that I'd kept bottled up for years.

'I'm here to listen,' he said.

Tom went down with dysentery: high fever, dehydration and those pitiful excursions every half hour to the bush. He'd lost so much weight and didn't have much resistance left. There's months more of this, I said to myself, and the food will get less across the desert: Christ, can he make it?

Gordon and I took on all the major chores, with masses of help from my father who just wouldn't stop. At 1a.m. one morning, I was woken up by the wind. There's always a strong wind before it rains – nature's way of giving you a few minutes to brace yourself before the deluge. I woke Gordon and we set to, putting up three tents and moving Tom.

My father woke up and started gathering the wood for tea. He was dog tired but switched onto automatic, thinking it was morning and time to get up. As I tried to direct him into a tent I was reminded of an old Zairois proverb: 'He who wishes to herd the elephant must first take into account which way the elephant are already heading.'

The landscape had become just sand and dust. The next village could be seen far away marked by its mosque – there were no schools or clinics, just mosques. The Fulani herd the animals to drink at the river. They'd come in their kind – first the donkeys, then the goats and then the shoats. And the Wolof herd their lamsies. So placid, they seemed to share the temperament of their herders. We spent our days looking for something cold to drink. The Katadyn water filter had clogged beyond repair so we boiled all our drinking water. It never got time to cool, so we drank it hot. They seemed surprised when we asked for beer. The locals drank it, but not *warm*.

Then we reached a stretch where, for the first time on my journey, the villagers had electricity and cold Coke! They also had masses of chocolate products in the little stores and all this sugar became quite unsettling for all of us. There were no fresh vegetables or fruit apart from the odd mango, but plenty of tins. We ate laxatives with each meal and crossed our fingers. Wood was in such short supply along the river that we'd douse the end of unburnt sticks, put them on the bonnet and take them with us. Unfortunately, as the boys drove, the wind acted as bellows on a cinder and the whole windscreen was obscured by smoke, then flames! There was a nasty smell coming from the burning wood.

'Did you pee on that?' my father asked.

'Yes,' said Gordon, 'I do it to save water.'

Then came a stretch of tarmac road and the villagers became unpleasant. I'd walk through and be surrounded by kids as usual, but they wouldn't play or hold my hand or respond to the growling game. They jeered and chased me out; then the stonings began. Tom felt incredibly protective of me, to such an extent that, lying semi-delirious on his camp bed, he had woken up and shouted: 'Fi should be here by now, another five minutes and you must go back for her, she'll be in trouble.'

Sure enough, I was just visible in the distance.

The reason for this sudden hostility had to be due to foreigners, and sure enough, we discovered that this was a stretch of the Paris/Dakar car rally and the cars ran over a lot of chickens. As my father walked with me through a village on blistered feet the chanting set up. It started low and out of time, then found a rhythm and got louder and more demanding. It was good to have someone else there to experience it but it spoiled the walk for him. It must have taken great restraint for him to let us handle it – he was my father, after all, and he was watching his daughter walk into trouble. But I walked out of it, with the help of my team.

It was the end of a week and we drove to the river. Night fell before we reached it, and picked out in the headlights we saw two stone columns with a bauble on top – the gateway to something. Driving in we saw the outlines of ornamental gardens and knew we were about to come across something pretty big. The house had obviously once been a wealthy colonial home, standing three stories high with columns and stone stairways, but it was now forlornly derelict.

We set up camp, figuring we'd go to find the river in the morning.

The caretaker arrived with a chicken in his pocket and told us the story of his establishment.

'The house was taken over in the battle for independence. We have left it standing to show our children what we fought and won!'

It was a familiar theme in Africa. The conquerors don't move into the houses of the ousted missionaries or colonials in the bush, they just wreck them and then live next door. It reminded me of heads on sticks.

We moved camp to the river where we weren't left alone at all by the kids. They wanted a fight, and baited, goaded and jeered until one cocky youngster came just too far. Tom ran after him at a mighty pace and headed him into the river. Gordon took over and swam after him. The boy was so scared, he swam to Mauritania! Some women came by later and I offered them our washing for an easy wage. This made the rest day quite fabulous – my socks would take me a couple of hours, let alone the dresses and sheets.

Tom and I talked of his continuing role that night, away from the camp. He couldn't let go of the responsibility of the Land Rover or for my safety and the stress was consuming him. He took it out on all of us at times and couldn't get a handle. He was also so physically weak now and would get weaker as we crossed the desert.

'You've got to get this stress under control,' I said. 'Think about it when you've calmed down and give me an answer when my father goes. Then he can instruct Shuna to find another driver.'

I didn't want him to go: it would mean spending a huge amount of money that I couldn't spare, and a lot of hassle for Shuna and us. And I wanted him to stay because I wanted him to finish the walk. Besides, I needed him for his energy, his humour and his incredible commitment to the walk.

Out walking with my father, on a dead straight gravel road lined by dead straight verges right up to the apex, far in the distance, I spoke of the build-up of stress to one who knew all about it.

'Can I offer some advice here?' he asked cautiously.

'Come on, give me a break will you?'

'When we were out on exercise, we could usually get a replacement in to take over if one of us was injured or losing it. I think you should consider sending him home and having a fresh pair of hands on board.'

'Yeah, I've asked him to think about it.'

The logistics also trawled up a whole mess of conflict: if I fired him I'd have to ask my father for a loan to cover the cost of getting him out and a new driver in. I hadn't been in the position more than twice in my life of having to ask him for money, and each time I had repaid him in full within two months. This time I had no guarantee that I'd have any money at the end – and five malachite ashtrays sure wouldn't square the account. But Tom's health and the success of the trip was more important than a bit of hurt pride.

'If he goes, I can't afford to get him out or a new driver in. The cost of the Land Rover and getting Gordon out has drained the contingency fund. How would you feel about a £1,000 loan? I must point out that I'm broke, I've got nothing and I might have to pay you back over a year.'

I braced myself.

'No problem. Just let me know and I'll get the money to Shuna.'

On the day my father left, as we waited for a bus for him to take to Dakar, I asked Tom for a decision.

'Can you get a handle on this stress shit?'

'I'll put everything into the walk, as I've always done. I want to stay.'

'OK,' I said, 'let's give it another shot.'

As I hugged my father goodbye, he asked if he could come to Tanger. It was as if he'd been saving it up; it was perhaps the first time he'd ever asked me if he could do something.

'Come to the party in London,' I said. I didn't want to hurt him, but with all the controversy over our relationship, it would over-shadow the achievement of everyone else if he was there. As he got on the bus I suddenly realized something. I was standing still as he was moving away.

13.5.93. I wrote in my diary: *Wind stops after dawn breeze. The air heats up. The road looks wet in streams. Hot on my chest. Drumming in my ears. The body pants. Search out shade. Must take the first bush, wait for another and I'll be battling and growing anxious and arguing with myself. Shade. Unzip behind, reach back, pull the water bottle, judge how much I have now for drink, little dribbles on my palm to wet my arms and face. Turn till I catch the slightest breeze and cool.*

Once the air gets to a particularly stagnant and suffocating pitch, the breeze begins, if from behind, I must keep turning to cool, my face beats beetroot. Water breaks become dancing stops. The shock of the breeze chilling my body when I douse, gasp, want to find the perfect temperature but it only lasts for moments. On the road west, I was on edge all day with increasing villages, gently pacifying and defusing, preempting BEING NICE takes concentration − it also distracts but it's fuelled by fear. Walk in, hear the first recognition before I see it − the 'ba' of Touba (tourist) or 'dam' of Madame or 'Eh!' that demanding grunt. I turn to it and lift my hand in a wave but don't say anything yet. Then the children swarm to the road, movement between the houses like the tide sucking back between the rocks, making their screaming, clapping, shrieking noises of delight. I wave to them and break into a broad smile and giggle 3 times to relax my face. I say 'Ça va?' they ask me back and I say 'Ça va bien' and keep walking, walking and greeting as I go − trying to look far into the shadows of the overhanging thatch, careful to be even and gentle.

But if I shake hands there is a break-down, I am no longer revered and they swarm, gathering momentum, noise and I must be careful not to do anything which they will imitate or gang up on − unite them against me, single me out, making them realize that this is something very vulnerable to play with.

The Land Rover had to wait for me at the end of each village because the stonings got so bad; a hit on the head could be pretty serious. The adults didn't give a shit and wouldn't control their kids. The women sat watching, the skin dyed purple around their mouths like Dibble on *Top Cat*.

The landscape changed: the ground was still yellow sand but there were more palm trees. I called them Medusa palm because their branches moved like snakes. It looked like a bedroom to me, there was no leaf litter, just sand with trees sticking up and the women padded along in there like it was indoors. Every relief in the landscape has a sand dune on the southwest side − every twig, every goat dropping, every branch.

We reached Richard Toll, where the shops mostly sold luggage, and discovered a bar with cold beer! When it hit the back of my throat I felt immense relief, as if I was sick and had made it to the doctor's surgery just in the nick of time.

We drank at a pink colonial hotel with half-buried tyres round the entrance like a cartoon of the Loch Ness Monster and bougainvillea on trestles out on the patio beside the Senegal River. For the first time in weeks, I found a door which locked. Instead of fresh croissants, the mark of civilization now, after months on end of going to the loo with kids watching, was simply being able to shut a door behind me and enjoy complete privacy. There were no windows.

I was out of sight of everyone. I stayed in there for a long while before I went back to the bar.

We could either stay a night there but not get pissed, or get pissed and worry about a campsite later. We chose the latter. That night I lost control – not over drink, but out of a build-up of my own stress. Not so much the stonings or anything black and white, but that grey mess of principles inside my head where there is no map.

Like standing on a soap box on Hyde Park corner, I just about covered everything I believed in or spat out everything I didn't in an effort to figure out just what I was supposed to do with Tom. When all this got mixed up in daydreams, I'd hit the major crisis, which usually happens at the end. In stark contrast, I spent my days walking past the lives of full families, where the young are surrounded by instruction on right and wrong. But they find this too, when they leave for the city: suddenly there isn't anyone who can keep them in line. Maybe they go crazy like I did, screaming out my rage, trawling through my mind for an issue. Christ, if only it was as simple as oppression.

I knew that I could calm down, but I didn't want to – like crying, sometimes you've just got to get it out. When I'd finished my theatricals I took myself off to the shore of the Niger and lay in a hammock. When Gordon and Tom felt like leaving we drove out to the bush and set up camp.

I walked to the border at Richard Toll the next morning and we took a ferry to Mauritania. It was the first time I'd congratulated us on a new country before we'd crossed the second border post. I shouldn't have done that.

The ferry chief wanted me to pay the amount for a truck because we had a trailer. This was out of order. I was explaining to him the weight difference, and that tourist vehicles were charged a tenth of that as per his tariff, when Tom charged in and starting shouting. You can't deal with Africans like that; they just start laughing. It gives them great pleasure to wind up a white because it's so easy. Eventually, I got him to accept the normal rate.

Then we handed in our passports. They were rejected, because our visas had expired: the consul in Bamako had issued them wrongly. I should have checked. Gordon's was still valid for a day, however, so they agreed to let him in to Nouakchott with our passports where they could be extended. Then they changed their minds and said we'd all have to go back to Dakar to get new ones. This meant waiting half a day for the ferry, driving eight hours down there, waiting two days till after the weekend, another two days to get them issued, driving eight hours back, waiting half a day for the ferry and another few hours to get through the border. We asked if there was any other way round the problem, but it was sod's law that the first border official we'd met who wouldn't take a bribe was this one.

While waiting for the return ferry, I went down to the river to wash out all the muck that had accumulated in my day bag. The cystitis pills had escaped and dyed everything a shocking jaundiced yellow.

I sat down on a concrete and shell jetty with a bar of basic soap and a scrubbing brush. I rarely used any of the toiletry products in the Land Rover, mainly because I had forgotten what I had, but also because I liked to treat myself to a pep-up occasionally by taking them out and turning them over like Mr Fox counting Jemima Puddleduck's nest of eggs.

A slip of a girl came to play at big sister's dressing table and once she'd scoured the pieces clean for me I let her experiment. She settled herself down, straight-backed, and knew what was what. Touching each piece lightly, she chose the shiniest one and pulled off the lid. She upped the lipstick expertly and peered at me for approval as she stroked her generous lower lip. As my Mummy had done for me, I rolled in my lips to even up the colour. She mirrored the movement then giggled, covering her mouth with her hand, a little shy. I daubed some scented oil on her filthy wrist, slipped on a bracelet and set about organizing her hair care treatment – shampoo and detangler for a bushy head, dreadlocked with bits of straw and browned by dust. The session wound up after a time when she looked at me questioningly with a tampax in her hand.

So, back we went to Dakar, leaving the trailer with the owners of the car in Richard Toll. We stayed there two days, during which time two major events occurred. The first was that Tom's behaviour hadn't changed in the least and I made the decision that he'd leave in Nouakchott. The desert lay ahead, and it doesn't forgive as we do. The second was that we ran yet again into the American of Agadez fame.

He'd kept his nose clean as far as Bamako where we'd last seen him, but had been arrested for four days down in Ghana for suspected espionage.

'You didn't tell them you were a journalist did you?' I asked.

'Sure I did.'

It turned out he wasn't even a journalist, but had been asked by some poxy little paper back home to write something about his travels when he got back.

I called Shuna. She'd already run through the list of contingency drivers and had a few other leads. She also faxed me instructions from Stan, an EO driver who'd crossed the Mauritania/OWS border recently.

We spent the weekend on the beach. It wasn't the one from the Bounty commercial. Old women bent straight-legged, making salt in round pools. Beyond them a concrete factory bellowed out dust which covered the trees till they were white like snow and the shocks from the mining cracked the houses. Nobody did anything about it, despite many cases of serious breathing problems in the area, because they didn't have a voice – not even a croaky one – against the mighty power of commerce and corruption.

I wished it didn't have to be so dragged out. I wanted Tom to be gone. I wanted to start afresh. I didn't want to hear about his plans for what he'd do next. Hell, I wanted to escape as well, but I couldn't. I felt his relief that he could go, saw the stress drain away from him and his spirits pick up. It was all I could do to keep to my decision when I saw him so relaxed.

The visas took a day to issue, the quickest I've ever experienced, and we drove back that night. We got the first ferry, crossed through the border and congratulated each other. When people in Senegal had asked for a 'cadeau' and we'd explained we had a long way to go, they asked us where we were going.

'To Mauritania.'

'Ah, then you will need all the things you have.'

Senegal was a wealthy country compared to Mauritania; the drivers now had to pay for water. For four days I walked due north to Nouakchott, 'the place of the winds.' The landscape was Hollywood desert, great yellow dunes that encroached on the road. And the wind! No matter which way you walk across a continent there will always be a head wind. This was cold, blowing straight from the Atlantic and blowing long into the night. There was salt in the air; we were nearing the sea. After the orange dunes, so perfectly sculpted like origami shapes, the grey white sand began, flat land and tufty grasses.

There was no wood, so we used camel dung and experimented with different ages of the stuff. It burned hot and quick and then crumbled to dusty powder, dampening the coals beneath. This was something to tell our grandchildren, Tom said – boiling tea on camel dung in the Sahara. I thought it might make a very saleable, environmentally friendly fuel in the west, especially as barbecue briquettes for yuppies.

I wore my kaffiyeh over my head at all times – I hadn't walked without it much anyway so it wasn't a big change. But my long dresses caused a problem – the head wind was so strong they acted like sails and pulled me backwards.

As I passed the nomads' tents, the women would raise an empty glass, offering me a drink. Sometimes I'd duck into the shade and enjoy the mint tea.

The children were still aggressive. They had a military-like demand to their calls, shouting 'Come here!' like little sergeant-majors. I'd call back that if they wanted to talk to me, they had to join me. It got so out of hand in one village that I went to find the chief. I greeted him as I would anywhere in Africa, using the local greetings and putting out my hand. He leapt back when he saw it, flinging his own hands in the air and making a sound like a schoolgirl finding a dead rat in her desk. I didn't know that it was their custom that men and women did not touch each other. It must have made sex interesting.

We reached Nouakchott, a low, dusty, windy city of grey concrete buildings and sand-covered roads, and picked up some mail at the poste restante. For the first time there were letters for Tom – up till now his friends hadn't known how to get hold of him. I knew what a bummer it had been for him to build up to a mail stop and then find there wasn't any for him.

I got Tom on standby for that night's flight, and we spent the rest of the day sorting out his kit and swiping away flies in an open air café as we wrote letters for him to take back home.

A couple of Europeans walked into the café and said they'd seen us in Kano at the Chinese restaurant. Angelo was a car trader; he drove them down from Europe to sell in West Africa.

'But the Algeria/Niger border is closed,' he said, 'so I have come down from Morocco.'

'We met some guys in Niamey who'd gone across the border with a military convoy,' I said.

Angelo hadn't heard this and didn't really believe it. Still, they were fun guys and told us of a place to camp outside town. They also knew the way to get onto the beach stretch which led to the desert crossing to Nouadibou in the north of Mauritania. They took Gordon to show him. When he got back, he looked worried.

'There is no way the Land Rover could get across that stretch of sand without massive digging,' he said, 'and that bit is just the start.'

It was 500 kilometres to Nouadibou: ten days' walk. The trailer would be full of water at the beginning, and impossibly heavy. There was another route going inland and then due west to the coast but it would add a month to the walk – and it would be impossible to carry a month's water.

I said, 'It might be that if I could find camels for the beach stretch the Land Rover could drive round and meet me on the other side.'

Night drew in and we drove Tom to the airport. We made light of it, remembering the good times.

'Well, while you guys cross the desert, I'm off to the land of Haagen Daaz.'

'Fuck you, Metcalfe,' I thumped him. 'I hope you choke on it.'

He got on the flight; we waved goodbye and turned back to the walk.

Gordon said, 'It's a loss.'

I said, 'It's for the best.'

It had been such an intense relationship, of incredible highs and desperate lows, it left me drained of energy.

As Gordon and I drove out to the desert and set up camp in the dark, I saw the plane take off. I knew that as the seconds passed, he got further and further away. And I knew that when I started walking again, every step would lessen the distance between us. All I had to do was walk 4,000 kilometres and I could see him again.

32

W e had a long way to go now and a lot of things to do before I could start walking.

G had left me a letter saying he couldn't cross the border and had flown home from Nouadibou. He hadn't met, or heard of, any other travellers going north. He urged us, if we were going to try an illegal crossing, to take a guide up to Nouadibou even before the minefield – he'd met a British guy there who had tried to cross with his Land Rover. He'd lost it in the quicksand and spent five weeks getting it out.

The next day we started on the permission trail to cross the border. We went to the British consul, a fabulous lady who ran her own camel milk factory. She was Scottish but had married a Mauritanian, spoke fluent Arabic and dressed like a local woman. She wrote us a letter of introduction to the Minister of the Interior.

We also went to see the Canadian consul, whom the EO drivers said was very clued up on the bureaucracy here and could get us in to see the Minister.

He sat us down and said, 'The border is closed. Some people were getting through with permission from the Minister but in February he sent a telex to all the consuls saying there would be no more permissions to cross.'

This was a pretty major blow. But the EO driver had crossed illegally by hiring a guide to take them through the minefield. We had the name of the guide, so if all other doors were closed, that was the one we'd try.

The land mines had been laid by the Spanish, the Mauritanians and the Moroccans, and dug up and replanted by the Polisario. Nobody knew where they were, except that they were in the sand and the dunes were on the move. The Western Sahara had been a Spanish colony. Overnight, Spain let it go but divided it up, giving two-thirds to Morocco and a third to Mauritania. The Mauritanians

let their third go to Morocco because they couldn't afford to fight
the Polisario, the freedom fighters for the Western Saharan people
who wanted their country back. They were fighting a seventeen-year-
old war against Morocco, funded by Algeria because they wanted an
Atlantic port. Morocco took the dispute to the International Court
of Justice and asked for a referendum to be held to settle the dispute.
The ICJ agreed and sent in the United Nations to make sure human
rights were upheld. Morocco, meanwhile, had planted thousands of
Moroccans in OWS to boost its voting base; until they were moved
out again, the Polisario wouldn't talk. To add to the confusion,
Mauritania had closed its border with OWS, for whatever reason,
but the OWS border was open. So you could cross quite easily from
north to south but not from south to north.

We faxed Shuna about the new driver. She had chosen Peter Gray,
whom I had interviewed but whose visa had been refused by the
Mauritanian Embassy in Paris. They were trying again. It looked as
if we'd be in Nouakchott for about ten days, getting the repairs made
to the Land Rover and preparing for the desert crossing – time
enough for him to reapply, get his visa and fly out.

We went out to the start of the desert stretch to camp and figure
out our plan of action. Angelo arrived with his friend Giorgio, who
was going to try to cross into Morocco that night. The first 170
kilometres of the route was straight up the beach, then he'd turn
inland and cross 355 kilometres of desert to the border. He had to
leave at night because of the tides: the water comes right up to the
deep sand dunes every four hours. When it came to our turn to try,
we knew we'd have real problems if the Land Rover couldn't get on
or off the dune wall. Fortunately, it wouldn't be a full moon.

After supper, Giorgio washed up his plate, got into his 4×4, lit a
cigarette, waved, and headed off – in the wrong direction. Some time
later he returned and we helped push him across the deep sand to
the beach.

A young Belgian guy joined the camp. He'd hoped to take his
motorbike up north but had also been stuck with the permission
problem. Aha – Gordon and I looked at each other – an extra pair
of hands! It would save me a lot of money if we found another
driver on the ground.

'Maybe we can do something here,' I said. 'We know a guide who
can take us over. We need an extra guy and we'd pay for your food.'

He said he'd think about it and come back later. But we met him the next morning and realized he wasn't the right type of character to move at our pace. He moved and spoke as if he was wired into the mains.

It was freezing cold out there that night, with furious winds blowing damp air off the sea, and I'd been feeling pretty unwell for a couple of days. After going into the town to find a garage where Gordon could work on the Land Rover, we drove back to the desert and set up camp around midday. I curled up on my bed against the driving sand and my temperature shot up. Angelo arrived with his friend Rosario, the Italian Consul and another Italian. He was flying home that night and had come to say goodbye.

Rosario said to his friend, 'Ah, but she's pretty.'

The reply, from what I could interpret was, 'Yes, but she should wash herself.'

They realized at once that I needed a doctor and took me into town. The doctor poked and prodded and then gave his learned diagnosis: 'Appendicitis.'

There was a sharp intake of breath from the men who'd brought me in.

'You will have to be evacuated to England,' Angelo said. 'They cannot perform such an operation here.'

The doctor looked at me with grave concern.

'I don't think that will be necessary,' I said.

'Why not?'

'I had my appendix removed eleven years ago.'

Tests showed it was amoebic dysentery. Rosario put me up at his house and drove out to tell Gordon.

I was violently ill for four days and four nights with stomach cramps and diarrhoea that were worse than I'd ever had before, probably because I was so much weaker. When I woke up, I suddenly realized that Tom had gone. I realized, too, that I had a desert and a minefield to cross, and that Gordon was a nerd.

I felt so low and empty. We went out for a Coke and a Dutchman walked into the café having spotted our Land Rover outside; he'd seen it in Kano at the tourist camp before Tom and I had arrived.

'Are you going north?' he asked.

'We are, but we're taking ten days instead of two.'

The Dutchman wasn't fazed by my reply. He introduced himself as Rene and brought in three friends – two girls called Helga and Karen and a guy called Hans. We bought a round of Cokes. They had travelled all over west Africa and were now due to go home.

Hans had a temperature and was getting pretty ill, so I sent them to
the doctor I'd seen and we planned to meet at a hotel in town later.

'Where's Hans?' I asked Rene when I saw him.

'Flown home. He has suspected typhoid.'

They were one male fewer so they were even more keen to join
us to cross the desert. It didn't matter to them that it would take so
much longer. Great! Now we had solved the problem of crossing
with only one driver – Peter's visa had been refused a second time
and he would meet us in Dakhla, Morocco. We'd also solved the
wood problem: the Dutch had a stove.

I got hold of a tide chart from the French Embassy so that we
could plan the quarters between tides for the first three and a half
days up the beach. We'd heard that we could get a guide to cross
the desert at the last village on the beach. There was no point in
hiring one from Nouakchott – they were extortionate even at the
normal pace.

We calculated the fuel, water and food supplies and split the loads
between the two vehicles. Theirs was a fairly new 110 Land Rover
(fortunately, also diesel) with an extra fuel tank, but it didn't like
sand any more than ours did. We had three sets of sand mats
between us and three spades.

While Gordon got the last of the mechanical jobs done, I walked
through Nouakchott to the start of the beach section. Rosario came
with me to drive me back. When I reached the sea, I realized that a
momentous occasion had passed uncelebrated – I hadn't even
recognized it as one. But I'd hit the sea for the first time on the
walk from Cape Town. Straight across the ocean was America; I had,
in fact, walked around the world!

We started at 5.30a.m. on 11 June 1993. Every step was hard. My
feet were sucked down by the sand, but as I kept telling myself:
'Each one counts!'

Our Land Rover had to be sandmatted right across the rough
stretch but once it was on the flat sand, no problem, they overtook
me and pulled up on the bank after twenty kilometres – the farthest
I could go before the tide turned. Dolphins jumped out of the water,
seeming to look across at me. Back and forth they dashed, sliding,
playing and feeding, against a pastel seascape of spray and yellow
sand.

I was ecstatic with the wind, the ocean and the easy walking. I
felt alive for the first time since being sick. The sand was littered

with little fish, both whole and bony, and dead sharks whose fins had been cut off by the fishermen for export to China. I'd never even seen a hammerhead, let alone stroked one – it was smooth in one direction, like sandpaper the other. The fishermen on this stretch traditionally have no boats since there is no wood, so they use the dolphins. By whacking the surface of the water they call them in, and they round up the fish into the men's nets. The deal they seem to have struck is that they share the catch.

On the second day out, my right knee started to ache. I didn't think much of it at the time; it was probably just a mild sprain or tendonitis, I thought, and could be treated with a bandage. But by day's end I couldn't stand without it giving way beneath me. Something had pulled in there, possibly because of the constant camber of the beach.

I set out the next morning after only a few hours' sleep because of the late tide, but could only manage twenty kilometres. Gordon had been an athlete and we both reckoned it just needed rest. He and the Dutch had built a camp by a shipwreck. We rested there out of the wind for six hours until the tide changed again. I set off in the dark, with my right shoe off to try to counterbalance the camber. It didn't work so I walked up on the dunes to lessen the thudding. That didn't work either; my knee just crumpled under me. I waited for the Land Rovers.

'It's no good,' I said, 'I need a longer rest.'

'We don't have enough water to rest up more than a day,' Gordon said.

Christ, another 100 kilometres of this and I couldn't even manage ten. And after that was 500 kilometres of soft desert.

It was viciously cold and the wind howled around the tents; they flapped like the cracking of a horse whip. All the bedding was damp and covered in sand.

Gordon woke me before dawn so I could set out with the tide. I took painkillers, bandaged my knee and limped off. The painkillers only worked for eight kilometres. Normally I would have steered clear of using them, but this time there was no other way. I swallowed a cocktail of Nurofen and tranquillizers washed down with coffee.

I walked the next ten kilometres without my right shoe. The soft sand was such hard going, and required constant concentration to place the left foot on higher mounds and tufts. Since the pain was numbed, I was also in danger of causing further injury, and had to remind myself of this when getting carried away with the great feeling of being able to walk again. With about forty minutes still to go, the painkillers began to wear off. I felt an overwhelming rush of misery and looked out to sea. An albatross floated on the ocean like a small boat.

We reached the village of Nouamghar, which was the last of the three along the beach and the beginning of the Parc National de Banc D'Arguin, a wilderness bird sanctuary. It was also on the most important fold on the map: crossing it meant we were on the northern half.

This was a serious fold and the fold party was serious. We took a rest day and spent the time topping up with water and cooking an amazing meal. Rene had bought two large fresh lobsters from the fisherman. Helga and Karen made mayonnaise and chips, and baked a chocolate cake with whipped-up tinned cream.

I couldn't move, partly because I was keeping my leg completely elevated, wrapped in a Spenco bandage and a sea-cooled towel, partly because I'd OD'd on painkillers and spun out. I fell asleep to the sound of Helga whisking egg yolk for the mayo and woke some time later to the same sound. She was walking around with a bowl and whisk, her bicep bulging like a fiddler crab's.

The camp site was plagued by flies desperate for food and moisture. Everything had to be covered, and even while chopping or whipping, someone else would have to swat the flies away from the cook. They crawled on our sweaty skin, in our hair and on our sores. Just like in the forest, sores will not heal in the desert. Any small cuts or abrasions had to be cleaned with salt water immediately.

Gordon went paddling and nearly lost his toe to a small shark. It couldn't get a bite on the flat surface, swam away, then came back for another look. Undeterred, Karen and I went in, and Helga eventually joined us. It was strange: I'd thought that the desert stretch in summer would be scorchingly hot, and that dips in the ocean would cool us off. In fact, we were so damp and cold most of the time, we couldn't bear the thought of getting wet in the choppy water. But it was refreshing that day; the ocean was deep green and the bright blue sky was reflected on the wet sand. The small waves left lines of fine shredded vegetation that reminded me of the peppercorns on the skin of salami.

We went to the office for the National Park to look for a guide. The chief offered the use of his private chauffeur – not of a limousine, as we expected when we heard the word, but of hardcore Land

Rover stuff. Galo, a charismatic, amusing guy who wore gold-rimmed airline pilot's sunglasses, was the best desert driver in the area.

He said there were two ways to cross – the short way meant three large sections of dunes, the long way meant some dunes but mostly piste. We opted for the short route. We needed a guide because it wasn't a question of just following any track – they simply get blown away – and there were several areas of quicksand.

Our Land Rovers were consuming far more fuel than expected, even allowing for the soft sand. We kept enough in reserve so that if one couldn't make it, the other would drive ahead to Nouadibou, collect fuel and return. We bought some diesel from a passing fuel truck, one of only three vehicles we'd seen since Nouakchott, and set off early the next morning.

My knee felt a hell of a lot better on even ground but it soon started to hurt again. I had a store of painkillers in my bumbag and popped them like candy. I felt nauseous from the drugs and weak once they started to wear off. The first day wasn't too bad, but once we encountered the yellow crescent shapes of stereotype Sahara the pain was excruciating. Our Land Rover had to be dug and sand-matted out only to sink again a few metres further. Helga, Karen and I dug while Galo gave directions and Gordon and Rene drove. We thought Galo had the easy job; he said he was saving his energy – things were going to get much worse.

The wind was relentless, roaring head-on in my ears like a train going through an endless tunnel. My dresses billowed like spinnakers until I cut them short. I wore my kaffiyeh tightly round my head and borrowed Gordon's wraparound shades to replace the ones I'd lost in Niamey, but still the rims of my eyes were gritted with grains of sand enveloped in mucus. I soon learned not to rub them or the mucus bag would split and the sand would scratch my eyes. The wind let up sometimes at lunch and the air became heavy and hot: we'd try to sleep then but the flies kept us fidgeting.

There were compensations. I saw beautiful, deep pink flamingoes, and fiddler crabs waving their nippers territorially – feisty little creatures, they didn't scuttle away but galloped. I also saw golden jackals resting up before they went hunting for crabs at night.

I got lost. As I topped a dune, the Land Rovers were nowhere to be seen; their tracks had been blown away. Your sense of perspective goes: it's impossible for the untrained eye to differentiate between a small object close and a large object far away. Several times I picked out the Land Rovers and walked towards them, finding after a few minutes it was just a gnarled old bush. I reached the top of another dune and scanned the horizon. I felt a rush of anxiety and sat down, calmed myself, drank some water and looked again, rejecting each dark object one by one. Something moved. I didn't look directly at it but on the periphery of my vision, where for some reason I could see clearer. It was the Land Rovers.

We decided from then on that they would wait for me at each rise. This put a heavy strain on them because it was easier if they got to a break and had plenty of time to fix up the tarps as wind breaks.

My nose had clogged with sand, forcing me to breathe through my mouth. I soon had a severely sore throat where the salt and sand had gathered. My knee felt as if it was held in a clamp with a blunt screw being driven into the side and sharp needles of pain were splitting out in all directions. Towards the end of one quarter the muscles in the knee locked completely straight. I could see the Land Rovers on the next rise but they were about five kilometres away. For an hour I used the leg as a kind of wooden appendage, swinging it out Douglas Bader fashion, unable to bend, and then stepping down on it while the other leg bent and took the next step. I was full-on into the wind.

When I reached the Land Rover I hauled myself up into the shelter of the cab and burst into tears. Gordon brought me a cup of tea and let me alone. I got a grip, got out and carried on.

There were times when I saw the light of the Land Rovers in the distance as I walked at night and I ran through everything I would do when I got there.

'Hi guys!'

'Hi Fi!'

'Boy that smells gooooood!'

'Come and take a seat, you look like shit.'

I sit down, humff!

'Oh it's so nice to sit down.'

'Coffee?'

'Please! And a smoke! Life doesn't get any better.'

Helga and Karen are getting the food ready.

'Pass some of that stuff,' I say, 'and let me do some chopping.'

I slip the smoke into the sand, take the knife and chop up the last of the tomatoes.

Galo, like a cat, has found the least draughty place and is very happy. Rene and Gordon are talking engines. Helga sings us a song.

I'm so happy to be in camp, sinking into my chair with my knee up, waiting for the painkillers to kick in. Oh fuck! The sudden realization that I'm not in camp, I'm still out in the desert: I've sat down and nodded off.

It has often happened that people die very close to camp and the survivors and rescuers wonder why they gave up, when they could see the camp. I formed the view that they don't give up: they thought they had arrived and sat down.

A good slap on the face gets you going, a good grinding step, treating the leg like normal, inflicting pain, makes you wake up and get a grip.

I got to camp and helped cook. It was an anticlimax and made me want to cry: there should have been bells tolling and birds of peace flying around or a sunrise or something. That was how back-up saw me much of the time: tired, hungry and relieved to be there. There was about five minutes of grumpy behaviour when I got in as a reaction to the battle – there was no energy to be fun and happy until I'd settled and let go, realizing this time it wasn't a dream.

We had no water for washing, just half a mug for our teeth. We used sand to clean the plates but it had to be done quickly or else the food would dry. As soon as we finished eating there'd be a plunge as the first plate hit the sand and then the scrub, scrub of grit on dirt. Having a second helping made the scrubbing even harder, but I figured a way round it – you squeeze the juice from your tea bag onto the dried food and it slips off very easily.

Up again before dawn, I excavated great clods of sand from my nose. My socks were like hardboard and all our clothes were starched crisp with sweat, salt and sand. We hadn't washed for five days. I pressed on.

Like a giant broom, the wind sweeps the land of loose sand and debris from NE to SW in the morning, then back again as the wind changes to NW–SE in the afternoon. The fruit had run out but we'd bought tins. A sugar rush from the syrup, even though most of it was drained off, tied my delicate intestines in knots.

It was halfway now and the days could be counted down. Out alone, I'd think about good things; the daydreams of old about fast cars were obsolete, they were no longer part of my world. I mulled over the happy times with Tom, I thought about food, and then Tom again. I'd hold one of his smiles in my mind and look at it like a photograph, and I'd remember his funny stories. When he was six he had a blazing row with his mother. He stormed up to her bedroom to get the small suitcase he'd often seen in her wardrobe. He tried to pull it out but it was incredibly heavy. His mother came in and asked him what he was doing.

'I'm running away.'

'What?' she said, 'with the sewing machine?'

I'd start up chuckling and then howling and remember his face grinning at me after the story. Then I'd fall over from the pain and write in the sand with my finger

HOME
TOM

with an arrow pointing due north. All across the desert I wrote this in the sand, on piste where it may never be eroded and in the dunes where I stumbled. I built a life for us together in a cottage where he'd go out to work and I would write my book and bake bread and feed the stray cats. I had learned in Australia that anger can push you on from behind but love can pull you on from ahead. I made a pact, as I always do about daydreams: 'You can dream of anything and make anything real, Fi, just as long as you get there. Leave the muddle of unravelling the mind games until the end.'

They say that something magical happens in the desert when you stand alone in nothingness and hear silence. The headwind had always prevented any kind of silence, or even standing upright, but one day it suddenly stopped. The crunching of my footsteps along a stretch of piste got so loud it reminded me to stop and listen. The engine note of the Land Rovers and the sound of double-declutching up ahead died down after several minutes until there was complete and utter silence. I heard only the rushing of the blood in my ears. I had once experienced complete darkness in a cave deep in the Mendip Hills. I had experienced complete wilderness in Mali. Now I had this silence. Such things make me feel I have a place, that I am part of something, not merely battling to dominate as in the city.

The desert was barren but for shells and brilliantly bleached white bones. I ground out the days and Gordon and our Dutch friends gave me full-on support. Galo injected his by saying a Frenchman had tried to walk across this desert but gave up after three days. We had great storytelling in the evenings – the best I'd ever had – because we all knew the score and nothing had to be explained.

One night after a particularly tough stretch of dunes which had taken five hours to cross, we camped in the lee of one and Galo started dancing. He took us out to the ridge and pointed northwest.

You couldn't see it by looking directly, but out of the bottom of our eyes we saw lights.

'Nouadibou! Nouadibou!' he chanted.

We laid bets on how far away it was to the military post on the railway line where we'd stop, drive down to Nouadibou on the peninsula, and hopefully return with a guide to cross the minefield.

Galo said 28; Gordon 45; Rene, Helga and Karen and I somewhere in between.

If it was twenty-eight kilometres we'd get there before lunch – time enough to travel fifty kilometres to Nouadibou in daylight. We set off the next morning in high hopes. Karen, a keen walker, came out with me for an hour. We travelled along white, hard, crisp formations of incredible beauty.

I walked on alone and got to the breakfast break, which was in the lee of a perfectly formed crescent dune.

'So, eleven kilometres to go Galo?'

Galo was beginning to look a little sheepish.

During the second quarter I reached the Land Rovers every four kilometres so we could keep each other in sight. This went on and on, hour after hour, grinding out the steps on the knee that had all but given up. At each meeting Galo had sunk a little further into the passenger seat. Then, after thirty-five kilometres, we spied the railway.

Yeeha!

I walked another six kilometres due west along the track to the military post, which had laid a wooden plank covered in nails across the track. I walked to it, touched it and hugged everyone. We'd crossed the worst part and won.

The military post was just a collection of low stone huts built into a hill: a bleak and terrible place to be posted. The men didn't even have proper uniforms and it appeared that they supplemented their meagre supplies by asking travellers for food.

Galo explained that we were on our way to Nouadibou but the chief didn't understand why it had taken us eleven days from Nouakchott. He was suspicious and took Rene and Gordon into one of the huts. I was tearing my hair out wanting to get in there but, being a woman, it was better that I didn't. It was a long time before they came out.

'The chief wants proof of what you are doing,' Galo said.

I showed him my witness book.

We had told Galo, and now we told these men, that we would try to get permission to cross into Morocco; if we couldn't we'd put the

Land Rovers on a boat for the Canary Islands and then to Casablanca and carry on from there. I didn't think Galo, who was employed by the government, believed this one bit – he'd seen me fight hard across that desert and he knew I wouldn't be missing out any steps. Still, to protect him and us, we kept to our story.

There is no road to Nouadibou – everything goes by train and boat. Galo drove in the lead at terrific speed over the sand, twisting the steering wheel quickly to let the tyres get a grip and using every scrap of hard-looking sand, bush and rock. We had to mat a couple of times and we got separated from Rene as Galo charged off before they could pick a route.

We gave a lift to a soldier who was walking to Nouadibou, but he didn't help push. On one occasion, we had just dug out and driven up onto a bank when Rene stopped. He got out of the Land Rover, waving what looked like a stick. As he got closer, we realized that it was indeed a stick – the gear stick. His Land Rover was now jammed in second gear.

Eight hours later, weary and in desperate need of simply arriving somewhere, we reached the military post on the outskirts of Nouadibou. They wanted to check our currency declarations and count our money, and discovered a discrepancy with mine of 50 francs – about 7p. They were virtually arresting me over this until I said I'd give them the note. They let us through and Galo directed us to a hotel.

We hadn't washed for ten days. The longest I'd been without a full wash was six weeks, but this was worse. My hair was one coarse clump with a centimetre of thick sand covering my scalp that made my hair stand up. My ears, too, were clogged, not to mention all the other little places.

When Helga and I went in, we hugged and laughed and danced. Yes, they had rooms! Yes, they had showers! Yes, they could do our laundry! And yes, they had cold beer!

We all gathered in the bar. We had probably all mentally rehearsed the phrase, yet everybody seemed reluctant to say it.

Finally, I piped up: 'Six cold beers please!'

They hit the back of the throat and numbed the eyeballs and the condensation on the bottle slipped over our fingers, and we sank into the comfy chairs out of the wind and sand and said our silent thanks to God.

Several rounds later I got up and said, 'I'm just going for a walk, I may be some time.'

I sank down under the shower and thought: this is real! I'd imagined it so often. It was absolute, indescribable luxury. I'd just got soaped up when the water slowed to a dribble and then stopped completely. Fuck you, Africa!

I stormed out, covered in soap and asked for the water to be turned back on. This wasn't civilization at all. That night I was so badly bitten by mozzies in my room that I couldn't sleep. So I went out to the bar and got so pissed that every mosquito that bit me probably died of alcohol poisoning.

The next day we went to the gendarmerie courthouse to try once again to get permission to cross. The chief kept us waiting for five hours. When we were finally granted an audience and explained what we were doing, he just said; 'No. The border with Morocco is closed.'

We tried to get hold of the guide, Mohammed, but he wasn't at the address we had, nor was the phone number correct. We kept getting hassled by dodgy brothers asking if we needed a guide, but we couldn't trust any of them because they might be spies: African paranoia must be contagious. One particularly tenacious character kept following us and darting up to show us pieces of paper from the bank. We brushed him off, and continued our search for Mohammed. At one stage, Gordon got so cross with this character that he asked him his name.

'Mohammed,' he said, 'I am Mohammed!'

33

W e would be leaving in two days' time. We found a camp ground in the lee of an escarpment on the beach. The wind didn't let up but at least we had firewood and kept warm. Helga went to bed with a temperature but her symptoms didn't follow the usual pattern of malaria or dysentery. We decided to cross the border together and if Helga hadn't got better, the Dutch would drive the 400 kilometres alone to Dakhla, the first town in OWS.

Nouadibou is the main shipping port for Mauritania; you can get pretty much anything there. All the fruit and veg is brought down from Morocco and Spain and it's pretty serious stuff. We'd been used to green oranges and black spotted bananas, but this fruit was something else – spherical oranges that were orange, firm yellow bananas that were so perfect they looked like plastic ones.

I called Shuna to tell her we'd arrived. Tom answered the phone: he was sharing the flat with her. God it was good to hear his voice – good to hear him say he loved me and missed me very much. Those words kept me going until we met Peter in Dakhla with a bag of mail. Shuna had one sad piece of news, however: she'd lost her job because she'd spent so much time on the walk.

'But don't worry, I'm actually much happier now that I'm temping,' she said.

I was sure she was telling me the truth, but I felt very bad.

So, out of the desert and into the minefield.

We got a laissez passer from the gendarmerie to show that we had permission to drive back to Nouakchott – this would at least get us through the military posts. We filled up with water and fuel and fresh fruit and bread, but we couldn't say goodbye to Galo. It really hurt; he might not have told the authorities, but we couldn't take the chance.

Mohammed climbed on board, furtive and excitable, and he

directed us with much less skill than Galo back out to the military post where I'd stopped. We explained to them that we were going back because we couldn't get permission, and that I would walk. We gave them some bread and out I got.

After six kilometres, the Land Rovers crossed the railway line into the minefield. Our vehicle was a bit of an embarrassment as it couldn't even clear the railway without being sand matted. We had to hurry: the military were probably watching us from the top of a sand dune.

I kept on the vehicle tracks, trotting rather than walking to get out of sight of the railway line. Soon I broke into a run, not because of the military but because I was desperate to have a pee.

Some time later, Mohammed pointed to a black, table-topped mountain far in the distance and said, 'That's the Moroccan military post.'

Then he demanded his money and said he wouldn't take us any further.

Someone burst into song: 'Don't pay the ferry man...'

No amount of haggling would make him go on. Something had frightened him and we didn't know what it was.

Tentatively I walked on. We joined a set of vehicle tracks and felt a little more safe. From the EO notes, we knew we would reach a tarmac road running perpendicular to us: we had to wait there for the Moroccans to come and escort us over the worst stretch. We reached the road – an old Spanish, crumbling ribbon of tarmac – and took out the binoculars. We could see the soldiers on the mountain and they could see us. They were waving.

'What do you think they mean?' I said. 'Stay put or come on?'

'Better safe than sorry,' Gordon said.

We stayed put for about half an hour. So did they. Stalemate.

'Come on, let's go!' I called, and walked ahead – it was all right for me, I was unlikely to be blown up because these would be anti-tank mines. The Land Rovers followed a little more gingerly. Eventually, we reached the mountain where three soldiers greeted us as if we'd just fled across the Berlin Wall.

We had lodged our details with the Moroccan embassy in Nouak-chott, who had radio'd them to Rabat, who in turn had contacted the main border post. The soldiers now took our details to check with the main post that we had clearance to proceed. I told them it was imperative that I walked and they should have details of my request along with our details from Rabat.

While they were checking, the chief brought us melons and dates, roasted almonds and fresh water. We offered him some soup but he didn't like it. It was all pretty nerve-racking; this was a war zone but we had come through too much to miss out any steps now.

Sabona's PR company had told Tom in London that they had a highly placed contact who could get me permission, but he couldn't give an undertaking. He was far too important. Tom finally took matters into his own hands and got on to the British embassy in Rabat and the Moroccan embassy in London. The former couldn't help because to give us permission would make it appear that they recognized Morocco's occupation of the Western Sahara, which they didn't. The latter had some influence and was keen, just like the embassy in Nouakchott, to see people crossing from Mauritania.

My father had checked to see if there was anyone he knew on the United Nations base whom he might ask for a favour. Luckily the head of the base was a Marine, Colonel Adrian Wray, who, having received an 'outstanding letter' from Tom, contacted the head of the Moroccan military with details of exactly what we needed.

The radio message came back that Gordon and I could go through and that I could walk! They wanted us to get to the main military post that night. It was dark, we were in a minefield, it was incredibly cold and windy and none of us felt like walking or driving two and a half hours to the main base sixteen kilometres away. Besides, it would take between twenty-four and forty-eight hours for permission to be granted for the Dutch and we wanted to stick together.

'Can we camp?' I asked.

More radio communication, during which the head of the main military base drove out to meet us.

'When you are chez Morocco,' he said, 'you are chez vous.'

More food came down from the mountain. The hospitality was genuine and the level of intelligence and training of these young soldiers was the best I'd come across since South Africa. They wore proper uniforms and their guns looked like they worked – and they had ammunition. No wonder these guys were winning the war against the Polisario.

The message eventually came through that we could camp and carry on the next morning. Gordon had a temperature and went to bed. Helga was still very sick but we were told there was a doctor at the main post who had been alerted we were coming. The next morning, we were given a guide to show us the way and kept well between the markers. I decided to wait till we got to the main post to pin down the imaginary blue ribbon behind me that marked the crossing of yet another border.

The Land Rovers were parked up on a large football pitch. We made day camp but the wind was ferocious: the main military base was stone built and looked so snug and sheltered. After some hours, the chief, Captain Hassan, came and invited us up to the base. He showed us into a long comfortable room with firmly shut windows, no wind, no noise, no damp air and no flies. The walls were lined with flat sofas with cushions and it nearly killed me when an orderly brought in a tray of hot mint tea!

We thanked him and, just before he left us to sleep, he said, 'The King knows you are coming.'

We all had a shower in hot water, after which we were called in to dinner. We feasted on a tremendous goat stew with flat Moroccan bread, fresh tomatoes and cucumbers, while watching football on TV. It was all a bit much. I was very tired as I climbed into bed; sometimes such immediate relief from hardship can make you very sleepy.

During the night, Captain Hassan tapped on the door to say that the Dutch had permission to go to Dakhla but would not be allowed to travel with us at our speed. It was probably for the best: Helga was still very sick and the military doctor had tentatively diagnosed diabetes.

I woke with a lump in my throat that our friends were leaving. We'd shared a lot of tough experiences but we agreed on a reunion after the walk. We'd get a trough of sand and a high-power fan, drink warm water then go down to the pub and get smashed.

We split up our things and the food. With them went the gas stove – sad for us, since there was no wood on the next stretch and no way of gathering small bush because of the mines. We shared our last cup of hot tea and were given our escorts – one soldier in each cab to make sure we didn't divert off the road and get ourselves blown up. Waving goodbye to Rene, Karen and Helga and to Captain Hassan, I stepped back into the head wind and pushed forward.

Rachid, our escort, was about to get married. The way he described it, a Moroccan wedding is a pretty serious affair: seven days of non-stop partying, with each day more excessive than the last.

The coastline bordered the richest untapped fishing grounds in the world. Fishermen came here for three months at a time, living in makeshift tents. Their catches were collected every day by refrigerated trucks. The drivers got used to seeing us, since there were no other cars. Rachid didn't know them but they and the fishermen often stopped to talk to him. They gave us fish and bread and oranges – hospitality that made me feel we were on the home stretch and that this walk would end as it began in South Africa, with incredible kindness and generosity.

For eight days I battled against the head wind and the damp cold, with nothing but kilometre posts to break the monotony of the horizons – and they, too, were all the same. It was a damned nuisance that each had the number to Tanger. Start at 2524; ten minutes of head wind later, 2523. Ten minutes of head wind later, 2522. I used them as water-stop posts – just low enough to sit on comfortably, and also just the right height to prevent splash back from the wind when I used them as loos, my butt over the lee side.

I watched the sea birds in the thermals but mostly I was deep in dreams. Gordon did a great job on cooking and finding wood. Rachid knew the most dangerous stretches of minefield and was able to go a short way from the road to gather small bush. One day they found an old crate – enough wood to bake scones and bread.

A saloon car towing a white caravan stopped at breakfast. They wanted the lowdown on the road to Nouakchott; they had sold their house and were driving down to buy a boat and sail round the world. They had about eighteen inches of clearance under their car, no four-wheel drive, no sand mats, not even a spade.

Gordon told them straight: 'You won't get through.'

But they carried on, as I would have done. People are always saying it's impossible and they're never right. But in this case, we were.

We met a camel merchant in a beat-up Land Rover who needed a few gallons of fuel to get to Dakhla. This we gave him, and he asked if he could buy us anything when he got there because he'd be coming back in a few days.

'Beer, that's all. A crate of beer!'

We gave him some money and shared our supper with him in the back of his Land Rover because it was sheltered. When the meal was done and Rachid and Gordon climbed out, I was making my way to the door when the nomad pulled me back. He made pathetic whimpering sounds and tried to kiss me. I shook him off.

Gordon was coping well, but he was very tired. It was a terrible strain on him to keep going at this pace when he knew he could reach Dakhla in two hours, not another four days. We got into a lovely habit at day's end after Rachid had washed up of snuggling into our tents with a mug of hot chocolate and reading for a bit. That hour at day's end when all was done was just about perfect – not so long as to get lazy, just enough to recharge before the dawn march. It was a time to clear the mind of anxieties, put the petty worries into perspective and take stock of where you were. The Africans do it too – using whatever brand of alcohol or drug is produced locally – like the stinging nettle and the dock leaf, stress relief grows nearby.

The head wind prevented the Land Rover from getting into top gear. My knee was well on the mend and the kilometre markers were counted down, one by one. The desert scrub looked like one large macaroon and sometimes I could look over the cliff edge to the pink sand on the beaches. To walk down there would have felt like being inside a seashell.

I felt a new sense of gentleness inside. It came through occasionally, like a voice breaking in adolescence; when I walked I pretended I was with my child, showing it the road through Africa. I've often conjured up a companion – back in Nigeria it had been a donkey, but there had been a long break without one while Tom was around. Instead of the *confidant* companions of Australia, they'd become people I took care of. The child on my back, carried like an African, would be fed and washed and nappies changed and introduced to people we met and talked to all the time.

Rachid's presence helped to alleviate the tension between Gordon and me. 'Gumby', as I'd re-christened him, was so boastful and up himself that I had given him a new name – 'Master of the Universe'. It didn't matter what story I told, Gordon always had a better one.

Sometimes I'd lay traps for him and piss myself laughing when I walked off.

Like, 'I think the first thing I drove was a tractor when I was twelve.'

Wait for the response: 'I drove my grandfather's tractor when I was four.'

He reminded me of a kid who falls off his bike in front of a bunch of people and says: 'I planned that.' Whenever anything went right – accidentally or not – Gordon could be relied upon to pipe up that he had planned it that way. He constantly boasted about his athletic prowess, his triathlons, his rowing, his sailing, his Dad, and even his mother's cheesecake. Everyone in his family was perfect.

And he was 'Master of the Universe' – he'd pumped himself up for a fall; I was just biding my time.

I found his nerdishness rather embarrassing at times – it could be stomached in private or amongst people who didn't speak English, but day after day of silent cringes had hunched my shoulders. I hoped Pete could give massages.

At a break one day, two white four-wheel-drive vehicles stopped. They were UN guys who said they were all waiting for us in Dakhla, and that Colonel Wray in Laayoune needed an ETA: he was going to take us all out to dinner when we got there. They opened their cool box and gave us the rest of their lunch – cold beers, cold Cokes, oranges and ham and cheese sandwiches. I could have had sex with all of them.

I overheard Gordon saying, 'Usually one of the drivers walks a quarter with Ffyona every day.'

I pulled him up on this when they'd gone.

'Gordon, how often have you walked with me?'

'Tom and I walked every other day through Senegal.'

'For how long?'

'A week.'

'So you walked three days and each day you walked eight kilometres, that's twenty-four kilometres out of 4,000. Do you think it's *usual* for drivers to walk with me?'

He admitted that it wasn't and then said it was just my paranoia that made me think people would assume drivers usually walked.

'Not paranoia, you just told them that.'

He sulked for the rest of the day.

I understood that he'd always been in the limelight as an athlete and that he was probably competing with me, and it had to be said that he had done a remarkable job in getting a twenty-six-year-old, beaten-up Land Rover across some of the toughest country in the world – something that would have been way beyond me. But he didn't take pride in that achievement.

On the night before we reached the turn-off for Dakhla, we camped on the cliff edge above pink sands and looked across the ocean to another peninsula where the lights of the town glistened against the setting sun.

'Pete's over there,' I said.

'And mail!'

We tried not to talk about it; the mere thought of post gave me an awful anxiety rush because I couldn't reach it. Patience!

I spent my days, hour after hour, calming myself to accept the pace. I let myself dream about the town but not fret. I'd be clean, my hair would be soft and moving in strands not one clump, and I'd be sitting in a clean little café with a waiter serving me cups of hot coffee, full packet of smokes in front of me, reading Tom's letters.

We reached the military post at the turn off and greeted them. We let out a cheer and all shook hands, then we drove to Dakhla to find Peter and read our mail.

We stopped along the way to take photographs of a spectacular pink ravine but the window fell out of the passenger door and smashed on the ground. Another thing to be fixed when we got there. Gordon had poured all his energy into nursing that aging Land Rover across the desert and he needed a rest. I promised at least one full day of doing nothing but what he wanted.

Rachid took us to the gendarmerie. There then followed a whole morning of bureaucracy – four different offices in three different buildings; God knows how many duplications of details, but at least each man knew what he was doing. If this had been down south, we'd have been there for days.

Rachid took us to a cheap hotel which put up many of the soldiers and we booked two rooms. Then it was back to the gendarmerie to drop off Rachid and fill in a few more forms.

When it was all done, I knew the end was possible. I'd got over the final physical hurdle: now it was just a short sprint of 2,000 kilometres to the Med.

34

I spotted a white guy with a day pack and wondered if it was Pete. But I didn't think so, or he would have come after us when the only blonde this side of the Sahara was walking past him.

As we got into the Land Rover, he came running over to us.

'Hi, I've been looking for you guys!'

He climbed on board to a round of cheers. Gordon and I were desperate to ask him if he'd brought our mail and I just couldn't hold out until it was polite enough to ask.

'You got any mail for us?'

'Ummm.'

'Peter!'

'Yes, got all your mail ... and chocolate ... and whisky...'

We drove round to his hotel to collect his gear. While we were waiting for him in the street, our friends with the car and caravan appeared: they hadn't even made it past the main military post before turning back. Gordon and I were desperately trying to stifle our giggles and pissed ourselves laughing when they drove off, looking for a place to sell their caravan and buy a boat.

We washed under power showers and went out for a full-on meal to read our mail. It was rather unfortunate for Pete that he had brought it with him – we were torn between wanting to chat with him and reading our letters. Max Arthur, the editor of *Feet of Clay*, sent me such a positive booster, as always. He said he saw much maturity in my recent letters and more of the real me which had been suppressed for so long. 'Remember that I love you and there are beautiful days ahead.'

Shuna's letters were full of gossip, which made me realize there was another world going on, one full of laughter and sex. It wasn't my world and I didn't want it, but I liked to hear her having fun.

Tom's letter was a side and a half he'd knocked out in his lunch hour. Bastard!

*

I had tried to get a green card insurance in Nouakchott for Morocco but because the border was closed they didn't issue them. I went to the only insurance office in Dakhla, but they couldn't issue one either. However, the guy said we couldn't continue without insurance. I pulled him up on the Catch 22 and eventually he suggested I get one in Laayoune, 550 kilometres to the north.

Dakhla is a military town. All the buildings are castellated, and adorned with Moroccan flags and posters of King Hassan II. It was built to establish the Moroccans' occupation of Western Sahara – the first stage in the expansion of the country into what Hassan calls 'Greater Morocco' – but when the battle is over, the town will disappear. Nothing has been said of what will happen to OWS when and if it becomes part of Morocco. There is no industry, no fertile land, nothing to mine except phosphates and the world market is way down on that resource. All the people they have shunted in to take residency to increase their vote base will have to be moved back out again. Fuel, food and accommodation are all heavily subsidized to get people to move down there, but all that will disappear.

We were invited to dinner with the UN people at the base on the edge of town. A bunch of really good guys! The Aussies provided the beer and we sank several cans of Fosters but tried to limit the intake – our bodies were so lean now, we got pissed very quickly. The daydreams started coming true when they produced chocolate mousse for pudding.

They gave us the lowdown on the route north and drew a map. There were patches of mines in the sand all the way up to Laayoune but nobody knew where they were. When the road had been built, the Moroccans had got a fair idea.

They let us use the radio phone for a patched call home. I spoke to Tom and kept forgetting to press the bloody thing on the handle. He sounded distant and it was awkward with all those people standing around.

The next day, Gordon was shopping for spares when he ran into Angelo. When you meet a face for the second time, you're buddies; the third time, you're family. Angelo invited us to the beach that night for dinner. He had returned with a truck with a 4×4 inside and was driving it down to sell in Niger. He'd brought his son with him and had a message for me from Rosario. I penned him a note back. Giorgio had made it across, too, and was heading back down.

These two nights out drinking gave us all a chance to relax in other people's company, and took the awkward edge off meeting a new driver. Pete had the streetwise streak in him; he had brought down umpteen pairs of shades to trade with the locals. He'd got a hotel room in Agadir at half price by handing over a pair of £2 sunglasses. He'd flown to Agadir and taken a bus down to Dakhla – a pity for him, I thought, because it meant he'd seen all the land we were going to walk through.

Gordon tried gauchely to get Pete on his side to be two against one. He asked me how much I'd spent in the market for groceries.

'You got ripped off,' he sniggered in front of Pete.

I pointed out that he didn't even know what I'd bought.

But Pete kept rejecting him anyway. He wanted the three of us to work together. He was open, down to earth and always looking for the fun in everything. He loved women and I immediately picked up on it. We could touch and it felt good. Vitality and humour were breathed back into the walk.

Well rested, we set out on the first of five stretches to Tanger – eleven days straight to Laayoune.

Two days out of the Dakhla turn off, Gordon directed me at day's end up and over an escarpment to the camp. Set amongst wind-shaped sandstone rocks, on a flat slab layer, Pete was making supper. He'd picked this camp site with tremendous views across the barren plain. We watched the sun set, drinking Kaluha which he'd brought down for us. Then came a chocolate cake. It was a fold party – our first going east – and I'd completely forgotten! We also celebrated crossing the Tropic of Cancer just before Dakhla, which we'd also forgotten about, being so preoccupied with getting to town.

When the washing up had been done, Pete got out his harmonica. Oh boy, the music echoed around the sandstone.

He told us about his safaris in Zimbabwe, where he'd run trips out to the national park taking tourists to the best sights. 'I'd point out a springbok to a bunch of greenhorns and some stupid German guy says, "Oooh! Does it bite?"'

He had the most amazing stories which distracted me from walking – he'd start one at a break but I'd have to go and couldn't hear the punchline for another two and a half hours.

He'd lost one of his fingers.

'I was fifteen and working on a prawn trawler,' he said with a twinkle in his eye. 'Sometimes we pulled in sharks with the catch and I'd mess with them. One time I was poking this shark's eye when the skipper called me. I looked round and the shark got hold of my finger. It was so mangled, the skipper had to cut it off.'

Gumby swallowed it hook, line and sinker.

Next morning, the Land Rover wouldn't start: the battery was flat. We tried pushing it but on soft sand we couldn't get up enough speed. Gumby waited by the road for a car to jump start it. He was ages down there; eventually a fishing truck stopped but it had no leads. They came and pushed it with us anyway. We gave them coffee with masses of sugar and got it going.

I realized just how much Gordon was enjoying having Pete around, so instead of meeting me halfway through the last quarter for water, I suggested they go ahead, set up camp and have time to play. I knew they'd play frisbee or set up their gym with rocks and rope; I liked to see them having fun. However, when I got into evening camp and nothing had been set up, I was furious.

I'm not very good at keeping my temper when something goes wrong and after so many weeks of good support without problems, I shouldn't have reacted so strongly. Gordon made an excuse that I was early, but I knew I was bang on time. Poor Pete didn't know what the heck was going on.

Pete had been badly bitten by bed bugs at the hotel in Dakhla. Red lumps started appearing all over his body and he began to shake. It was a potentially life-threatening situation because wounds do not heal easily in the desert. I had started this stretch with three sores which were now deep, swollen and badly infected, despite frequent cleaning and antibiotic powder. Pete cleaned his sores with Betodine, and I took over with the ones he couldn't reach. We laughed as I swabbed his backside, but I knew that if his body continued to react to the poison it would become one big tropical ulcer and we'd have to get him to a doctor quickly.

At times when we couldn't find the bottle opener, I'd prised the tops off Coke bottles with my molar teeth. My teeth are very strong – I don't have any fillings – but one day, as I tore off the metal cap, my tooth broke. It continued to crumble until there was just one corner left sticking up like a peg and a hole big enough to lose an olive stone in. Served me right, but the Sahara is not a good place to be in need of dental treatment and there was nothing I could do about it.

The coastline was incredibly beautiful along that stretch: sheer crusty cliffs crumbling down to a coral red plain almost shining in the morning dew. Like coins in an amusement arcade game, the shell layers were poised, about to return to the sea from whence they'd come. We'd camp beside them, looking out over the Atlantic sunset.

One evening, the boulders were irresistible. Pete and I went on an expedition to the beach and did some pretty good climbing. He brought his improvised fishing gear; I watched his well-proportioned body as he played the line, half naked. His large, bronzed, deeply defined muscles moved well. A thought crossed my mind, but I dismissed it. You just couldn't take the guy seriously, he was such a live wire.

The next day, Pete took up my suggestion to walk a quarter with me. He actually jogged the distance beside me and got to lunch exhausted. I took a long drink of heavily chlorinated water from my bottle.

'Anyone want a swig of swimming pool?'

I passed it to Pete. He looked inside at the rim of green algae around the top.

'Fi, this is disgusting, it looks like a Ninja hangout.'

As I was getting ready to get up and go on again, he said, 'Can I do the next quarter as well?' It blew me away.

By day's end he was very tired: the perfect time to teach a new driver about the importance of being in the right place, and how valuable their job was to me. I pointed to a kilometre marker in the distance and said: 'That's the end.'

I felt him relax with relief beside me, his eyes straining for the marker. When we got to it, I said: 'Sorry, got it wrong, it's another half an hour.'

He nearly broke my head.

Not to be outdone by Pete, Gordon asked to walk with me through the last quarter of the following day. He wanted to walk a full day at least once, as Tom had done the day before he left. 'I could teach you a thing or two about walking,' he said.

I was delighted when he decided to walk a quarter in preparation for a full day. I could still remember what Tom had said of his day's walk: 'I had no idea what you go through out here.'

We set off and I kept up my normal pace, expecting him to fall in time since he was so fit. However, he soon lagged back. I kept stopping for him, but he waved me on. Usually, I'll keep drivers in sight in case they fall, but Gordon was a triathlon athlete. He'd driven his grandfather's tractor when he was four. His mother's cheesecake was without equal.

I reached day's end camp having left Gordon some way back in the heat haze. I waited for half an hour and then said, 'You'd better go back for him, Pete.'

Pete set off in the Land Rover and was gone a long time. They eventually returned an hour later. Gordon had collapsed from lack of salt, his muscles convulsing. Pete had scraped him off the hard shoulder and laid him across the front of the Land Rover like a dead moose; his body couldn't fold up to sit in the seat. We nursed him back to health with Bovril, salt tablets, sugar and water.

I took Pete aside and said, 'I don't think Gordon will be walking a full day.'

'Nah,' said Pete, 'we haven't got enough salt in the Land Rover.'

The advance welcoming party from the UN base in Laayoune arrived one lunch time three days before the town. I felt very awkward in the presence of strangers of my own kind, but loosened up after they opened a cool box of beer packed in ice and handed out bars of chocolate. They said there was a Red Cross medical contingent of fourteen Swiss nurses in Laayoune – news that had Gordon and Pete on a high all the way until we arrived and found they were all paired off.

The morning of the day we were going to hit town, Jim, one of the UN guys, arrived again with a couple of others bringing a basket of croissants. I gorged but the flies did their usual best to spoil the fun.

The road into town had no hard shoulder. The wind started to gust strongly, throwing me off balance onto the tarmac. I picked up two large stones and carried one in each hand as stabilizers. From time to time a truck would stop suddenly to offer a lift, but the drivers never paid any attention to the cars behind them. On several occasions I came pretty close to being the meat in a metal sandwich.

Colonel Wray was waiting for us on the outskirts. He was open, highly amusing, warm and on the ball.

'I'm going to have to escort you in,' he said.

Sod's law: we had arrived on the day of the first peace talks between the Polisario and the Moroccans in seventeen and a half years. The place was crawling with men with dark glasses and hearing problems.

The town was beautifully laid out in rows of palm trees above pink and white tiled walkways and gardens with fountains. As the Land Rover chugged along one of the elegant boulevards, it broke down. For Gordon, who really needed a break, it was the last straw. He put it into the UN garage but knew he would have to work on it during the rest day.

I walked to the hotel where most of the Australians were staying and there, bang in the middle of the desert, they'd set up an Aussie bar. The K Club was kitted out with flags, cork hats, cartoons, darts and footie machines, and the bar stocked everything from Fosters to chocolate bars. I tried one of each, several times.

We were put up at the hotel courtesy of the Aussie contingent, borrowing a couple of rooms from people out on exercise. We had a serious power shower – nobody organizes their showers better than the Australians – then went out for dinner with Colonel Wray. He took a whole party of us to a traditional, Moroccan open-air restaurant for a traditional, British good time.

Pete's bites had healed, but mine were badly infected and needed treatment. The Red Cross contingent were so bored they were desperate to get their hands on anything sick. The dentist spent three hours fixing my broken tooth. It was the first dental work I'd ever had done; he was so gentle I found myself nodding off in the chair.

The Australians also gave us a load of kit when they saw that ours just wasn't man enough to keep us warm in the cold damp days and nights. They lavished us with hospitality; every night there was a barbecue, every morning after a bad head.

But there were rumblings on the team front again. Gordon was tired and wanted a break but, instead of coming to me to talk about it, he whinged to Pete. Pete told me, and I had to decide what to do. There was a UN flight to the Canary Islands every week, taking soldiers over for compulsory R&R. Gordon wanted to see if he could go out there. He asked Colonel Wray who, after checking out the availability of seats, agreed. He'd be away for about a week.

During his absence, Pete and I had a fabulous time. We set up the camp the way we liked it, spending time in creating an ambience. I really felt I had come home. Gordon had been so used to setting up camp as a wind break that it had lost any warmth.

Pete found the most amazing campsites among rock formations. One night we camped in an amphitheatre-shaped feature and kicked back with a round of freshly baked banana bread cooked on a crate I'd found on the road. We set up our camp beds side by side under the awning and chatted quietly until something silenced us: the sky was ablaze with shooting stars.

Music came back to camp. Pete set up his hammock at breaks, we made really great meals, we laughed and told stories all through the day.

The UN guys came out again and let us make a radio patched

phone call home. I called my parents and spoke to my mother for the first time in six months.

We camped for the rest day in a secluded bay where a slow stream ran into the sea, sheltered from the north wind. We had a hell of a time getting across the sand but Pete got us through by unhooking the trailer and towing it out on a strop. We set up house and I baked croissants; we named the place 'The Bay of Croissants'. We played frisbee and went beach combing. It was sad to see the amount of trash that littered such a beautiful place – everything from washing-up liquid bottles to syringes, and mostly from Spain. But there was so much driftwood we could keep the fire going all the time. The cliff face was formed by several layers of different rock; some had been shaped into natural seats like bracket fungus. I climbed up a few stories and sat on one for a while like a frog.

Pete solved our lighting problem that night. Our outside light had broken, and although we'd bought several hurricane lamps, none of them had worked. Pete's motto – improvise, adapt, overcome. He wrapped rags around the top of a metal spike and soaked them in diesel. It burned magnificently. We called it the 'Al Haji Torch' after the Muslim headgear.

Something had burrowed into Pete's foot and, by the light of 'Al Haji Torch', I tried to dig it out. It seemed to be a barb from a fish or plant and had its own devious means of not coming out. The operation went on for hours because I had to keep stopping to give him a break from the pain. In the end he decided to let it grow out.

The open ulcers on my foot, calf and hand were not healing despite two deep cleansing treatments in Laayoune and my daily saline washes. Small volcanoes of pus had sprouted around them and my foot was swollen, hot and red. I'd walk with my hand up which helped to keep the poison from settling in there but I couldn't do the same with my foot.

It became apparent to both of us that we were very happy, we were home, and we could carry on like this until the end. Neither of us wanted Gordon back. Maybe he would be more rested when he returned, but Pete and I made a pact that if he couldn't fit into this system, he would have to go. For all I knew, Gordon was perhaps thinking along these lines anyway but couldn't see a way out, in which case I would offer it to him carefully. I didn't feel bad about this conspiracy; Gordon had been a first-class driver, but he'd made it clear he didn't believe in what I was doing. He thought it should benefit some greater cause than me and Survival International.

It seems ridiculous to me that the press and members of the public cannot accept that the expedition members should be the only beneficiaries of their hard work. Instead, the expedition has to benefit the world. They seem to think that people who embark on expeditions do it for fame, but I haven't met anyone yet who has gone through hell in search of fame: it isn't pleasant to be seen as a freak, misunderstood and ogled at.

Expeditions started as explorations, but the world has been explored. What remains is exploration of self, the need to make a journey. Native people understand this as part of life. Western people search for a philosophical answer to the big 'Why?' question to the human race and the universe. I've pondered the question myself and never come up with an answer in words. But I've felt it – when I realized I was part of something very big and there was a natural place for me in it.

During that week with Pete, I reached a place inside which I'd experienced only once before, between Ouaga and Bamako: a state of peace. Our life was so simple, so gentle, honest, pure and full of laughter and challenges pushed hard for each day and won. It had direction and purpose and a rhythm.

A sign for travellers going in the opposite direction read 'Doorway to the Sahara'. As I passed it, I closed the door behind me. Beyond it lay a ploughed field, a line of gum trees as a windbreak for an orchard with a man tending his crops in irrigated squares. When I smelt again and heard a tractor and felt the sun warm and saw its pretty warm light of evening, I realized I had walked across the Sahara Desert.

Gordon was in camp when I reached day's end. He'd hitched a ride on a truck and looked pale and spotty. His first words were that he was disgusted by the state of the Land Rover.

Pete and I put up the awning for day's end camp, which we liked because it made a home, gave definition to our special place like walls.

'What's that for?' Gordon asked.

When I told him, he sniggered. The week's R&R had done nothing for Gumby. He picked at the new changes to the system which Pete and I had worked out to make our lives more comfortable and more enjoyable. He said that the 'Al Haji Torch' wasn't environmentally friendly – probably because he hadn't thought of it himself. We all realized it would be difficult for him to come back into a unit which had worked well without him.

He'd brought a bottle of Pimms from Colonel Wray, which we drank neat around the fire. I asked him to talk frankly.

'My job is done,' he said. 'This is all too boring for me now. There is no more challenge. I want to leave.'

I accepted his resignation, thanked him for the hard work he'd put into the walk and suggested he stay till Agadir, a week away, where he could get a flight back. I said I'd pay for it even though he was leaving voluntarily, but just as with the money I had given him to go and play in the Canary Islands, he didn't say thank you.

During the next week, the same atmosphere developed which had prevailed before Gordon's holiday. This time, tensions were heightened because Pete and I had had such a good relationship. Something else began, too, which made life very difficult.

It began near Tan Tan, the first large town after the desert, and in true Morocco. I had diarrhoea and was squatting behind a bush. A car stopped and I waved it off, shuffling further behind the scant bush. But the guys in the car just stayed there, staring at me. I gave them hell.

Later that day, I was followed out of town by two guys, walking quickly. I wanted them to overtake me so I could duck behind a bush in privacy. I walked way off the road and got down behind some bushes just in time. One of the guys left the road and came down to me.

'Stay there!' I shouted. 'You can see what I'm doing!'

He kept coming. He came right up to about ten metres away and stood there watching me have diarrhoea. Loo paper was hard to come by in the north. I was so sore, I felt as if I'd been buggered by a lavatory brush.

'Leave me alone!' I called out.

Still he just watched.

When I'd finished I walked up to him and told him to fuck off. He just stared at me.

It baffled me for some days why vehicles stopped ahead and the drivers got out, checked their tyres and had a pee. Surely this was too much of a coincidence, that they should all need to urinate right under my nose? Then, as I passed one, I finally realized that these guys weren't peeing, they were masturbating.

A Merc stopped. I'd actually seen him going the other way, but he must have turned, driven ahead of me and got out. Sure enough, his fist was a blur of action. He called me over to watch; I carried on walking.

Later that day, I'd just left the Land Rover at a water stop when a cyclist overtook me on a hill, turned round and cycled back down towards me with his robe open and an erection on display. When the Land Rover went past soon afterwards on its way to set up the next break, I told Pete and Gordon what had happened. They chased after the flasher, through a village and down the back streets, eventually cornering him in a courtyard. He said he'd never seen them before, that it must have been someone else, but his bike was propped up by the wall. According to the boys, he looked very shaken.

I decided to change my clothes in case that was the problem, even though I had never had any sexual harassment in the other eight Muslim countries I'd walked through so far. With my shoulders, legs and head covered, I set out at 5.30a.m. Almost at once, a cyclist rode by, stopped ahead of me, and got his penis out. Christ, I thought, what is it with this country?

The same stuff carried on happening all day, so I went back to wearing what was comfortable; long robes are very difficult to walk in at speed, trousers caused hot, wet rubs and fungal infections, and sleeves caused underarm rubs when they got wet. I wore my kaffiyeh under my bumbag to protect my bones from being bruised by the water bottle.

We arrived in Guelmim, where all the houses were deep pink with blue doors and shutters. The inhabitants wore identical white robes. The market, however, was like all the others I'd walked through: the stalls were staffed by cocky young boys who mimicked me, despite my smiles and 'hellos'. And when I looked in the shadows at the back of the stalls for adults to help me should things get out of hand, they just looked at me and made sexual gestures.

Gordon had brought a fax from Pat, the woman who ran the PR company for Sabona. She said I was to be featured in the Moroccan Tourist Board's push to get Brits over to Morocco; they were putting a lot of money into advertising. Why should I, I wanted to know?

It opened a whole can of worms. It appeared that the PR people had brought in some eight companies to provide services like hotel accommodation, flights, and another Land Rover, in order to offset Sabona's costs in sponsoring me. In return, they wanted my endorsement.

Tom had an emergency meeting with Detmar in London, explaining that this was completely unacceptable. Detmar didn't understand the strange world of sponsorship and there was no reason why he should – that's why he'd hired a PR company. He agreed to a further injection of cash to cover the loan I'd had to take out, but the payoff was that I would have to agree to keep my mouth shut about what was happening to me in Morocco. Three press conferences were arranged – in Marrakech, Casablanca and Rabat, and at none of them must I mention the harassment.

I complied, but not because the PR people wanted me to. It had suddenly occurred to me that the Moroccans could very easily kick me out of their country if they wanted to, and I wouldn't be able to finish.

Gordon left the walk in Agadir, and it wasn't a tearful farewell. Pete and I continued. Pat wanted me to go to Marrakech for a Sabona press conference, which would entail a long and exhausting detour over the Atlas Mountains. If I had known that Sabona didn't actually have a market in Morocco and that this press conference was to promote tourism in Morocco, I wouldn't have climbed a 1,400 metre mountain range from sea level in midsummer to meet with her request.

Not far out of Agadir, the road took me past a bunch of kids lounging under the olive trees, their goats in the branches feeding above them.

'Ay! Donnez-moi d'argent!' they demanded.

I greeted them cordially, but they repeated the demand.

'Where is the money that I'm supposed to give you?' I smiled as I walked on. One of them stood up and ran along beside me. He threw a stone; I ignored it. He threw another. It hit a car that was passing at speed in the other direction and the windscreen shattered. The vehicle careered off the road.

I ran back down the road to help, and the kids continued to stone me. And this was the country whose tourism industry I was supposed to be promoting. These were not just 'simple hill dwellers', they were positively interbred. They had bulbous foreheads, squint eyes and demented demeanours. Many seemed to spend their days just sitting under the twisted thorny trees amongst the red stony earth, or against the dry stone walling, staring.

It was hard to appreciate the scenery when so much unpleasantness was going on around me, but it was quite Mediterranean. Cactus mounds like sea anemones sprouted from the sand. Ranges of conical hills sat on the horizon in pale pastel strips.

Up a steep hill which I'd hoped would give me a superb view, I approached three girls with back baskets full of straw. They stood and stared at me, then started to imitate my wide arm swing. As I reached them, more girls came down the slopes to join in the baiting of this new thing. I waved. One of them shoved me from behind. I turned and shoved her back. A boy grabbed me, but I shook him off. It happened again and again, his grip getting harder each time to dislodge. The screaming jeers echoed around the canyon with a beat, getting faster and more furious. A stone was thrown, then whole volleys.

A Mercedes shrieked to a halt in front of me and I asked for help. He spoke little French, but sussed out the situation and went over to speak to the ring leader. He took the boy to one side and spent some time explaining I was a tourist. The rest of the gang grouped on the other side of the road, silent at first then giggling and jeering. The driver told me I could continue in peace.

I set off again, but near the summit another group was waiting to pick up the baiting. They came in viciously, pushing me, trying to trip me up, stoning me. As soon as I reached them they crowded in around and behind me. I tried to ignore their pulsating, hysterical chant and walked on. One child was pushing a trolley toy on a stick in front of him. He held it across my path to trip me, and I suddenly decided I'd had enough. I grabbed it and smashed it down hard on the road, again and again and again, until there was nothing left of it but a roadful of smithereens.

Then I saw Pete running towards me. He'd heard the terrible noise and knew I was in trouble. He bent for a stone. I thought he was going to throw it at the kids, but it was destined for a dog that was snapping at his heels. He charged over to me and the kids scattered up the hillside – but he caught one. She started screaming, but in this land of cowards none of her friends returned to help. I went up to her and let rip right in her dumb face.

Peter looked at me differently. Whenever I'd told him about the abuse, he'd reminded me of the hospitality we'd enjoyed from these people – at one night camp at a farm, young men had brought us courgettes, squashes, apples, olive oil, fresh milk and honeycomb. 'Yes, Pete,' I'd said, 'but only when we are seen together.'

Now he understood.

35

At every village I was laughed at and stoned. Just as a smile is a universal white flag, so a snigger is a universal rejection. I dealt with it by trying to understand that they saw me as an odd thing. But at the same time, I had a lump in my throat and I was crying inside: being stoned reaches something very primitive. At a time when I was beginning to feel a bit proud of what I had done, 2,000 kilometres of ridicule was pretty hard to bear. I felt I couldn't hold my head high.

Prickly pear was for sale at the side of the roads. I'd shake hands with the vendors as I'd always done, but learned not to after I was pulled into the bush several times and had to fight my way out. I learned to pick up stones when a driver pulled over for a Moroccan-style pee. As soon as they saw this, they got back inside and drove off quickly.

One guy on a motorbike played with himself as he rode slowly past. I called him a pig – the greatest insult to a Muslim. He stoned me. I stoned him back. He rode ahead and waited for me, I picked up large stones not to throw but to beat him off close up if it came to it. He pushed me, I pushed him back so he fell off his bike. He came on again and punched me on the back as he rode past. I'd had enough of this. He waited ahead. I walked up to him and broke his nose.

Pete wanted to trail me but I didn't want him to. What little energy we had must be put into our work, not sapped by crawling along at six kilometres an hour for eight hours a day. I could defend myself, I had my stones and they were cowards.

Way out on an open plain, a man came running after me. I'd asked him and his father how far it was to Marrakech because I had been lost in daydreams, drunk all my water and didn't know how far the Land Rover was to pace myself. I worked out it was about eight kilometres away. The man said he wanted 'Nik Nik'. I told him my husband wasn't far away and thanked him for escorting me to him. He stoned me, the stones shattered on the tarmac and the splinters hit my legs. His face contorted with rage. I calmed him, figuring I just had to keep this going until a car came. I turned back and started walking to his house saying that if he had some water, I would be very pleased to accept his invitation and asked him about his father and his farm. He broke off, screamed again for 'Nik Nik' and stoned me again.

He was coming towards me up the bank, snarling. I picked up a couple of stones very quickly and stoned him back. A car came and I waved it down, but they were frightened and wouldn't stop. Christ, this was getting serious. I calmed and soothed and told him about my husband.

A truck came by and the guy ran off.

'Are you OK?'

'I'm fine.'

I could have accepted their lift and gone to get Pete to come back and trail me but I thought: FUCK YOU ARSEHOLE, you're not going to destroy my walk. I walked on alone, glancing behind me when I thought I heard footsteps. He didn't return.

I got to the camp just as Pete was about to come back for me because I was so late. I told him what had happened and asked him to keep me in sight from now on. He agreed; in fact, he'd been itching for me to ask.

We reached Marrakech the next day. For two days we had to suffer the crap from the Moroccan dignitaries who were gathered to meet us: 'I hope you have a wonderful time in our country and you invite many British people to spend their holiday here.'

I took aside the head of the Tourist Board in the UK, the man who had organized all these people and a cheap hotel for Pete and me to stay in. I told him about all the trouble I was having and he asked me to direct it to the head of tourism in Marrakech.

When I did, the official said, 'This sort of thing doesn't happen in Morocco! You must understand, in recent years we have had a severe drought and people change at times of drought.'

I said, 'I have met many people throughout Africa who have suffered drought and I can assure you the last thing on their minds is sex.'

Much of the hassle I was getting was due to the huge numbers of Europeans who'd come to Morocco since the 1960s. Drugs and free love was the rage then, and prostitution of every mix was still in great demand by the tourists. Moroccans feel that white women are out for sex; hardly surprising from what they've seen of us. And they think that if a woman is alone she must have turned her back on all other moral codes. It did not matter what I wore, I'd worked that out; I was a woman alone and they thought I was out for sex.

Pat arrived in Marrakech. I was furious that she had allowed Land Rover to jump on the band wagon when they had refused to help me whenever I'd asked them in the past. My drivers had nursed an ageing wreck across the Sahara – a huge amount of responsibility on young shoulders – and now Land Rover, Morocco, had provided a brand new 110 for the press to drive around in, and splashed huge logos all over the vehicle and its driver.

'I don't want it anywhere near us,' I said. 'If they want it for the press, fine, but it isn't going to be in any shots of me and it isn't going to follow me.'

Pat said she wanted it to follow me from now on because of the problems.

'And how are you going to explain to the press that I have to have two vehicles following me, when I've never had one follow me before except in game areas and areas of severe attack? You'll have to explain that Morocco is a dangerous country for a woman to walk alone in and how will that go down with your chums at the Tourist Board? Send the driver back where he came from, I will not have it follow me. We will finish this walk in the way it has always been – me and that piece of junk.'

Pat's response nearly floored me: 'But what are we going to tell the driver?' she said. 'He's so sweeeet!'

Without batting an eyelid, she went on to say that she wanted me to stay in Tanger for four days at the end of the walk because she had set up lots of drinks parties at galleries and famous peoples' houses.

'This is a news story,' I said. 'If Sabona is to get any coverage out of this, I have to get back immediately. Nobody is going to be interested in 'Four days ago, Ffyona Campbell finished her walk through Africa.'

It took me two days to convince her.

Tom had spoken to the news desks of various papers. He discovered that nobody had heard from the PR company about me or the walk.

I raged for days. Pete, too, was furious. We made up a song which

I beat out on the road: 'If you're Patricia and you know it slash your wrists...'

We tried to keep ourselves together: another week to Casablanca, another ridiculous press conference after hard days when Pete trailed me. We'd get to a break, set it up quickly, leaving only half an hour to rest from the sun. At midday we took two hours off so that Pete could set up his Fred Flintstone gym of rocks, rope, sand mats and tent poles to do bench presses, flies, jerks and on the 'hell machine' at the back of the trailer using a strop, he'd do sit ups holding a boulder. He'd pop a Nicorette and go for a six-kilometre run, drink a shit load of water and relax with a smoke. Kept me inspired! His body was in fine condition – it had to be, he'd had to punch guys off me several times and be prepared to do it at any moment all day long.

We got to Casablanca and stayed at the Hyatt, who'd sent out press releases about their sponsorship. They had been written by Pat. They said I was twenty-two metres tall and had started the walk from Nigeria.

We could have spent another night in the hotel but decided we'd rather go back to the bush. We camped on a hill overlooking the city and looked at the tower of the Hyatt in the distance. We were much happier in the bush, where things were straight, down to earth, and free of the screeching voice of PR women in bright red lipstick, thrusting exaggerations down our throats. Perhaps this encounter was there to show me what I had learned. It reminded me so much of the story I had heard about Eric Taberly, the solo round-the-world yachtsman. Approaching Brest harbour at the end of his epic voyage, he took one look at the brass bands and cheering crowds on the quayside, leant on the tiller, and sailed straight back out to sea.

Pete and I laid out our camp beds, side by side with the water bottle and knife and stick at easy reach in the gap between us and fell into a light sleep looking out at the stars over the water and the city. We'd wake sometimes and reach out an arm to be sure of each other. 'Love you Fi.' 'Love you Pete.' I remembered the bit in *The House at Pooh Corner* when Piglet sidled up to Pooh from behind.

'Pooh!' he whispered.

'Yes, Piglet?'

'Nothing,' Piglet had said, taking Pooh's paw. 'I just wanted to be sure of you.'

*

We slept badly over the next three days to Rabat. My dreams were violent again, full of maiming, but I'd feel refreshed in the morning. Pete later told me that he had them for several months after the walk. He drove behind me, watching everything that happened. He saw the wanking for himself and the kids in formation, streaming down from the houses in hostility. He had to charge ahead many times to get men off me. 'This is shit, Fi, feels like we're punching our way through Morocco.'

At camps we were intimidated, and at night we were on edge after kids had stoned us, knowing they could come back in the night. Pete would take out his stick, holding it like a pump action shot gun and the kids would scatter. He'd leap up several times from sleep, punching his way out of his bag when he heard a noise. It wasn't till I was looking for a packet of cheese sauce mix one evening, deep in the guts of the Land Rover, that I found the cause of the noises which woke him. A rat. Pete spent much of his time inventing new ways to outsmart the bastard, but he always got away.

We climbed a hill to camp one evening after seven incidents of sexual perversity and stonings in fifteen kilometres and were followed by a small boy selling prickly pear. I bought some from him in exchange for a pen, and gave him a couple of smokes for his grandfather who was coming up the hill on a donkey. He rested at the top with us and he said, when I told him I didn't have any children yet, 'My son is your son.' All the horrors and fear of the day melted away with his words. Pete and I were so relieved that it hadn't turned into a racial thing as it could have, so easily and with justification – if you get harassed by the same people in the same way for enough time, you begin to get weary of those people when you meet new ones.

We could have gone straight to the Hyatt in Rabat for an extra day because we were early, but we decided to spend the rest day in the bush. Even though this was farmland, we found a ravine amongst pine trees and we set up our last camp. It was so out of line with the surrounding countryside it seemed to have been made for us. We spent the day in our house, baking, cleaning and laughing. Pete got more cocky with his boomerang – throwing it over the ravine and it came back. The second time, it didn't. It was way down in the ravine. He set off with his water bottle to find it. Some hours later, I called to him. He looked up when he heard the echo and saw his boomerang in a tree.

That day I had to face the inevitable: my walk was going to end.

I'd have to leave this way of life for one in that dreadful world of phonies. It wouldn't be like moving house, my house wouldn't exist any more, I couldn't go back to it unless I made another walk. But the home inside would still be there, I would just have to learn to carry it with me.

I was broke, too. Everything I'd ever earned had gone into the walks; there was nothing back in the UK, just a bunch of old clothes in plastic bags stored in someone's damp little flat. I remembered my life there during the evacuations and I was scared. I'd have to make some money quickly so I could go on my next journey without sponsors, without PR people – and then afterwards, build a life the way I wanted, in the outdoors some place where the sun shines. Australia, perhaps.

Pete came up the bank with his boomerang. We cleared out the Land Rover of all the things we wouldn't need in the next week. Most of it was broken; only one of the chairs was still working, the red one which had got the Land Rover out of the salt pans in Botswana. We put them in a pile for the village nearby. The locals came very quickly and took it all away. One of them, his arms full of goodies, stayed behind and asked for a pen. You've just got to laugh.

Pete made another trap for the rat. It had been eating our fruit and veg, taking a small bite out of each piece, chewing through plastic containers and leaving droppings everywhere. I'd seen it but was scared that Pete would – not because it might bite him but in case it was a lot smaller than I'd said!

We got into Rabat the next day, met Pat at the Hyatt and tried to block out her screeching voice. We met a Russian cyclist who was cycling around the edges of each continent. He'd started in Norway and had got this far after two years. He had been refused permission to enter Libya and had to overfly. Now Mauritania had refused him entry because the border was closed. I gave him the low down. I wanted to encourage him, but his journey had already been broken and I saw in him the same despair I'd felt while struggling with the cart.

We had dinner with Sir Allan Ramsay, the British Ambassador to Morocco. He and his wife are tremendous people and the Deputy of the Mission, Gordon Pirie, is the father of Andy, a very old friend of mine from the 'wild days'.

It was arranged that I would meet the Minister of Sport and hold a press conference in his office. This we did and I bit my tongue when he again expressed his hopes that I would encourage women to visit their wonderful country. He asked me if there was anything he could do for me. I asked the cameras and reporters to leave the room and explained, through Mr Pirie's diplomatic interpretation, just what was going on – the stonings, the masturbating, the hauling off the road, the men staring when I went to the loo. The Minister replied that he was very sorry that this had happened – he was sure it *had* happened, but he didn't think it would happen again.

'Morocco just isn't like that,' he explained.

What made me so angry was that Morocco was spending millions of pounds on advertising in Britain, inviting people to spend their holidays there with one hand and sweeping the dangers under the magic carpet with the other. I didn't know then just how far this failure to acknowledge the problems would go.

I phoned Tom. He had written an article for *You* magazine, who had bought the rights to cover the walk from the beginning. But they wouldn't run it, they didn't want the story or even to cover the end. So Tom sold it to the *Daily Telegraph*. He broke the story of my walk with that article. The media started calling. They had ignored the PR press releases, but they took note when they saw Tom's story.

After Pete and I had been on the local TV, everyone hooted and waved as I walked out of Rabat and along the main road while Pete followed me. This was Morocco at its best. But the road got busy with fast cars, and a few near misses made me realize the Land Rover was going to get hit. I persuaded Pete to go ahead and pull off the road.

'Everyone knows us here,' I convinced him, 'nothing's going to happen.'

Reluctantly he drove a few kilometres ahead to where he could pull off.

I walked through a village, my waves returned by everyone. I stopped and signed my autograph for a kid in a car, chatted with fruit sellers, tripping along. Perhaps the press conference had been a good idea after all.

A young man came running up behind me. I turned and greeted him. He greeted me in return. He was in his late twenties, my height, medium to light build, with shaggy long hair. He offered me his hand, which I refused. He pointed at the bushes at the roadside and motioned, 'You and me?'

'No,' I said. 'Fuck off.'

I picked up a stone to show I meant business and two guys on a motorbike stopped to watch the fun.

He grabbed my arms but I wasn't going to wait for the inevitable and I lashed out, thumping his face, squeezing his cheeks with my nails. He punched me to the ground and started dragging me by my hair up a bank. I screamed for help to the guys on the motorbike. They laughed, kicked the bike into life, then drove off.

Many cars passed, but nobody stopped. Eventually, I managed to break free and ran into the road. My clothes were ripped and I was bleeding as I tried to flag down a car. A taxi stopped. My attacker promptly ambled over to the driver's window and seemed to be indicating that we were friends. More cars stopped and he just walked away. A well-dressed man who was a passenger in a taxi started to follow him. I followed *him*, and when I caught up he said, 'We need gendarmes.'

The taxi gave us a lift to the Land Rover. Pete was angry and ready to go ten rounds, but I assured him that the most sensible thing to do was for the three of us to drive to Kenitra, a large town a few kilometres away. Our friend, who introduced himself as Armed, a photographer, pleaded our case at the gendarmerie but it was clear that nobody gave a toss. They just looked at me and shrugged, saying it wasn't their district.

'Go back to Bouknadel,' they said.

We did and just about a kilometre from where the incident had happened we came across the site of a road accident. We spoke to two gendarmes in a police car, but they waved us away. I spoke to another one on a motorbike; he told us to take Armed to look for the man, since their hands were full with the accident. 'Or go to the gendarmerie in Kenitra,' he added. 'It's their district.'

We'd had enough and decided to go to the British embassy in Rabat to see if they could convince the gendarmes to look for the guy. After all, I had a good description of him and had scratched his face.

Mr Pirie saw us at once. He made sure I was OK and got on the phone. It took him, a senior diplomat, a whole day to get the gendarmes in the first town to admit that the scene of the crime was within their jurisdiction and to convince them they should go out and look for the guy.

With an interpreter from the embassy, Stephanie Sweet, we went back to the gendarmerie and gave a full account of what had happened and a description. It was now a good forty-eight hours after the event.

'We will find him,' they said.

We sat in the station for the next ten hours, with Stephanie living up to her surname but showing a hell of a strong streak when needed. Finally, we drove back to Rabat but on the way, a police car skidded to a halt on the hard shoulder. Two gendarmes hauled a guy from the bush and brought him to me. They shone a torch on him.

'Is this the guy?'

I looked at him. It was pretty hard to tell in the torchlight but he did have the same height and build, the same long curly hair and clothes, but I didn't want to make a mistake. I wasn't absolutely certain it was him, until the torch shone full on his face and I saw the marks I'd made.

'Yes, that's him.'

I will remember that in future – always leave a mark. He admitted to the crime, but didn't seem to understand what he had done wrong.

When I confronted the chief about why they had turned us away in the first place he said, 'If we had known you were famous, we would have helped straight away.'

I never did find out what happened to the guy, but the unfortunate upshot of the incident was that I had to accept an escort of gendarmes to trail me and Pete all the way to Tanger. Neither Morocco nor I could stand another attack.

'Fuck it Pete, this means I'll never walk alone in Africa again.'

'After this, mate, neither will I.'

I had to get there on 1 September, and I'd already wasted two days having my face stitched up and getting this guy nailed. We stayed with Mr and Mrs Pirie on our last night before returning to the road. The Piries, and most of the other couples I'd met at the Ambassador's party, had lived in other Muslim countries. They all told me this one was unique: the women could not go anywhere alone without the risk of being stoned.

For the next 278 kilometres, Pete and I fought to keep hold of the walk as we knew it. Night camp was terrible with the noise of the gendarmes, their loud music blaring out in the night and their constant talking until the small hours. We had to sleep in our clothes because they watched us get up in the morning. Walking through villages with my battered face, followed by gendarmes, was humili-

ating. The villagers looked at me as though I was being paraded
through the streets for being a bad woman.

Pat arrived with Sandra Parsons, a reporter from the *Mail*. She
wanted to walk with me and do an interview.

Oh God, I thought, here we go: little by little they want a piece,
they'll suck me dry.

We set off.

'I might look like something from your life,' I said, 'but I am very
different inside.'

She responded with some phoney comment.

I turned to her and said, 'You've come with your questions and
your preconceived ideas. Drop them now and listen to what I have
to say – or fuck off.'

Sandra left her crap by the side of the road and walked in time
with me, listening. She wrote a very good story.

Two days before the end, we'd camped way up on a ridge and
knew it was our last night alone before Pat arrived with her entourage.
We couldn't even say goodbye to the walk the way we knew it
because the gendarmes set up their racket. Pete went and told them
to be quiet.

We made a good camp, almost solemnly, and lit the fire. I left the
camp for a while and scuffed down the track in the light of a full
moon – my twenty-third African full moon.

Sometimes I'd looked too hard for Africa's magic and felt cheated
and empty. But after Kano, I'd relaxed and built my home there on
the road and let the tempo and rhythm flow through me. Without
looking for it, I had felt contentment. I saw it in the faces of women
in the villages, young and old. This is Africa's magic: if only they
could send missionaries to the West.

We had a peaceful night. We held hands for a while, to be sure
of each other, and were woken by the worst noise I'd ever heard –
worse than the high-pitched whine of a mozzie, worse than chanting
kids, worse than the sound of someone farting.

'Ffyona, Ffyona are you there? It's Patricia! Wakey wakey! We're
here!'

She'd arrived with two film crews from the BBC and ITN. They
wanted to film us getting up – well sure, but can we just get dressed
off camera?

We shook hands and made them coffee. During that day of filming,
they kept their distance; they were a great bunch of people. When
we gave them an interview at lunch, they asked good questions and

listened to us. Pete and I hung on to our time alone, neither of us wanted it to end, but we were both getting frustrated – there was something huge about to happen and the waiting was heavy going.

Through the next day they kept with us. We tried to explain our way of life but it didn't sound right. So much of it was a feeling inside and that was private and inexplicable.

That night, the last night of the walk, we camped up on a hill. John Passmore from the London *Evening Standard* arrived: he had flown in with Tom and Shuna and Max; they'd had an horrendous twelve-hour journey instead of four hours direct. Pat had got GB Airways on board but they would only fly them to Gibraltar, so they had to take a ferry across from Spain. We invited them all into camp.

Pete spent an hour hunting for wood. The land was so well gleaned that there was nothing left but thorn twigs. It was important for both of us that they be given a good meal and experience a good camp. But the wood was such poor quality that the quiche didn't rise. It hurt Pete, too. Soon all this knowledge would be useless. What would I do in a modern kitchen? Quiche just wouldn't taste the same without woodsmoke and burnt bits in a dented oven. However, they brought beers! We hadn't had beer in camp for thousands of kilometres.

When they'd gone, Pete and I set out the camp beds, side by side with the sticks and the knife in the middle and talked for a while, looking out over another African night.

I said, 'We'll be going to sleep looking at a wall tomorrow.'

Pete didn't say anything.

'But at least you won't have to look at a girl with permanent bed-head.'

He gave me a silver pendant of Africa with my route engraved on it and he hung it round my neck. It was to protect me: good medicine.

I was torn up inside. I didn't want this to end. I wanted the walking to end because I was tired, but I wanted to be like this always. I couldn't trade it in, I didn't want what was waiting for me after the beach. I didn't want to dance for sponsors or talk about my journey. I'd give them anecdotes of slave merchants, cannibals and evacuations, of missionaries and disease, lion tracks, tsetse fly and crossing minefields, but they couldn't have the private things.

Pete and I woke up the next morning and cleared up the camp. We said the things we always did, packed everything away as we always did, only this was for the last time. I ate my melon and Pete watched me from the corner of his eye as I chucked it out of the camp with the girlie throw that always made him crack up. He climbed into the driver's seat and I walked down to the road. We were seventeen kilometres from Tanger.

I'd crossed the Sahara with a vision pulling me on, and today it would come true. All I wanted was to hug Tom; I couldn't see past that. I played it over in my mind for the thousandth time: I'd walk into the sea, shout 'I made it!' and then hug him. Hug Tom. Hug Tom. Round and round, hugging Tom.

The reporters came back, looking dead tired. Fiona Hanson from the Press Association joined us, taking photos. Some time later, they left. Pete and I were alone and I walked beside his window for a while. We took the piss out of Pat and sang our song. Then I walked up ahead.

I thought back over the walk, over all the drivers, the border crossings, the memorable camps, all the seemingly small triumphs along the way which were far greater than this one. I thought about Blake making pancakes for me in the tsetse swarm, and Bill talking calmly through our arrest when I could see his heart thumping through his T-shirt. I thought about the second night in CAR when I felt I was beaten and Raymond, slumped over his sticks, struggling with the fire. I remembered when Johann refused to let a group of armed, aggressive officials look in my washbag during a full search of the Land Rover. And Tom, calling out from the throes of delirium that I should be there by now, and G pumping away at the filter until the wee small hours. I remembered giving Gordon a choice to put the Land Rover on a boat and meet me on the other side of the minefield, but he wouldn't go. And Pete, taking my word for it and pummelling the shit out of a guy who'd attacked me out of sight. And I thought about the time I had picked some poison leaves and ground them up in my hand and I remembered why I hadn't eaten them: because we'd found a tin of milk powder and were having milk for breakfast.

We reached the outskirts of Tanger and Pete let out a hoot on the horn. A guy passed me and said he wanted to fuck me. *Let it go, Fi, it doesn't matter any more, you can hold your head up now!*

The gendarmes' siren went off and gave me a fright. We'd got to an intersection and they sped off ahead and stopped the traffic. Other gendarmes joined the convoy. I looked back and there was Pete, trundling behind me but many other cars too, their lights flashing. It all got so loud. I felt so small, walking gently down the road, surrounded by all these cars making such a racket and stopping the traffic. I felt so damn fragile.

We were to be on the beach at 10a.m.; it was 9.30 when we reached the bottom of the hill. Pete parked the Land Rover and we went into a café to kill time. We had a Coke. Pete started to cry, and I held his hands in mine.

'Love you, Pete.'

Patricia came in at that moment. Somehow, she'd found us. God knows what she was saying, it was just a noise. She left.

I looked at Pete and took a deep breath.

'You wanna go for a swim?'

'You bet.'

I walked out of the café and Pete got into the Land Rover and drove behind me. The gendarmes gathered around and set up their sirens. I walked to the end of the road and turned left towards a gate in the beach wall where a funnel of people was directing me. Someone gave me a bunch of flowers.

I saw the sand and started to cry.

I was hyperventilating, letting out ridiculous sobs, my face all screwed up and I tried to get a grip. *For fuck's sake, Fi, hang on to it, not yet, just a bit further.*

I couldn't see where I was going for the tears, but I was aware of people running beside me. On to the deep sand, sucking me down, I switched into my own four wheel drive like I had done in the desert. They were calling out to me to walk diagonally across the sand.

I scanned the shore for a sign of my people and made out a dense group. Then I realized it was going to be over. I stopped and waited for Pete to catch up. He gunned Jagga Jagga across the sand. I held out my hand and said, 'Goodbye Pete.'

I walked for a bit holding his hand through the window and then turned back to the walk. Each step, I was trying to get a grip, but I was just convulsing. I thanked each of my drivers in turn and then said, 'Quarter's end, day's end, week's end, country's end, walk's end.'

I saw the water coming very quickly towards me but I couldn't wait for it. I started to run and as soon as my feet hit the water of the Mediterranean I screamed: 'YES! YES! YES I MADE IT!'

I spun round searching for Tom. Through all the shouting press people, I saw him running towards me. Then he was hugging me, spinning me round and round in the water.

I hugged Shuna and Max and Vanessa and Pete and then I walked back into the water, turned away from all of it and looked out across the sea for a moment and said: 'Thank you.'

I took the small film canister of sand I'd gathered from the beach in Cape Town and filled it with sand from the beach in Tanger. Then Pete and I took down the wood we'd gathered that morning and lit the last in a chain of fires which stretched 16,800 kilometres all the way back to Cape Town.

Appendix 1

Date	To	Daily distance in kms		Date	To	Daily distance in kms
From Camps Bay, Cape Town				9.5	8km before Sannieshof	48
2.4.91	Goodwood	27		10.5	16km before Lichtenburgh	48
3.4	14km before Paarl	36				
4.4	10km past Wellington	40		11.5	34km past Lichtenburgh	50
5.4	50km past Wellington	40				
6.4	16km past Ceres	40		12.5	7km past Zeerust	50
7.4	32km past Ceres	16		13.5	58km past Zeerust	51
9.4	72km past Ceres	40		14.5	6km past Botswana border	49
10.4	112km past Ceres	40				
11.4	141km past Ceres	29				
12.4	14km before Sutherland	40		**Botswana**		
13.4	26km past Sutherland	40		18.5	31km past Gaborone	47
14.4	66km past Sutherland	40		19.5	78km past Gaborone	47
16.4	Fraserburg	47		20.5	126km past Gaborone	48
17.4	40km past Fraserburg	40		21.5	174km past Gaborone	48
18.4	80km past Fraserburg	40		22.5	222km past Gaborone	48
19.4	14km before Canarvon	45		23.5	270km past Gaborone	48
20.4	31km past Canarvon	45		24.5	8km past Serowe	49
21.4	76km past Canarvon	45		26.5	154km before Orapa	48
22.4	121km past Canarvon	45		27.5	106km before Orapa	48
23.4	11km before Prieska	45		28.5	57km before Orapa	49
24.4	33km past Prieska	45		29.5	41km before Orapa	16
26.4	78km past Prieska	45		30.5	28km north Letlakane	48
27.4	7km before Douglas	45		31.5	11km before Lost City	48
28.4	38km past Douglas	45		1.6	33km north Lost City	44
29.4	25km before Kimberley	45		2.6	81km north Lost City	48
30.4	13km past Kimberley (7km through town)	45		3.6	129km north Lost City	48
				4.6	16km north Nata	48
4.5	Warrenton	56		6.6	64km north Nata	48
5.5	Christiana	47		7.6	112km north Nata	48
6.5	47km before Schweize-Reneke	47		8.6	160km north Nata	48
				9.6	206km north Nata	46
7.5	Schweize-Reneke	47		10.6	256km north Nata	50
8.5	48km past Schweize-Reneke	48		11.6	Kazangula ferry	44

Date	To	Daily distance in kms
Zambia		
18.6	18km west Kazangula ferry	18
19.6	66km west Kazangula ferry	48
20.6	Masese	48
21.6	48km north Masese	48
22.6	96km north Masese	48
23.6	144km north Masese	48
24.6	192km north Masese	48
25.6	224km north Masese	32
30.6	40km south Luampa	48
1.7	8km north Luampa	48
2.7	30km west Kaoma	48
3.7	10km north Kaoma (8km through town)	48
4.7	58km north Kaoma	48
5.7	106km north Kaoma	48
6.7	154km north Kaoma	48
8.7	202km north Kaoma	48
9.7	24km north Kasempa	48
10.7	82km north Kasempa	48
11.7	130km north Kasempa	48
12.7	34km south Solwezi	43
14.7	7km north Solwezi	41
15.7	23km north Solwezi	16
16.7	'Zaire border'	12
22.7	66km west Solwezi	43
23.7	8km west Kipushi	49
Zaire		
24.7	Lubumbashi	41
25.7	48km north Lubumbashi	48
26.7	96km north Lubumbashi	48
27.7	16km west Likasi	48
29.7	2km west Kakansa	48
30.7	50km west Kakansa	48
31.7	99km west Kakansa	49
1.8	16km past Kolwezi	48
2.8	Kanzenze	32
3.8	48km north Kanzenze	48
6.8	80km north Kanzenze	32
7.8	100km north Kanzenze	20
8.8	148km north Kanzenze	48

Date	To	Daily distance in kms
9.8	196km north Kanzenze	48
10.8	Luebo	49
11.8	Kamina	48
13.8	48km north Kamina	48
13.4	96km north Kamina	48
15.8	148km north Kamina	52
16.8	9km south Kabongo	48
17.8	2km north Kambo	48
18.8	3km north Kitenge	48
20.8	49km north Kitenge	46
21.8	97km north Kitenge	48
23.8	137km north Kitenge	40
24.8	45km north Kakuyu	50
25.8	93km north Kakuyu	48
29.8	9km south Lubao	48
30.8	39km north Lubao	48
31.8	88km north Lubao	49
1.9	4km south Samba	48
8.9	44km north Samba	48
9.9	92km north Samba	48
10.9	21km north Kibombo	48
11.9	69km north Kibombo	48
12.9	37km south Kindu	48
13.9	Kindu	37
14.9	16km past Kindu	16
15.9	64km north Kindu	48
16.9	112km north Kindu	48
17.9	160km north Kindu	48
18.9	208km north Kindu	48
19.9	Punia	38
20.9	48km north Punia	48
21.9	96km north Punia	48
22.9	Lubutu	48
24.9	48km north Lubutu	48
25.9	96km north Lubutu	48

Evacuation

Pushing cart, Central African Republic (distances approx)

Date	To	Daily distance in kms
20.11	22km west Bangassou	22
21.11	62km west Bangassou	40
22.11	Gambo	15
24.11	30km west Gambo	30

Date	To	Daily distance in kms	Date	To	Daily distance in kms
25.11	Dimbe	35	**Central African Republic**		
26.11	Ngama	38	30.3	50km west Bangui	50
27.11	Pavica	30	31.3	100km west Bangui	50
28.11	Alindao	20	1.4	150km west Bangui	50
29.11	25km west Alindao	25	2.4	200km west Bangui	50
30.11	Puju	30	3.4	250km west Bangui	50
			4.4	300km west Bangui	50
Zaire			6.4	350km west Bangui	50
21.12	110km north Lubutu	14	7.4	400km west Bangui	50
22.12	160km north Lubutu	50	8.4	450km west Bangui	50
23.12	208km north Lubutu	48	9.4	491km west Bangui	41
24.12	Kisangani	48	10.4	541km west Bangui	50
30.12	49km north Kisangani	49	11.4	591km west Bangui	50
31.12	97km north Kisangani	48	12.4	Garoua-Boulai	37
1.1.92	6km north Banalia	48			
2.1	54km north Banalia	48	**Cameroun**		
3.1	56km north Banalia	2	25.4	50km past Garoua Boulai	50
4.1	104km north Banalia	48	26.4	1km north Meidougou	50
5.1	152km north Banalia	48	27.4	34km north Meidougou	50
6.1	Buta	48	28.4	84km north Meidougou	50
9.1	48km west Buta	48	29.4	134km north Meidougou	50
10.1	93km west Buta	45	30.4	15km north Ngaoundere	50
11.1	Aketi	41	2.5	55km north Ngaoundere	40
13.1	48km west Aketi	48	3.5	107km north Ngaoundere	52
14.1	96km west Aketi	48			
15.1	144km west Aketi	48	4.5	157km north Ngaoundere	50
16.1	4km east Bumba	48			
18.1	12km west Bumba	16	5.5	106km north Ngaoundere	49
19.1	60km west Bumba	48			
20.1	108km west Bumba	48	6.5	42km south Garoua	41
21.1	150km west Bumba	42	7.5	50km west Ngong	50
23.1	40km north Lisala	48	9.5	11km west Nigeria border	43
24.1	88km north Lisala	48			
25.1	136km north Lisala	48	**Nigeria**		
26.1	20km south Businga	48	10.5	Yola	50
28.1	28km north Businga	48	11.5	50km north Yola	50
30.1	108km north Businga	32	13.5	20km north Numan	40
31.1	4km east Gemina	48	14.5	60km north Numan	40
2.2	44km west Gemina	48	15.5	110km north Numan	50
3.2	92km west Gemina	48	16.5	151km north Numan	41
4.2	140km west Gemina	48	19.5	14km north Gombe	50
5.2	20km north Boyabo	48	20.5	64km north Gombe	50
6.2	68km north Boyabo	48	21.5	20km south Darazo	50
7.2	Bangui	31			

Date	To	Daily distance in kms		Date	To	Daily distance in kms
22.5	4km south Darazo	16		16.3	25km west Koupela	50
31.5	46km north Darazo	50		17.3	69km west Koupela	46
1.6	96km north Darazo	50		18.3	119km west Koupela	50
2.6	144km north Darazo	48		19.3	Ouagadougou	17
3.6	194km north Darazo	50		21.3	50km west Ouagadougou	50
4.6	244km north Darazo	50		23.3	Koudougou	50
5.6	8km north Kano	40		24.3	50km west Koudougou	50
6.6	58km north Kano	50		25.3	100km west Koudougou	50
7.6	108km north Kano	50		26.3	10km west Dedougou	50
8.6	Niger border	26		27.3	60km west Dedougou	50
				28.3	8km east Tansilla	50
Evacuation				30.3	Yorosso, Mali border	50
5.2.93	40km west Kano	40				
6.2	80km west Kano	40		**Mali**		
7.2	20km west Dayi	40		31.3	50km west Yorosso	50
8.2	66km west Dayi	46		1.4	10km west Katiala	50
9.2	6km west Tsafi	50		2.4	14km west Konseguela	50
10.2	17km west Gusau	50		3.4	64km west Konseguela	50
12.2	16km west Kanoma	50		4.4	45km west Beleko	50
13.2	Anka	31		6.4	18km west Fana	50
14.2	50km west Anka	50		7.4	70km east Bamako	34
15.2	100km west Anka	50		13.4	20km east Bamako	50
16.2	135km west Anka	35		14.1	3km east Bamako	17
17.2	185km west Anka	50		18.4	42km west Bamako	50
19.2	40km west Jega	50		19.4	30km west Negala	50
20.2	27km east Kamba	45		20.4	10km west Sebekoro	50
21.2	12km west Niger border	46		21.4	10km west Kita	50
				22.4	7km east Toukoto	50
Niger				23.4	16km west Fangala	51
22.2	40km west Gaya	50		26.4	66km west Fangala	50
23.2	80km west Gaya	50		27.4	3km west Mahina	43
25.2	20km west Falmey	50		28.4	53km west Mahina	50
26.2	Birni Garare	42		29.4	73km west Mahina	20
27.2	34km past Birni Garare	34		30.4	8km east Kayes	50
28.2	Moli	50		1.5	42km west Kayes	50
4.3	7km past Moli/Kohe	7		2.5	Kidira, Senegal border	55
5.3	7km past Say	35		5.5	13km before Bakel	52
6.3	Tamou – Burkina Faso border	46		6.5	37km west Bakel	50
7.3	50km west Tamou	50		7.5	80km west Bakel	43
8.3	18km west Kantchari	50		8.5	4km west Kanel	50
9.3	68km west Kantchari	50		9.5	54km west Kanel	50
11.3	118km west Kantchari	50		10.5	Galoye	50
12.3	5km west Fada	41		13.5	50km west Galoye	50
14.3	55km west Fada	50		14.5	100km west Galoye	50

Date	To	Daily distance in kms	Date	To	Daily distance in kms
15.5	3km west Thile-Boubakar	34	12.7	250km north turn off	50
			13.7	300km north turn off	50
16.5	15km east Dagana	50	14.7	350km north turn off	50
17.5	Richard Toll	42	15.7	400km north turn off	50
20.5	Rosso, Mauritania border	17	16.7	450km north turn off	50
			17.7	Laayoune	42
Mauritania			18.7	34km north Laayoune	34
25.5	34km north Rosso	34	21.7	84km north Laayoune	50
26.5	84km north Rosso	50	22.7	34km north Tarfaya	50
27.5	134km north Rosso	50	23.7	84km north Tarfaya	50
28.5	184km north Rosso	50	24.7	134km north Tarfaya	50
29.5	Nouakchott	19	26.7	184km north Tarfaya	50
10.6	Atlantic Ocean	9	27.7	25km north Tan-Tan	50
11.6	59km north Nouakchott	50	28.7	75km north Tan-Tan	50
12.6	96km north Nouakchott	37	29.7	5km south Guelmim	50
13.6	99km north Nouakchott	3	30.7	7km north Guelmim	12
14.6	134km north Nouakchott	35	31.7	16km north Boulzakarn	50
			1.8	Tiznit	50
15.6	Nouamghar	35	2.8	50km north Tiznit	50
17.6	48km north Nouamghar	48	3.8	8km east Ait-Melloul	40
18.6	98km north Nouamghar	50	6.8	66km north Agadir	50
19.6	140km north Nouamghar	42	7.8	116km north Agadir	50
			8.8	14km north Imi-n-Tanoute	50
20.6	190km north Nouamghar	50	9.8	64km north Imi-n-Tanoute	50
21.6	236km north Nouamghar	46	10.8	Marrakech	39
22.6	Mauritania military post	41	13.8	17km north Marrakech	17
			14.8	67km north Marrakech	50
Occupied Western Sahara			15.8	117km north Marrakech	50
27.6	Moroccan military post 1	9	16.8	Settat	50
28.6	Moroccan military post 2	16	17.8	46km south Casablanca	25
29.6	50km north post 2	50	20.8	Casablanca limits	43
30.6	105km north post 2	55	21.8	50km east Casablanca	50
1.7	155km north post 2	50	23.8	Rabat	33
2.7	205km north post 2	50	26.8	9km south Kenitra	29
3.7	255km north post 2	50	28.8	41km north Kenitra	50
4.7	305km north post 2	60	29.8	91km north Kenitra	50
5.7	Dakhla turn off	23	30.8	64km south Tanger	39
8.7	50km north turn off	50	31.8	14km south Tanger	50
9.7	100km north turn off	50	1.9.93	Tanger, Mediterranean Sea	14
10.7	150km north turn off	50			
11.7	2000km north turn off	50			

Between 2 April 1991 and 1 September 1993, Ffyona Campbell walked every step from Cape Town to Tanger, a total distance of 16,088 kilometres.

Appendix 2

Kit list for pushing the cart

Unless indicated, we each had the following. Several items were doubled up in case we lost a rucksack or were separated. Everything had its own bag.

1 Berghaus rucksack
1 Rab sleeping bag
1 Thermorest
1 freestanding Northface tent (shared)
1 headtorch with batteries
1 Ventile jacket
1 neck knife
1 Swiss army knife
1 set Coleman stainless steel stacking saucepans with bowl lid (shared)
1 mug
1 spoon
1 water bottle (1 ltr Nalgene)
1 pair shoes
1 pair long trousers
1 pair shorts
2 T-shirts
1 sweatshirt
1 notebook
1 tube suncream
1 tube mozzie milk
1 shampoo and conditioner
1 hand-sized towel
1 sleeping bag inner
1 Michelin map (laminated)
1 compass
1 shortwave radio (shared)
1 French/English dictionary (shared)
1 money belt – travellers' cheques, cash, insurance, air ticket, passport

1 Millbank bag (should be washed in detergent)
2 water bags 1 ltr, 2 ltr
1 20 ltr plastic jerry (shared)
3 dehydrated meals
1 FM2 Nikon, 24mm lens, 35–105mm lens, SB15 flash
20 rolls Fujicrome 100 ASA film
1 medical kit (shared): Flagyl, erythromycine, oxytetracyclin, Paludrine, Avlaclore, Piriton, Halfan, Neurofen, Temgesic, Fentezin, Immodium, potassium permanganate, Chloromin T. All drugs decanted into labelled Nalgene bottles
1 tweezers
1 scissors
4 scalpel blades
1 bottle Betadine
adhesive Elastoplast
1 eye patch
steri strip
crepe bandage
triangular bandage
ankle support
thermometer
1 cart with chain and padlock (just about shared)

My House – Kano to Tanger kit list

This camp kit list was compiled after eighteen months on the road to provide the most comfort for sleeping and eating – about the only two things you have any control over. Everything had a place in a Curver stacking box or drawstring bag.

THE BEDROOMS

The following sleeping kit gave us a choice to sleep outside or in a tent

2   freestanding tents with mozzie netting and fly (roof tents were fabulous if your roof was strong enough, make sure it's water and mozzie proof)
3   Thermorests (¾ length)
3   camp beds – military (big was best, with legs which fit easily)
3   mozzie nets – No See Um
2   sleeping bags
1   duvet with sheet and cover
3   pillows with cases
1   canvas envelope for sleeping kit

MY WARDROBE

6   100% cotton long dresses
6   pairs 100% cotton socks
6   pairs 100% cotton undies
1   pair shorts
1   pair sweat pants
1   100% cotton headscarf
1   decent dress
1   jumper
1   Ventile jacket
1   down vest
1   bathing suit
1   pair thongs
4   pairs cheap running shoes
2   pairs orthotic insoles
1   pair wraparound shades
1   bumbag with water bottle, talc, loo paper

THE DINING ROOM

1   fold-down table
3   fold-down chairs (padded ones were better than netting)
1   hammock – fabric with string

THE KITCHEN

10   plastic tubs for leftovers, tea, coffee, flour, beans, etc.
2   string bags for fruit and veg

1   bottle crate of empty coke bottles (to exchange for full)
1   axe
1   machete
1   carbon steel knife (not of heroic proportions)
1   serrated knife

Day box: cutlery, chopping board, condiments, ceramic plates and mugs (metal ones burn your mouth)

Food box: most important food items brought from UK: hot chocolate, Marmite, instant mashed potato mix, cheese sauce mix, dried soups, pasta, veggie burger mix

Metal cook box: large frying pan, 1 large stainless steel saucepan, 1 small saucepan without handle (for baking), 1 iron pot with lid (used as oven) with 3 used tomato paste tins in the bottom, 2 iron tripods, 1 sieve; 1 four-sided, collapsible metal fire guard; 1 grill (for putting over two tripods)

THE GLORY HOLE

1   ball string

THE SINK AND LAUNDRY ROOM

3   laundry bags
Wash box:
1   washing powder in plastic tub
2   scrubbing brushes
1   potassium permanganate (small Nalgene bottle) for cleaning fruit and veg
1   Chloromin T (small Nalgene bottle) for purifying water
3   plastic washing bowls
1   plastic tarp (as draining board)
1   soap in box
1   bottle washing-up liquid
1   pegless washing line

We used the side of a jerry can for scrubbing clothes if washing rocks not around.

THE LOO

6   rolls loo paper (most soft)
1   spade

THE MEDICINE CABINET

As in kit list for pushing cart, except much more of it.

ELECTRICS, PLUMBING AND WALLS

3   headtorches (with normal bulbs and choice of 2 battery sizes)
1   strip light (with cigarette lighter plug)
3   1 litre water bottles

5 water jerry cans – plastic (draped with wet towel to keep cool)
1 Katadyn water filter hand pump – not a good idea, electric ones are better
1 heavy canvas awning with side flaps, cross poles and guy ropes
  mallet

THE LIBRARY AND ENTERTAINMENT

1 books box – *Africa on a Shoestring*, local guide books, novels, etc.
1 cassette player with tapes box
1 shortwave radio with alarm clock
1 cool bag for film
1 Olympus OM4 camera with 50mm and 50–250mm lenses

THE GYM

1 sand mat
2 rocks with ropes
1 boulder with rope
2 strops
1 tent pole

THE OFFICE

1 waterproof document case with carnet, ownership document, insurance (personal and vehicle), passports, vaccination certificates, log book, accounts book
1 letter writing case
1 box Bic pens
1 calculator
1 Michelin map, laminated
1 safe
Local money, US dollars and French francs in cash and major travellers' cheques
1 Visa card
3 hardback notebooks with elastic band

THE GARAGE

Information on choice of vehicles, trailers, spares, tools, etc. are widely available.

THE GARDEN AND NEIGHBOURS

Information on countries, attractions and people are widely available. But if you're lucky enough to come across unknown places of extreme beauty, keep them quiet.

Survival

25 years for tribal peoples

Ffyona Campbell's walk across Africa aimed to highlight the work of Survival International which campaigns for the rights of tribal peoples around the world. From the Yanomami in the Brazilian Amazon to the Bushmen of the Kalahari Desert, tribal peoples are seeing their lands, environments, and way of life stolen from them. Many face death.

'It's vitally important for us all to stand with tribal peoples – particularly now when they are faced with so much oppression'   *Ffyona Campbell*

If you believe in human rights, please join Ffyona in supporting Survival. Please send a donation – however small. If you would like more information about the work of Survival and how you can become a member, please return the coupon. Thank you.

....

☐ I would like to make a donation of: ☐£10 ☐£25
☐ £50 ☐other £. ... ...

☐ Please send me more information about Survival's work.

Please make cheques payable to 'Survival International'.
Please return this form to: Ffyona Campbell, Survival International, 310 Edgware Road, London W2 1DY, UK. Tel: 071–723 5535.

Survival International is a worldwide movement to support tribal peoples. It stands for their right to decide their own future and helps them protect their lands, environment and way of life.